Global Pathways to Abolishing Physical Punishment

Routledge Research in Education

For a full list of titles in this series please visit www.routledge.com

21. Participatory Learning in the Early Years
Research and Pedagogy
Edited by Donna Berthelsen, Jo Brownlee, and Eva Johansson

22. International Perspectives on the Goals of Universal Basic and Secondary Education
Edited by Joel E. Cohen and Martin B. Malin

23. The Journey for Inclusive Education in the Indian Sub-Continent
Mithu Alur and Michael Bach

24. Traveller, Nomadic and Migrant Education
Edited by Patrick Alan Danaher, Máirín Kenny and Judith Remy Leder

25. Perspectives on Supported Collaborative Teacher Inquiry
Edited by David Slavit, Tamara Holmlund Nelson and Anne Kennedy

26. Mathematical Relationships in Education
Identities and Participation
Edited by Laura Black, Heather Mendick and Yvette Solomon

27. Science, Society and Sustainability
Education and Empowerment for an Uncertain World
Edited by Donald Gray, Laura Colucci-Gray and Elena Camino

28. The Social Psychology of the Classroom
Elisha Babad

29. Cross-Cultural Perspectives on Policy and Practice
Decolonizing Community Contexts
Edited by Jennifer Lavia and Michele Moore

30. Education and Climate Change
Living and Learning in Interesting Times
Edited by Fumiyo Kagawa and David Selby

31. Education and Poverty in Affluent Countries
Edited by Carlo Raffo, Alan Dyson, Helen Gunter, Dave Hall, Lisa Jones and Afroditi Kalambouka

32. What's So Important About Music Education?
J. Scott Goble

33. Educational Transitions
Moving Stories from Around the World
Edited by Divya Jindal-Snape

34. Globalization, the Nation-State and the Citizen
Dilemmas and Directions for Civics and Citizenship Education
Edited by Alan Reid, Judith Gill and Alan Sears

35. Collaboration in Education
Edited by Judith J. Slater and Ruth Ravid

36. Trust and Betrayal in Educational Administration and Leadership
Edited by Eugenie A. Samier and Michèle Schmidt

37. Teaching and Learning with Technology
Beyond Constructivism
Edited by Concetta M. Stewart, Catherine C. Schifter and Melissa E. Markaridian Selverian

38. Gender Inclusive Engineering Education
Julie Mills, Mary Ayre and Judith Gill

39. Intercultural and Multicultural Education
Enhancing Global Interconnectedness
Edited by Carl A. Grant and Agostino Portera

40. Systemization in Foreign Language Teaching
Monitoring Content Progression
Wilfried Decoo

41. Inclusive Education in the Middle East
Eman Gaad

42. Critical Issues in Peace and Education
Edited by Peter Pericles Trifonas and Bryan Wright

43. Children's Drawing and Writing
The Remarkable in the Unremarkable
Diane Mavers

44. Citizenship, Education and Social Conflict
Israeli Political Education in Global Perspective
Edited by Hanan A. Alexander, Halleli Pinson and Yossi Yonah

45. Emerging Teachers and Globalisation
Gerry Czerniawski

46. Social Studies as New Literacies for Living in a Global Society
Relational Cosmopolitanism in the Classroom
Mark Baildon and James S. Damico

47. Education Policy, Space and the City
Markets and the (In)visibility of Race
Kalervo N. Gulson

48. Memory and Pedagogy
Edited by Claudia Mitchell, Teresa Strong-Wilson, Kathleen Pithouse and Susann Allnutt

49. Universities and Global Diversity
Preparing Educators for Tomorrow
Edited by Beverly Lindsay and Wanda J. Blanchett

50. Equity and Excellence in Education
Towards Maximal Learning Opportunities for All Students
Edited by Kris Van den Branden, Piet Van Avermaet and Mieke Van Houtte

51. Global Pathways to Abolishing Physical Punishment
Realizing Children's Rights
Edited by Joan E. Durrant and Anne B. Smith

Global Pathways to Abolishing Physical Punishment

Realizing Children's Rights

Edited by Joan E. Durrant and Anne B. Smith

Routledge
Taylor & Francis Group
New York London

First published 2011
by Routledge
711 Third Avenue, New York, NY 10017

Simultaneously published in the UK
by Routledge
2 Park Square, Milton Park, Abingdon, Oxon OX14 4RN

Routledge is an imprint of the Taylor & Francis Group, an informa business

First issued in paperback 2013

Typeset in Sabon by IBT Global.

Library of Congress Cataloging-in-Publication Data

Global pathways to abolishing physical punishment : realizing children's rights / edited by Joan E. Durrant, Anne B. Smith.
p. cm. — (Routledge research in education ; 51)
Includes bibliographical references and index.
1. Corporal punishment of children—Cross-cultural studies. 2. Discipline of children—Cross-cultural studies. 3. Children's rights—Cross-cultural studies. I. Durrant, Joan E. II. Smith, Anne B.
HQ770.4.G56 2011
362.76—dc22
2010031289

ISBN13: 978-0-415-87920-0 (hbk)
ISBN13: 978-0-203-83968-3 (ebk)
ISBN13: 978-0-415-84798-8 (pbk)

Contents

Boxes, Figures, and Tables

BOXES

FIGURES

TABLES

Foreword

Paulo Sérgio Pinheiro

The process of the UN Secretary-General's Study on Violence against Children, which I led from 2003–2007, was a voyage of discovery, not least for me. I was well aware of the extreme forms of violence that adults perpetrate on children—sexual exploitation, trafficking, female genital mutilation. But I was not so aware of the extent of the daily, routine onslaught of punitive violence against children, in their homes and also in many countries in schools, other institutions, penal systems, and in child labor. Nor was I aware of the degree of legality of this violence disguised as discipline.

The history of childhood is indeed a nightmare from which we have only recently begun to awaken (as Lloyd de Mause prefaces his celebrated history). But awakening we are, and not least because children themselves are now telling us of the misery it causes them, in particular when the violence is administered by adults closest to them. My many meetings with children in all regions during the course of the study were upsetting, but also highly motivating: "No violence against children is justifiable—all violence against children is preventable" became the mantra of the study. This violence has to stop—now.

Our slow but accelerating awakening is a direct result of the recognition that children are individuals and holders of human rights. The UN Secretary-General's Study, proposed originally by the Committee on the Rights of the Child, endorsed by the General Assembly, was rights-based. In a priority recommendation, I urged states to prohibit all forms of violence, including all corporal punishment. I submitted my report to the General Assembly in 2006, and in the same year the Committee on the Rights of the Child issued its General Comment on the right of the child to protection from corporal punishment and other cruel or degrading forms of punishment, which provides detailed guidance on how States should fulfill their obligations to prohibit and eliminate this most common form of violence.

I very much welcome this documentary account of the impressive progress that is now being made in all regions. The book valuably documents the strong and growing human rights consensus for prohibition and elimination. It brings together the social science evidence of the dangers of corporal punishment to all societies. It highlights that law reform to clearly ban all corporal punishment is fundamental—but that it must be linked to comprehensive awareness-raising and the promotion of positive, non-violent forms of child-rearing and education.

But the book also indicates—through the monitoring work of the Global Initiative to End All Corporal Punishment of Children—how far we are from achieving a world in which it is at least as unlawful and unacceptable to hit a child as to hit anyone else. I hope all who read it will feel motivated to work, or work harder, towards this goal.

Professor Paulo Sérgio Pinheiro, Independent Expert who led the UN Secretary-General's Study on Violence against Children; and Commissioner and Rapporteur on the Rights of the Child, Inter-American Commission on Human Rights, Organization of American States.

REFERENCES

de Mause, L. (1991). The history of childhood—the untold story of child abuse. London: Bellew Publishing.

Acknowledgments

The process of editing this book has been a remarkable journey in itself. We have been privileged to work with passionate, creative, and dedicated people around the globe who have had a real and lasting positive impact on children's lives. We are deeply grateful to each of the authors who have contributed to this book—for their enthusiasm, knowledge, and willingness to contribute their precious time to this project.

This book has been a truly international endeavor, requiring coordination and communication across all regions of the world. We, the editors, live on opposite sides of the planet. We have been fortunate to have received funding support from two sources—the University of Otago William Evans Visiting Fellowship Program, and the Royal Society of New Zealand Bilateral Research Activities Program—which enabled us to travel across hemispheres to bring this book to fruition.

We are very grateful to Max Novick at Routledge who has always understood the complexities involved in producing this book. He has provided helpful guidance and great patience with the unexpected challenges along the way.

We could not have completed this book without the cheerful, meticulous, and dedicated assistance of Rachael Brinsdon. She managed to keep track of the various versions of chapters flying through cyberspace and across time zones to produce a coherent, perfectly formatted manuscript. We are deeply indebted to Ashley Stewart-Tufescu for coming to our rescue at the last moment and helping us with the index.

We are fortunate indeed to have been able to consult with Peter Newell and Dominique Pierre Plateau as the book developed and took root. Their vast knowledge of the many dimensions of law reform helped us to sort through the complex cultural and legal issues that arose along the way. We are most grateful for their generous support of this project. We also wish to thank Nicola Taylor and Bruce Ryan who gave so generously of their time to provide useful comment and feedback on some of the chapters.

Finally, we express our heartfelt gratitude to our families—John, Gregg, and Jonah—who have shown tremendous understanding and forbearance throughout this editing journey. They have provided all of the emotional and instrumental support we have needed to bring the book to completion. We thank you from the bottoms of our hearts.

Part I

The Rationale for Eliminating Physical Punishment of Children

1 Introduction to the Global Movement to Ban Physical Punishment of Children

Anne B. Smith and Joan E. Durrant

> All inputs change the potential future. That we no longer hang children, burn them as witches or brand them as vagrants is not the victory of a few reformers, it is the victory of a whole society which has overcome the constructions that made such actions possible. The killings and maimings of children that our society still generates can also be consigned to the history book—by the same processes which have made possible the worlds in which we now live.
>
> (Stainton Rogers, 1989, p. 29)

The rights of children to protection from sexual abuse, neglect, discrimination, and exploitation are reasonably well accepted and uncontroversial. There is one right, however, which still remains extraordinarily controversial in many places: the child's right to protection from physical violence in the family when it takes the form of physical punishment.[1] Historically, most societies have rejected the idea that children have the same fundamental right to protection as adults. We have failed to give children equal respect and protection under the law and, in doing so, have put many of their other rights at risk.

This book, however, marks a historic turning point. Three important anniversaries took place while this book was being written: the 60th anniversary of the *Universal Declaration on Human Rights*; the 20th anniversary of the *Convention on the Rights of the Child*; and the 30th anniversary of the world's first ban on all physical punishment of children. These events have led many people all over the world to reflect on the state of children's rights—to recognize how far we have progressed, and how far we have yet to go.

Until 30 years ago, the near-universal practice of hitting children was considered appropriate, necessary, and a parental right in every country of the world. Children, like women historically, have been considered to belong to the private world of the family rather than participants in public life, which has justified their different and unequal treatment, and the non-recognition of their citizenship rights. But just as the women's movement has helped make domestic violence towards women anathema in many parts of the world, so the current movement to uphold children's rights has energized changes to policies and laws to make violence against children equally unacceptable in many countries. Nevertheless, the belief that governments should not meddle in private family matters continues to be a major barrier to such changes. While physical punishment of students is no longer allowed in the schools of most countries, lack of respect for children's physical integrity within the confines of the family has been harder to challenge. In many places, the debate about physical punishment continues to be framed in terms of parents' rights to treat their children as they see fit. This book shows, however, that the world is moving to a greater recognition that children too have rights, and that it is possible to uphold for children the same right that adults take for granted—not to be assaulted or hurt by others.

At the time of this book's publication, 29 countries have prohibited all physical punishment of children: Austria, Bulgaria, Costa Rica, Croatia, Cyprus, Denmark, Finland, Germany, Greece, Hungary, Iceland, Israel, Kenya, Latvia, Liechtenstein, Luxembourg, Moldova, the Netherlands, New Zealand, Norway, Poland, Portugal, Romania, Spain, Sweden, Tunisia, Ukraine, Uruguay, and Venezuela. (See www.endcorporalpunishment.org for the legal status of physical punishment in all countries, continuously updated.) In addition, High Courts in Italy and Nepal have ruled that physical punishment in childrearing is unlawful. Many other countries, such as Lithuania and Serbia, are committed to full prohibition and are in the process of bringing it about.

This is an astonishing rate of change that signals a paradigm shift in conceptions of childhood, and a redefinition of physical punishment as violence and a violation of children's rights to physical integrity and dignity. But the stories telling why and how these changes have been taking place are very rarely heard. In this book, individuals who have been witness to this movement in countries around the globe describe the process of change—in some cases successful, in others stalled—to help us better understand the underpinnings and trajectory of this social movement. To provide a foundation for understanding the motive for change in these countries, this book first provides an examination of the three main rationales for prohibition: (1) human rights; (2) theoretical; and (3) empirical.

The United Nations *Convention on the Rights of the Child* (CRC; 1989) and other human rights instruments have been powerful forces in confronting this issue. In its Preamble, the CRC states that children "should grow up in a family environment, in an atmosphere of happiness, love and understanding". Article 19 requires "measures to protect the child from all forms of physical or mental violence" and Article 37 requires states to ensure that no child is subjected to "cruel, inhuman or degrading treatment or punishment". In its *General Comment No. 8* (2006), the Committee on the Rights of the Child explicitly states that corporal punishment conflicts with children's rights to dignity and physical integrity, that it is incompatible with children's best interests, and that ratifying countries[2] are obligated to eliminate it (paras. 2, 3, 21, 26). In Chapter 2, Peter Newell documents the origins of these instruments, how they have been interpreted in domestic and international arenas, and their role in facilitating global change.

The human rights imperative is becoming increasingly resonant with evolving theories of childhood, which accord respect, dignity, rights, and personhood to children. Constructions of childhood have important implications for the actions that societies take for and against children, and for children's survival and quality of life. Considering children as the possessions of their parents to be moulded into a form of the parents' choosing, makes it easier to justify the pain and indignity of physical punishment. But positioning children as partners in improving their lives and viewing them as social actors recognizes their status as persons in their own right, deserving of respect and able to contribute to their own families and societies. In Chapter 3, Anne Smith presents several major theories that explain the impact of physical punishment on children's development, from traditional learning theories to critical theories of childhood.

The growing base of social science research demonstrating that physical punishment predicts negative long-term outcomes, whether measured in terms of social, emotional, intellectual, or physical development, shows a degree of consistency that is unusual in the social sciences. These findings have helped to clarify for decision makers the reasons why it is so important—at individual, family, and societal levels—to eliminate physical punishment from children's lives. Yet, in many places, this large body of research continues to be ignored, overlooked or resisted. In Chapter 4, Joan Durrant provides an overview of this research and explores its relevance to the human rights and theoretical foundations of prohibition.

In the second section of the book, the stories of 18 countries and 1 continent are told by writers who were (or are) "on the ground" as their governments took on the challenge of prohibition. They include academics, lawyers, educators, clinicians, program directors of non-governmental organizations, researchers, a pediatrician, and an advisor to a Children's Ombudsman. Their cases were selected to represent as many regions of the world as possible, as well as a wide range of cultural contexts, political systems, levels of industrialization, and approaches to law reform. Of the 19 cases, 11 have prohibited all physical punishment of children. Their stories describe how the issue emerged, the forces that promoted and resisted law reform, and how families have been supported in their efforts to raise their children without violence. The remaining 8 cases remain at various places along the pathway to prohibition. Their stories describe their progress towards prohibition, barriers to achieving it, the lessons they have learned and their plans for the future.

Most of these stories have not been heard before. They provide valuable cultural and historical lessons about the factors that drive and inhibit social change towards a world where children's right to protection is affirmed.

Our aims are to provide a better understanding of how the movement to abolish physical punishment of children has unfolded, and to document this historic movement and the social policy changes accompanying it, as it spreads around the globe.

The third section of the book ties these stories together. In Chapter 24, Kai-D. Bussman, Claudia Erthal, and Andreas Schroth present the findings of the first multi-country study to assess the impact of law reform. Its findings provide useful answers to the question of whether law reform is necessary and/or sufficient to promote attitudinal and behavioral changes. The book concludes with a chapter summarizing what has been learned from the movement so far, highlighting the commonalities and differences among countries' approaches and outcomes, and identifying pathways to the global elimination of physical punishment of children.

Although this book is about research, history, law, policy, and social change, it was born from a recognition of how children feel when they are intentionally hurt by those entrusted with their care. As expressed by a 12-year-old, "Being smacked is like being treated like something very little and not important to the rest of the world" (Saunders & Goddard, 2010, p. 153). The contributors to this book collectively assert the value and worth of children as persons and citizens with rights, who are entitled to special care, dignity, happiness, love, and freedom from the physical and emotional pain of physical punishment.

NOTES

1. Physical or corporal punishment has been defined as "any punishment in which the use of physical force is used and intended to cause some degree of pain or discomfort, however light" (Paragraph 11, Committee on the Rights of the Child, 2006).
2. All countries of the world, except the United States and Somalia, have ratified the CRC.

REFERENCES

Committee on the Rights of the Child. (2006). *General Comment No. 8: The right of the child to protection from corporal punishment and other cruel or degrading forms of punishment*. Retrieved from www.unhchr.ch/tbs/doc.nsf/(Symbol)/CRC.C.GC.8.En?OpenDocument

Saunders, B., & Goddard, C. (2010). *Physical punishment in childhood: The rights of the child*. Chichester, UK: Wiley-Blackwell.

Stainton Rogers, R. (1989). The social construction of childhood, in W. Stainton Rogers, D. Hevery, J. B. Roche & E. Ash (Eds.), *Child abuse and neglect: Facing the challenge* (pp. 23–29). Batsford: London.

United Nations. (1989). *Convention on the Rights of the Child*. Retrieved from www.un.org/documents/ga/res/44/a44r025.htm

2 The Human Rights Imperative to Eliminate Physical Punishment

Peter Newell

Corporal punishment is a direct assault on the human dignity of the child and a direct invasion of the child's physical integrity. Respect for human dignity is the foundation of human rights, of the *Universal Declaration of Human Rights* and successive core human rights instruments.

The universality of rights is expressed in all the early human rights instruments—the *Universal Declaration*, the *European Convention on Human Rights*, and the two *International Covenants on Civil and Political Rights* and *Economic, Social and Cultural Rights*. The particular purpose of the *Convention on the Rights of the Child*, adopted by the United Nations General Assembly in 1989, has been to re-emphasize that universality includes children: that children are holders of human rights alongside adults, including the right to respect for their human dignity and physical integrity and to equal protection under the law. While there are evidence-based reasons for prohibiting and eliminating all corporal punishment and other cruel or degrading forms of punishment of children, it is human rights that provide the urgent imperative in the form of obligations under international law.

Without some awareness of the traditional status of children in human societies, as possessions rather than individual people—let alone rights-holders—it is hard indeed to understand why the human rights community has taken so long to accept and promote children's equal right to protection from all violence. The existence in many states' legislation of authorizations or defenses (e.g., "reasonable punishment", "lawful correction") for deliberate violence against children disguised as "discipline" is highly symbolic of children's persisting low status. But now there is a strong human rights consensus across all systems and regions, speeding the prohibition and elimination of punitive violence against children.

ESTABLISHING THE HUMAN RIGHTS FOUNDATION

It appears the European Court of Human Rights (ECHR) was the first international human rights mechanism to address corporal punishment of children, in a case brought against the United Kingdom concerning the flogging of a young offender (European Court, 1978). Anthony Tyrer was a 15-year-old living in the Isle of Man, a UK Crown Dependency. He was convicted of assault in 1972 and sentenced to be birched. The ECHR judgment states: "After waiting in a police station for a considerable time for a doctor to arrive, Mr. Tyrer was birched late in the afternoon of the same day. His father and a doctor were present. The applicant was made to take down his trousers and underpants and bend over a table; he was held by two policemen whilst a third administered the punishment, pieces of the birch breaking at the first stroke. The applicant's father lost his self-control and after the third stroke 'went for' one of the policemen and had to be restrained" (para. 10).[1] The European Court found, by 6 votes to 1, that the punishment amounted to degrading punishment in breach of Article 3 of the Convention (European Court, 1978). The British judge in the Court at the time, Sir Gerald Fitzmaurice, dissented from the judgment and annexed a lengthy separate opinion, arguing that the punishment was not degrading. He explained that his view

> may be colored by the fact that I was brought up and educated under a system according to which the corporal punishment of schoolboys (sometimes at the hands of the senior ones—prefects or monitors—sometimes by masters) was regarded as the normal sanction for serious misbehavior, and even sometimes for what was much less serious. . . . Moreover, these beatings were carried out without any of the safeguards attendant on Mr. Tyrer's: no parents, nurses or doctors were ever present. They also not infrequently took place under conditions of far greater intrinsic humiliation than in his case. Yet I cannot remember that any boy felt degraded or debased. Such an idea would have been thought rather ridiculous . . . indeed, such is the natural perversity of the young of the human species that these occasions were often seen as matters of pride and congratulation.[2]

Such attitudes, although more frequently now addressed in less extreme terms, persist today. This should be a very simple issue—hitting people is wrong and children are people too. But, as Sir Gerald's statement suggests, the reason it remains so difficult and controversial is the personal dimension. It is easy enough to condemn the extreme forms of violence against children—sexual exploitation, trafficking, and so on-because they are perpetrated by other, different people. When it comes to corporal punishment, it is still the case that a majority of children in almost every country have been hit by their parents; most parents have hit their own children. We do not like to think badly of our parents or of our own parenting and it is that which makes it so challenging, and for some so painful, to move on and see this as an issue of equality and human rights.

By the time the Tyrer case came before the European Court, applications concerning school corporal punishment in the UK had been submitted to the European Commission on Human Rights by two Scottish mothers (until 1998, there was a two-stage process in the Council of Europe for considering individual applications alleging breaches of rights—starting with the Commission). The Court, in a 1982 judgment, found that the UK was in breach of the *European Convention* by not respecting parents' objections to school corporal punishment (so this early judgment was about parents', not children's, rights). The mothers had asserted that corporal punishment used in their sons' schools (striking the palm of a child's hand with a leather strap called a tawse) breached their sons' right to protection from inhuman or degrading punishment (Article 3). As neither boy had in fact received corporal punishment, the Court did not find an Article 3 violation. It did, however, find that the UK had failed to respect the parents' philosophical convictions against the use of corporal punishment, in breach of Article 2 of Protocol 1 to the Convention which states: "No person shall be denied the right to education. In the exercise of any functions which it assumes in relation to education and to teaching, the State shall respect the right of parents to ensure such education and teaching in conformity with their own religious and philosophical convictions." One of the boys, Jeffrey Cosans, aged 15, had been suspended from his school when he refused to accept corporal punishment and the Court found that this amounted to denial of his right to education (European Court, 1982).

Following this judgment, during the 1980s more than 20 other applications concerning school corporal punishment were made by UK schoolchildren and their parents, alleging breaches of their rights under Article 3 or Article 8 (respect for family and private life) or both. After being declared admissible by the European Commission on Human Rights, in most cases "friendly settlements" were reached, with the UK Government making *ex gratia* payment to the families involved, effectively "buying off" the applicants and avoiding further Court judgments against the UK. In 1993, the Court issued a judgment on private school corporal punishment in which, by 5 votes to 4, it found that the punishment of a 7-year-old boy, Jeremy Costello-Roberts, did not reach the necessary "level of severity" to breach Article 3 (degrading punishment; Jeremy had been given "three 'whacks' on the bottom through his shorts with a rubber-soled gym shoe", causing no marks or bruising). The Court did say in its judgment that it did not wish "to be taken to approve in any way the retention of corporal punishment as part of the disciplinary regime of a school" (European Court, 1993).

Sweden became the first state explicitly to prohibit corporal punishment in the home in 1979 (see Chapter 19). A challenge to this ban led to another significant decision by the European Commission on Human Rights in 1982, when it rejected as "inadmissible" an application by a group of Swedish parents (European Commission on Human Rights, 1982). They alleged that the Swedish ban on parental corporal punishment breached their right to respect for family life and to freedom of religion. These parents, belonging to a Protestant free church congregation in Stockholm, believed in the necessity of corporal punishment, justifying their beliefs with references to Biblical texts. The Commission concluded that the Swedish law on assault was not unusual or in any way Draconian:

> The fact that no distinction is made between the treatment of children by their parents and the same treatment applied to an adult stranger cannot, in the Commission's opinion, constitute 'an interference' with respect for the applicant's private and family lives since the consequences of an assault are equated in both cases. . . . The Commission finds that the scope of the Swedish law of assault and molestation is a normal measure for the control of violence and that its extension to apply to the ordinary physical chastisement of children by their parents is intended to protect potentially weak and vulnerable members of society.

In a similar decision in September 2000, the European Court rejected unanimously and without a hearing an application by individuals associated with a group of Christian private schools in the UK, who had alleged that the implementation of a ban on corporal punishment in private schools breached parents' rights to freedom of religion and family life (European Court, 2000).

It was not until September 1998 that the European Court issued its first judgment concerning parental corporal punishment. It found unanimously that severe caning of a young English boy by his stepfather had breached Article 3, and that the UK was responsible because the domestic law allowing "reasonable chastisement" failed to provide children with adequate protection, including "effective deterrence" (European Court, 1998).[3] The European Court has emphasized that it regards the European Convention as a "living instrument" which "must be interpreted in the light of present-day conditions". In its decisions, the Court now increasingly refers to the UN *Convention on the Rights of the Child* (CRC). For example, in a 2003 judgment it stated: "The human rights of children and the standards to which all governments must aspire in realizing these rights for all children are set out in the Convention on the Rights of the Child" (European Court, 2003). In the A v UK judgment the Court referred, without further comment, to Articles 19 and 37 of the CRC, requiring protection from all forms of violence and from cruel, inhuman or degrading treatment or punishment (para. 22).

It seems clear that if another application is made to the European Court concerning the legality of corporal punishment in the home, it will uphold children's right to equal legal protection of their human dignity and physical integrity. Another Council of Europe human rights mechanism—the European Committee of Social Rights, monitoring compliance of member-states with the *European Social Charter* and *Revised Social Charter*—has since 2001 been consistently asserting the need for explicit prohibition of corporal punishment, including in the home (see page 17).

THE UN CONVENTION ON THE RIGHTS OF THE CHILD AND ITS MONITORING COMMITTEE

It is the adoption of the CRC and its almost universal ratification (full acceptance) by 193 States[4] that has led to rapid acceleration towards a consensus that all corporal punishment is a human rights violation. The Committee on the Rights of the Child, the internationally-elected group of experts established by the CRC to monitor progress towards its full implementation, has paid special attention to children's right to protection from all forms of violence, including all corporal punishment. Ratifying Governments (States parties) are required to submit a report to this Committee 2 years after ratification, and every 5 years thereafter. State representatives are examined about their reports by the Committee at a session in Geneva. Non-governmental organizations (NGOs), UN agencies, and others also contribute reports to brief the Committee.

The Committee started to examine reports from States parties in 1993. From early on, the Committee showed particular concern over the persisting legal and social acceptance of corporal punishment of children, in their homes, schools, other institutions, and penal systems. In its concluding observations adopted following examination of states' reports, the Committee has recommended prohibition of all corporal punishment and education campaigns to encourage positive, nonviolent child-rearing and education to more than 140 states in all continents.[5]

In 2001 the Committee adopted its first *General Comment*,[6] on the Aims of Education (Article 29[1] of the CRC), in which it states:

> Children do not lose their human rights by virtue of passing through the school gates. Thus, for example, education must be provided in a way that respects the inherent dignity of the child, enables the child to express his or her views freely in accordance with article 12(1) and to participate in school life. Education must also be provided in a way that respects the strict limits on discipline reflected in article 28(2) and promotes non-violence in school. The Committee has repeatedly made clear in its concluding observations that the use of corporal punishment does not respect the inherent dignity of the child nor the strict limits on school discipline. Compliance with the values recognized in article 29(1) clearly requires that schools be child-friendly in the fullest sense of that term and that they be consistent in all respects with the dignity of the child. (Committee on the Rights of the Child, 2001)

In June 2006, the Committee issued a *General Comment on the Right to Protection from Corporal Punishment and Other Cruel or Degrading Punishment* (see Box 2.1). This document consolidated the Committee's guidance to States on how to implement their immediate obligation to prohibit and eliminate all corporal punishment (Committee on the Rights of the Child, 2006).

Box 2.1 Excerpts from the Committee on the Rights of the Child's Landmark General Comment No.8. on the Right of the Child to Protection from Corporal Punishment and Other Cruel or Degrading Punishment (2006).

The Committee's definition of "corporal" or "physical" punishment:

> *Any punishment in which physical force is used and intended to cause some degree of pain or discomfort, however light. Most involves hitting ('smacking', 'slapping', 'spanking') children, with the hand or with an implement - a whip, stick, belt, shoe, wooden spoon, etc. But it can also involve, for example, kicking, shaking or throwing children, scratching, pinching, biting, pulling hair or boxing ears, forcing children to stay in uncomfortable positions, burning, scalding or forced ingestion (for example, washing children's mouths out with soap or forcing them to swallow hot spices). . . . In the view of the Committee, corporal punishment is invariably degrading. In addition, there are other non-physical forms of punishment that are also cruel and degrading and thus incompatible with the Convention. These include, for example, punishment which belittles, humiliates, denigrates, scapegoats, threatens, scares or ridicules the child (para. 11).*

The purpose of the General Comment:

> *To highlight the obligation of all States parties to move quickly to prohibit and eliminate all corporal punishment and all other cruel or degrading forms of punishment of children and to outline the legislative and other awareness-raising and educational measures that States must take. Addressing the widespread acceptance or tolerance of corporal punishment of children and eliminating it, in the family, schools and other settings, is not only an obligation of States parties under the Convention. It is also a key strategy for reducing and preventing all forms of violence in societies (paras. 2 & 3).*

The Committee's position on defining a "reasonable" level of violent punishment of children:

> *In the view of the Committee, corporal punishment is invariably degrading (para. 11). The dignity of each and every individual is the fundamental guiding principle of international human rights law (para. 16).[T]he practice directly conflicts with the equal and inalienable rights of children to respect for their human dignity and physical integrity. The distinct nature of children, their initial dependent and developmental state, their unique human potential as well as their vulnerability, all demand the need for more, rather than less, legal and other protection from all forms of violence (paras. 20 & 21).*
>
> *Article 37 of the Convention requires States to ensure that "no child shall be subjected to torture or other cruel, inhuman or degrading treatment or punishment." This is complemented and extended by article 19, which requires States to "take all appropriate legislative, administrative, social and educational measures to protect the child from all forms of physical or mental violence, injury or abuse, neglect or negligent treatment, maltreatment or exploitation, including sexual abuse, while in*

(*continued*)

the care of parent(s), legal guardian(s) or any other person who has the care of the child". There is no ambiguity: 'all forms of physical or mental violence' does not leave room for any level of legalized violence against children. Corporal punishment and other cruel or degrading forms of punishment are forms of violence and States must take all appropriate legislative, administrative, social and educational measures to eliminate them (para. 18).

The Committee's position on prohibiting corporal punishment of children:

Eliminating violent and humiliating punishment of children, through law reform and other necessary measures, is an immediate and unqualified obligation of States parties . . . Other treaty bodies, including the Human Rights Committee, the Committee on Economic, Social and Cultural Rights and the Committee against Torture have reflected the same view in their concluding observations on States parties' reports . . . For example, the Committee on Economic, Social and Cultural Rights, in its general comment No. 13 (1999) on "The Right to Education" stated: "In the Committee's view, corporal punishment is inconsistent with the fundamental guiding principle of international human rights law enshrined in the Preambles to the Universal Declaration and both Covenants: the dignity of the individual. Other aspects of school discipline may also be inconsistent with school discipline, including public humiliation" (para 22).

The Committee's advice to States on how legislation needs to be reformed and implemented in the best interests of children:

The Convention requires the removal of any provisions (in statute or common—case law) that allow some degree of violence against children (e.g., "reasonable" or "moderate" chastisement or correction in their homes/families or in any other setting (para. 31).

In some States, the Committee has observed that while there is no explicit defence or justification of corporal punishment in the legislation, nevertheless traditional attitudes to children imply that corporal punishment is permitted. Sometimes these attitudes are reflected in court decisions (in which parents, teachers or other carers have been acquitted of assault or ill-treatment on the grounds that they were exercising a right or freedom to use moderate "correction") (para 33).

In the light of the traditional acceptance of violent and humiliating forms of punishment of children, a growing number of States have recognized that simply repealing authorization of corporal punishment and any existing defences is not enough. In addition, explicit prohibition of corporal punishment and other cruel or degrading forms of punishment, in their civil or criminal legislation, is required in order to make it absolutely clear that it is as unlawful to hit or 'smack' or 'spank' a child as to do so to an adult, and that the criminal law on assault does apply equally to such violence, regardless of whether it is termed 'discipline' or 'reasonable correction' (para. 34).

Once the criminal law applies fully to assaults on children, the child is protected from corporal punishment wherever he or she is and whoever the perpetrator is. But . . . given the traditional acceptance of corporal punishment, it is essential that the applicable sectoral legislation - e.g. family law, education law, law relating to all forms of alternative care and justice systems, employment law - clearly prohibits its use in the relevant settings. In addition, it is valuable if professional codes of ethics and guidance for teachers, carers and others, and also the rules or charters of institutions, emphasize the illegality of corporal punishment and other cruel or degrading forms of punishment (para. 35).

(*continued*)

The Committee's position on prosecution of "minor" assaults:

> *The principle of equal protection of children and adults from assault, including within the family, does not mean that all cases of corporal punishment of children by their parents that come to light should lead to prosecution of parents. The de minimis principle —that the law does not concern itself with trivial matters—ensures that minor assaults between adults only come to court in very exceptional circumstances; the same will be true of minor assaults on children. States need to develop effective reporting and referral mechanisms. While all reports of violence against children should be appropriately investigated and their protection from significant harm assured, the aim should be to stop parents from using violent or other cruel or degrading punishments through supportive and educational, not punitive, interventions (para. 40).*
>
> *Children's dependent status and the unique intimacy of family relations demand that decisions to prosecute parents, or to formally intervene in the family in other ways, should be taken with very great care. Prosecuting parents is in most cases unlikely to be in their children's best interests. It is the Committee's view that prosecution and other formal interventions (for example, to remove the child or remove the perpetrator) should only proceed when they are regarded both as necessary to protect the child from significant harm and as being in the best interests of the affected child. The affected child's views should be given due weight, according to his or her age and maturity (para. 41). Where, despite prohibition and positive education and training programmes, cases of corporal punishment come to light outside the family home—in schools, other institutions and forms of alternative care, for example—prosecution may be a reasonable response. The threat to the perpetrator of other disciplinary action or dismissal should also act as a clear deterrent. It is essential that the prohibition of all corporal punishment and other cruel or degrading punishment, and the sanctions that may be imposed if it is inflicted, should be well disseminated to children and to all those working with or for children in all settings. Monitoring disciplinary systems and the treatment of children must be part of the sustained supervision of all institutions and placements which is required by the Convention. Children and their representatives in all such placements must have immediate and confidential access to child-sensitive advice, advocacy and complaints procedures and ultimately to the courts, with necessary legal and other assistance. In institutions, there should be a requirement to report and to review any violent incidents (para. 43).*

The Committee's position on public education:

> *Given the widespread traditional acceptance of corporal punishment, prohibition on its own will not achieve the necessary change in attitudes and practice. Comprehensive awareness-raising of children's right to protection and of the laws that reflect this right is required (para. 45). States must ensure that positive, non-violent relationships and education are consistently promoted to parents, carers, teachers and all others who work with children and families. The Committee emphasizes that the Convention requires the elimination not only of corporal punishment but of all other cruel or degrading punishment of children (para. 46).*

The General Comment is available at http://www2.ohchr.org/english/bodies/crc/comments.htm.

[1] The Committee notes that at one time in many States similar defences were also available to justify the chastisement of wives by their husbands and of slaves, servants and apprentices by their masters (para. 31).

In 2000 and 2001, the Committee's annual days of general discussion focused on violence against children and in recommendations issued following these days, it reiterated the obligation to prohibit all corporal punishment (Committee on the Rights of the Child, 2000/2001). Another outcome of these discussions was a proposal from the Committee that the United Nations Secretary-General should be requested, through the General Assembly, to carry out an in-depth international study on violence against children. This was taken forward between 2003 and 2006, and resulted in new recommendations for the global prohibition and elimination of all violence against children, including all corporal punishment (see next section).

In its examination of States' reports, the Committee has singled out for particular criticism legislation that justifies or defends some level of violent punishment of children—"reasonable chastisement", "moderate correction", and so on. For example, when it examined Spain's first report in 1994, it expressed concern "at the wording of article 154 of the Spanish *Civil Code* which provides that parents 'may administer punishment to their children reasonably and in moderation', which may be interpreted to allow for actions in contradiction with article 19 of the Convention" (Committee on the Rights of the Child, 1994, paras. 10, 18). By 2010, some States had received three recommendations on this issue from the Committee, each delivered with deepening concern.

For example, when the Committee examined the UK's first report in 1995, it expressed concern about "the national legal provisions dealing with reasonable chastisement within the family". The Committee recommended "that physical punishment of children in families be prohibited in the light of the provisions set out in articles 3 and 19 of the Convention" (Committee on the Rights of the Child, 1995, paras. 16, 31, 32). In 2002, the Committee expressed deep regret "that the State Party persists in retaining the defense of 'reasonable chastisement' and has taken no significant action towards prohibiting all corporal punishment of children in the family". Again the Committee recommended that the UK should "with urgency" adopt legislation "to remove the 'reasonable chastisement' defence and prohibit all corporal punishment" (Committee on the Rights of the Child, 2002, paras. 35–38). In 2008, following the third examination, the Committee expressed its concern again, "at the failure of the State party to explicitly prohibit all corporal punishment in the home and emphasizes its view that the existence of any defense in cases of corporal punishment of children does not comply with the principles and provisions of the Convention, since it would suggest that some forms of corporal punishment are acceptable". It recommended that the UK "prohibit as a matter of priority all corporal punishment in the family, including through the repeal of all legal defences" (Committee on the Rights of the Child, 2008, paras. 40–42). Many other States have similarly received two or three successive recommendations from the Committee to prohibit all corporal punishment.

The CRC and its consistent interpretation by the Committee on the Rights of the Child has been taken up by other international human rights treaty bodies, by regional human rights mechanisms, and also increasingly in judgments of high-level constitutional and other courts in all regions, accelerating the condemnation, prohibition, and ultimate elimination of all corporal punishment. The Human Rights Committee; Committee on Economic, Social and Cultural Rights; Committee against Torture; and most recently the Committee on the Elimination of Discrimination against Women have all condemned the legality of corporal punishment and recommended prohibition of it in some or all settings of children's lives. The Geneva-based Human Rights Council introduced in 2008 a new process of "Universal Periodic Review" of states' overall human rights record. In this process, too, children's right to protection from all corporal punishment has been taken up frequently, with further recommendations urging prohibition (Human Rights Council, 2008).

THE UNITED NATIONS SECRETARY-GENERAL'S STUDY ON VIOLENCE AGAINST CHILDREN

Another context for the accelerating progress towards prohibiting all corporal punishment has been the *UN Secretary-General's Study on Violence against Children*. This Study was proposed to the UN General Assembly by the Committee on the Rights of the Child following its two General Discussion Days on violence against children in 2000 and 2001. The then-UN Secretary-General, Kofi Annan, appointed Professor Paulo Sérgio Pinheiro as the Independent Expert to lead the Study in 2003.

This was the first comprehensive global study on the issue, and also the first United Nations exercise of this kind to attempt to involve children themselves directly in its work. Nine regional consultations for the Study were held around the world in 2005. Children participated actively in each and prepared their own recommendations and statements. Professor Pinheiro also made a point of meeting privately with them. Their presence helped to ensure that adults, including government representatives, did not remain in denial about the scale of violence; the children highlighted not only extreme forms of violence including sexual exploitation, trafficking, and female genital mutilation, but also the "routine", legalized violence that so many of them suffered daily in their homes and in many cases also in schools and other institutions.

When the Study report (Pinheiro, 2006) was submitted to the General Assembly one of its key overarching recommendations was that States should prohibit all violence—including all corporal punishment, setting an over-ambitious deadline of the end of 2009. Another recommendation was that the Secretary-General should be requested to appoint a Special Representative to act as a global advocate and to follow-up on the Study recommendations (Pinheiro, 2006). This recommendation was endorsed by the General Assembly in 2007. In September 2009, Marta Santos Pais, a well-known children's rights advocate, former member of the Committee on the Rights of the Child, former Director of UNICEF's Innocenti Research Centre, and strong supporter of the prohibition of all corporal punishment, was appointed as Special Representative.

RECENT REGIONAL DEVELOPMENTS

Building on the consistent interpretation of the CRC and the progressive global condemnation of corporal punishment, regional human rights mechanisms are now working against it.

The Council of Europe

The Strasbourg-based Council of Europe, with 47 Member States, is the first inter-governmental organization to pursue with energy the elimination of corporal punishment. The Council is rooted in human rights, democracy, and the rule of law. The progressive condemnation of corporal punishment by the European Court of Human Rights was documented earlier in this chapter.

Observations of the European Committee of Social Rights. The European Committee of Social Rights (ECSR), monitoring Member States' compliance with the *European Social Charter* and *Revised Social Charter*, concluded in a general observation issued in 2001 "that Article 17 requires a prohibition in legislation against any form of violence against children, whether at school, in other institutions, in their home or elsewhere. [The Committee] furthermore considers that any other form of degrading punishment or treatment of children must be prohibited in legislation and combined with adequate sanctions in penal or civil law" (European Committee of Social Rights, 2001, p. 26). The Committee notes that its observation was prepared "in the light of the case-law developed under other international treaties as regards the protection of children and young persons, such as the United Nations Convention on the Rights of the Child and the European Convention on Human Rights. It has also taken into account developments in national legislation and practice as regards the protection of children" (European Committee of Social Rights, 2001, p. 26). Since then, as the Committee examines reports from Member States on their implementation of the Charters, it has systematically asked about the legality of corporal punishment, and has found many States to be not in conformity with Article 17 because it is not fully prohibited.[7]

Complaints by the World Organization against Torture. In 2003, "collective complaints" were submitted against five Member States by the World Organization against Torture (OMCT), under a procedure established by an *Additional Protocol to the Social Charters* (by 2010, this procedure had been accepted by 12 Member States). The complaints alleged non-compliance with the Charters because the States had not prohibited all corporal punishment. In 2004, the ECSR found a violation in three of the cases (Greece, Belgium, and Ireland), and the Committee's decisions on the merits of the complaints were made public in May 2005 (European Committee of Social Rights, 2005).

In its decision against Greece, the Committee found that there was a breach of Article 17 on the grounds that corporal punishment was not adequately prohibited in the home, in secondary schools and in institutions caring for children. It highlighted that even if violence against the person is punished under criminal law provisions and subject to increased penalties where the victim is a child, this does not constitute sufficient prohibition to comply with the Charter.

Similar decisions were reached against Ireland and Belgium. In the case of Ireland, the Committee noted that corporal punishment of children in the home is permitted because of the existence of the common law defense of reasonable chastisement, although the criminal law protects children from very serious forms of violence. For children in foster care, residential care, and some child-minding settings, the Committee identified the existence of guidelines, standards and inspections, but noted that these did not have the force of law and so the common law defense of "reasonable chastisement" remained applicable.

In response to the complaints against Italy and Portugal, the Committee found no violation. The Committee noted that in Italy, the law (both criminal law and civil law) as interpreted by the courts adequately prohibited all forms of violence, wherever it occurs and whoever the perpetrator; there had been a Supreme Court of Cassation decision to this effect in 1996. Similarly, the Committee noted that in Portugal the law, as interpreted by the country's Supreme Court, was sufficient: ". . . according to a series of Supreme Court decisions even a simple slap causing no bodily injury is considered as a corporal assault falling into the scope of Section 143. . . . Given Section 143 of the Criminal Code as interpreted by the Supreme Court, the Committee holds that in Portugal the prohibition of all forms of violence has a legislative basis" (European Committee of Social Rights, 2005, paras. 38, 42).

But in April 2006, the Supreme Court in Portugal, in a case concerning cruelty and ill-treatment of mentally disabled children in a children's institution, ruled that slaps and spankings are "legal" and "acceptable" in childrearing, and that failure to use these methods of punishment could even amount to "educational neglect". In May 2006, OMCT submitted another collective complaint alleging that domestic law in Portugal does not explicitly nor effectively prohibit all corporal punishment of children.

After rapid consideration of this second complaint, the Committee stated in its landmark decision on the merits, released in December 2006:

> To comply with Article 17, states' domestic law must prohibit and penalize all forms of violence against children, that is acts or behaviour likely to affect the physical integrity, dignity, development or psychological well being of children. The relevant provisions must be sufficiently clear, binding and precise, so as to preclude the courts from refusing to apply them to violence against children. Moreover, states must act with due diligence to ensure that such violence is eliminated in practice. . . . The conclusion to be drawn from the Supreme Court's decision of 5 April 2006 is that Portuguese law does not include such provisions, even though this was the interpretation that had been drawn from a previous decision of that court. In addition, the Government has not supplied information to show that the measures in practice are likely to result in the eradication of all forms of violence against children. For these reasons, the Committee concludes unanimously as to the violation of Article 17 of the Revised Charter. (European Committee of Social Rights, 2006, paras. 19–23)

What happened in Portugal illustrates that court decisions, even at the highest level, are not adequate to achieve prohibition of all corporal punishment, because a subsequent decision can always reverse a judgment. Prohibition needs to be achieved in legislation. The governments of Greece and Portugal, following these complaints and long-term campaigns for law reform in both countries, moved quickly to effectively prohibit all corporal punishment. But, as of March 2010, Belgium and Ireland had taken no action in response to the Committee's decisions.

Parliamentary Assembly of the Council of Europe. In 2004, the Parliamentary Assembly of the Council of Europe issued a recommendation calling for a "Europe-wide ban on corporal punishment of children":

> The Assembly considers that any corporal punishment of children is in breach of their fundamental right to human dignity and physical integrity. The fact that such corporal punishment is still lawful in certain member states violates their equally fundamental right to the same legal protection as adults. Striking a human being is prohibited in European society and children are human beings. The social and legal acceptance of corporal punishment of children must be ended. . . . The Assembly notes the success of the Council of Europe in abolishing the death penalty and the Assembly now calls on the Organization to work in the same way to make Europe, as soon as possible, a corporal punishment-free zone for children. (Parliamentary Assembly, 2004, paras. 5, 7)

The Council of Europe has become the first inter-governmental organization to launch an explicit campaign for prohibition of all corporal punishment in its 47 Member States. In April 2006, the Council launched a 3-year action program, "Building a Europe for and with Children". Among its aims was combating all forms of violence against children. In June 2008, an explicit campaign to achieve universal prohibition of corporal punishment was launched in Zagreb, Croatia. The Council also made available in many languages handbooks and other materials on the detail of law reform and a TV spot, "Raise your hand against smacking" (Council of Europe, 2008a).

Commissioner for Human Rights. The Commissioner for Human Rights for the Council of Europe, Thomas Hammarberg (who also launched the Global Initiative to End All Corporal Punishment of Children in 2001 with the author of this chapter), has been actively encouraging prohibition across the region. In 2006 he published an Issues Paper, *The Right Not To Be Hit, Also a Right of Children.* In it, he writes:

> The imperative for removing adults' assumed rights to hit children emanates from human rights principles. Therefore, it should not be necessary to prove that alternative and positive means of socializing children are more effective. However, research into the harmful physical and psychological effects of corporal punishment in childhood and later life, and into its links with other forms of violence do indeed add further compelling arguments for banning the practice, thereby breaking the cycle of violence. . . . How can we expect children to take human rights seriously and to help build a culture of human rights, while adults not only persist in slapping, spanking, smacking and beating them, but actually defend doing so as being 'for their own good'? Smacking children is not just a lesson in bad behaviour: it is a potent demonstration of contempt for the human rights of smaller in size, and thus, more vulnerable people (pp. 7–8).

The Commissioner also raises the issue of banning all corporal punishment when he pays formal visits to Member States. For example, following formal visits to the UK in 2008, he presented a memorandum on corporal punishment to the UK Government. The press release accompanying it was headlined: *"UK must improve children's protection and ban corporal punishment" reports Commissioner Hammarberg".* It continued:

> The UK is one of the few European countries which have neither achieved full prohibition of corporal punishment nor committed themselves publicly to it. Worse, it is in a small minority whose laws actually persist in allowing parents and some other carers to justify some level of violence as 'reasonable' when it is regarded as discipline. This situation is unacceptable and must be changed. Criticizing the specific national legislative provisions on corporal punishment, Thomas Hammarberg emphasizes that "laws allowing the definition of 'justifiable assaults' and 'reasonable punishments' on children are not compliant with international human rights standards. Moreover, the fact that

children, uniquely, should have less protection under the criminal law from assault is additionally discriminatory and unimaginable" (Council of Europe, 2008b).

INTER-AMERICAN HUMAN RIGHTS SYSTEM

In December 2008, the Inter-American Commission sent a request to the Inter-American Court of Human Rights for an Advisory Opinion on whether the legality and practice of corporal punishment of children was compatible with regional human rights standards. The Court declined to provide a new Opinion, stating that its existing jurisprudence, together with the CRC and its interpretation by the Committee on the Rights of the Child, already clarified the incompatibility of corporal punishment with human rights standards.

In August 2009, the Inter-American Commission of Human Rights issued a *Report on Corporal Punishment and Human Rights of Children and Adolescents*, prepared by the office of the Commission's Rapporteur on the Rights of the Child (Professor Paulo Sérgio Pinheiro, who also led the *UN Secretary General's Study on Violence against Children*). It calls on all Member States of the Organization of American States (OAS) to:

> act immediately on the problem of corporal punishment by placing explicit and absolute legal bans on its use in all contexts and, in parallel, by adopting such preventive, educational and other measures that may be necessary to ensure the eradication of this form of violence, which poses a serious challenge to the wellbeing of children in the Hemisphere. (Inter-American Commission on Human Rights, 2009, para. 3)

The Commission asks OAS Member States to report back to it "on the measures adopted to eradicate corporal punishment as a way of disciplining children and adolescents and to make the Americas a region free of child corporal punishment by 2011" (Inter-American Court of Human Rights, 2009, para. 120[5]).

AFRICAN HUMAN RIGHTS MECHANISMS

All states in Africa have ratified the *African Charter of Human and Peoples' Rights* (African Commission on Human and Peoples' Rights, 1981). It asserts equal protection before the law, respect for dignity and physical integrity, and protection from cruel or degrading punishment. States are also required "to ensure the protection of the rights of the child as stipulated in international declarations and conventions" (African Commission on Human and Peoples' Rights, 1981, in particular Articles 3, 4, 5, 18).

In 2000, a complaint was submitted to the African Commission on Human and Peoples' Rights regarding the sentencing of eight students in the Sudan to 25 to 40 lashes for "public order" offences under the 1991 *Sudanese Criminal Law*. In its decision the Commission stated: "There is no right for individuals, and particularly the government of a country to apply physical violence to individuals for offences. Such a right would be tantamount to sanctioning State sponsored torture under the Charter and contrary to the very nature of this human rights treaty" (African Commission on Human and Peoples' Rights, 2003, para. 42). The Commission concluded that the Sudanese legislation permitting flogging violated Article 5 of the *Charter on Human and Peoples' Rights*, and requested that the government of Sudan immediately amend its law, abolish the punishment of lashes and ensure compensation for the victims.

The majority of states in the region have also ratified the *African Charter on the Rights and Welfare of the Child* (Organization of African Unity, 1990). The African Committee of Experts on the Rights and Welfare of the Child in 2008 committed itself to telling all states that they have an obligation to prohibit all corporal punishment and to provide advice, in collaboration with civil society, on the promotion of positive discipline. In late 2009, the Committee issued its first "concluding observations", following examination of Egypt's initial and first periodic report under the Charter. It noted the resistance to eliminating corporal punishment and "recommends the State party to take the necessary measures to abolish the practice" (African Committee of Experts, 2009, para. 10).

CONCLUSION

All corporal punishment of children is now clearly recognized as a human rights violation by both international and regional human rights monitoring bodies and mechanisms. The days of impunity for deliberate adult punitive violence against children should be numbered. As Paulo Pinheiro concluded when he presented his report to the UN General Assembly in 2007: "Children are tired of being called 'the future': they want to enjoy their childhoods, free of violence, now."

But, despite the almost universal acceptance of the CRC, the systematic recommendations of the Committee on the Rights of the Child, the concurring recommendations of other Treaty Bodies, and the judgments and decisions of regional human rights mechanisms and high level supreme and constitutional courts in all regions, adults are still resisting and delaying the realization for children of a right which adults take for granted for themselves.

The *Universal Declaration of Human Rights* demands that everyone has an effective remedy for acts which violate fundamental rights (Article 8). The Committee on the Rights of the Child emphasizes this in its

General Comment No. 5 *on General Measures of Implementation for the Convention on the Rights of the Child*: "For rights to have meaning, effective remedies must be available to redress violations. . . . Children's special and dependent status creates real difficulties for them in pursuing remedies for breaches of their rights" (Committee on the Rights of the Child, 2003, para. 24).

In most states, children still lack effective remedies to protect them from corporal punishment in all settings, including their family home. We adults who like to think of ourselves as advocates for children have to admit (to children and to ourselves) that children's rights advocacy—20 years after the adoption of the CRC—is still in its infancy; it lags behind the women's rights movement, the movement on environmental rights, and others. Most advocacy remains soft advocacy.

But the CRC is a *legal* instrument which places legal obligations on States which ratify it. Use of the CRC as a legal instrument has begun tentatively. Beyond national courts, so far international and regional human rights mechanisms have only been used systematically to challenge corporal punishment in Europe—the stream of applications to the European Commission on Human Rights and Court against the UK from 1972 and the more recent use of the collective complaints procedure under the *European Social Charter*.

Now that the scale of this adult assault on children is almost everywhere visible and is so plainly identified as a human rights violation, children must not be kept waiting any longer. What is needed now—and the Global Initiative to End All Corporal Punishment of Children (www.endcorporalpunishment.org) is embarking on this with appropriate partner organizations—is a systematic analysis of the situation in each of the States where corporal punishment remains legal in one or more setting (home, school, alternative care, penal system). The analysis will review the compatibility of the legality of corporal punishment with each state's constitution and other relevant domestic laws, and also with the CRC and other relevant international and regional human rights instruments which the state has ratified. Then consideration must be given to whether challenging the legality of corporal punishment in domestic courts is possible; if it is impossible or fails, then relevant international or regional human rights mechanisms could be used.

New partnerships must be formed to work collectively wherever corporal punishment is still authorized, to creatively review possible domestic, regional, and international remedies, to draft detailed legal advisory opinions, prepare cases, threaten and initiate action. We need a new-style of advocate and innovative, human rights-based lawyers, supported internationally with technical legal and other assistance. Strategic use of litigation must be added to all the other forms of advocacy—continuously lobbying governments and parliaments, using the media, petitions by children and others, formation of broad professional alliances, multi-faith action, and so on. This should speed the ultimate elimination of deliberate, legalized adult violence against children.

The potential of success for the peaceful future of human societies and human relationships is boundless. The price of adult delay is all around us in the daily misery, suffering, injury, harmed development, and insulted dignity of yet another generation of children.

NOTES

1. All judgments of the Court are available at: http://hudoc.echr.coe.int/hudoc/
2. Separate Opinion of Judge Sir Gerald Fitzmaurice, annexed to ECHR Tyrer v UK.
3. A fuller account of this case, and its failure to date to persuade the UK Government to remove completely the "reasonable chastisement" defense to give children equal protection, is given in Chapter 20.
4. The CRC has been ratified by every UN state except the United States and Somalia. Both of these countries have signed the Convention, signifying intent to ratify.
5. The website of the Global Initiative to End All Corporal Punishment of Children provides details of all treaty body recommendations concerning corporal punishment, in individual reports on each state worldwide. See: www.endcorporalpunishment.org
6. General comments are authoritative statements of the Committee's interpretation of states' obligations under the CRC. For details, see: http://www.coe.int/T/E/

REFERENCES

African Commission on Human and Peoples' Rights. (1981). *African Charter on Human and Peoples' Rights*. Available at http://www.achpr.org/english/_info/charter_en.html

African Commission on Human and Peoples' Rights. (2003). *Curtis Francis Doebber v Sudan*, 236/2000, 33rd Ordinary Session, Niger.

African Committee of Experts on the Rights and Welfare of the Child. (2009, November). *Concluding observations on Egypt's initial and first periodic reports under the African Charter issued during the Committee's 14th Session*, Addis Ababa.

Committee on the Rights of the Child. (1994, October). *Concluding observations on Spain's initial report under the Convention on the Rights of the Child*. CRC/C/15/Add.28.

Committee on the Rights of the Child. (1995, February 15). *Concluding observations on the UK's initial report under the Convention on the Rights of the Child*. CRC/C/15/Add.34.

Committee on the Rights of the Child. (2000/2001). *General Discussion Days*. Reports available from http://www2.ohchr.org/english/bodies/crc/discussion2008.htm

Committee on the Rights of the Child. (2001). *General comment no. 1: The aims of education*. CRC/GC/2001/1. Available from http://www2.ohchr.org/english/bodies/crc/comments.htm

Committee on the Rights of the Child. (2002, October). *Concluding observations on the UK's first periodic report under the Convention on the Rights of the Child*. CRC/C/15/Add.188.
Committee on the Rights of the Child. (2003). *General comment no. 5: General measures of implementation of the Convention on the Rights of the Child*. CRC/GC/2003/5. Available from http://www2.ohchr.org/english/bodies/crc/comments.htm
Committee on the Rights of the Child. (2006). *General comment no. 8: The right of the child to protection from corporal punishment and other cruel, inhuman or degrading treatment or punishment*. CRC/C/GC/8. Available from http://www2.ohchr.org/english/bodies/crc/comments.htm
Committee on the Rights of the Child. (2008, October). *Concluding observations on the UK's third and fourth periodic reports*. CRC/C/GBR/CO/4.
Council of Europe. (2008a). *Building a Europe with and for children*. Available from http://www.coe.int/t/dc/files/themes/chatiments_corporels/default_en.asp
Council of Europe. (2008b, October). *UK must improve children's protection and ban corporal punishment*. Strasbourg: Council of Europe Press Division.
European Commission on Human Rights. (1982). *Admissibility Decision: Seven Individuals v. Sweden*, Application no. 8811/79.
European Court of Human Rights. (1978). *Tyrer v UK*. Available from http://hudoc.echr.coe.int/hudoc/
European Court of Human Rights. (1982). *Campbell and Cosans v. UK*. Available from http://hudoc.echr.coe.int/hudoc/
European Court of Human Rights. (1993). *Costello-Roberts v. UK*. Available from http://hudoc.echr.coe.int/hudoc/
European Court of Human Rights. (1998, September 23). *A v. UK*. Available from http://hudoc.echr.coe.int/hudoc/
European Court of Human Rights. (2000). *Decision on Admissibility: Philip Williamson and Others v. UK*. Application no. 55211/00. Available from http://hudoc.echr.coe.int/hudoc/
European Court of Human Rights. (2003, July 8). *Grand Chamber Judgment: Sahin v. Germany*. Available from http://hudoc.echr.coe.int/hudoc/
European Committee of Social Rights. (2001). *General observations regarding article 7, paragraph 10, and article 17. Conclusions XV–2*, Vol. 1, General Introduction.
European Committee of Social Rights. (2005). *Collective Complaints:* 17/2003 *World Organization against Torture (OMCT) v. Greece*; 18/2003 *OMCT v. Ireland*; 19/2003 *OMCT v. Italy*; 20/2003 *OMCT v. Portugal*; 21/2003 *OMCT v. Belgium*. Decisions on the merits and all details are available from http://www.coe.int/t/dghl/monitoring/socialcharter/Complaints/Complaints_en.asp
European Committee of Social Rights. (2006). *Decision on the Merits: Collective Complaint 34/2006, OMCT v. Portugal*.
Hammarberg, T. (2008). Issue Paper 2006/1, updated version January 2008, *Children and corporal punishment: The right not to be hit, also a children's right*, CommDH/IssuePaper(2006)1REV. Available from https://wcd.coe.int/ViewDoc.jsp?Ref=CommDH/IssuePaper(2006)1&Language=lanEnglish&Ver=REV
Human Rights Council. (2008). *Universal Periodic Review process*. Reports and recommendations available from http://www.ohchr.org/EN/HRBodies/UPR/Pages/UPRmain.aspx
Inter-American Commission on Human Rights. (2009, August 5). *Rapporteurship on the rights of the child: Report on corporal punishment and human rights of children and adolescents*. OEA/Ser.L/V/II.135. Available from www.cidh.org

Inter-American Court of Human Rights. (2009, January 27). *Resolution in response to the request for an advisory opinion from the Inter-American Commission of December 29 2008*. See http://www.cidh.org
Organization of African Unity. (1990). *African Charter on the Rights and Welfare of the Child*. OAU Doc. CAB/LEG/24.9/49. Available at http://www.africa-union.org/root/au/Documents/Treaties/Text/A.%20C.%20ON%20THE%20RIGHT%20AND%20WELF%20OF%20CHILD.pdf
Parliamentary Assembly of the Council of Europe. (2004). *Recommendation 1666: Europe-wide ban on corporal punishment of children*. See http://assembly.coe.int/ASP/Doc/ATListing_E.asp
Pinheiro, P. S. (2006). *World report on violence against children*. Geneva: United Nations. Available from http://www.violencestudy.org/IMG/pdf/English.pdf.
United Nations. (1989). *Convention on the Rights of the Child*. Available at www.un.org/documents/ga/res/44/a44r025.htm.

3 The Theoretical Rationale for Eliminating Physical Punishment

Anne B. Smith

"Every question concerning the child depends on some theoretical framework if it is to provide any sort of answer" (Honig, 2009, p. 66). A lack of theoretical grounding for research has hampered the study of physical punishment in the past (Straus & Donnelly, 2005), so it is important to look at theoretical perspectives about childhood and society and children's well-being, quality of life, learning, and development, which support the human rights imperative described by Peter Newell in Chapter 2. This chapter will outline theories about children and childhood, which suggest that physical punishment fails to recognize children's personhood, competency and agency, and is an ineffective and harmful means of influencing children's development and learning.

THEORIES OF THE CHILD IN SOCIETY

Childhood Studies

Childhood Studies emerged out of a critique of traditional psychological perspectives on children, which tend to ignore the contribution that children themselves make to their growing up (Qvortrup, Corsaro, & Honig, 2009).

> Childhood Studies is about a more integrated approach to research and teaching about children's lives and well-being, a more 'joined-up' view of the 'child in context', which has become a priority for policy and for professional training. . . . Childhood Studies is built around a rejection of the essentialism endemic in traditional theorizing, in favor of recognizing the multiple ways childhood is socially constructed and reconstructed in relation to time and place, age, gender, ethnicity etc. Childhood Studies also represents a critique of the way children's lives are regulated in modern societies, an emphasis on recognizing children as social actors, and empowering their participatory rights in all areas of social life. (Woodhead, 2004, pp. x–xi)

The discipline of Childhood Studies and the growth of the Children's Rights movement have developed on a parallel course, sharing an emphasis on children's agency, their right to participate, and how they construct their social worlds; children as subjects not objects of control or concern; and children as individuals and persons rather than as a collective undifferentiated class or immature beings (Alanen, 2010; Freeman, 1998). Relationships between adults and children are of central importance in Childhood Studies, and also in the consideration of the use of physical punishment within families. As Mayall (2009) points out, "if children are understood as competent, knowledgeable and morally reliable, their parents will be less required to, and will see less reason to, control their children's every move" (pp. 176–177). Parent–child relationships are located in particular historical and social contexts, and provide opportunities for, and limit, children's agency (Honig, 2009; Mayall, 2009; Qvortrup et al., 2009). Their nature determines how each successive generation of parents interacts with their children.

In the past, children were expected to obey immediately and unquestioningly, not expressing their own views (Mayall, 2009). But the increasing democratization of the family in Western societies diminishes the social space between children and parents, and is a central influence in the global movement to eliminate physical punishment. It is no accident that the Nordic countries were the first to reform their laws on physical punishment, because they have long upheld the values of democratic and participatory relationships between adults and children, and they have had a sense of collective responsibility for children's well-being (Dahlberg, 2009; Lindahl, 2008). The strength of a democracy is sometimes judged by how well it treats its weakest members, so the growing rejection of physical punishment, may be seen as a sign of strengthening democracies, and increasing respect for children's well-being and dignity (Kaufmann & Rizzini, 2009). Societies in which adults have unlimited rights to do what they want with their children are places "where violence against children persists as a permanent threat" (Pinheiro, 2006, p. xvii). All indications are that such authoritarian parenting is on the wane, as evidenced by the ever-growing number of countries prohibiting physical punishment.

A central tenet of Childhood Studies is that childhood is not a natural or universal feature of human societies, but a social construction (Mayall, 2002; Prout & James, 1997). Complex culturally constructed belief systems inform us about the 'right' way for children to develop, be cared for and disciplined (Woodhead, 2005). This book provides numerous examples of how culturally embedded views about appropriate power relationships between adults and children become barriers to law reform. Much of the research literature on physical punishment ignores the role of children as social actors, viewing them as the passive objects of their parents' socialization efforts. Children are perceived as immature beings who are shaped or molded into 'appropriate' behavior, and therefore as a legitimate target of physical discipline (Gough & Reavey, 1997). While the social science literature on physical punishment (see Chapter 4) provides compelling evidence that there are harmful long-term consequences of physical punishment, Phillips and Alderson (2003) believe that the issue cannot be resolved solely on the basis of compiling evidence against it. They argue that the problem lies in the dominant view of childhood "that constructs children as human becomings rather than human beings, and a power system that upholds 'parents' rights' over children's human rights" (Phillips & Alderson, 2003, p. 175).

Viewing children as the property of their parents and the passive recipients of socialization helps to rationalize the use of violence to control them. If children are considered less valuable and less important than adults, and as owned by their parents, then violence against them can be "considered an acceptable, private matter" (Saunders & Goddard, 2010, p. 230). Although children are social actors and experiencing subjects, with a viewpoint of their own about issues such as fairness, justice, punishment, and rules, respecting children as persons is not a salient part of many countries' social constructions of childhood. But the growing debate about physical punishment challenges traditional perspectives, and we can see from many of this book's chapters, indicates that a social reconstruction of childhood is well underway.

The neglect of children's perspectives on physical punishment leaves a substantial gap in the research literature. Even researchers who have not explored children's perspectives believe that children's understanding and experience of family discipline mediates its effects (e.g., Deater-Deckard & Dodge, 1997). If parental messages are to guide children's behavior "the child must perceive the message as appropriate, the child must be motivated to comply with the message, and the child must feel the message has not been imposed but rather has been self-generated" (Grusec & Goodnow, 1994, p. 17). It is only recently that the invisibility and voicelessness of children in this area of research has been questioned. A few studies have emerged that focus on children's perspectives on physical punishment and challenge commonly held adult beliefs about its effects and value (e.g., Dobbs, Smith, & Taylor, 2006; Horgan, 2002; Saunders & Goddard, 2010; Taylor, 2005; Willow & Hyder, 1998). As Garbarino (2005) has noted, "the power of children to articulate their experiences and have their account validated in public settings may play an important role in changing values and practices with respect to corporal punishment" (p. 16).

Childhood Studies provides a useful starting point for a theoretical framing of physical punishment and its prohibition, because of its compatibility with human rights principles and its emphasis on children's personhood and agency. This approach centers on the notion that childhood and intergenerational relationships are socially constructed within particular historical and social contexts. As societies move towards valuing democratic and participatory generational relationships over hierarchical and authoritarian relationships, they should become increasingly amenable to law reform respecting children's equal rights to justice and freedom from violence.

Ecological Theory

Ecological theory (Bronfenbrenner, 1979) emphasizes the impact on children's development of the interactions among many contextual layers or systems. The child's immediate environment or "microsystem" (e.g., home, school, playground) is where the child's development is most directly affected by the quality of social interactions. Their experiences within their microsystems involve not only activities, roles, and interpersonal relationships as they are objectively measured, but as they are understood subjectively by the participants. For microsystems to sustain and enhance development, they should be emotionally validating for children.

Bronfenbrenner (1979) considered that interpersonal relationships which supported development were those in which there is a balance of power between adult and child, where one partner does not dominate the relationship, where the child is gradually given more opportunity to take control, and where there is warmth and reciprocity between parent and child.

> Learning and development are facilitated by the participation of the developing person in progressively more complex patterns of reciprocal activity with someone with whom that person has developed a strong and enduring emotional attachment and when the balance of power gradually shifts in favor of the developing person. (Bronfenbrenner, 1979, p. 60)

Physical punishment "diminishes the partnership nature of the socialization process" (Garbarino, 2005, p. 14) and is antithetical to the reciprocity, warmth and balance of power which Bronfenbrenner considered optimal in parent–child relationships.

Connections between the family and other microsystems are called mesosystems. These systems allow communication among microsystems and the messages communicated can have an impact on the child. For example, child care centers may support or discourage parents' reliance on physical punishment.

The family (and other microsystems) is nested within a wider framework of social and economic influences—the "macrosystem"—which affects its capacity to nurture children's well-being. This means that the well-being of children can be affected profoundly by events occurring in settings in which they are never present. Risk and resiliency research (Masten, 2001) has demonstrated that factors associated with hostile and supportive parenting are found not only within individuals and families, but also in past family history, cultural and religious values and beliefs, family support systems, economic circumstances, law, and public policy. The macrosystem values and practice around violence provide a climate of support for, or opposition to, physical punishment. Macrosystems reflect people's shared assumptions about how things such as bringing up children should be done in a culture or sub-culture (Garbarino, 2005). Straus (1996) has found evidence of their importance in the positive correlation between countries' homicide rates and physical punishment rates.

Law is part of the macrosystem. It influences all of the other ecological systems affecting the child. This effect is seen in the impact of law reform aimed at eliminating physical punishment, particularly when it is accompanied by intensive and ongoing public information (see Chapter 24). For example, in Sweden, where successive law reforms have made the unacceptability of physical punishment increasingly explicit, its incidence has declined steadily and child maltreatment fatalities have become extremely rare (Durrant & Janson, 2005). "Cultural support for physical punishment is most concretely evident in legislation governing its use" (Durrant, Broberg, & Rose-Krasnor, 1999, p. 28).

Xu, Tung, and Dunaway (2000) have developed an integrated theoretical model of the determinants physical punishment, identifying the four main determinants as cultural capital, human capital, social capital, and exogenous factors. Cultural capital includes the symbolic meanings, intergenerational beliefs, religious and cultural values, and norms which guide parenting, such as cultural acceptability of responding to conflict with violence. Human capital is people's skills and capacities to change and the resources from which parents may draw, such as education, employment, and income. Social capital is found in interpersonal relationships, such as informal support networks, child care, assistance with domestic work, and emotional support from partners, extended family members, neighborhood networks, and outside agencies. Exogenous factors include family demographics, such as family size, marital status of parents, and parental age. These four sources of capital interact to determine the likelihood of physical punishment.

The ecological perspective suggests that intervention at more than one level is likely to be the most effective way of ending physical punishment of children: legal prohibitions; educational campaigns; agencies and services which support families; family friendly employment conditions; reduced economic disparities; increased social inclusion; and supportive connections and shared values among families, schools, childcare centers, and communities are all components of ecological systems will all have influence if they enhance warmth, strengthen reciprocity and equalize the balance of power in parent–child relationships.

THEORIES OF DEVELOPMENT AND LEARNING

Attachment and Moral Internalization

Attachment—the affectional tie which binds the child to the parent/caregiver across space and time—is central to learning and development, most particularly in the formation of identity and social relationships. On the basis of interactions with their attachment figures (caregivers), young children develop internal working models of self which allow them to regulate their own behavior, interpret the behavior of others, anticipate the future, and make plans (Bretherton & Mulholland, 1999; Cassidy, 1999).

The formation of secure attachments in early childhood is the essential foundation for the development of relationships throughout life. Attachment provides a secure base of trust from which children explore their physical and social worlds. Secure attachments derive from caregivers'availability, sensitivity and responsiveness, which help children to understand when it is safe to explore and when they should seek protection (Crittenden, 2005; Kochanska & Aksan, 2006). Attachment security is vital to children's sense of well-being and their feeling of safety within and outside the boundaries of their family (Garbarino, 2001).

The development of secure attachment is impeded by negative and punitive parental responses (Coyl, Roggman, & Newland, 2002; Lyons-Ruth & Jacobvitz, 1999; Posada & Pratt, 2008). From this perspective, physical punishment is deleterious to the formation of secure attachments, interfering with children's exploration and learning, as well as their capacity to develop trusting relationships with their parents and others. By arousing anxiety, physical punishment undermines children's "confidence in the caregiver's availability as a haven of support" (Posada & Pratt, 2008, p. 16).

Attachment plays an important role in the development of conscience and the internalization of rules and moral values (Kochanska, 2002; Kochanska & Aksan, 2006; Laible & Thompson, 2000), which are promoted by reciprocal, emotionally supportive, interpersonal parent–child interactions. The development of internal control is an important long-term parenting goal. While young children are initially dependent on external regulation, they gradually "become increasingly guided by inner mechanisms and, thus, self-regulated" (Kochanska & Aksan, 2006, p. 1588). Even young preschool children are now believed to be capable of having a rich conscience, allowing them to understand and abide by moral rules and standards. Power assertive parental responses, such as physical punishment, are less successful in promoting moral internalization than the use of induction or reasoning (e.g., Grusec & Goodnow, 1994; Kochanska & Aksan, 2006).

Some developmental psychologists (Hoffman, 1994; Larzelere, 1996) have argued that a combination of power assertive and inductive disciplinary techniques can encourage moral internalization. According to Hoffman, a focus on the cognitive social information processing involved in a disciplinary encounter, risks ignoring the importance of affective components. He believes that power assertion can provide the motivation and arousal to direct the child's attention to the message, which should then be given inductively. But he points out that while a low level of arousal may result in the child ignoring the parental message, too high a level will result in fear, anxiety, and resentment which will direct the child's attention not to the message but to the consequence for him/herself. Because pain generally induces a high level of arousal, physical punishment is unlikely to be helpful in conveying a rational message to the child.

In summary, developmental theory predicts that sensitive, responsive caregiving in warm, reciprocal relationships will promote secure attachment and moral internalization. Children are more likely to develop autonomy and self-regulation in a warm, supportive family context.

Sociocultural Theory

Sociocultural theory (Karpov, 2005; Rogoff, 1990; Tomasello, 1999; Vygotsky, 1978) holds that children gradually come to know and understand the world through their own activities within the context of social relationships. Out of sensitive and reciprocal early interactions between infants and caregivers arise episodes of joint attention—where children and caregivers focus on a common reference point, such as an object, person, or event. These episodes underlie cognitive and language development, as the foundation of communication, shared meaning, and mutual understanding (Karpov, 2005; Smith, 1999; Tomasello, 1999). While joint attention episodes begin in the first year of life, they become increasingly important to learning through early childhood (Carr et al., 2009), as well as to the development of a sense of self; identity is forged through the negotiation and co-construction of meaning in interpersonal communication (Wenger, 1998). Therefore, cognitive development is based in early attachment (Karpov, 2005), which may help explain why children who are physically punished tend to demonstrate poorer academic outcomes (Shumow, Vandell, & Posner, 1998).

While they are developing skills, children perform more competently with assistance. Help and guidance can be gradually withdrawn as children become increasingly able to act independently. In the process of learning through scaffolding[1] and guidance from adults, children internalize the modes of social interaction which they experience. According to a sociocultural view, if children experience pain and negativity from their caregivers, they will internalize these modes of interaction, and apply them in their interactions with others.

Ideally, families provide 'responsive learning contexts' which allow children to gradually take more and more initiative in controlling their own behavior. Responsive learning contexts develop when family members are aware of children's current levels of competence and understanding, and can judge when and where they need support. The key elements of responsive learning contexts are dialogue, social interaction, and graduated assistance. While in the early years there is a major role for the more skilled family member in the scaffolding process, responsive learning contexts give the learner increasing opportunities for self regulation, responsibility, and initiative. Physical punishment is antithetical to this process, as it involves coercive external control, not supportive communication. According to Infante (2005), physical punishment is a failure of communication resulting from parents' communicative incompetence, and it is unlikely to lead to the internalization of messages.

Language helps children relate to and understand others, and it enables them "to reflect on, represent, and communicate about the self and others" (Laible & Thompson, 2000, p. 1424). When caregivers refer to feelings and moral evaluations in conversations with children, those children are more likely to be sensitive to the feelings of others, be aware of the consequences of their actions, and feel guilty if they have harmed others (Laible & Thompson, 2000). Establishing a dialogue within shared conversations during early childhood is the starting point of an ongoing disposition towards reciprocity, which is the foundation for children being able to work collaboratively with others, master challenge and stretch their thinking (Carr et al., 2009).

Sociocultural theory predicts that the lack of emotional support and failure in communication characterizing physical punishment diminish children's opportunities to internalize parental messages, learn to regulate their own behavior, and develop their ability to engage reciprocally with others.

Learning Theory

Classical Learning Theory

Classical learning theory explains the process of associative learning which begins when a stimulus (the unconditioned stimulus) automatically evokes a physiological response in the learner. If another stimulus is presented at the same time, or slightly before the unconditioned stimulus, it comes to be associated with the unconditioned stimulus and, over time, evokes the same response. Classically conditioned responses were studied by Pavlov who presented food (unconditioned stimulus) to dogs, causing them to salivate. By ringing a bell shortly before he presented the food, and doing this a number of times, he was able to elicit salivation solely by ringing the bell. Watson and Rayner (1920) demonstrated that emotional responses can also be learned through association. In a notorious experiment, they presented a white rat to a young child shortly before striking a steel bar behind his head. He quickly came to associate the rat with the sound of the steel bar and responded with fear to the sight of the rat. His fear generalized to similar objects, including a rabbit, a dog, a fur coat and a Santa Claus mask.

It has been empirically demonstrated that a wide range of positive and negative emotional responses, such as fears and dislike of food, people, or places, are learned through classical conditioning. A particularly powerful unconditioned stimulus is physical pain, which elicits fear, anxiety, and hostility, and defensive behaviors such as withdrawal, avoidance, and retaliation. Those responses can become associated with other stimuli present at the time the pain is inflicted, including the parent and the home. If such a conditioned negative emotional response is generated, this can interfere with the development of attachment. "The association of fear or pain with a specific target may lead to systematic avoidance of that object for the rest of one's life" (Newman & Newman, 2007, p. 132).

Operant Learning Theory

Operant learning theory explains the process of learning through consequences. If an individual's behavior is followed by something that the individual likes, desires, or finds pleasant, the behavior that produced it is likely to increase in frequency (positive reinforcement). For example, if a baby vocalizes and her mother responds by smiling and talking to the baby—and the baby enjoys her response—the baby's vocalizing is likely to increase (Smith, 1998). If a behavior is followed by the removal of something the individual doesn't like or finds unpleasant, that behavior also is likely to increase (negative reinforcement). For example, if a child is told that if he practices the piano after dinner he does not have to wash the dishes—and he dislikes washing dishes—his piano practicing is likely to increase. If a behavior is followed by something that the individual dislikes or finds unpleasant, that behavior is likely to decrease in frequency (punishment). For example, if a toddler touches an expensive object and her father shouts at her—and she dislikes being shouted at—she is less likely to touch that object in the future.

Parents who use physical punishment expect that it will operate according to operant learning principles; that is, it will decrease the frequency of behaviors they do not like. However, empirical evidence demonstrates that punishment has lasting effects only when it is immediate, severe, and consistent (Domjan, 2000, cited in Holden, 2002). While this might induce compliance, it also risks injury to the child and a conditioned negative emotional response to the parent.

Social-interactional Theory

Social Interactional theory describes the development of coercive processes in families (Patterson, 1982, 1995; Patterson, Dishion, & Chamberlain, 1993; Stoolmiller, Patterson, & Snyder, 1997)—the moment-by-moment interactions in which the parent and child reinforce each other's coercive behaviors. These interactions begin when the parent makes a demand of the child. If the child responds by acting out—and if the parent stops making the demand—the child is negatively reinforced by the parent. If the child then stops acting out, the parent is negative reinforced by the child. Alternatively, a child who is seeking a parent's attention might do something the parent dislikes until the parent pays attention to him. The parent's attention might be in the form of scolding, shouting, or physical punishment.

While the parent believes that he is punishing the child, the child values the attention so it actually positively reinforces his behavior. If the child then stops the disliked behavior, the parent is negatively reinforced for shouting at or hitting him. Over time, the child and parent become "trained" in using aggressive or other antisocial behavior to control others.

> The discipline reflects parents' desperate effort to control a child who is essentially socially unskilled. Presumably, this is because the parent is nonsupportive for prosocial-skill behaviors. As a result, they issue three or four times as many commands, threats, and scoldings; but the punishments they use tend to be ineffective. (Stoolmiller et al., 1997, p. 223)

Social Learning Theory

Social learning theory (Bandura, Ross, & Ross, 1961) explains the vast amount of learning that occurs without direct reinforcement or punishment. It focuses on the role of observational learning or modeling. Albert Bandura conducted a series of experiments in which he would expose one group of children to an aggressive model and another group to a non-aggressive model. Later, he would observe their behavior with a doll. Those children who observed the aggressive model were more aggressive towards the doll than the children who observed the non-aggressive model.

> Most human behavior is learned observationally. Through modeling, observing others, one forms an idea of how new behaviors are performed, and on later occasions this coded information serves as a guide for action. (Bandura & Walters, 1977, p. 82)

Children learn complex new patterns of behavior, including aggressive behavior, by watching others. Through modeling, societies and families pass on patterns of behavior to the next generation. Children are most likely to repeat observed behaviors if they are performed by models who are powerful, prestigious, and in control of resources, and who are themselves rewarded for the behavior (Newman & Newman, 2007).

Families provide many powerful opportunities for children to learn through modeling, often not deliberately. Parents can be models of a wide array of maladaptive and harmful behaviors, such as smoking, consuming alcohol, speeding, insulting others, showing poor sportsmanship, lying, shirking responsibility, and many more—including interpersonal violence. When parents respond to other family members with hitting or other physical force, they provide models of aggressive behavior which are observed and encoded by their children who are then much more likely to engage in such behavior themselves. Chapter 4 summarizes the evidence that supports this theoretical position by demonstrating that physical punishment is consistently associated with increased child aggression.

Attribution Theory

A cognitive behavioral perspective (Caselles & Milner, 2000; Nix et al., 1999; Weiner, 1986) suggests that physical punishment is often the result of particular parental attributions for children's behavior. For example, if parents believe that their children's transgressions are intentional and controllable they are more likely to respond with anger and punishment than if they believe that the behavior was developmentally normative, unintentional, or uncontrollable (Durrant et al., 1999). For example, if a parent believes that his 3-year-old daughter is having a tantrum because she is "spoiled" or trying to make him mad, he is likely to punish her. On the other hand, if he believes that she is not yet able to regulate her emotions, and is tired and feeling frustrated, he is likely to respond by staying calm, removing her from the situation, and talking with her afterward. When parents have unrealistic expectations of their children and punish them for not meeting those expectations, the children are likely to feel misjudged, becoming resentful and hostile—or anxious and fearful. If the parents continue to attribute these behaviors to intentional controllable factors, the punishment is likely to escalate over time.

SUMMARY

A range of theories, from rights-based to systems-focused to classical learning theories, predict that physical punishment will be detrimental to children's cognitive, social, and emotional development. The Childhood Studies perspective argues physical punishment disrespects the child's agency, reflecting an outmoded construction of the child as the possession of parents and the objects of adult power. Ecological theory locates the child within the immediate framework of the family, but also within broader social, economic, cultural, and legal contexts, suggesting that children's well-being is affected by parental beliefs and actions, cultural values and traditions, and their legal status. Attachment theory predicts that children's well-being and development will be best supported by sensitive, responsive caregiving, characterized by reciprocity between children and adults within a safe and secure environment. Learning theories explain why physical punishment can produce fear, hostility, aggression, and withdrawal in children, and how it can escalate to increasingly severe levels and be transmitted across generations. Whatever the nature of the theory on which we base our intervention, it will support the elimination of physical punishment, whether on the basis of children's rights or their healthy development.

NOTES

1. Scaffolding refers to giving children the opportunity to do as much as possible alone, while the adult fills in what the child cannot do (Bruner, 1985).

REFERENCES

Alanen, L. (2010). Taking children's rights seriously. *Childhood, 17*(1), 5–8.

Bandura, A., Ross, D., & Ross, S. A. (1961). Transmission of aggression through imitation of aggressive models. *Journal of Abnormal and Social Psychology, 63*, 575–582.

Bandura, A., & Walters, R. H. (1963). *Social learning and personality development.* New York: Holt, Rinehart, & Winston.

Bretherton, I., & Mulholland, K. A. (1999). Internal working models in attachment relationships: A construct revisited. In J. Cassidy & P. R. Shaver (Eds.), *Handbook of attachment theory, research and clinical* applications (pp. 89–114). New York: Guilford.

Bronfenbrenner, U. (1979). *The ecology of human development.* Cambridge, MA: Harvard University Press.

Bruner, J. (1985). Vygotsky: A historical and conceptual perspective. In J. V. Wertsch (Ed.), *Culture, communication and cognition: Vygotskian perspectives* (pp. 21–35). Cambridge: Cambridge University Press.

Carr, M., Smith, A. B., Duncan, J., Jones, C., Lee, W., & Marshall, K. (2009). *Learning in the Making: Disposition and design in early education.* Rotterdam, The Netherlands: Sense Publishers.

Caselles, C. E., & Milner, J. S. (2000). Evaluations of child transgressions, disciplinary choices, and expected child compliance in a no-cry and a crying infant condition in physically abusive and comparison mothers. *Child Abuse & Neglect, 24*(4), 477–491.

Cassidy, J. (1999). The nature of the child's ties. In J. Cassidy & P. R. Shaver (Eds.), *Handbook of attachment theory, research and clinical applications* (pp. 3–20). New York: Guilford.

Coyl, D. D., Roggman, L. A., & Newland, L. A. (2002). Stress, maternal depression, and negative mother–infant interactions in relation to infant attachment. *Infant Mental Health Journal, 23*(1–2), 145–163.

Crittenden, P. (2005). The origins of physical punishment: An ethological/attachment perspective on the use of physical punishment by human parents. In M. Donnelly & M. A. Straus (Eds.), *Corporal punishment of children in theoretical perspective* (pp. 73–90). New Haven, CT: Yale University Press.

Dahlberg, G. (2009). Policies in early childhood education and care: Potentialities for agency, play and learning. In J. Qvortrup, W. A. Corsaro, & M.-S. Honig (Eds.), *The Palgrave handbook of childhood studies* (pp. 228–237). Basingstoke, Hampshire: Palgrave MacMillan.

Deater-Deckard, K., & Dodge, K. A. (1997). Spare the rod, spoil the authors: Emerging themes in research on parenting and child development. *Psychological Inquiry, 8*(3), 230–235.

Dobbs, T., Smith, A. B., & Taylor, N. (2006). 'No, we don't get a say, children just suffer the consequences': Children talk about family discipline. *International Journal of Children's Rights. 14*(2), 137–156.

Durrant, J., Broberg, A., & Rose-Krasnor, L. (1999). Predicting mothers' use of physical punishment during mother–child conflicts in Sweden and Canada. *New Directions for Child and Adolescent Development, 86*, 25–41.

Durrant, J. E., & Janson, S. (2005). Law reform, corporal punishment and child abuse: The case of Sweden. *International Review of Victimology, 12*, 139–158.

Freeman, M. (1998). The sociology of childhood and children's rights. *International Journal of Children's Rights, 6*, 433–444.

Garbarino, J. (2001). An ecological perspective on the effects of violence on children. *Journal of Community Psychology, 29*(3), 361–378.

Garbarino, J. (2005). Corporal punishment in ecological perspective. In M. Donnelly & M. A. Straus (Eds.), *Corporal punishment of children in theoretical perspective* (pp. 8–20). New Haven, CT: Yale University Press.
Gough, B., & Reavey, P. (1997). Parental accounts regarding the physical punishment of children: Discourses of dis/empowerment. *Child Abuse & Neglect, 21*(5), 417–430.
Grusec, J. E., & Goodnow, J. J. (1994). Impact of parental discipline methods on the child's internalization of values: A reconceptualization of current points of view. *Developmental Psychology, 30*(1), 4–19.
Hoffman, M. L. (1994). Discipline and internalization. *Developmental Psychology, 30*(1), 26–28.
Holden, G. W. (2002). Perspectives on the effects of corporal punishment: Comment on Gershoff (2002). *Psychological Bulletin, 128*(4), 590–595.
Honig, M.-S. (2009). How is the child constituted in Childhood Studies? In J. Qvortrup, W. A. Corsaro, & M.-S. Honig (Eds.), *The Palgrave handbook of childhood studies* (pp. 62–77). Basingstoke, Hampshire: Palgrave MacMillan.
Horgan, G. (2002). *It's a hit, not a 'smack'*. Belfast, Ireland: Save the Children.
Infante, D. A. (2005). A communication theory perspective. In M. Donnelly & M. A. Straus (Eds.), *Corporal punishment of children in theoretical perspective* (pp. 183–198). New Haven, CT: Yale University Press.
Karpov, Y. V. (2005). *The neo-Vygotskian approach to child development*. Cambridge: Cambridge University Press.
Kaufmann, N., & Rizzini, I. (2009). Closing the gap between rights and the realities of children's lives. In J. Qvortrup, W. A. Corsaro, & M.-S. Honig (Eds.), *The Palgrave handbook of childhood studies* (pp. 422–434). Basingstoke, Hampshire: Palgrave MacMillan.
Kochanska, G. (2002). Committed compliance: Moral self, and internalization: A mediational model. *Developmental Psychology, 38*, 339–351.
Kochanska, G., & Aksan. N. (2006). Children's conscience and self regulation. *Journal of Personality, 74*(5), 1587–1617.
Laible, D. J., & Thompson, R. A. (2000). Mother–child discourse, attachment security, shared positive affect, and early conscience development. *Child Development, 71*(5), 1424–1440.
Larzelere, R. E. (1996). A review of the outcomes of parental use of nonabusive or customary physical punishment. *Pediatrics, 98*(4), 824–828.
Lindahl, M. (2008). Children's right to democratic upbringings. *International Journal of Early Childhood, 37*(3), 33–47.
Lyons-Ruth, K., & Jacobvitz, D. (1999). Attachment disorganization: Unresolved loss, relational violence, and lapses in behavioral and attentional strategies. In J. Cassidy & P. R. Shaver (Eds.), *Handbook of attachment theory, research and clinical applications* (pp. 520–554). New York: Guilford.
Masten, A. S. (2001). Ordinary magic: Resilience processes in development. *American Psychologist, 56*(3), 227–238.
Mayall, B. (2002). *Towards a sociology of childhood*. Buckingham, UK: Open University Press.
Mayall, B. (2009). Generational relations at family level. In J. Qvortrup, W. A. Corsaro, & M.-S. Honig (Eds.), *The Palgrave handbook of childhood studies* (pp. 176–187). Basingstoke, Hampshire: Palgrave MacMillan.
Newman, B. M., & Newman, P. R. (2007). *Theories of human development*. Mahwah, NJ: Lawrence Erlbaum Associates.
Nix, R. L., Pinderhughes, E. E., Dodge, K. A., Bates, J. E., Pettit, G. S., & McFadyen-Ketchum, S. A. (1999). The relation between mothers' hostile attribution tendencies and children's externalizing behavior problems: The mediating role of mothers' harsh discipline practices. *Child Development, 70*(4), 896–909.

Patterson, G. R. (1982). *Coercive family process: A social interactional approach.* Eugene, OR: Castalia.
Patterson, G. R. (1995). Coercion as a basis for early age of onset for arrest. In J. McCord (Ed.), *Coercion and punishment in long-term perspectives* (pp. 81–105). Cambridge, UK: Cambridge University Press.
Patterson, G. R., Dishion, T. J., & Chamberlain, P. (1993). Outcomes and methodological issues relating to treatment of antisocial children. In T. R. Giles (Ed.), *Effective psychotherapy: A handbook of comparative research* (pp. 43–88). New York: Plenum.
Phillips, B., & Alderson, P. (2003). Beyond 'anti-smacking': Challenging violence and coercion in parent–child relations. *International Journal of Children's Rights, 115,* 175–197.
Pinheiro, P. (2006). *World report on violence against children.* Geneva: United Nations Secretary-General's Study on Violence against Children. Available at: www.unviolencestudy.org
Posada, G., & Pratt, D. M. (2008). Physical aggression in the family and preschoolers' use of the mother as a secure base. *Journal of Marital and Family Therapy, 34*(1), 14–27.
Prout, A. & James, A. (1997). A new paradigm for the sociology of childhood? Provenance, promise and problems. Chapter 1 in A. James & A. Prout (Eds.) *Constructing and reconstructing childhood: contemporary issues in the sociological study of childhood.* London and New York: RoutledgeFalmer (pp. 7–33).
Qvortrup, J., Corsaro, W. A., & Honig, M.-S. (2009). Why social studies of childhood? An introduction to the handbook. In J. Qvortrup, W. A. Corsaro, & M.-S. Honig (Eds.), *The Palgrave handbook of childhood studies* (pp. 1–18). Basingstoke, Hampshire: Palgrave MacMillan.
Rogoff, B. (1990). *Apprenticeship in thinking: Cognitive development in social context.* New York: Oxford University Press.
Saunders, B. J., & Goddard, C. (2010). *Physical punishment in childhood: The rights of the child.* Chichester, UK: Wiley-Blackwell.
Shumow, L., Vandell, D. L., & Posner, J. K. (1998). Harsh, firm, and permissive parenting in low-income families: Relations to children's academic achievement and behavioral adjustment. *Journal of Family Issues, 19*(5), 483–507.
Smith, A. B. (1998). *Understanding children's development* (4th ed.). Wellington, New Zealand: Bridget Williams Books.
Smith, A. B. (1999). Quality childcare and joint attention. *International Journal of Early Years Education, 7*(1), 85–98.
Stoolmiller, M., Patterson, G. R., & Snyder, J. (1997). Parental discipline and child antisocial behavior: A contingency-based theory and some methodological refinements. *Psychological Inquiry, 8*(3), 223–229.
Straus, M. A. (1996). Spanking and the making of a violent society. *Pediatrics, 98*(4), 837–841.
Straus, M. A., & Donnelly, M. (2005). Theoretical approaches to corporal punishment. In M. Donnelly & M. A. Straus (Eds.), *Corporal punishment of children in theoretical perspective* (pp. 1–7). New Haven, CT: Yale University Press.
Taylor, N. (2005). Children and young people's perspectives. In A. B. Smith, M. M. Gollop, N. J. Taylor, & K. A. Marshall (Eds.), *The discipline and guidance of children: Messages from research* (pp. 79–86). Wellington and Dunedin, New Zealand: Office of the Children's Commissioner and Children's Issues Centre.
Tomasello, M. (1999). *The cultural origins of human cognition.* Cambridge, MA: Harvard University Press.

Vygotsky, L. S. (1978). *Mind in society: The development of higher psychological processes*. London: Harvard University Press.
Watson, J. B., & Rayner, R. (1920). Conditioned emotional reactions. *Journal of Experimental Psychology, 3*, 1–14.
Weiner, B. (1986). *An attributional theory of motivation and emotion*. New York: Springer-Verlag.
Wenger, E. (1998). *Communities of practice: Learning, meaning and identity*. Cambridge: Cambridge University Press.
Willow, C., & Hyder, T. (1998). *It hurts you inside: Children talking about smacking*. London: National Children's Bureau Enterprises in association with Save the Children.
Woodhead, M. (2004). Foreword. In M. J. Kehily (Ed.), *An introduction to childhood studies* (pp. x–xi). Maidenhead, NY: Open University Press.
Woodhead, M. (2005). Early childhood development: A question of rights. *International Journal of Early Childhood, 37*(3), 79–98.
Xu, X., Tung, Y.-Y., & Dunaway, R. G. (2000). Cultural, human, and social capital as determinants of corporal punishment: Toward an integrated theoretical model. *Journal of Interpersonal Violence, 15*(6), 603–630.

4 The Empirical Rationale for Eliminating Physical Punishment

Joan E. Durrant

The prohibition of physical punishment is based foremost on the human rights imperative to provide children with equal protection and equal respect for their dignity and personhood (see Chapter 2). In many countries, however, this principle has become buried beneath debates about whether children learn from physical punishment or are harmed by it, and whether physical punishment is equal to, or different from, physical abuse. As Anne Smith demonstrated in Chapter 3, a range of theoretical perspectives predict that physical punishment will be harmful to children's development in a number of ways. However, in many places, developmental and learning theories alone have not proved sufficient to reframe the issue as one of healthy child development. Instead, academic debates rage, particularly in North America, over the type and amount of data necessary to decide when a theory has been adequately tested. With each study published, controversy ensues over questions of causality, confounding variables, measurement, and sample sizes (see *Pediatrics*, 1996, Vol. 98[4]; *Psychological Bulletin*, 2002, Vol. 128[4]). As these debates continue, children's rights principles disappear into the shadows.

It should not be necessary, on an issue of fundamental human rights, to demonstrate conclusively that violation of those rights leads invariably to harm before ensuring that those rights are protected. Nor should the putative "benefits" of a rights violation be used to justify the violation. For example, a woman who is hit once by her partner may not suffer any serious long-term harm, yet we would not argue that the law should therefore allow hitting of women. And if a study found that hitting elderly people for walking slowly can increase their walking speed, we would not argue that the law should therefore allow hitting of elderly people. We can easily see the rights dimensions of these scenarios—rights to protection, physical security, and dignity. But if a study should find that children who are physically punished might not always be harmed, or that some moderating factor might reduce the degree of harm they sustain, prohibition is questioned, challenged, and resisted.

This phenomenon is particularly perplexing in light of the overwhelming amount of evidence that has accumulated over past decades to demonstrate that physical punishment predicts negative developmental outcomes with remarkable consistency. Across cultures, samples, measures, and outcomes, the literature supports the theoretical propositions outlined in Chapter 3, showing that physical punishment can interfere with attachment, moral internalization, mental health, and cognitive development; that it promotes aggression and risks escalation; and that children generally experience it as a negative force in their lives. In this chapter, I will examine the empirical findings related to each of the theoretical perspectives described in Chapter 3 and consider this research within the larger landscape of constructions of childhood.

THEORIES OF DEVELOPMENT AND LEARNING

Attachment and Moral Internalization

Attachment is considered by most developmental scientists to be the primary building block of healthy child development (see McCain, Mustard, & Shanker, 2007). It underpins self-regulation, identity formation, and social relationships. It is founded on a trusting relationship with a nurturing caregiver, which allows the child to explore the world with a sense of security, knowing that the caregiver will be there to support, protect, and respond sensitively to the child. Attachment theory would predict that caregiver-inflicted pain will disrupt the attachment process, as it violates the child's trust in that person as "a haven of support" (Posada & Pratt, 2008, p. 16). This hypothesis has been supported by the findings of several studies. Physical punishment predicts insecure attachment in toddlers (Coyl, Roggman, & Newland, 2002), preschoolers (Barnett, Kidwell, & Leung, 1998), and adolescents (Palmer & Hollin, 2001). In a meta-analysis of the physical punishment literature, Gershoff (2002) found that all of the 13 studies examining physical punishment and parent–child relationship quality found this association to be a negative one.

When attachment is disrupted, the child's trust and sense of safety are damaged, contributing to insecurity, anxiety, depression, and poorer mental health. This process may help to explain why physical punishment is associated with a range of mental health problems in children and youth. These include depression, unhappiness, anxiety, feelings of hopelessness, alcohol and drug use, and general psychological maladjustment (Csorba et al., 2001; Du Rant et al., 1994; Eamon, 2001; Lansford et al., 2005; Lau et al., 1999; Lau, Chan, Lam, Choi, & Lai, 2003; Rodriguez, 2003; Steely & Rohner, 2006; Turner & Finkelhor, 1996). Moreover, the relationship between physical punishment and mental health problems (depression, substance abuse, post-traumatic stress symptoms, and suicidal tendencies) continues into adulthood (Afifi, Brownridge, Cox, & Sareen, 2006; Lau et al., 2003; Medina, Mejia, Schell, Dawson, & Margolin, 2001; Turner & Muller, 2004). There is some research to suggest that this relationship might be mediated by a neurological process; violence in childhood can leave "chemical markers" that inhibit the brain's stress-regulation mechanism (McGowan et al., 2009).

According to attachment theory, the quality of the caregiver–child relationship contributes to the development of the child's self-regulation. Through feeling safe in exploring her external and internal worlds, the child learns self-control, comes to understand the reasons for limits and boundaries, and internalizes the caregiver's moral standards. If attachment is impeded by physical punishment, this theory would predict that the child will have more difficulty with self-control and demonstrate weaker moral internalization. Research findings support this hypothesis. Physical punishment is associated with lower levels of resistance to temptation, altruistic behavior, empathy, and moral judgment and regulation (Grinder, 1962; Kerr, Lopez, Olson, & Sameroff, 2004; Lopez, Bonenberger, & Schneider, 2001). In fact, Gershoff (2002) found that physical punishment was associated with weaker moral internalization in 13 of the 15 studies examining this relationship.

Sociocultural Theory

According to sociocultural theory (Rogoff, 1990; Vygotsky, 1978), children's learning is rooted in their social relationships. Whereas attachment theory focuses on the role of the caregiver–child relationship in emotional development, sociocultural theory emphasizes the importance of social interactions and relationships to cognitive and language development. When adults communicate sensitively and meaningfully with children, they engage them in learning. With the caregiver's graduated assistance (or "scaffolding"), the child becomes increasingly competent and confident, able to master complex tasks, and comfortable taking initiative in solving problems.

According to this theory, physical punishment would be antithetical to scaffolding, as it is coercive rather than supportive, and distancing rather than engaging. If so, physical punishment will be associated with slower cognitive and linguistic development, and with lower levels of intellectual achievement. Indeed, the frequency of physical punishment has been found to be inversely related to IQ (Aucoin, Frick, & Bodin, 2006; Smith & Brooks-Gunn, 1997), cognitive ability (Parkinson, Wallis, Prince, & Harvey, 1982), and language comprehension (Gest, Freeman, Domitrovich, & Welsh, 2004).

Recently, researchers have examined the relationship between physical punishment and cognitive development longitudinally. For example, in a study of 5,715 children from birth to age 13, spanking predicted lower levels of receptive vocabulary and reading recognition (Bradley, Corwyn,

Burchinal, McAdoo, & Coll, 2001). A later study of 806 2- to 4-year-olds and 704 5- to 9-year-olds (Straus & Paschall, 2009) found that, in both age cohorts, children who were never or rarely spanked gained on cognitive ability relative to children who were spanked—and the more children were spanked, the more they fell behind children who were not spanked. Moreover, there was an inverse relationship between physical punishment and scaffolding: The less mothers spanked their children, the more cognitive stimulation they provided (e.g., reading; talking about colors, shapes, and letters; providing books).

Learning Theories

Classical Learning Theory

According to classical learning theory, our emotional responses can be "conditioned" through a process of association. For example, pain automatically elicits a stress response, manifested physiologically in higher levels of the hormone cortisol, and behaviorally in withdrawal or aggression. Any stimulus that accompanies the sensation of pain can become associated with it psychologically: Over time that stimulus will come to elicit the same stress response, even when it is not accompanied by the physical sensation of pain. Therefore, the pain of being physically punished could become associated with the caregiver who inflicts it: Over time, the presence of the caregiver will come to elicit the stress response originally triggered by the pain. There is evidence that this associative learning can occur quickly and early in childhood. For example, 1-year-olds who experience frequent physical punishment show elevated levels of cortisol in reaction to anxiety-provoking interactions with their mothers (Bugental, Martorell, & Barraza, 2003) and 2-year-olds who are physically punished are more likely to distance themselves from their mothers than those who are not (Crockenberg, 1987).

Furthermore, pain is an elicitor of reflexive aggression (Azrin, Hake, & Hutchinson, 1965; Ulrich & Azrin, 1962). Reflexive pain-elicited aggression can be conditioned to animals or objects not involved in the delivery of the painful stimulus (Berkowitz, 1983) and aversive events can "prime anger, irritation, and hostility across a variety of contexts" (Stein & Levine, 1990, p. 69). According to Berkowitz (1993),

> One of the widespread illusions in our society is that suffering is ennobling. . . . This thought is comforting—but, unfortunately, actually has little empirical justification. Few of us become more virtuous and kinder as a result of our suffering. Quite to the contrary, a mounting body of evidence indicates that people afflicted by a decidedly unpleasant occurrence are all too apt to become hostile and aggressive. (p. 277)

This process may help to explain the relationship consistently found between physical punishment and child aggression (see next section).

Classical conditioning does not only happen to children. It also affects caregivers in a way that can cause their aggressive responding to generalize. Wolfe (1987) has suggested that a caregiver can develop a conditioned emotional response to a child's behavior. For example, when a child whines, the caregiver might become irritated and slap the child. Over time, the child's facial expression as he begins to whine can elicit the caregiver's irritation and impulse to slap the child. In this way, the caregiver becomes conditioned to respond to cues that have been associated with the disliked behavior, responding with anger and aggression to a broader range of child behaviors. Such a process might help to explain Gil's (1970) finding, in the first national study of physical child maltreatment in the United States, that a substantial proportion of maltreatment incidents

> derive from a general attitude of resentment and rejection on the part of the perpetrator toward a child. In these cases, not a specific act but the "whole person," or a specific quality in the person . . . is the object of rejection. In these cases, too, specific acts of the child may precipitate the acting out of the underlying attitude of rejection. (p. 127)

Operant Learning Theory

Operant learning theory predicts that a behavior followed by something that the individual likes will increase (reinforcement), whereas a behavior followed by something that the individual dislikes will decrease (punishment). It might be assumed, then, that if physical punishment is an effective punisher, it will reduce children's noncompliant or otherwise undesired behavior. It is this assumption that most often underlies the justification of its use.

A few studies have found that physical punishment can increase immediate compliance. For example, in a controlled laboratory study, Bean and Roberts (1981) found that physical punishment could motivate behavior disordered preschoolers to stay on a time-out chair for 2 minutes. But an average of eight spankings was required in a single experimental session to elicit this level of compliance, calling its "effectiveness" into question.

The relationship between physical punishment and compliance is not a reliable one. Physical punishment has been found to predict *lower* levels of compliance (Roberts & Powers, 1990) and to be *unrelated* to compliance (Day & Roberts, 1983). Some research has found that physical punishment is no more effective than time-out, taking away privileges, threats, ignoring, or reasoning in inducing compliance (Larzelere & Kuhn, 2005). Together, these findings indicate that physical punishment is not justified on the basis of effectiveness in increasing children's immediate compliance.

Social-interactional Theory

According to social-interactional theory, parents and children influence each other's behavior through ongoing bidirectional learning. The process through which coercive family interactions develop has been well-documented (Patterson, 1982; Snyder & Patterson, 1995; Wolfe, 1987). Briefly, if a child ends a disliked behavior when struck by a caregiver, the caregiver is reinforced for striking the child. But physical punishment is not reliable in inducing compliance, so it might not "work" next time. However, the caregiver believes that it works because it was successful earlier, and so increases its intensity. If the child resists or retaliates, the caregiver might escalate the intensity of the punishment further—or might end the interaction. In the former case, the child learns to submit to the punishment and the caregiver learns to inflict harsher punishment at an earlier stage of the interaction. In the latter case, the child learns to overpower others. In either case, the child is learning to control others through coercion.

> There is certainly some element of truth in the parent's perception that they are "trapped" into continuing to use harsh forms of control with the child. Some children may easily habituate . . . so that more and more harsh forms of discipline are required to attain the previous level of compliance. . . . [T]he short-term consequences for the parent may serve to maintain strict control over the child. For example, such control may ease the parent's tension and frustration (i.e., negative reinforcement), and provide the parent with immediate obedience from the child. . . . These immediate "gains" may outweigh the less noticeable, long-term consequences of this negative cycle: The need to increase the intensity of the punishment to maintain strict control, the child's avoidance of the parent and susceptibility to emotional and physical harm, and the failure of this process to teach the child the desired behaviours that would eliminate much of the need to rely on punishment methods. (Wolfe, 1987, p. 66)

Support for this theory comes from four decades of research on child physical maltreatment. Gil (1970) examined all of the cases of child maltreatment reported throughout the United States over a 2-year period. His findings revealed that nearly 63% were "incidents developing out of disciplinary action taken by caretakers" (p. 126) in response to a real or perceived act of the child. Similarly, Kadushin and Martin (1981) found in a study of more than 800 substantiated cases of child maltreatment that "most instances . . . were, in effect, extensions of disciplinary actions" (p. 263). Most maltreating parents in this study saw their actions as "primarily instrumental" and a "legitimate use of force"; a large percentage said they would do it again. As one mother in this study said,

> Then I started spanking her and she wouldn't cry—stubborn, she's just like I am, she just wouldn't cry—like it was having no effect, like she was defying me. So I spanked her all the harder. (p. 173)

Kadushin and Martin (1980) concluded that, "no factor was so universal, so ubiquitous, as some identifiable behavior on the part of the child which precipitated the parent–child interactional sequence culminating in abuse" (p. 254).

The role in child maltreatment that is played by a caregiver's intent to punish has been documented in other large studies, as well. For example, data from the *Canadian Incidence Study of Reported Child Abuse and Neglect* (Durrant, Trocmé, Fallon, Milne, & Black, 2009; Trocmé et al., 2001; Trocmé et al., 2005) show that most substantiated incidents of physical maltreatment are acts of punishment. In her meta-analysis of the physical punishment literature, Gershoff (2002) found that all of the 10 studies examining the relationship between physical punishment and physical harm found it to be a positive one.

Social Learning Theory

According to social learning theory (Bandura & Walters, 1963), much learning takes place not through direct reinforcement or punishment, but through observing the behavior of others and its consequences for them. It has been 50 years now since Bandura and his colleagues (Bandura, Ross, & Ross, 1961) first established empirically that observing others' aggression can increase children's own levels of aggression. Since then, all of the studies examining the relationship between physical punishment and child externalizing behavior have found this relationship to be a positive one. As of 2002, 27 studies of this relationship had been published (Gershoff, 2002). For example, in an early experimental study (Fairchild & Erwin, 1977), first-grade boys who watched a 1-minute video of a boy being yelled at, shaken, and spanked with a paddle for misbehaving showed more aggression in doll play than boys who watched a 1-minute video of nonviolent responses to misbehavior. In a more recent prospective study of 6- to 9-year-old children controlling for initial level of child antisocial behavior, as well as child-rearing style and socioeconomic status, physical punishment predicted higher levels of antisocial behavior 2 years later across ethnic groups and regardless of parental warmth (Straus, Sugarman, & Giles-Sims, 1997).

Since then, evidence of this relationship has continued to accumulate. Physical punishment has been consistently associated with higher levels of physical aggression (Fine, Trentacosta, Izard, Mostow, & Campbell, 2004; Gershoff & Bitensky, 2007; Li, Shi, Wan, Hotta, & Ushijima, 2001; Nelson, Hart, Yang, Olson, & Jin, 2006; Pagani et al., 2004; Sim & Ong,

2005), verbal aggression (Pagani et al., 2004), physical fighting and bullying (Ohene, Ireland, McNelly, & Borowsky, 2006), dating violence (Douglas & Straus, 2006), antisocial behavior (Grogan-Kaylor, 2004), and general behavior problems (Aucoin et al., 2006; Javo, Rønning, Heyerdahl, & Rudmin, 2004; Kerr et al., 2004; McLoyd & Smith, 2002; Olsen, Ceballo, & Park, 2002). And the relationship between physical punishment and child aggression has been documented across cultures (see Durrant, 2008; Lansford et al., 2005).

Increasingly, these studies are being designed to answer the question of whether children's aggression elicits or is elicited by physical punishment. Several large longitudinal studies that have controlled for children's aggression at Time 1 have found that physical punishment does indeed contribute to increased levels of aggression at Time 2 (Grogan-Kaylor, 2005; Mulvaney & Mebert, 2007; Slade & Wissow, 2004; Taylor, Manganello, Lee, & Rice, 2010). Gershoff & Bitensky (2008) provide a full analysis of this debate and conclude that even after child behavior is accounted for, physical punishment continues to predict increased child behavior problems.

Attribution Theory

Heider (1958) proposed that our behavior involves inferences about why people act as they do. In any personal interaction, we make judgments about the other's intentions and our response reflects that attribution. For example, if we attribute the other's behavior to an intentional desire to harm us, we are more likely to respond with fear or anger than if we attribute the other's behavior to an unintended accident. This theory explains how our behavior is influenced by a complex interweaving of cognition and emotion, based in our perceptions of others' intent.

Parents continually make attributions for their children's behavior—and they are not always correct. Parents, like everyone, are subject to a number of perceptual biases. One of these is the *self-serving bias*, which occurs when we attribute our successes to internal, controllable factors, but ascribe our failures to external, uncontrollable factors. For example, a mother might attribute her son's good manners to her parenting while attributing his tantrums to his difficult nature. Another is the *fundamental attribution error* (Ross, 1977), which is the tendency to over-attribute others' behavior to internal, personality-based factors, and under-attribute others' behavior to external, situational factors. For example, a father might attribute his daughter's refusal to go to bed to her defiant personality, failing to consider that the darkness might be frightening her.

A study of incarcerated mothers' perceptions of their fatally maltreated children (Korbin, 1987) highlights the importance of parents' attributions to their emotions and actions. A primary theme of these women's perceptions was rejection. For example, immediately after giving birth, one mother believed that the infant looked at her husband, not at her; that he actively refused her breast; and that he "squirmed and moved around too much" in "protest" (p. 403). She attributed this newborn baby's behavior to internal, intentional, controllable causes, which aroused feelings of hurt and anger, eventually leading to her fatal maltreatment of the child.

Daphne Bugental and her colleagues (e.g., Bugental, Blue, & Cruzcosa, 1989) have documented the role of attribution in parents' coercive or violent responses to their children: Coercive and violent mothers are less likely than nonviolent mothers to believe that they can prevent negative outcomes—and more likely to believe that children can control those outcomes.

> Cognitive inferences regarding the controllability of interpersonal events have important implications for the ways in which caregivers interpret and affectively respond to potentially stress-inducing child behavior. If, for example, a child engages in aversive behavior, very different outcomes can be anticipated for adults who believe that this is a controllable or "wilful" act on the part of the child as opposed to adults who simply believe that the child is responding to some aspect of the environment or is tired, or so forth. (p. 538)

Others studies have revealed similar findings. For example, in a study of 73 violent caregivers, Dietrich, Berkowitz, Kadushin, & McGloin (1990) found that these individuals were more likely to interpret the child's behavior preceding the violent event as intentional than accidental—and all of those who viewed the behavior as intentional believed that it had been aimed at them personally. More than 60% of the sample believed that their actions were justified. The authors conclude: "The abusers seemed to be saying it was entirely proper to hit their young charge if he/she had defied their authority or even if the child had done something to annoy them when they had been under a great deal of stress" (p. 343). They go on to explain, "confronted by the child disobedience (or whatever the annoying action was), they may have wanted consciously to coerce (i.e., influence) and even punish (i.e., hurt) the offender" (p. 344).

A primary aim of prohibition of physical punishment is to interrupt this process by: (1) placing the responsibility for caregivers' violent actions onto the caregivers themselves, rather than onto the child; and (2) providing an inhibitory mechanism in situations of conflict. Consistent with what attribution theory would predict, prohibition has been most successful when accompanied by public education that shifts caregivers' understanding of the reasons behind children's behavior (Chapter 24). In Sweden, for example, parents are provided with information about each developmental stage as it occurs so that they understand the important functions of crying, tantrums, negativism, exploration, and so on (see Ateah, Durrant, & Mirwaldt, 2004). This information is intended to shift parents' attributions for conflict with their children from "defiance" to developmentally normative. With such a shift, parents' responses would be expected to become less angry and punitive, and more consistent with guidance, scaffolding and teaching.

THEORIES OF THE CHILD IN SOCIETY

Childhood Studies

The childhood studies perspective provides a framework for recognizing, considering, and understanding the child's viewpoint (Qvortrup, Corsaro, & Honig, 2009). It also illuminates the social and historical contexts within which the concept of childhood is constructed, optimizing or diminishing children's opportunities for participation and agency.

From this perspective, the very nature of research on physical punishment is called into question. We begin to recognize that this research is driven, conceptualized, conducted, and interpreted by adults whose histories and values shape their definition of the issue. For example, one of the main debates in this area focuses on whether physical punishment can induce children to comply with parental commands. The three studies that have been relied upon by some (Baumrind, 2001; Larzelere, 2000) to demonstrate physical punishment's effectiveness in this regard were conducted by a team of researchers whose aim was to determine whether spanking could increase the length of time children would remain seated on a time-out chair, decrease their number of "escapes" and increase their compliance on a laboratory task (Bean & Roberts, 1981; Day & Roberts, 1983; Roberts & Powers, 1990). The children participating in these studies were all clinic-referred preschoolers with serious behavior problems who were put into a frustrating situation to ensure their noncompliance.

From a childhood studies perspective, these studies would be challenged on several bases. First, the salience of immediate compliance as a desirable outcome would be reframed in terms of power, which has been defined by Giddens (1995, cited in Robinson & Kellett, 2004) as "the ability of individuals or groups to make their own concerns count, even when others resist" (p. 54). In any adult–child interaction, the adult holds the power. Giddens goes on to state that "power sometimes involves the direct use of force, but is almost always accompanied by the development of ideas (ideologies) which justify the actions of the powerful" (p. 54). From this perspective, justifying physical punishment on the basis of its ability to elicit compliance is a means of preserving the power imbalance between children and adults. Moreover, while it could be argued that immediate compliance in a situation of danger or urgency could be critical to the child's safety, the justification of using physical punishment to secure it is questionable. As this review demonstrates, compliance may be gained at the expense of trust, secure attachment, moral internalization, self-regulation, cognitive development, and mental health.

Second, the methodology of these compliance studies is subject to critique. Far from being active participants in these studies, the children involved were manipulated to optimize their resistance to parental coercion so that they would "need" to be punished. The childhood studies perspective would point to the rights of these children—to consent, to dignity, and to physical security—that were violated by this process. Like the vast majority of studies in this area, these studies defined children as subjects, meant to reveal the effects of physical punishment upon them, rather than as persons in their own right.

In contrast, the childhood studies perspective emphasizes the child's perspective, capacity for insight, and participation in social change. It is only very recently that researchers have considered asking children for their perspectives on physical punishment, their experiences, and their thoughts about prohibition. Willow and Hyder (1998) were among the first to do so. They developed a method for capturing the unbiased viewpoints of children as young as 5, and their sample of 76 included children from diverse ethnic and socioeconomic groups. Their findings revealed children's negative physical and emotional experiences of physical punishment (e.g., "It's horrible." "You feel sad and like running away."), its impact on children's behavior (e.g., "They smack somebody else." "They might break something or hurt their parents. . . . It's like getting your own back."), their insight into adults' emotions (e.g., "They sometimes feel they want to say sorry."), the parent–child power differential (e.g., "Little children aren't bigger than adults, but the adults are bigger than them, so the adults can smack the little ones and the little ones can't smack the adults."), and how to end physical punishment:

> If they changed the law then a lot of people will realize what they had done to their child and they would probably . . . be happy that the law was changed. If they don't change the law they will think "oh well, the child doesn't mind so we can keep on doing it." But if they realize that children have been talking to adults about it then I think they will definitely realize that it hurts their child and they will be very upset with themselves. (p. 86)

In recent years, a number of researchers have extended this approach, collecting qualitative data from children about the meaning of physical punishment in their lives. Dobbs (2005) adapted Willow and Hyder's (1998) methodology to explore New Zealand children's attitudes, feelings, beliefs and experiences. These children reported being hit with spatulas, tennis rackets, spoons, belts, canes, and "The Whacker", as well as having unpleasant substances placed in their mouths. They were punished by parents and their girlfriends/boyfriends, step-parents, siblings, grandparents, uncles, cousins, and caregivers. They described feeling scared, sad, ashamed, unloved, and "like you've been adopted or something and you're not part of the family." Following the punishment, many children felt angry and hateful towards their parents (e.g., "I just like to tell my parents that I hate them and stuff. 'I hate you; you are so mean' and stuff like that."), wanted to avoid their parents or pushed them away, and wanted "payback" and revenge. These children also recognized the power differential between children and adults (e.g., "The Police would come and get you if you smacked your parents." "Adults don't let children smack them 'cause most adults are selfish and think that they are higher than all the children."). Similar findings have been obtained in Wales (Crowley & Vulliamy, n.d.), Scotland (Cutting, 2001); Ireland (Horgan, 2002) and Cambodia (Save the Children Norway, 2005). In Brazil (Azevedo & de Azevedo, 2001), younger children primarily expressed pain and sadness in response to physical punishment, while older children primarily expressed rage. This growing body of child-focused research demonstrates that studies conducted solely from an adult perspective fail to capture the nature of the experience for children, and highlight the impacts of physical punishment that extend far beyond simple compliance.

Most recently, Saunders and Goddard (2010) carried out a qualitative study with Australian children, parents and grandparents, and professionals. Their findings demonstrate that questionnaires intended to measure the prevalence and outcomes of "spanking" are inadequate to capture the reality of physical punishment. Adults' definitions of "a good smack" included: "bordering on beating", "a real strong whack", "a really hard slap in the face", "smack[ing] intensively . . . painfully", "inflicting pain", and "leav[ing] a couple of finger marks" (pp. 67–68). Adults recalled their own experiences of physical punishment as children within the context of power: "a child is at their mercy", "It hurt and I was scared . . . you are so powerless", "I certainly felt . . . lesser than them, like not as important", "Adults don't listen . . . don't respect you" (pp. 69–70). They also articulated the affective underpinnings of compliance: "Living with a single parent you have only got one source of love and care. . . . I just became a completely compliant child", "It made me more wary of being caught, perhaps a bit sneaky. . . . I was very angry but [never] dared to show that" (p. 72).

The children in Saunders and Goddard's (2010) study were very much aware of the symbolic meaning of physical punishment. An 8-year-old child said:

> Adults have more power. . . . They can get really mad and swear . . . and stuff. . . . Children can't do anything like that because they don't have enough power. We have to do what they say. Adults can . . . hurt them. (p. 135)

A 10-year-old child declared, "It's what keeps us apart, adults are more important than children" (p. 136). And a 13-year-old explained, "Adults have basically more power. They have a greater say. . . . It really frustrates me when . . . I will have an opinion but I can't do much with it" (p. 137).

Ennew (2003) has called attention to the importance of language in research, as particular labels, such as "spanking", can have different meanings among children and across cultures. She and her colleagues have developed a method for developing a culturally relevant punishment vocabulary that can form the basis of talking with children about their experiences (Beazley, Bessell, Ennew, & Waterson, 2005). It involves asking children to draw pictures of the acts they consider to be punishment, and then discussing with them the words they use to identify those acts. This method contrasts sharply with traditional approaches to designing questionnaires intended to investigate children's physical punishment experiences. A number of guides and toolkits have been developed for researchers planning to involve children in research that are contributing to a shift in this area (e.g., Feinstein, Karkara, & Laws, 2004; Save the Children, 2003, 2004a, 2004b, 2006; Save the Children Sweden, 2006; Willow, 2010).

Child-focused research also has shed light on the realities of physical punishment in schools. For example, a qualitative interview study involving 200 students in 20 Kenyan schools (Human Rights Watch, 1999) yielded a wealth of information about children's everyday experiences of corporal punishment, including the range of punishments imposed, the frequency with which they were administered, the types of implements used, the language the children use to describe these experiences, the reasons for the punishments, and the psychological and emotional dimensions of the punishments. Children participating in qualitative research in Cambodia (Miles & Varin, n.d.) reported being beaten by teachers with sticks; being forced to stand on one leg, kneel, stand on sharp objects, or stand outside in the heat; having clothespins pinned into their lips or ears; and having their heads pushed into walls. Many of these acts are excluded from standard measures of physical punishment designed without consulting children. Child-focused research conducted in Mongolian schools and institutions (Odgerel et al., 2005) revealed that 71% of children had been beaten—mostly by teachers, but also by cooks, guards, and other school employees. Although 78% of these children believed that adults have a duty to discipline children, 90% favored explanations over beatings and only 25% believed that children must be punished in order to learn proper behavior.

Ecological Theory

Ecological theory (Bronfenbrenner, 1979) describes a child's world in terms of nested layers or "systems", all of which interact simultaneously to influence the child's development. This perspective interweaves psychological, sociological, anthropological, political, and legal research to understand the complexity of the forces affecting children's well-being, ranging from genes to ideology.

According to ecological theory, "physical punishment" is much broader than a particular act at a particular point in time, or a simple stimulus-response chain (i.e., child behavior → caregiver punishment → child response). Rather, from this perspective physical punishment is laden with affective, relational, intergenerational, historical, religious, political, and legal meanings, all of which play a role in its use and impact.

The *microsystem* is made up of the child and his or her immediate environments. It includes the child's genetics, temperament, learning capacities, competencies, information processing style, social skills, and a myriad of other characteristics. It also includes children's and adults' conditioned emotional responses, attributions, modeling, coercive family patterns, stress, and social support. And it includes all members of the family, the school environment, peers, and neighborhoods, as well as affect, nonverbal communication, vocal intonation, and other subtle features of parent–child interactions. Even at this initial level, we can recognize the complexity of any given parent–child conflict. The particular confluence of child and caregiver characteristics within a given setting at a specific time will influence the likelihood of physical punishment occurring, and can affect its outcome.

An example of the importance of microsystem factors is provided by the work of Philip Davis (1991, 1996) who has conducted observational studies of physical punishment in public places. He has documented the verbal aggression and denigration that can accompany it; the words that adults use to label it; adults' demeanor, statements, gestures, and vocal intonations in punitive interactions; the intimidation and public humiliation that can accompany adults' threats and use of physical punishment; and children's reactions in these situations.

Other researchers have found links between physical punishment and other elements of the child's microsystem. For example, physical punishment is positively associated with family size (Straus & Asdigian, in press; De Zoysa, 2005), interparental violence (Fergusson & Horwood, 1998), and the level of violence in the neighborhood (Winstock & Straus, 2008). Recognition of the dynamics among elements of the microsystem enhances our understanding of physical punishment's impact on the child, its meaning to the adult, the intent that underlies it, and the role it plays in the developing relationship between children and their social worlds.

Perhaps the most significant contribution made by ecological theory to our understanding of physical punishment is its focus on the *macrosystem*, which refers to the broad social, cultural, religious, political, and ideological contexts in which it occurs. The macrosystem is made up of shared understandings, values, and beliefs among members of the culture, such as the saying, "Beating is from Heaven" (Chapter 16); historical contexts, such as colonization (Chapters 5 and 7), communism and the transition to democracy (Chapter 17), or the Enlightenment (Chapter 19); religion (Chapters 14 and 15); and social movements, such as the human and child rights movements (Chapters 9 and 12).

The elements of the macro- and micro-systems exist in a constantly interacting, fluid relationship—the *mesosystem*—which allows change and evolution within systems. It is this process that this book seeks to document. We know that the prevalence of physical punishment is influenced by macrosystem factors. For example, Sweden's ever-declining prevalence rate has accompanied increases in democratization, child-rights-focused policy, and cultural rejection of violence (Durrant, 2003, 2006; Durrant & Olsen, 1997). Across nations, the prevalence of physical punishment is positively related to approval or acceptance of other types of violence (Straus, forthcoming; Levinson, 1989), frequency of warfare (Ember & Ember, 1994), social stratification (Ember & Ember, 2005), homicide rates (Straus, 1996), and level of social development (Straus, forthcoming).

We also know that the legal status of physical punishment is related to its prevalence. Out of 32 nations examined by Straus (forthcoming), the 4 with full prohibition had the lowest percentage of students who were spanked or hit a lot as young children. Chapter 24 of this volume provides systematic comparative evidence that a combination of prohibition and public education is associated with more negative attitudes toward, and less use of use of, physical punishment by parents. And data from New Zealand indicate that when parents understand prohibition, they are more likely to support it (Lawrence & Smith, 2008).

But we have limited understanding of how micro- and macro-system factors converge to make prohibition not only possible, but realized. For a nation to progress to the point where a previously normative act becomes formally abolished is a remarkable social change. Yet we know little about how such change is generated. The chapters in this volume constitute a step towards this understanding.

CONCLUSION

Over the past 50 years, evidence has been steadily accumulating of the risk that physical punishment poses to children's social, emotional, intellectual and physical development. These relationships obtain across research designs, sample sizes, family structures, child ages, and cultures. This should come as no surprise: All of the major theories would predict that physical punishment will be a negative force in children's development. We take for granted that pain, intentionally inflicted by one person on another, will have a negative impact on that person—if the victim is an adult, or if the perpetrator is a child. Most societies invest resources into preventing such acts between adults and between children, and refer to such acts as aggression, violence, abuse, bullying and antisocial behavior. It is only in the case of adult-to-child aggression that we seek to justify it, resist eliminating it, and call it "punishment" as though the victim is to blame for the perpetrator's aggression. The deep entrenchment of the beliefs and justifications for punitive violence in most cultures makes its eradication exceedingly difficult.

For this reason, the stories that are told in this book may indicate that we are nearing the "global turning point" described by Paolo Pinheiro (2006) that will bring "an end to the justification of violence against children, whether accepted as 'tradition' or disguised as "discipline" (p. 3). The following pages tell the story of a remarkable social change that reflects an ever-growing recognition of the personhood of children.

REFERENCES

Afifi, T. O., Brownridge, D. A., Cox, B. J., & Sareen, J. (2006). Physical punishment, childhood abuse and psychiatric disorders. *Child Abuse & Neglect, 30*, 1093–1103.

American Academy of Pediatrics. (1996). The short- and long-term consequences of corporal punishment. *Pediatrics, 98*.

Ateah, C. A., Durrant, J. E., & Mirwaldt, J. (2004). Physical punishment and physical abuse of children: Strategies for prevention. In C. A. Ateah & J. Mirwaldt (Eds.), *Within our reach: Preventing abuse across the lifespan* (pp. 11–29). Halifax, Nova Scotia: Fernwood Publishing and RESOLVE (Research and Education for Solutions to Violence and Abuse).

Aucoin, K. J., Frick, P. J., & Bodin, S. D. (2006). Corporal punishment and child adjustment. *Journal of Applied Developmental Psychology, 27*, 527–541.

Azevedo, M. A., & de Azevedo Guerra, V. N. (2001). Hitting mania: Domestic corporal punishment of children and adolescents in Brazil (Sao Paulo: IGLU Editora.

Azrin, N. H., Hake, D. F., & Hutchinson, R. R. (1965). Elicitation of aggression by a physical blow. *Journal of the Experimental Analysis of Behavior, 8*, 55–57.

Bandura, A., Ross, D., & Ross, S. A. (1961). Transmission of aggression through imitation of aggressive models. *Journal of Abnormal and Social Psychology, 63*, 575–582.

Bandura, A., & Walters, R. H. (1963). *Social learning and personality development*. New York: Holt, Rinehart, & Winston.

Barnett, D.,Kidwell, S. L., & Leung, K. H. (1998). Parenting and preschooler attachment among low-income urban African American families. *Child Development, 69*, 1657–1671.

Baumrind, D. (2001, August). *Does causally relevant research support a blanket injunction against disciplinary spanking by parents?* Invited address to the 109th Annual Convention of the American Psychological Association, San Francisco, CA.

Bean, A. W., & Roberts, M. W. (1981). The effect of time-out release contingencies on changes in child noncompliance. *Journal of Abnormal Child Psychology, 9*, 95–105.

Beazley, H., Bessell, S., Ennew, J., & Waterson, R. (2005). *Comparative research on physical and emotional punishment of children in Southeast Asia and the Pacific 2005: Regional protocol*. Bangkok: Save the Children Sweden.

Berkowitz, L. (1983). Aversively stimulated aggression: Some parallels and differences in research with animals and humans. *American Psychologist, 38*, 1135–1144.

Berkowitz, L. (1993). Pain and aggression: Some findings and implications. *Motivation and Emotion, 17*, 277–293.

Bradley, R. H., Corwyn, R. F., Burchinal, M., McAdoo, H. P., & García Coll, C. (2001). The home environments of children in the United States Part II: Relations with behavioral development through age thirteen. *Child Development, 72*, 1868–1886.

Bronfenbrenner, U. (1979). *The ecology of human development*. Cambridge, MA: Harvard University Press.

Bugental, D. B., Blue, J., & Cruzcosa, M. (1989). Perceived control over caregiving outcomes: Implications for child abuse. *Developmental Psychology, 25*, 532–539.

Bugental, D. B., Martorell, G. A., & Barraza, V. (2003). The hormonal costs of subtle forms of infant maltreatment. *Hormones and Behavior, 43*, 237–244.

Coyl, D. D., Roggman, L. A., & Newland, L. A. (2002). Stress, maternal depression, and negative mother–infant interactions in relation to infant attachment. *Infant Mental Health Journal, 23*, 145–163.

Crockenberg, S. (1987). Predictors and correlates of anger toward and punitive control of toddlers by adolescent mothers. *Child Development, 58*, 964–975.

Crowley, A., & Vulliamy, C. (n.d.). *Listen up! Children talk: About smacking*. Save the Children UK (Wales).

Csorba, J., et al. (2001). Family and school-related stresses in depressed Hungarian children. *European Psychiatry, 16*, 18–26.

Cutting, E. (2001). *"It doesn't sort anything!" A report on the views of children and young people about the use of physical punishment*. Edinburgh: Save the Children UK (Scotland).

Davis, P. (1991). Stranger intervention into physical punishment in public settings. *Social Problems, 38*, 227–246.

Davis, P. W. (1996). Threats of corporal punishment as verbal aggression: A naturalistic study. *Child Abuse & Neglect, 20*, 289–304.

Day, D. E., & Roberts, M. W. (1983). An analysis of the physical punishment component of a parent-training program. *Journal of Abnormal Child Psychology, 11*, 141–152.

De Zoysa, P. T. (2005). *Parental use of physical force towards school children in the Colombo district: Prevalence, psychosocial correlates and psychological consequences*. University of Colombo, Sri Lanka.

Dietrich, D., Berkowitz, L., Kadushin, A., & McGloin, L. (1990). Some factors influencing abusers' justification of their child abuse. *Child Abuse & Neglect, 14*, 337–345.

Dobbs, T. (2005). *Insights: Children and young people speak out about family discipline*. Wellington, New Zealand: Save the Children New Zealand.

Douglas, E. M., & Straus, M. A. (2006). Assault and injury of dating partners by university students in 19 countries and its relation to corporal punishment experienced as a child. *European Journal of Criminology, 3*, 293–318.

DuRant, R. H., Cadenhead, C., Pendergrast, R. A., Slavens, G., & Linder, C. W. (1994). Factors associated with the use of violence among urban Black adolescents. *American Journal of Public Health, 84*, 612–617.

Durrant, J. E. (2003). Legal reform and attitudes toward physical punishment in Sweden. *International Journal of Children's Rights, 11*, 147–174.

Durrant, J. E. (2006). From mopping up the damage to preventing the flood: The role of social policy in the prevention of violence against children. *Social Policy Journal of New Zealand*, *27*, 1–17.

Durrant, J. E. (2008). Physical punishment, culture and rights: Current issues for professionals. *Journal of Developmental and Behavioral Pediatrics, 29*, 55–66.

Durrant, J. E., & Olsen, G. M. (1997). Parenting and public policy: Contextualizing the Swedish corporal punishment ban. *Journal of Social Welfare and Family Law, 19*, 443–461.

Durrant, J. E., Trocmé, N., Fallon, B., Milne, C., & Black, T. (2009). Protection of children from physical maltreatment in Canada: An evaluation of the Supreme Court's definition of reasonable force. *Journal of Aggression, Maltreatment and Trauma, 18*, 1–24.

Eamon, M. K. (2001). Antecedents and socioemotional consequences of physical punishment on children in two-parent families. *Child Abuse & Neglect, 25*, 787–802.

Ember, C. R., & Ember, M. (1994). War, socialization, and interpersonal violence: A cross-cultural study. *Journal of Conflict Resolution, 38*, 620–646.

Ember, C. R., & Ember, M. (2005). Explaining corporal punishment of children: A cross-cultural study. *American Anthropologist, 107*, 609–619.

Ennew, J. (2003). Research design. In M. Childe, J. Ennew, D. P. Plateau, & C. Trimmer (Eds.), *Towards a strategy to address corporal punishment of children in Southeast, East Asia and Pacific* (pp. 109–125). Bangkok: International Save the Children Alliance, Southeast, East Asia and Pacific Region.

Fairchild, L., & Erwin, W. M. (1977). Physical punishment by parent figures as a model of aggressive behavior in children. *Journal of Genetic Psychology, 130*, 279–284.

Feinstein, C., Karkara, R., & Laws, S. (2004). *A workshop report on child participation in the UN Study on Violence against Children.* London: International Save the Children Alliance.

Fergusson, D. M., & Horwood, L. J. (1998). Exposure to interparental violence in childhood and psychosocial adjustment in young adulthood. *Child Abuse & Neglect, 22*, 339–357.

Fine, S. E., Trentacosta, C. J., Izard, C. E., Mostow, A. J., & Campbell, J. L. (2004). Anger perception, caregivers' use of physical discipline, and aggression in children at risk. *Social Development, 13*, 213–228.

Gershoff, E. T. (2002). Corporal punishment by parents and associated child behaviors and experiences: A meta-analytic and theoretical review. *Psychological Bulletin, 128*, 539–579.

Gershoff, E. T., & Bitensky, S. (2008). The case against corporal punishment of children: Converging evidence from social science research and international human rights law and implications for U.S. public policy. *Psychology, Public Policy, and Law, 13*, 231–272.

Gest, S. D., Freeman, N. R., Domitrovich, C. E., & Welsh, J. A. (2004). Shared book reading and children's language comprehensive skills: The moderating role of parental discipline practices. *Early Childhood Research Quarterly, 19*, 319–336.

Giddens, A. (1995). *Sociology.* Cambridge, UK: Polity Press.

Gil, D. G. (1970). *Violence against children: Physical child abuse in the United States.* Cambridge, MA: Harvard University Press.

Grinder, R. E. (1962). Parental child-rearing practices, conscience, and resistance to temptation of sixth-grade children. *Child Development, 33*, 803–820.

Grogan-Kaylor, A. (2004). The effect of corporal punishment on antisocial behavior in children. *Social Work Research, 28*, 153–161.

Grogan-Kaylor, A. (2005). Corporal punishment and the growth trajectory of children's antisocial behavior. *Child Maltreatment, 10*, 283–292.

Heider, F. (1958). *The psychology of interpersonal relations.* New York: John Wiley & Sons.

Horgan, G. (2002). *It's a hit, not a 'smack'.* Belfast, Ireland: Save the Children.

Human Rights Watch. (1999). *Spare the child: Corporal punishment in Kenyan schools.* New York: Human Rights Watch.

Javo, C., Rønning, J. A., Heyerdahl, S., & Rudmin, F. W. (2004). Parenting correlates of child behavior problems in a multiethnic community sample of preschool children in northern Norway. *European Child and Adolescent Psychiatry, 13*, 8–18.

Kadushin, A., & Martin, J. A. (1981). *Child abuse: An interactional event.* New York: Columbia University Press.

Kerr, D. C., Lopez, N. L., Olson, S. L., & Sameroff, A. J. (2004). Parental discipline and externalizing behavior problems in early childhood: The roles of moral regulation and child gender. *Journal of Abnormal Child Psychology, 32*, 369–383.

Korbin, J. E. (1987). Incarcerated mothers' perceptions and interpretations of their fatally maltreated children. *Child Abuse & Neglect, 11*, 397–407.

Lansford, J. E., et al. (2005). Physical discipline and children's adjustment: cultural normativeness as a moderator. *Child Development, 76*, 1234–1246.

Larzelere, R. E. (2000). Child outcomes of non-abusive and customary physical punishment by parents: An updated literature review. *Clinical Child and Family Psychology Review, 3*, 199–221.

Larzelere, R. E., & Kuhn, B. R. (2005). Comparing child outcomes of physical punishment and alternative disciplinary tactics: A meta-analysis. *Clinical Child and Family Psychology Review, 8*, 1–37.

Lau, J. T. F., Chan, K. K., Lam, P. K. W., Choi, P. Y. W., & Lai, K. Y. C. (2003). Psychological correlates of physical abuse in Hong Kong Chinese adolescents. *Child Abuse & Neglect, 27*, 63–75.

Lau, J. T. F., Liu, J. L.Y., Cheung, J. C. K., Yu, A., & Wong, C. K. (1999). Prevalence and correlates of physical abuse in Hong Kong Chinese adolescents: A population-based approach. *Child Abuse & Neglect, 23*, 549–557.

Lawrence, J., & Smith, A. B. (2008). Aotearoa/New Zealand families: Their perspectives on child discipline and recent legislative changes. *Childrenz Issues, 12(2)*, 17–24.

Levinson, D. (1989). *Family violence in cross-cultural perspective.* Newbury Park, NJ: Sage.

Li, Y., Shi, A., Wan, Y., Hotta, M., & Ushijima, H. (2001). Child behaviour problems: Prevalence and correlates in rural minority areas of China. *Paediatrics International, 43*, 651–661.

Lopez, N. L., Bonenberger, J. L., & Schneider, H. G. (2001). Parental disciplinary history, current levels of empathy, and moral reasoning in young adults. *North American Journal of Psychology, 3*, 193–204.

McCain, M. N., Mustard, J. F., & Shanker, S. (2007). *Early years study 2: Putting science into action.* Toronto: Council for Early Child Development.

McGowan, P. O., et al. (2009). Epigenetic regulation of the glucocorticoid receptor in human brain associates with childhood abuse. *Nature Neuroscience, 12*, 342–348.

McLoyd, V. C., & Smith, J. (2002). Physical discipline and behavior problems in African American, European American, and Hispanic children: Emotional support as a moderator. *Journal of Marriage and the Family, 64*, 40–53.

Medina, A. M., Mejia, V. Y., Schell, A. M., Dawson, M. E., & Margolin, G. (2001). Startle reactivity and PTSD symptoms in a community sample of women. Psychiatry Research, *101*, 157–169.

Miles, G., & Varin, S. (n.d.). *"Stop violence against us!" A preliminary national research study into the prevalence and perceptions of Cambodian children to violence against children in Cambodia.* Phnom Penh: Tearfund.

Mulvaney, M. K., & Mebert, C. J. (2007). Parental corporal punishment predicts behavior problems in early childhood. *Journal of Family Psychology, 21*, 381–397.

Nelson, D. A., Hart, C. H., Yang, C., Olsen, J. A., & Jin, S. (2006). Aversive parenting in China: Associations with child physical and relational aggression. *Child Development, 77*, 554–572.

Odgerel, T., et al. (2005). *Corporal punishment of children: Views of children in some schools, kindergartens and institutions.* Ulaanbataar: Gender Center for Sustainable Development and Save the Children UK Mongolia Program.

Ohene, S. A., Ireland, M., McNeely, C., & Borowsky, I. W. (2006). Parental expectations, physical punishment, and violence among adolescents who score positive on a psychosocial screening test in primary care. *Pediatrics, 117*, 441–447.

Olson, S. L., Ceballo, R., & Park, C. (2002). Early problem behavior among children from low-income mother-headed families: A multiple risk perspective. *Journal of Clinical Child and Adolescent Psychology, 31*, 419–430.

Pagani, L. S., Tremblay, R. E., Nagin, D., Zoccolillo, M., Vitaro, F., & McDuff, P. (2004). Risk factor models for adolescent verbal and physical aggression toward mothers. *International Journal of Behavioral Development, 28*, 528–537.

Palmer, E. J., & Hollin, C. R. (2001). Sociomoral reasoning, perceptions of parenting and self-reported delinquency in adolescents. *Applied Cognitive Psychology, 15*, 85–100.

Parkinson, C. E., Wallis, S. M., Prince, J., & Harvey, D. (1982). Research note: Rating the home environment of school-age children: A comparison with general cognitive index and school progress. *Journal of Child Psychology and Psychiatry, 23*, 329–333.

Patterson, G. R. (1982). *Coercive family process: Social interactional approach.* Eugene, OR: Castalia.

Pinheiro, P. (2006). *World report on violence against children.* Geneva, Switzerland: United Nations Secretary-General's Study on Violence Against Children.

Posada, G., & Pratt, D. M. (2008). Physical aggression in the family and preschoolers' use of the mother as a secure base. *Journal of Marital and Family Therapy, 34*(1), 14–27.

Qvortrup, J., Corsaro, W. A., & Honig, M.-S. (2009). Why social studies of childhood? An introduction to the Handbook. In J. Qvortrup, W. A. Corsaro, & M.-S. Honig (Eds.) *The Palgrave handbook of childhood studies* (pp. 1–18). Basingstoke, Hampshire: Palgrave MacMillan.

Roberts, M. W., & Powers, S. W. (1990). Adjusting chair timeout enforcement procedures for oppositional children. *Behavior Therapy, 21*, 257–271.

Robinson, C., & Kellett, M. (2004). Power. In S. Fraser, V. Lewis, S. Ding, M. Kelett, & C. Robinson (Eds.). *Doing research with children and young people* (pp. 81–96). London: Sage.

Rodriguez, C. M. (2003). Parental discipline and abuse potential effects on child depression, anxiety, and attributions. *Journal of Marriage and Family, 65*, 809–817.

Rogoff, B. (1990). *Apprenticeship in thinking: Cognitive development in social context.* New York: Oxford University Press.

Ross, L. (1977). The intuitive psychologist and his shortcomings: Distortions in the attribution process. In L. Berkowitz (Ed.), *Advances in experimental social psychology* (vol. 10, pp. 173–220). New York: Academic Press.

Saunders, B. J., & Goddard, C. (2010). *Physical punishment in childhood: The rights of the child.* Chichester, UK: Wiley-Blackwell.

Save the Children. (2003). *So you want to consult with children? A toolkit of good practice.* London: International Save the Children Alliance.

Save the Children. (2004a). *How to research the physical and emotional punishment of children.* Bangkok: International Save the Children Alliance.

Save the Children. (2004b). *So you want to involve children in Research? A toolkit supporting children's meaningful and ethical participation in research relating to violence against children.* Stockholm: Save the Children Sweden.

Save the Children. (2006). *Voices against violence.* Stockholm: Save the Children Sweden.

Save the Children Norway. (2005). *Children's view on domestic violence: Research into physical and emotional punishment of children in Cambodia.* Phnom Penh: Save the Children Norway.

Save the Children Sweden. (2006). *What children say: Results of comparative research on the physical and emotional punishment of children in Southeast Asia and the Pacific, 2005.* Bangkok: Save the Children Sweden.

Sim, T. N., & Ong, L. P. (2005). Parent physical punishment and child aggression in a Singapore Chinese preschool sample. *Journal of Marriage and Family, 67*, 85–99.

Slade, E. P., & Wissow, L. S. (2004). Spanking in early childhood and later behaviour problems: A prospective study of infants and young toddlers. *Pediatrics, 113*, 1321–1330.

Smith, J. R., & Brooks-Gunn, J. (1997). Correlates and consequences of harsh discipline for young children. *Archives of Pediatric and Adolescent Medicine, 151*, 777–786.

Snyder, J. J., & Patterson, G. R. (1995). Individual differences in social aggression: A test of a reinforcement model of socialization in the natural environment. *Behavior Therapy, 26*, 371–391.

Steely, A. C., & Rohner, R. P. (2006). Relations among corporal punishment, perceived parental acceptance, and psychological adjustment in Jamaican youths. *Cross-Cultural Research, 40*, 268–286.

Stein, N. L., & Levine, L. J. (1990). Making sense out of emotion: The representation and use of goal-structured knowledge. In N. L. Stein, B. Leventhal, & T. Trabasso (Eds.), *Psychological and biological approaches to emotion* (pp. 45–73). Hillsdale, NJ: Lawrence Erlbaum Associates.

Straus, M. A. (1996). Spanking and the making of a violent society. *Pediatrics, 98*(4), 837–841.

Straus, M. A. (forthcoming). Prevalence and societal causes of corporal punishment by parents in world perspective. *Law and Contemporary Problems.*

Straus, M. A., & Asdigian, N. (in press). There was an old woman who lived in a shoe: Number of children and corporal punishment. In M. A. Straus, E. M. Douglas, & R. A. Medeiros (Eds.), The primordial violence: Corporal punishment by parents, cognitive development, and crime. Walnut Creek, CA: AltaMira.

Straus, M. A., & Paschall, M. J. (2009). Corporal punishment by mothers and development of children's cognitive ability: A longitudinal study of two nationally representative age cohorts. *Journal of Aggression, Maltreatment, and Trauma, 19*, 459–483.

Straus, M. A., Sugarman, D. B., & Giles-Sims, J. (1997). Spanking by parents and subsequent antisocial behavior of children. *Archives of Pediatric and Adolescent Medicine, 151*, 761–767.

Taylor, C. A., Manganello, J. A., Lee, S. J., & Rice, J. C. (2010). Mothers' spanking of 3-year-old children and subsequent risk of children's aggressive behavior. *Pediatrics, 125*, 1087–1065.

Trocmé, N., et al. (2005). *Canadian Incidence Study of Reported Child Abuse and Neglect—2003: Major Findings.* Ottawa: Minister of Public Works and Government Services Canada.

Trocmé, N., et al. (2001). *Canadian Incidence Study of Reported Child Abuse and Neglect: Final Report.* Ottawa: Minister of Public Works and Government Services Canada.

Turner, H. A., & Finkelhor, D. (1996). Corporal punishment as a stressor among youth. *Journal of Marriage and the Family, 58*, 155–166.

Turner, H. A., & Muller, P. A. (2004). Long-term effects of child corporal punishment on depressive symptoms in young adults: Potential moderators and mediators. *Journal of Family Issues, 25*, 761–782.

Ulrich, R. E., & Azrin, N. H. (1962). Reflexive fighting in response to aversive stimulation. *Journal of the Experimental Analysis of Behavior, 5*, 511–520.

Vygotsky, L. S. (1978). *Mind in society: The development of higher psychological processes.* London: Harvard University Press.

Willow, C. (2010*). Children's right to be heard and effective child protection.* Bangkok: Save the Children Sweden.

Willow, C., & Hyder, T. (1998). *It hurts you inside: Children talking about smacking.* London: National Children's Bureau Enterprises in association with Save the Children.
Winstock, Z., & Straus, M. A. (2008). *Neighborhood violence and use of corporal punishment, verbal aggression, and physical abuse by a national sample of parents in Israel.* Durham, NH: University of New Hampshire, Family Research Laboratory.
Wolfe, D. A. (1987). *Child abuse: Implications for child development and psychopathology.* Newbury Park, NJ: Sage.

Part II

Stories of Progress Towards Prohibition

5 Africa

Growing Momentum Towards the Prohibition of Corporal Punishment

Sonia Vohito

HISTORICAL CONTEXT

During the colonial period, there was widespread use of corporal punishment in the context of slavery and military occupation across the continent; corporal punishment using canes and whips was institutionalized in schools and in penal systems, including for young offenders; and much missionary teaching promoted its use among parents. A close study of the laws authorizing and justifying corporal punishment across Africa shows how the legality of corporal punishment in most states, as in Asia and the Caribbean and other regions, has its origins in legal frameworks imposed during the colonial era.[1] The traditional English common law defense of "reasonable chastisement" is found in many of the states of southern and eastern Africa; others have adopted the French, Spanish, Portuguese and Dutch "right of correction".

For example, Lesotho's *Child Protection Act 1980* punishes ill-treatment of children but confirms the right "to administer reasonable punishment"; Mali's *Family Relations Code 1973* confirms a "right of correction"; Senegal's *Family Code 2000* gives the right to the person having parental authority to inflict correction to a degree compatible with the child's age and the correction of its behavior. Sierra Leone's *Prevention of Cruelty to Children Act 1926* confirms the right "to administer punishment"; Swaziland's *Constitution 2005* confirms that children may be subjected to "lawful and moderate chastisement for purposes of correction"; the *Constitution* in Zimbabwe (1979, amended 1990) allows for "moderate corporal punishment"; in Zambia the *Juveniles Act 1956* punishes cruelty but confirms the right "to administer lawful punishment".[2]

PREVALENCE OF CORPORAL PUNISHMENT ACROSS AFRICA

Studies typically point to a high prevalence of corporal punishment in the home and schools in African countries, as they do in states in all regions where it has not been systematically challenged over a long period. A series of studies commissioned by Save the Children Sweden in 2004–2005 in South Africa, Swaziland and Zambia confirmed this trend; in each case large numbers of boys and girls, respectively 2,750 in Swaziland and 2,705 in Zambia, aged 6 to 18 years were surveyed, and there were also in-depth interviews with a smaller sample of children. In Swaziland, the study found that 28% of children had been beaten with objects such as sticks, belts, sjamboks (a traditional heavy leather whip) and whips over a two-week period, and 18% of children had been hit with a hand in the home during the same period.

> My mother beat me with a belt on my back. I came home late from playing with friends. (Boy, 9- to 12-year age group, Soneson, 2005b, p. 13)

In Zambia, although corporal punishment is prohibited in schools, 38% of children reported being hit with objects and 32% being hit with a hand at school during a 2-week period.

> I never wrote my homework. I got whipped on my bum with a hosepipe. (Boy, Lusaka Province, Soneson, 2005a, p. 13)

The South African study on children aged 6 to 18 years revealed that corporal punishment was common in all schools situated in low income environments, irrespective of age and gender, but that boys experienced corporal punishment more than girls. Also, many boys and girls, of all ages (6 to 18 years) and social backgrounds, experienced corporal punishment at home (Soneson, 2005).

> Sometimes my mommy or daddy hit me, sometimes with their hands or sometimes with a belt. (Boy, Gauteng, Soneson, 2005a, p. 13)

A similar survey in Mozambique found that 42% of children reported experiencing physical and humiliating[3] punishment at school over a period of two weeks, while 43% of children reported experiencing it at home over the same period (Kleynhans, 2009). In Ethiopia, 72% of 18- to 24-year-olds reported having been physically punished as a child at school (African Child Policy Forum, 2006b).

UNICEF carried out an optional module on child discipline during the third cycle of the agency's "Multiple Indicator Cluster Surveys" (see UNICEF, 2009) which collected data from 37 states. The data reveal that 86% of children aged 2 to 14 had experienced physical punishment and/or psychological aggression in the home. Two out of three children were subject to physical punishment. Of the African countries included in the study, the percentage of children experiencing both physical punishment and psychological aggression varied from 53% in Burkina Faso, to 69%

in Cameroon, Central African Republic, Côte d'Ivoire, and Sierra Leone. These and other research findings, not only make the prevalence of corporal punishment more visible, but they are also valuable tools in convincing African governments to fully meet their international human rights obligations to children.

HUMAN RIGHTS CONTEXT

In Africa, as throughout the world, the *Convention on the Rights of the Child* (CRC) provides the fundamental human rights benchmark for protecting children from all forms of violence, including corporal punishment (see Newell, Chapter 2, this volume). All states in Africa have ratified the CRC with the exception of Somalia, which signed it in 2002, and in 2009 stated its intention to ratify it (Child Rights Information Network, 2009). But several regional human rights instruments also support prohibition.

The African Charter on Human and People's Rights

The *African Charter* (African Commission on Human and Peoples' Rights, 1981) has been ratified by all states in the region except Morocco. It contains a number of provisions which together support the imperative to prohibit all corporal punishment of children:

- The Member States of the Organization of the African Unity parties to the present Charter shall recognize the rights, duties and freedoms enshrined in the Charter and shall undertake to adopt legislative or other measures to give effect to them (Article 1).
- Human beings are inviolable. Every human being shall be entitled to respect for his life and the integrity of his person. No one may be arbitrarily deprived of this right (Article 4).
- Every individual shall have the right to respect of the dignity inherent in a human being and to the recognition of his legal status. All forms of exploitation and degradation of man, particularly slavery, slave trade, torture, cruel, inhuman or degrading punishment and treatment shall be prohibited (Article 5).
- The State shall ensure the elimination of every discrimination against women and also ensure the protection of the rights of women and children as stipulated in international declarations and conventions (Article 18.3).

In 2000, a complaint was submitted to the African Commission on Human and Peoples' Rights, which monitors the implementation of this *Charter*, concerning the sentencing of eight students in Sudan to corporal punishment for "public order" offences. In its decision, the Commission stated that its task was not to interpret Shari'ah law but to establish whether the lashes were consistent with human rights standards. It concluded: "There is no right for individuals, and particularly the government of a country to apply physical violence to individuals for offences. Such a right would be tantamount to sanctioning State sponsored torture under the *Charter* and contrary to the very nature of this human rights treaty" (African Commission on Human and Peoples' Rights, 2003, p. 6). The Commission recommended that the government of Sudan should "immediately amend the *Criminal Law* of 1991, in conformity with its obligations under the *African Charter* and other relevant international human rights instruments; abolish the penalty of lashes; and take appropriate measures to ensure compensation of the victims" (African Commission on Human and Peoples' Rights, 2003, p. 7).

The African Charter on the Rights and Welfare of the Child

By March 2010, this *Charter* (Organization of African Unity, 1990) had been ratified by 45 states. It requires states to:

- take all appropriate measures to ensure that a child who is subjected to school or parental discipline shall be treated with humanity and with respect for the inherent dignity of the child and in conformity with the present Charter (Article 11.5);
- take specific legislative, administrative, social and educational measures to protect the child from all forms of torture, inhuman or degrading treatment and especially physical or mental injury or abuse, neglect or maltreatment including sexual abuse, while in the care of a parent, legal guardian or school authority or any other person who has the care of the child (Article 16.1);
- ensure that no child who is detained or imprisoned or otherwise deprived of his/her liberty is subjected to torture, inhuman or degrading treatment or punishment (Article 17.2.a); and
- ensure that domestic discipline is administered with humanity and in a manner consistent with the inherent dignity of the child (Article 20.1) and assist parents and others responsible for the child in the performance of child-rearing and ensure the development of institutions responsible for providing care of children (Articles 20.1 and 20.2)

Article 1 emphasizes that nothing in this *Charter* "shall affect any provisions that are more conducive to the realization of the rights and welfare of the child contained in the law of a State Party or in any other international Convention or agreement in force in that State." The implementation of this *Charter* is overseen by the African Committee of Experts on the Rights and Welfare of the Child, which held its inaugural meeting in 2002. In

2009, in the first concluding observations it had issued following examination of States' reports, the Committee of Experts noted that Egypt's report indicated "some resistance to put[ting] an end to [corporal punishment] and recommend[ed] the State party to take the necessary measures to abolish the practice" (African Committee of Experts on the Rights and Welfare of the Child, 2009, recommendation 10).

REGIONAL MOVEMENT TOWARDS PROHIBITION

There is a growing movement supporting the full prohibition of corporal punishment of children in all settings of their lives, across Africa. This has been initiated by civil society organizations in individual states—non-governmental organizations (NGOs), human rights institutions, and faith-based groups—working together with international NGOs, and increasingly with Pan-African bodies. The movement, as elsewhere, highlights the human rights imperative for reform. The CRC has been ratified by all but one African state (Somalia). Nelson Mandela described the CRC as "that luminous living document that enshrines the rights of every child without exception to a life of dignity and self-fulfillment" (Mandela, 2000). From 1990 onwards, judgments of Supreme and Constitutional Courts in several states have condemned corporal punishment of children in penal systems and schools.

As active national campaigns have developed, research studies—including interviews with children—have made the extent of corporal punishment in the home, school, and other institutions more visible. The Global Initiative to End All Corporal Punishment of Children, with the support of national NGOs, UN agencies, and others, has mapped the legal status of corporal punishment across Africa and identified the reforms required to effectively prohibit it (Global Initiative to End All Corporal Punishment of Children & Save the Children Sweden, 2009, p. 24ff).

The need to review laws against international human rights standards has been recognized in Africa, and has begun to lead to reform. By October 2010, two of the 54 African states had achieved full prohibition; at least 23 had prohibited corporal punishment in schools; 40 had prohibited corporal punishment as a sentence for crimes committed by under-18-year-olds, and 21 had prohibited it as a disciplinary measure in penal institutions; and very few have banned it in all forms of alternative care outside the family.

Southern Sudan has achieved full reform through the adoption of its *Interim Constitution* in 2005 and a *Child Act* in 2008. Article 21 of the *Constitution* states: "Every child has the right . . . to be free from corporal punishment and cruel and inhuman treatment by any person including parents, school administrations and other institutions". Section 21 of the *Child Act* states that "no child shall be subjected to corporal punishment by chiefs, police, teachers, prison guards or any other person in any place or institution, including schools, prisons and reformatories". But Southern Sudan has an interim government and at the time of writing a referendum on achieving independence is still to be held. In Togo, the *Children's Act 2007* appears to prohibit corporal punishment, and laws against assault appear to apply equally to children and adults, but it has proved difficult to get official confirmation that the law is interpreted as prohibiting all corporal punishment.

Fourteen African states are currently reviewing and reforming their children's legislation. In every case this process provides key opportunities for achieving full prohibition of corporal punishment. African civil society organizations are increasingly collaborating—nationally, regionally, and across the continent—in developing strategies to achieve prohibition and to promote positive, nonviolent forms of discipline in schools and the family.

WITHIN-COUNTRY PROGRESS TOWARDS FULL PROHIBITION

Although the prohibition of corporal punishment of children in all settings is yet to be achieved through legal reforms in the majority of states across Africa, there has been significant within-country progress in many states. Some examples are Nigeria, Zambia and South Africa.

Tunisia

In July 2010, Tunisia became the first African state to prohibit corporal punishment of children in all settings, including the home with the enactment of *Law No. 2010-40 of 26 July 2010* amending the *Penal Code*. Article 319 of the *Code* punished assault and violence which did not lead to serious or lasting consequences for the victim, but stated that "correction of a child by persons in authority over him is not punishable". This clause was explicitly repealed by the new law, criminalizing even light assault of a child. When the law was published in the Official Gazette in July 2010, it was accompanied by a statement from the Constitutional Council asserting that it effectively makes the provisions against light assault in article 319 of the *Penal Code* equally applicable to "correction" of children.

Kenya

In August 2010, Kenya adopted its new *Constitution*, which protects every person from corporal punishment. Article 29 states that every person "has the right to freedom and security of the person, which includes the right not to be ... (c) subjected to any form of violence from either public or private sources; (d) subjected to torture in any manner, whether physical or psychological; (e) subjected to corporal punishment; or (f) treated or punished in a cruel, inhuman or degrading manner". Article 20.1 states: "The Bill of Rights applies to all law and binds all State organs and all persons." And article 53 confirms that every child has the right "to be protected from abuse, neglect, harmful cultural practices, all forms of violence, inhuman treatment and punishment, and hazardous or exploitative labour". Article 2.4 renders void any law, including customary law, that is inconsistent with the *Constitution*.

Various legal provisions in other Kenyan laws justify or authorize corporal punishment and will need to be reviewed and amended to bring legislation into line with the new *Constitution*, including repeal of "the right of any parent or other person having the lawful control or charge of a child to administer reasonable punishment on him" from article 127 of the *Children Act 2001* and of the authorization of corporal punishment in schools in article 11 of the *Education (School Discipline) Regulations*. Civil society organizations are collaborating in efforts to ensure that the prohibition is publicized, understood and implemented. A press statement was issued on behalf of child rights civil society organizations highlighting the prohibition and calling on the government to ensure these are enforced through further legal reform to harmonize existing legislation with the new *Constitution*.

Nigeria

The Child Rights Network (CHIRN)—a civil society organization—launched *Discipline*, a bi-monthly bulletin, which is distributed to children's organizations, schools, NGOs, and parliamentarians. The bulletin includes the voices of children who have experienced corporal punishment, and aims to increase information sharing and build alliances around the recommendation of the UN's *World Report on Violence against Children* (Pinheiro, 2006) to promote prohibition in all settings, including the home.

Zambia

At a 2006 meeting organized by the Zambia Civic Education Association, the Solicitor General, Mr. Sunday Nkonde, noted that "despite the wish, and indeed resolve, to consign corporal punishment to history, the reality is that it still exists". He noted the global context of the UN's *World Report on Violence against Children* (Pinheiro, 2006), with its recommendation that all violence, including all corporal punishment be prohibited, and acknowledged his own passion for achieving prohibition. He stressed that, for children, corporal punishment instills fear, and that fear retards development in children, inhibiting their ability to express themselves. He questioned how society could expect children to grow up to be responsible adults, capable of steering much-needed national development, when corporal punishment was so widely used.

In 2008, the Zambia Coalition on Ending Corporal Punishment was formed. This coalition is composed of civil society organizations, media representatives, and governmental bodies such as Child Protection Units and Victim Support Units. In 2009, the Alliance developed an Advocacy Plan proposing strategic activities to end corporal punishment and promote positive parenting, which is expected to be implemented in 2010.

South Africa

In post-apartheid South Africa, there were rapid moves to limit and prohibit corporal punishment of children—and indeed in 2007 complete prohibition of all corporal punishment, including in the home, was almost achieved. One of the early cases to be heard by the new Constitutional Court in 1995 challenged the sentencing of juveniles to whipping. Statistics in Ministry of Justice annual reports up to 1993 had recorded between 30,000 and 40,000 sentences of whipping each year, most of them whippings of juveniles (EPOCH South Africa, 1995, p. 13). Declaring the sentence of whipping to be unconstitutional, the leading judge stated: "it is my view that at this time, so close to the dawn of the 21st century, juvenile whipping is cruel, it is inhuman and it is degrading" (*S v Williams and others 1995 [3] SA 632 [CC]*, para. 91). The judge commented:

> Courts do have a role to play in the promotion and development of a new culture 'founded on the recognition of human rights', in particular, with regard to those rights which are enshrined in the Constitution. It is a role which demands that a court should be particularly sensitive to the impact which the exercise of judicial functions may have on the rights of individuals who appear before them; vigilance is an integral component of this role, for it is incumbent on structures set up to administer justice to ensure that as far as possible, these rights, particularly of the weakest and the most vulnerable, are defended and not ignored. One of the implications of the new order is that old rules and practices can no longer be taken for granted; they must be subjected to constant re-assessment to bring them into line with the provisions of the Constitution. . . . The Constitution now offers an opportunity for South Africans to join the mainstream of a world community that is progressively moving away from punishments that place undue emphasis on retribution and vengeance rather than on correction, prevention and the recognition of human rights.[5]

The judgment quoted the condemnation of the flogging of juveniles by the European Court of Human Rights in a 1978 case against the UK[6] (*Tyrer v UK*—see Newell, Chapter 2, this volume). It also referred to earlier decisions of the Supreme Courts of Namibia and Zimbabwe, noting them to be of "special significance. Not only are these countries geographic neighbors, but South Africa shares with them the same English colonial experience which has had a deep influence on our law" (para. 31), as well as the Roman-Dutch legal tradition. The 1991 judgment of Namibia's Supreme Court arrived at the conclusion that the infliction of corporal punishment, whether on adults or juveniles, was inconsistent with Article 8 of the Namibian *Constitution* and constituted "inhuman or degrading" punishment.[7] Juvenile whipping had also been held to constitute inhuman and degrading punishment by Zimbabwe's Supreme Court in 1990, with the judge characterizing it as "inherently brutal and cruel; for its infliction is attended by acute physical pain. After all, that is precisely what it is designed to achieve. . . . In short, whipping, which invades the integrity of the human body, is an antiquated and inhuman punishment which blocks the way to understanding the pathology of crime."[8]

Sadly, the response of the Zimbabwe government to the Supreme Court judgment was immediately to amend the 1979 *Constitution*'s Article 15, which states in subsection (1): "No person shall be subjected to torture or to inhuman or degrading punishment or other such treatment." A new subsection was inserted:

> (3) No moderate corporal punishment inflicted:
>
> a. in appropriate circumstances upon a person under the age of eighteen years by his parent or guardian or by someone *in loco parentis* or in whom are vested any of the powers of his parent or guardian; or
> b. in execution of the judgment or order of a court, upon a male person under the age of eighteen years as a penalty for breach of any law;
>
> shall be held to be in contravention of subsection (1) on the ground that it is inhuman or degrading. (Subsection as inserted in Article 15 of the Zimbabwe Constitution by Section 5 of Act 30 of 1990—Amendment No. 11).

Following the end of judicial corporal punishment for juveniles in South Africa, in 1996 corporal punishment was prohibited in all schools. The legislation states that "No person may administer corporal punishment at a school to a learner". Anyone who contravenes this "is guilty of an offence and liable on conviction to a sentence which could be imposed for assault" (South African Schools Act, 1996, Section 10).

There was an unsuccessful attempt to challenge the schools ban in the Constitutional Court in 2000. The application was brought by a voluntary association, which was the umbrella body for 196 independent Christian schools in South Africa with a total of approximately 14,500 pupils. According to the judgment, its parent body was originally established in the United States "to promote evangelical Christian education", and had been operating in South Africa since 1983. The application argued that the schools maintained an active Christian ethos. It asserted that "corporal correction" is an integral part of this ethos and that the blanket prohibition of its use invades their individual, parental, and community rights freely to practice their religion. The Constitutional Court dismissed the application, just as the European Court of Human Rights dismissed an application from a very similar group of Christian schools in the United Kingdom, also in 2000 (see Newell, Chapter 2, this volume).[9]

In 2002, the South African Law Reform Commission, during a review on the amendment of children's legislation, recommended that parents and others should no longer be able to use the "reasonable chastisement" defense if charged with assault on a child. The Commission also recommended awareness-raising and educational measures to promote positive, nonviolent discipline (South African Law Commission, 2002). A strong civil society campaign persuaded the South African Parliament to include explicit prohibition of corporal punishment by parents and others in an amending Bill during its parliamentary passage, but in the final stages in 2007, these provisions were removed, leaving only a requirement that prevention and early intervention programs must focus on, among other things, "developing appropriate parenting skills and the capacity of parents and caregivers to safeguard the well-being and best interests of their children, including the promotion of positive, non-violent forms of discipline" (Children's Amendment Act, 2007, amending the Children's Act, 2005, Section 144[1;b]).

PAN-AFRICAN DEVELOPMENTS

During 2005, three regional consultations for the *UN Secretary-General's Study on Violence against Children* (Pinheiro, 2006) were held in East and Southern Africa, West and Central Africa, and the Middle East and North Africa. Children played an active role in each consultation and their recommendations and the outcome documents included support for the prohibition of all corporal punishment. For each, the Global Initiative to End All Corporal Punishment published and distributed regional reports on *Ending Legalised Violence against Children* (www.endcorporalpunishment.org).

In 2006, the African Child Policy Forum, a Pan-African organization, held its second international policy conference, focusing on violence against girls in Africa. The resulting 2006 *African Declaration on Violence Against Girls* urged all member states of the African Union and the African Union itself, to take all necessary measures for the effective prohibition of all forms of violence against children, including corporal and other humiliating forms of punishment; to place the issue of violence against children and especially girls on the African Union Summit's agenda as soon as possible; and to establish a Special Envoy on Violence Against Children to serve as a mechanism for preventing, reporting and monitoring violence against children in collaboration with the African Committee of Experts on the Rights and Welfare of the Child, the monitoring body for the *African Charter on the Rights and Welfare of the Child* (African Child Policy Forum, 2006a).

In an *All-Africa Report*, the then-Chairperson of the African Committee of Experts, Jean-Baptiste Zoungrana, wrote:

> Millions of African children are victims of violence despite the fact that their States have ratified international and regional legal instruments protecting children and have integrated the provisions of those instruments into their internal legal systems. . . . Although some legislative measures have been taken to ban violence against children in schools, care institutions and penal systems in many African states, not much has been done to end corporal punishment administered to children by their families, in their homes, where violence seems to be culturally accepted. In fact, thousands of homes have become real laboratories of violence against children, and the media have reported many cases. That is unacceptable. The African Committee of Experts on the Rights and Welfare of the Child is particularly concerned by this situation. (Global Initiative to End All Corporal Punishment of Children & Save the Children Sweden, 2007, p. 4)

In 2006, a Southern African Network was formed, with the support of Save the Children Sweden, to end corporal punishment and other humiliating forms of punishment, and to promote positive discipline. It includes NGOs and human rights institutions from seven southern African states and meets annually.[10] The Network's first major project was to develop and deliver, with the African Child Policy Forum, a detailed submission to the 12th session of the African Committee of Experts, held in November 2008 in Addis Ababa, Ethiopia. The submission noted that corporal punishment had been identified as one of the most serious forms of violence against children, widely practiced across the length and breadth of Africa. It urged the Committee of Experts to provide leadership on the issue by adopting a written statement urging African states to prohibit corporal punishment and other forms of humiliating punishment of children in all settings, and to ensure that member states provide information on their progress in eradicating the use of corporal punishment in their periodic reports to the Committee. Individual members of the Committee were urged to promote a ban on corporal punishment of children in their own countries.

The submission was endorsed by more than 30 NGOs and human rights institutions from across Africa. At the end of its session, the Committee of Experts stated that it would write to all the states parties to the *African Charter on the Rights and Welfare of the Child* urging them to prohibit corporal punishment and other forms of humiliating punishment of children; before doing so, it wished to develop guidelines on positive discipline to circulate to states.

In March 2010, in a statement on violence against children in Africa to the Committee of Experts at its 15th Session, the African Child Policy Forum highlighted African countries' "weak legal and policy frameworks and response mechanisms", illustrated through the "absence of provisions on specific forms of violence such as corporal punishment in the home and school environment" (African Child Policy Forum, 2010, p. 6). The organization called on the Committee to promote national policy and legal reforms in order to meet the obligations of the *African Charter on the Rights and Welfare of the Child* and the CRC. The newly-appointed UN Secretary-General's Special Representative on Violence Against Children, Marta Santos Pais (see Newell, Chapter 2, this volume), also called on the Committee during its session to develop an "advocacy campaign to call for an explicit ban on all violence against children, including corporal punishment" (Pais, 2010).

FAITH-BASED SUPPORT FOR PROHIBITION

As noted above, there has been at least one legal challenge to prohibition of corporal punishment by an organization representing Christian schools—in South Africa. In several countries, corporal punishment has been strongly defended from Christian or Islamic perspectives. But there are growing numbers of faith-based bodies and influential individuals advocating in favor of the prohibition of all corporal punishment of children in Africa. In 2007, the South African Council of Churches (SACC), an umbrella organization representing over 16 million Christians of 26 denominations in South Africa, issued a report calling for the abolition of corporal punishment and encouraging the use of positive discipline and nonviolent communication as alternative dispute resolution measures within the home, community, and nation (South African Council of Churches, 2007). At the same time, the Southern Catholic Bishops' Conference made a submission to the South African Parliament also arguing for prohibition of all forms of corporal punishment.

In a 2007 message for the Global Initiative's *All Africa Report*, Emeritus Archbishop Desmond M. Tutu stressed the need "to build communities of trust where all children are respected, where home and school are safe places to be and where discipline is taught by example". He wrote:

> I support the Global Initiative to eliminate all corporal punishment at home, in institutions and community. This worldwide movement has gained prominence through the United Nations Global Study on Violence against Children. Since the launch of the UN Global Report there has been good progress towards eliminating corporal punishment. . . . Millions of the world's children still suffer from humiliating acts of violence and these violations of their rights as human beings can have serious and lifelong effects. Violence begets violence and we shall reap a whirlwind. Children can be disciplined without violence that instils fear and misery, and I look forward to church communities working in solidarity with others and using the context of the Study

> to make further progress towards ending all forms of violence against children. (Global Initiative to End All Corporal Punishment of Children & Save the Children Sweden, 2007, p. 3)

During the 9th Assembly of the All Africa Conference of Churches (AACC), held in Mozambique in December 2008, AACC member churches were called on to ensure that their respective countries pass legislation that outlaws all forms of corporal and other humiliating punishment of children (All Africa Council of Churches, 2008).

Twenty-seven African countries are member states of the Organization of the Islamic Conference (OIC). In 2009, to mark the 20th year of the CRC, a conference was organized by the Egyptian Ministry of State for Family and Population and co-sponsored by the OIC and UNICEF. The conference put special emphasis on the relevance of principles of Islamic Shari'ah to the purposes and objectives of the CRC. The resulting *Cairo Declaration on the Convention and Islamic Jurisprudence* included recommendations calling on all OIC Member states to "urgently review and reform their legislation to ensure the prohibition of all forms of violence against children and to link law reform with promotion of positive, non-violent forms of discipline" (p. 6). Participants "recommend that OIC Member States prohibit all corporal punishment and other cruel or degrading forms of punishment or treatment of children, in all settings including within schools and within the family, linking law reform with the promotion of positive, non-violent forms of discipline" (Organization of the Islamic Conference, 2009, p. 7).

In June 2009 in Mauritania, following a social, educational, and legal study of the negative impact of corporal punishment, and of the rules governing it in Islamic Shari'ah, a Fatwa was issued, which stated that it is necessary to desist immediately and finally from physical punishment, regardless of the pretext given; this is not only required by law and piety, but is also essential for the good of the child, the educator, the family, and society. The Fatwa notes the need to adopt positive, proven educational methods for the upbringing of children (Al-Salek[11], 2009).

LOOKING TO THE FUTURE

The Global Initiative to End All Corporal Punishment of Children and the African Child Policy Forum initiated a project in 2009 to promote law reform and support national campaigns in all regions of Africa with information and strategies. The joint project is building a continent-wide network of supporters of prohibition of corporal punishment of children in Africa. Save the Children Sweden has been particularly active in supporting national organizations in many African countries to carry out research into the prevalence of corporal punishment, campaign for law reform, and pilot programs promoting positive, nonviolent discipline. The first technical workshop on law reform to prohibit all corporal punishment was held in Nairobi for East and Central African states in May 2009, bringing together governmental and non-governmental representatives from Ethiopia, Kenya, Sudan, Rwanda, Tanzania, and Uganda. National strategies to pursue law reform to achieve prohibition were developed, and the workshop led to the formation of the East and Central Africa Network to End Corporal Punishment of Children (Save the Children Sweden, 2009). Other workshops are planned for the Middle East and North Africa, and for West Africa.

In 2010, there are various opportunities for achieving full prohibition of corporal punishment across the continent. In Namibia, the current *Draft Child's Act* will, if enacted, outlaw corporal punishment in all settings except within the home. The semi-autonomous archipelago of Zanzibar—part of the United Republic of Tanzania—is drafting new children's legislation with a view to incorporate the provisions of international human rights instruments into domestic laws, to ensure compliance with the CRC and the *African Charter on the Rights and Welfare of the Child*. This process provides a tremendous opportunity for achieving full prohibition of corporal punishment—including in the home.

There are other opportunities for law reform in Cameroon, Guinea-Bissau, Liberia, Mali, Niger, Senegal, Swaziland, and Uganda; in each country family and/or children's law is under discussion. Civil society organizations in these countries—including the African Network for the Prevention and Protection against Child Abuse and Neglect (ANPPCAN)—Liberia Chapter; Coalition des ONG Africaines en Faveur des Enfants (CONAFE)—Senegal; and the Uganda Child's Rights NGO Network (UCRNN)—are mobilizing and campaigning for robust legal provisions on violence against children, including the elimination of corporal punishment in all settings.

Significant progress has been made towards the prohibition of corporal punishment of children in Africa. The active engagement of civil society organizations, the monitoring role of the African Committee of Experts on the Rights and Welfare of the Child, together with the support of the UN Secretary-General's Special Representative on Violence against Children for a ban on all corporal punishment, will undoubtedly compel African states to place this issue high on their agenda. Law reform is a prerequisite for the effective elimination of all corporal punishment of children, in the home and other settings. The pioneering judgments of high-level African courts and strong supportive statements from faith-based bodies and inter-governmental organizations encourage law reform. The large number of states currently engaging in review and reform of relevant legislation constitutes a key opportunity for maintaining and increasing the momentum to achieve full prohibition of corporal punishment of children in Africa.

NOTES

1. Details from individual State reports are on the website of the Global Initiative at: www.endcorporalpunishment.org
2. Details from individual State reports are on the website of the Global Initiative at: www.endcorporalpunishment.org
3. In the survey, corporal punishment in school in front of peers was defined as humiliating punishment.
4. Isaac Mwangi Wachira v Republic High Court of Kenya (Nakuru) Criminal Application No. 185 of 2004 (Unreported).
5. S v Williams and others 1995 (3) SA 632 (CC), paras. 8 and 50.
6. Tyrer v UK (1978).
7. SA 76 (NmSC) 1991(3).
8. SA 151 (ZSC) 1990(4).
9. BCLR 1051 (CC). 2000 (10).
10. For details see: http://www.rapcan.org.za/sanchpc/default.asp
11. Imam of the Old Mosque, Nouakchott, and President of the Imams and Ulema Coalition for the Rights of Women and Children in Mauritania.

REFERENCES

African Child Policy Forum. (2010). *Violence against children in Africa: The challenges and priorities for action.* Document prepared for the 15th Session of the African Committee of Experts on the Rights and Welfare of the Child, March 15–19, 2010, Addis Ababa, Ethiopia: African Child Policy Forum.

African Child Policy Forum. (2006a). *Second International Policy Conference on the African Child, Violence against Girls in Africa, May 11–13, 2006, Record of the Conference Proceeding.* Addis Ababa, Ethiopia: African Child Policy Forum.

African Child Policy Forum. (2006b). *Violence against girls in Africa: A retrospective survey in Ethiopia, Kenya and Uganda.* Addis Ababa, Ethiopia: African Child Policy Forum.

African Commission on Human and Peoples' Rights. (1981). *African Charter on Human and Peoples' Rights.* Available at: http://www.achpr.org/english/_info/charter_en.html

African Commission on Human and Peoples' Rights. (2003). *Curtis Francis Doebber v Sudan*, 236/2000, 33rd Ordinary Session, Niger.

African Committee of Experts on the Rights and Welfare of the Child. (2009). *Concluding observations on Egypt's initial report.* Addis Ababa, Ethiopia.

All Africa Council of Churches. (2008). *9th General Assembly draft report,* pp. 39–42, Pretoria, South Africa .

Al-Salek, H. A. O. (2009). Abstract of *A comprehensive social, educational and legal study of the negative impact of child beating, and the rules governing it in Islamic Shariah (Law).* Prepared by Professor Imam Hadd Amin Ould Al-Salek.

Child Rights Information Network. (2009, November 23). *Somalia plans to ratify Convention.* Reuters news release.

Children's Amendment Act. (2007). *Amending the Children's Act 2005, Section 144(1:b)*: South Africa.

EPOCH South Africa. (1995). *Hitting people is wrong—and children are people too.* South Africa.

Global Initiative to End All Corporal Punishment of Children & Save the Children Sweden. (2009). *Ending legalised violence against children: Global report 2009.* London, UK.

Global Initiative to End All Corporal Punishment of Children & Save the Children Sweden. (2007). *All Africa special report: ending legalised violence against children—A contribution to the UN Secretary-General's Study on violence against children.* London: Author.

Kleynhans, D. (2009). *Ending corporal punishment of children in Mozambique.* Save the Children Sweden Regional Office for Southern Africa.

Mandela, N. (2000). Statement by Nelson Mandela on building a global partnership for children, Johannesburg, May 6, 2000. Accessed October 15, 2010, from: http://www.sahistory.org.za/pages/people/special%20projects/mandela/speeches/2000s/2000_statement_global_partenership.htm

Organization of African Unity. (1990). *African Charter on the Rights and Welfare of the Child.* OAU Doc. CAB/LEG/24.9/49. Available at: http://www.africa-union.org/root/au/Documents/Treaties/Text/A.%20C.%20ON%20THE%20RIGHT%20AND%20WELF%20OF%20CHILD.pdf

Organization of the Islamic Conference. (2009, November). *Cairo Declaration on the Convention and Islamic Jurisprudence.* Cairo, Egypt.

Pais, M. S. (2010). *Statement by the United Nations Special Representative of the Secretary General on Violence against Children to the African Committee of Experts on the Rights and Welfare of the Child.* United Nations.

Pinheiro, P. S. (2006). *World report on violence against children*: Geneva: UN Secretary-General's Study on Violence against Children. Available at: www.unviolencestudy.org

Save the Children Sweden. (2009). *East and Central Africa regional technical workshop on law reform to prohibit all corporal punishment—Nairobi, Kenya.* Available at: www.endcorporalpunishment.org

Soneson, U. (2005a). *Ending corporal punishment of children in South Africa.* Save the Children Sweden Regional Office for Southern Africa. Pretoria, South Africa.

Soneson, U. (2005b). *Ending corporal punishment of children in Swaziland.* Save the Children Sweden Regional Office for Southern Africa, Pretoria, South Africa.

Soneson, U. (2005c). *Ending corporal punishment of children in Zambia.* Save the Children Sweden Regional Office for Southern Africa, Pretoria, South Africa.

South African Council of Churches. (2007). *Religions, the promotion of positive discipline and the abolition of corporal punishment.* South Africa.

South African Law Commission. (2002). *Project 110: Review of the Child Care Act, report.* South Africa.

UNICEF. (2009). *Progress for children: A report card on child protection.* Number 8 (September). New York: UNICEF.

Zimbabwe Constitution. (1990). Section 5, Act 30—Amendment No. 1.1.

6 Australia

The Ongoing Debate about Ending Physical Punishment

Bernadette Saunders and Judy Cashmore

Population:	22,497,810
Type of government:	Democracy, Constitutional monarchy
Governing structure:	Federal government, 6 state governments, 2 territory governments
Child protection system in place:	Yes
Legal system:	Criminal Code (based on British Common Law) and Child Protection Acts at the state and territory level, family law at the federal level.
Major religion:	Christianity
Official national language:	English
Ratified United Nations Convention on the Rights of the Child:	1990
Federal Children's Commissioner/ Ombudsman:	No, but Children's Commissioners and Children's Guardians at the state level.

HISTORICAL BACKGROUND

Aboriginal people have inhabited Australia for at least 50,000 years. In the late 18th century, the British set up penal colonies in Australia; between 1788 and 1868 160,000 convicts were transported. At this time, up to 1,000,000 Aboriginal people lived a hunter/gatherer lifestyle across Australia in 300 clans and speaking 250 languages. In the mid 1800s, gold was discovered and farms flourished, resulting in wealth, investment, and migration. In 1901, Australia became a federation comprising six states and territories with the British monarch as Head of State. Australia's Indigenous people were denied land rights until the 1992 High Court decision re Mabo, and continue to be adversely affected by paternalistic 'welfare' policies and practices.

In addition to over half a million Aboriginal and Torres Strait Islander people, Australia's population of around 22 million people consists of approximately 16 million born in Australia and 5.5 million people who have come to Australia predominantly from the United Kingdom, New Zealand, China, India, Italy, Vietnam, the Philippines, South Africa, Greece, and Germany (ABS, 2009). There has been significant immigration to Australia from Britain and Mediterranean Europe and by dispossessed peoples from Central Europe following the Second World War, and there is continuing immigration from Asia and elsewhere.

Australia is a developed country with a high standard of living relative to the rest of the world and a prosperous economy. It is rich in natural resources and farming produce. Australia's educational facilities and health services are accessible and well-resourced. Australians may freely express their views, crime rates are relatively low, and civil liberties and political rights are embedded in state and federal legislation.

The parenting practices of Australia's diverse population are varied. In many cultural groups, physical punishment persists as a common and valued response to conflict with children (see, for example, Kolar & Soriano, 2000). However, it does not appear to be a traditional child-rearing practice of Aboriginal Australians (Franklin, 2008); rather traditional discipline likely involved various methods of verbal communication and withdrawal of communication (Malin, Campbell, & Agius, 1996). European settlement resulted in a break-down of traditional Indigenous cultures and laws, leading to public perceptions of Aboriginal children as out of parental control, and disproportionate numbers of Aboriginal children being subjected to unprecedented family violence and abuse (Hunter, 2008; Lawrence, 2006). In light of this, it has been recently proposed that Indigenous communities should be informed "of their right to use physical correction that is reasonable in the circumstances" (Northern Territory Government, 2007, p. 73).

Many Australians believe that parents should have the right to use physical punishment (Tucci, Mitchell, & Goddard, 2006) and there are few signs of urgency about a reform agenda. Apart from some pockets of interest in academia, and among advocates and some professional bodies, concern about physical punishment and its potential impact on children and families gets little attention.

Although Australia was one of the first countries in the world to ratify the United Nations *Convention on the Rights of the Child* (CRC) in 1990, the Australian government has shown little response to criticism from the UN Committee on the Rights of the Child in relation to this issue. In the Committee's *Concluding Observations on Australia* (Committee on the Rights of the Child, 2005, paras. 35–36) "concern" was expressed "that corporal punishment in the home is lawful throughout Australia under the defense of 'reasonable chastisement' and other similar provisions in states' legislation". The Committee expressed further concern that "while corporal punishment has been prohibited in government schools and some private schools in most states and territories, it is still lawful in many private education institutions and in both government and private schools in South Australia and the Northern Territory". The Committee recommended that the Australian Government should "take appropriate measures to prohibit corporal punishment at home, in public and private schools, detention centers and all alternative care settings in all States and Territories", and involve children in strengthening "awareness-raising and education campaigns . . . in order to promote positive, non-violent forms of discipline and respect for children's rights, while raising awareness about the negative consequences of corporal punishment." Similarly, in 2008, the UN Committee against Torture (para. 31) observed that corporal punishment had not been "explicitly prohibited" in Australian States and Territories "and may still be applied as 'reasonable chastisement'." The Committee advised all governments in Australia to "adopt and implement legislation banning corporal punishment at home and in public and private schools, detention centers and all alternative care settings". The United Nations *World Report on Violence against Children* (Pinheiro, 2006) recommended full prohibition in all countries by 2009.

Australia's most recent *Periodic Report* to the Committee (2009) does not address the Committee's criticisms or recommendations. It makes no reference to physical punishment in the home, stating only that "the Australian Government does not endorse corporal punishment as an approach to developing values and respect in *students*", and it provides only three paragraphs outlining the *National Safe Schools Framework* and moves by three states in relation to schools, child care and out-of-home-care (Australian Government, 2008, paras. 106–108, emphasis added). The recent *National Framework for Protecting Australia's Children 2009–2020* (Council of Australian Governments, 2009) similarly disregards physical punishment, although it does include strategies to assess community attitudes towards the value of children and to educate and engage the public about child abuse. It also affirms children's right to participate in decision making that affects them.

LEGAL CONTEXT

A challenge for the Australian Government is that while it is responsible as the State Party for compliance with the CRC, it has limited jurisdiction over law, policy, and practice in the relevant areas. Australia has a federal democratic system of government comprising six independent state and two territory governments, as well as the federal government. Federal legislation guides family law matters relating to children's care following their parents' separation; the states and territories are responsible for legislation relating to child protection, education, and child care, and for criminal law provisions. The defense of "lawful correction" to civil action and to a criminal charge of assault applies under common law provisions in Victoria[1] and the Australian Capital Territory, and has been codified in the other jurisdictions.

The Australian picture is therefore a non-uniform patchwork of legislation, regulation, and policy concerning corporal punishment in the home, or in loco parentis, in government and independent schools, and in other forms of care for children such as child care, out-of-home care and juvenile detention:

> *Schools*: Corporal punishment in schools is regulated at state level. Corporal punishment is prohibited in government and independent schools in Australian Capital Territory, New South Wales, Tasmania and Victoria. It is prohibited in government schools in Western Australia . . . In Queensland, corporal punishment by schoolteachers is lawful . . . There is no explicit prohibition of corporal punishment in Northern Territory education law . . . [In South Australia] draft legislation . . . is due to be introduced into the South Australian Parliament.
>
> *Penal system*: Corporal punishment is prohibited as a sentence for crime in all states and territories. Corporal punishment is unlawful as a disciplinary measure in penal institutions in New South Wales, Northern Territory, Queensland, South Australia, Tasmania and Victoria. In the Australian Capital Territory [it] is not explicitly prohibited. It is not prohibited in Western Australia.
>
> *Alternative care*: Corporal punishment is prohibited in child care centres in New South Wales, Queensland, South Australia, Victoria and Western Australia . . . Corporal punishment is lawful in the Northern Territory, Tasmania, Australian Capital Territory. (Global Initiative to End All Corporal Punishment of Children, formatting added). Retrieved August 28, 2009, from http://www.endcorporalpunishment.org/pages/frame.html.

In relation to criminal law, the *Model Criminal Code* (MCC)[2] has attempted to achieve some consistency across states but rather than promoting physical punishment law reform, the MCC Officers' Committee report (1998) concluded that "it goes too far to criminalize a corrective smacking by a parent or guardian, so long as the force used is reasonable" (p. 13). The Committee recommended that a legislative standard of "reasonableness" be established, and that the use of objects in such a way as to cause or risk causing injury be prohibited.

States with *Criminal Codes* provide for a defense of reasonable force for "correction" (*Criminal Code Western Australia*) or for "correction, discipline, management or control" (s.280 *Criminal Code Queensland*). Only New South Wales (NSW) has explicitly limited "reasonable" chastisement. In 2001, it amended its *Crimes Act* 1900 to define unreasonable physical punishment by a parent or caregiver as "force" that "is applied: (a) to any part of the head or neck of the child or (b) to any other part of the body of the child in such a way as to be likely to cause harm to the child that lasts for more than a short period" (s61AA). A "short period" was not defined. A clause in the initial Bill had defined as unreasonable and therefore unlawful both the use of implements, such as a belt or stick, and the use of a closed fist but a lack of parliamentary support led to the withdrawal of these explicit limitations. A group of politicians, supported by a vocal lobby from Christian schools, the NSW Council of Churches, the Salvation Army, and the Centre for Independent Studies, a conservative think tank, opposed the Bill on the grounds of undesired intrusion on parents' rights to choose how they rear their children (Milfull & Schetzer, 2000). The result was a compromise, and a bill that was weakened, retaining "as before, an element of uncertainty and confusion" (Corbett, 2001:14063). Despite several moves since the NSW amendment to abolish the reasonable correction defense from both the criminal and civil law, particularly a recommendation in 2003 by the Tasmanian Law Reform Institute and private members' bills in South Australia and Queensland in 2007, law reform does not appear imminent.

LEGAL RESPONSES TO PHYSICAL PUNISHMENT

Physical assaults upon children are commonly dealt with as child protection matters via the Children's Courts[3] rather than as criminal matters, although it is difficult to obtain reliable statistics on the number of cases heard by either system. The imprecision of Australian laws concerned with physical punishment allows considerable prosecutorial discretion and there is little information available about the way that discretion is handled or the extent to which the common law defense is relied upon (Tasmanian Law Reform Institute, 2003). Most cases are heard in lower courts which are not courts of record so case law is limited.

Recent research (Naylor, Saunders, Alexander, & Antolak-Saper, 2009) draws attention to cases where physical punishment of a child has been (a) the subject of criminal proceedings; (b) raised in Family Court disputes about children's residence and contact, and in child protection proceedings; and (c) considered in tribunal proceedings related to foster parents who have used physical punishment (see, for example, *QW and QX v Minister for Community Services*, 2005). It also appears to have been taken into account as a mitigating factor in the sentencing of adult offenders (see for example *R v Jelisavac*, 2003), and as an aggravating factor in criminal cases where a child has been coerced into a sexual act (see for example *R v Tuitavake*, 1993). The approach to the issue varies markedly in these contexts. For example, while suffering physical punishment in childhood may be taken into account in sentencing (suggesting that it may predispose towards criminality). A parent's use of physical punishment may influence Family Court decisions related to children's living arrangements (see examples below). At the same time, parents who are charged with the physical assault of their child may have recourse to the defense of lawful correction and may be found not guilty (see for example *R v Bresnehan*, 1992). Foster carers, however, may not use physical punishment nor may staff employed in juvenile justice settings or teachers in most, but not all, Australian schools.

Charging and Prosecution

With regard to the prosecution of such cases, a review of Queensland Police Service data (Queensland Department of Justice and Attorney-General, 2008), however, provides some rare insights in a report about the use of the common law defense in Queensland assault cases. The review analyzed 198 "parent/child assault" cases in 2006–2007. Twenty-nine were "identified" as child abuse matters, 35 as domestic violence, and 134 as excessive discipline. In the 120 finalized matters, 95 accused persons were convicted, mostly after pleading guilty and not challenging their "unreasonable" use of force. Many of these assaults (80) involved implements such as "belts, brooms, sticks, kitchen utensils, pieces of hose and cattle prods" (p. 4). In 85 cases, children received blows to the head, 36 were punched, and 13 were kicked. The prosecution was discontinued in 23 cases but in only three cases did the common law defense in s.280 appear to have any bearing on the decision. In one case, "it was considered that a restorative justice approach was suitable because it was more appropriate for the parent to receive guidance and parenting skills" and "the children's mother did not want the children to have to go to court". In another, "the police offered no evidence on the grounds that section 280 was available". Of course, this review dealt with cases in which charges were laid—what is not known is how often "police decide not to charge a parent with assault because they think section 280 will be successfully raised on the evidence" (p. 5).

Conviction and Sentencing

In April 2009, the media reported that an Adelaide father who kicked his 3-year-old son for running to answer a knock at the front door of his home received a suspended sentence. The child suffered liver damage. The judge reportedly justified the sentence on the basis that the father was not likely to repeat his actions, and had attended anger management and counseling (Australian Associated Press, 2009). At the more severe end of sentencing, assault in the guise of discipline may result in a jail term. Recently, a Queensland mother was reportedly imprisoned for 6 years for three counts of cruelty and one count of grievous bodily harm for reportedly standing by as her de-facto partner "by way of so-called discipline" caused severe bruising and injuries to the brain, body, head, and limbs of her 2-year-old son. The prosecutor reportedly observed, "It was only a matter of fortune this is not a murder" (Keim, 2008).

Family Court Orders

Recent reported Family Court decisions indicate that some judges and magistrates are making orders restraining one or both parents and new partners from physically punishing children aged between 2 and 15 years of age. In some cases, the orders arose from one parent's concern about the other parent's skills and practices; in others, as a result of overall concerns about the parenting of both parents (see for example Higginson-Swann & Higginson-Swann, 2008; Re Michael and John [Children contact; 2003]). Interestingly, several judges and magistrates expressed a view about the inappropriateness of corporal punishment for older children—those over the age of 10 or 12. In M and J, for example, which involved children then aged 13 and 6, the magistrate accepted evidence that the mother had used a strap, particularly on the younger boy. His orders restrained "the mother from using corporal punishment against the older boy" who had "reached an age where it is inappropriate to use corporal punishment," and against the younger child "other than the use of the open hand on the posterior."

THE MEDIA CONTEXT

Newspaper articles commonly report legal professionals' comments and penalties enforced by magistrates in lower courts, as well as outcomes of the few cases that proceed to higher courts. Media reports of cases involving physical punishment and abuse frequently lead to heated public debate about parents' right, and even absolute need, to physically punish children and children's right to physical and emotional integrity and protection from harm. Differing opinions about the boundaries between lawful or tolerable physical punishment and child abuse or assault also spark controversy.

The media frequently trivialize the issue of physical punishment in headlines such as "Parents Slap Happy" (O'Brien, 2005), and when the "smacking" debate ensues, tabloid newspaper opinion polling inevitably occurs. Even when hitting children is linked with child deaths (Niellsen, Large, Westmore, & Lackersteen, 2009), prompting headlines such as "Deadly link to hitting a child" (McArthur, 2009), most respondents assert that "smacking" should not be banned (93.4% of 2.064 respondents in a recent poll; Voteline, 2009).

Cases in which corrective force resulted in fatal assault, include 2-year-old Daniel Valerio in 1992 whose step-father and murderer, imprisoned for 22 years, perceived him to be "naughty" (Rayner, 1994, p. 22). Five-year-old Amanda Clark died in 1994, reportedly as a result "of massive brain injuries" when violently shaken for wetting her bed (Ferguson & Webber, 1996, p. 4). Her mother reportedly "lost her grip", pleaded guilty to conduct endangering life, and received a 3-year good behavior bond (Houlihan & Drill, 2009, p. 6). In 2000, 2-year-old Jed Britton, who was unwell, "had not been toilet-trained and was still drinking from a baby's bottle", was “shaken savagely” to the point where his head forcefully “struck the floor” (R v Gary Stanley Kesic, 2001). In 2005, the de facto partner of 5-year-old Cody Hutchins’ mother, who perceived himself as a “disciplinarian” and had modified “a belt to become a heavy strap for . . . corporal punishment”, fatally assaulted Cody after frequent beatings in response to behaviors like not sitting down when told or being too fidgety. To no avail, Cody would plead: “Don’t call the strap man, Dad” (R v McMaster, 2007). Also in 2005, Jackson Daloisio, aged 6 weeks, was punched, shaken, and “clouted . . . in the ear hole” by his father for “whinging” and spitting out his pacifier (R v Douglas D’Aloisio, 2006).

A recent study (Nielssen et al., 2009) examined 165 child homicides in NSW from 1987 to 2001. The authors found that 36% of the children were fatally abused: bashed, thrown, or shaken by their mothers or step-fathers. They concluded that children’s lives could be saved by banning physical punishment. However, when the extreme consequences of physical punishment cannot easily be dismissed, commonly the media attribute greater clarity to the fuzzy line between the ill-defined “smack” and child abuse.

PUBLIC ATTITUDES TOWARDS PHYSICAL PUNISHMENT

Community acceptance of physical punishment appears to be declining but many parents’ strong defense of their perceived right to rear their children as they see fit, without ‘unnecessary’ outside interference, continues to undermine law reform efforts. In 1995, a National Child Protection Council survey of 1,200 parents found that 80% of respondents thought it “unharmful to hit a child, with 20% believing it acceptable to use an implement such as a ruler, leather strap or wooden spoon, and 50% of respondents believed it was every parent’s right to discipline children in any way they see fit” (Editorial: Australia, 1995). More recent telephone surveys have found that 75% of adults in a representative sample in 2002, and 69% in 2006, agreed that “it is sometimes necessary to smack a naughty child” (Tucci et al., 2006), with one in 10 respondents in 2006 saying it was appropriate to use implements such as canes, sticks, belts, or slippers. In a Queensland telephone survey of 4,010 parents with a child under 12 (Sanders, Markie-Dadds, Rinaldis, Firman, & Baig, 2007), 43.4% of parents reported being likely or very likely to give their child a single smack with their hand, and 7.7% indicated they were very likely to hit their child more than once or with an object.

PUBLIC EDUCATION INITIATIVES

Findings on public attitudes towards physical punishment have provided a good base for community education. In 2007, the federal government funded a $2.5 million (US $2.25 million) positive parenting education program, initiated by the Australian Childhood Foundation, which actively promotes nonviolent discipline. Parenting information and advice has been distributed in over one million free booklets in 16 languages, and parenting seminars have been attended by over 10,000 parents. Child protection services have also disseminated clear deterrence messages. For example, the New South Wales Department of Community Services produced a fact sheet for parents stating that "hitting, punching or striking your child is unacceptable. It won't solve the problem or help the situation. Above all, it will teach your child that violence is a solution to conflict" (NSW Government, n.d.). In Western Australia, the Department of Community Development's brochure *Protecting Children* states that "hitting a child can often cause problems: when you are angry or have been drinking or taking drugs, you can't tell how hard you hit, after a while you seem to need to hit more often and smacks just don't work; hitting children doesn't make them learn, it makes them frightened, angry and aggressive [and] you feel guilty after hitting" (Government of WA, n.d.).

THE FLEDGLING CAMPAIGN FOR LAW REFORM

Despite some efforts to educate the public about the harms of physical punishment, the articulation of the case for prohibition in Australia has been fairly muted in contrast with that of the Office of the Children's Commissioner and academics at the Children's Issues Centre in neighboring New Zealand (Smith, Gollop, Taylor, & Marshall, 2004). In Australia, several Commissioners for Children, particularly in Tasmania, have sought or supported legal reform, as have the former Chief Justice of the Family Court and some academics (including Boss, 1995; Cashmore & de Haas, 1995; Milfull & Schetzer, 2000; Naylor & Saunders, 2009; Sanders, 2008; Saunders & Goddard, 1998, 2010), several of whom have called for law reform in government and non-government reports and discussion papers. The current Tasmanian Children's Commissioner has recently argued that the Australian Government should "accept responsibility" if the states and territories are not prepared to do so and enact "appropriate legislation in reliance on its external affairs power" (Mason, 2008). Professional associations such as the Australian Psychological Association and some non-government associations concerned with children have position statements against physical punishment but have not acted upon this issue in any visible way. Organizations such as the Australian Childhood Foundation (ACF) and the End Physical Punishment Alliance have been more vocal and played a more visible role.

Few politicians have taken leadership on this issue. In NSW, Alan Corbett of the Better Future for our Children party successfully initiated legislative reform via a Private Member's Bill. Similarly, but unsuccessfully,

South Australia's Family First MP, Dennis Hood, introduced the Criminal Law consolidation (Reasonable Chastisement of Children) Amendment Bill 2007, and Dean Wells, former Queensland Attorney General and Labor Government MP, publicly supported the repeal or amendment of s.280 of that state's *Criminal Code*. However, a review of that section found that it was little used in defense of parental assaults upon children and that is likely to have undermined his call for reform despite its value for educational rather than prosecutorial purposes.

To date, an organized campaign has not evolved and sporadic actions to date have failed to gain any real traction. According to Nicholson, euphemistic language—"smacking"—which fails to take seriously physical punishment and its inherent lack of respect and discrimination against children, has derailed the debate. Law reform advocates, he observed, can "be easily characterized as do-gooders" intruding upon parents' "legitimate role" and "potentially criminalizing their actions as part of the much reviled Nanny State". Using this stereotype, many politicians, journalists, and others resistant to change undermine or "trivialize the significance of physical punishment of children", and suggest that any restraints on parents' rights "to correct a toddler in this way represents a serious interference with their rights as parents to protect their children, leaving them liable to potential prosecution" (2008, p. 12).

CHILDREN'S VIEWS

Children's views are an essential but largely neglected element of the physical punishment debate. While Article 12 of the CRC clearly stipulates the importance of providing opportunities for children to comment on matters that affect them, in Australian research and social commentary on physical punishment, children are rarely consulted. When given the opportunity to describe their experiences and to express their views, however, children provide important insights into the physical and emotional impact of physical punishment and its effect on their sense of self and well-being. Indeed, "suffering physical punishment, and being forced to live with other children's physical punishment at home and in public, may continually reinforce children's perception of themselves as lesser beings" (Saunders & Goddard, 2010).

In Saunders' (2005) study in Victoria, 31 children aged 8 to 17 years described physical punishment at home and in public, and expressed their views on why it occurs, its effects, effectiveness, and legitimacy. In individual semi-structured interviews in their homes or in one of four small focus groups in their schools, this small sample of predominantly Anglo-Saxon children, three quarters of whom had been physically punished, revealed a range of experiences and a diversity of opinions. Some children readily justified and acknowledged parents' 'right' to 'smack' children to teach "right from wrong" or if children's behavior frustrates them. Most children, however, imposed some age and severity restrictions, and all of the children disapproved of using implements and hitting children "too hard". While it might, according to one 9-year-old, be "okay to be smacked" when aged "like five and six, seven, eight, nine and ten" to prevent children "growing up with bad habits", the line was drawn for older children in terms of their personhood. A 13-year-old, for example, questioned the appropriateness of her parents continuing to physically punish her "'cause I think I am becoming a bit of a person, not a child any more".

The pain and distress associated with disrespectful treatment appeared foremost in most children's thoughts. Several talked about "really hard" hitting that "hurts a lot" and the need to respect and respond to children "like you treat yourself". Many children rejected the idea that "smacking" or physical punishment was either justified or effective, seeing it as not only physically and emotionally hurtful but unnecessary and unenlightened. Children remarked that "instead of adults using their mind and their head they use action" (9-year-old), and "a smack doesn't make them learn anything except [that] they're naughty" (8-year-old). A 13-year-old noted that parents "feel bad . . . guilty" and "I don't think there is any point of an adult punishing a child physically". A 9 year-old similarly observed that hitting a child is "giving the message that it's okay to smack" and "it's just a big cycle. . . . People are gonna get smacked until someone finally doesn't smack in your family".

Children also suggested alternatives to physical punishment, especially talking to children about what they have done wrong. Some wanted changes in the law and education for parents to encourage them to use better disciplinary methods. A 10-year-old child said, "it's easier to talk so then you can like settle it, and it doesn't like turn into an argument with crying and stuff, 'cause it's hurting." A 12-year-old similarly rejected the notion that hitting is constructive discipline: "I just find it a bit funny, a bit silly [that] . . . to get a person to do [something], rather than talk to them, you have to use physical violence. . . . I just think there might be a better way than doing that." Another 12-year-old said "they should make the law that you're not allowed to smack [because] smacking is wrong and it hurts".

Other 12-year-olds observed:

> Children are small and can't fight back [but] children have rights too. Adults are there to teach their children and if they do it the right way it can be some of the happiest times of your life, but if treated badly it can wreck your life.

> The Aboriginals [had] a walk to make John Howard [former Australian Prime Minister] say sorry. I think we should have a walk . . . to say: "Stop hitting children, it's not doing anything to help the kid. . . . This is not the way to . . . discipline, by hitting a child. Why? Think about it. . . . Any hitting, you can see a bruise but you can't see how

it mentally affects someone and they'll carry that right through their childhood, right through their adulthood".

CONCLUSION

There are as yet few signs that children's voices are being heard in Australia's debate or that any of its governments are prepared to repeal the "reasonable chastisement" provision. There are also few signs that the other states and territories see much mileage in the partial reform recommended by the *Model Criminal Code* or as codified in the NSW 2002 amendment. Indeed, this is a polarizing and polarized debate with which most politicians are reluctant to engage. The Australian government has yet to address the criticisms leveled by several UN Committees in relation to Australia's international commitments to children, or with regard to civil and political rights, and torture. Consequently, in its forthcoming appearance before the UN Committee on the Rights of the Child, the Australian government is expected to again come under pressure. Interested Australian advocates and academics are taking note of the campaign in New Zealand, the first English-speaking country to remove the criminal defense to corrective force of a child. Banning parental physical punishment of children together with education about positive discipline would be a significant acknowledgment of children's vulnerability and an important step towards ensuring children's optimal physical and emotional development.

NOTES

1. In Victoria, the common law defense emanates from a 1955 judgment which states: "there are strict limits to the right of a parent to inflict reasonable and moderate corporal punishment on his or her child for the purpose of correcting the child in wrong behaviour . . . the punishment must be moderate and reasonable . . . it must have a proper relation to the age, physique and mentality of the child, and . . . it must be carried out with a reasonable means or instrument" (*R v Terry*, 114, 116).
2. The Model Criminal Code is a co-operative project between the Commonwealth, State and Territory governments which aims to develop uniform national criminal laws and provides an opportunity to review the current state of the criminal law in Australia and to develop legislation based on best practice.
3. Children's Courts in Australia deal with matters related to the care and protection of children who have allegedly been abused and/or neglected, as well as criminal matters involving children and young people as alleged offenders.

REFERENCES

Australian Associated Press (2009) 'Subliminal forces' made dad kick son. *The Australian*. Retrieved 24th October, 2010, from http://www.theaustralian.

com.au/news/nation/subliminal-forces-made-dad-kick-son/story-e6frg6nf-1225701647060

ABS. (Australian Bureau of Statistics). (2009). *Migration Australia*, 3412.0, 2007–2008. Retrieved November 26, 2009, from http://www.ausstats.abs.gov.au/Ausstats/subscriber.nsf/0/33A138F3B3CD34C7CA25760000175284/$File/34120_2007-08.pdf

Australian Government. (2008). *Fourth report under the Convention on the Rights of the Child*. Retrieved August 28, 2009, from http://www.ag.gov.au/www/agd/rwpattach.nsf/VAP/%28084A3429FD57AC0744737F8EA134BACB%29~Fourth+Australian+CRC+Report+-+Proofread+Version+-+May+2009.pdf/$file/Fourth+Australian+CRC+Report+-+Proofread+Version+-+May+2009.pdf

Boss, P. (1995). Physical punishment in child rearing. *Children Australia, 20*(3), 27–32.

Cashmore, J., & de Haas, N. (1995). *Legal and social aspects of the physical punishment of children*. Canberra, Australia: Australian Government Publishing Service.

Committee on the Rights of the Child. (2005). *Concluding observations: Australia*. October 20, 2005. CRC/C/15/Add.268. Retrieved August 28, 2009, from http://www.unhchr.ch/tbs/doc.nsf/%28Symbol%29/CRC.C.15.Add.268.En?Opendocument

Corbett, A. (Australia, House of Representatives, 2001). *Debates*. 14063. Retrieved August 28, 2009, from http://www.parliament.nsw.gov.au/prod/PARLMENT/hansArt.nsf/V3Key/LC20010531006

Council of Australian Governments. (2009). *Protecting children is everyone's business: National framework for protecting Australia's children 2009–2020*. Retrieved August 28, 2009, from http://www.coag.gov.au/coag_meeting_outcomes/2009-04-30/docs/child_protection_framework.pdf.

Crimes Act 1990 (NSW). Retrieved November 21, 2009 from http://www.austlii.edu.au/au/legis/nsw/consol_act/ca190082/s61aa.html

Editorial: Australia. (1995, September 15). *Times Educational Supplement*.

Ferguson, S., & Webber, N. (1996, October 31). They got it wrong, says Gran. *Herald Sun*, p. 4.

Franklin, J. (2008). The cultural roots of Aboriginal violence. *Quadrant*, November, 22–25.

Global Initiative to End All Corporal Punishment of Children. Retrieved August 28, 2009 from http://www.endcorporalpunishment.org/pages/frame.html

Government of Western Australia, Department of Community Development. *Protecting children: Information for parents, families and friends*. Retrieved November 21, 2009, from http://www.community.wa.gov.au/NR/rdonlyres/A457BDFB-B570-4380-B913-8635C4EEBC6F/0/DCDPLNProtectingChildrenFinal.pdf

Higginson-Swann & Higginson-Swann. (Family Court of Australia, 2008).

Houlihan, L., & Drill, S. (2009). Act now, protect. *Sunday Herald Sun*. Retrieved August 28, 2009, from http://www.childhood.org.au/Assets/Files/599cd06c-dd04-4377-9808-cbe4c61ae5d0.pdf

Hunter, S. (2008). Child maltreatment in remote Aboriginal communities and the northern Territory emergency response: A complex issue. *Australian Social Work*, *61*(4), 372–388.

Keim, T. (2008). Beenleigh District Court told toddler was bashed, tied, beaten. *Courier Mail, 15 December*. Retrieved 24 November, 2010, from http://www.news.com.au/national/abused-tots-bound-legs-turned-purple/story-e6frfkwr-1111118327371#ixzz13KFhkJjo

Kolar, V., & Soriano, G. (2000). *Parenting in Australian families: A comparative study of Anglo, Torres Strait Islander, and Vietnamese communities*, Melbourne: Australian Institute of Family Studies.

Lawrence, C. (2006). A national disgrace: Violence against women and children in Indigenous communities. *Aboriginal and Torres Strait Islander Health Worker Journal, 30*(5), 29–33.

Malin, M., Campbell, K., & Agius, L. (1996). Raising children in the Nunga Aboriginal way. *Family Matters, 43*, 43–47.

Mason, P. (2008). Response to the development of a national plan to reduce violence against women and children. Retrieved 24 November, 2010, from http://www.childcomm.tas.gov.au/uploads/file/submissiondevelopmentofanationalplantoreduceviolenceagainstwomenandchildren.pdf.

McArthur, G. (2009, January 5). Deadly link to hitting a child. *Herald Sun,* p. 5. Retrieved 24 November, 2010, from Factiva Database http://global.factiva.com.ezproxy.lib.monash.edu.au/ha/default.aspx.

Milfull, C., & Schetzer, L. (2000). *Sufficient protection for Australian children's rights? Beyond the Corbett Bill: A comparative analysis of attitudes and legal responses to corporal punishment in the home.* Sydney: National Children's and Youth Law Centre.

Model Criminal Code Officers Committee. (1998). *Model Criminal Code Chapter 5 Non fatal offences against the person.* Barton, ACT: Criminal Law Division, Attorney-General's Department.

Naylor, B., & Saunders, B. (2009). Whose rights? Children, parents and discipline. *Alternative Law Journal, 34*(2), 80–85.

Naylor, B., Saunders, B., Alexander, R., & Antolak-Saper, N. (2009). *Taking the physical punishment of children seriously: Judicial approaches to physical punishment in criminal law, family law and child welfare proceedings in Australia.* Children and the Law International Conference, Prato, September, 2009.

Nicholson, A. (2008). Choose to hug, not hit. *Family Court Review, 46*(1), 11–36.

Nielssen, O., Large, M., Westmore, B., & Lackersteen, S. (2009). Child homicide in New South Wales from 1991 to 2005. *Medical Journal of Australia, 190*(1), 7–11.

Northern Territory Government. (2007). *Ampe akelyernemane meke mekarle "Little children are sacred".* Report of the Northern Territory Board of Inquiry into the Protection of Aboriginal Children from Sexual Abuse.

NSW Government pamphlet. *Toddlers are great fun. Tantrums are not.* Retrieved November 21, 2009, from http://www.community.nsw.gov.au/docswr/_assets/main/documents/tantrum_fact.pdf

O'Brien, S. (2005), 'Parents slap-happy', *Herald Sun*, 11 February, p.11.

Pinheiro, P. (2006). *World report on violence against children.* Geneva: United Nations Secretary-General's Study on Violence against Children.

Queensland Department of Justice and Attorney-General. (2008). *Review of section 280 of the Criminal Code.* Retrieved 24 November, 2010, from http://www.justice.qld.gov.au/corporate/community-consultation/community-consultation-activities/past-activities/review-of-s280-of-criminal-code-domestic-discipline.

QW and QX v Minister for Community Services. (NSW Administrative Decisions Tribunal, 2005).

R v Bresnehan. A 78/92. (Tasmania, 1992).

R v Douglas D'Aloisio. (Supreme Court of Victoria, 2006).

R v Gary Stanley Kesic. (Victorian Supreme Court of Appeal, 2001).

R v Jelisavac. (NSW Criminal Court of Appeal, 2003).

R v McMaster. (Supreme Court of Victoria, 2007).

R v Terry. (Supreme Court of Victoria, 1955).

R v Tuitavake. (Supreme Court of Queensland Court of Appeal, 1993).

Rayner, M. (1994, June 29). The ugly truth about the hand that wields the power. *The Age,* p. 22.

Re Michael and John (Children—contact). (Federal Magistrates Court of Australia 2003).
Sanders, M. (2008). Triple P-Positive Parenting Program as public health approach to strengthening parenting. *Journal of Family Psychology, 22*(3), 506–517.
Sanders, M., Markie-Dadds, C., Rinaldis, M., Firman, D., & Baig, N. (2007). Using household survey data to inform policy decisions regarding the delivery of evidence-based parenting interventions. *Childcare, Health and Development, 33*, 768–783.
Saunders, B. J. (2005). *'Because there's a better way than hurting someone': An exploratory study of the nature, effect and persistence of 'physical punishment' in childhood*. Unpublished Ph.D., Monash University, Melbourne.
Saunders, B. J., & Goddard, C. (1998). Why do we condone the physical punishment of children? *Children Australia, 23*(3), 23–28.
Saunders, B. J., & Goddard, C. (2010). *Physical punishment in childhood: The rights of the child*. Chichester, UK: John Wiley & Sons.
Smith, A., Gollop, M., Taylor, N., & Marshall, K. (2004). *The discipline and guidance of children: a summary of research*. Dunedin and Wellington, New Zealand: Children's Issues Centre and Office of the Children's Commissioner.
Tasmanian Law Reform Institute. (2003). *Physical punishment of children*. Hobart, Tasmania, Australia: Tasmanian Law Reform Institute.
Tucci, J., Mitchell, J., & Goddard, C. (2006). *Crossing the line: Making the case for changing Australian laws about the physical punishment of children*. Ringwood, Victoria, Australia: Australian Childhood Foundation.
United Nations Committee against Torture. (2008). *Consideration of reports submitted by States Parties under Article 19 of the Convention*. Retrieved 28 August, 2009, from http://hrlibrary.ngo.ru/cat/observations/australia2008.pdf
Voteline. (2009, January 6) *Herald Sun*, p. 17.

7 Canada

The Rocky Road of Repeal

Anne McGillivray and Cheryl Milne

Population:	33,739,900
Area:	9,093,507 square kms
Type of government:	Democracy, Constitutional Monarchy
Governing structure:	Federal government, 10 provincial governments, 3 territorial governments
Child protection system in place:	Yes
Legal system:	Criminal Code (based on British Common Law) at the federal level; Child Protection Acts at the provincial/territorial level
Major religions:	Christianity, Judaism
Official national languages:	English, French, regional languages recognized
Ratified United Nations Convention on the Rights of the Child:	1991
Children's Commissioner/ Ombudsman:	No, but Children's Advocates at the provincial/ territorial level.

HISTORICAL BACKGROUND

Canada is an immigrant nation and home to 53 First Nations speaking dozens of distinct languages. The population is highly diverse. Settlement began shortly after European discovery, beginning with the foundation of French and English colonies in Atlantic and central Canada. With the *Treaty of Paris* in 1763, French Canada passed into English hands. Western Canada, under the control of the Hudson's Bay Company from 1670 to 1880, was rapidly settled by immigrants from across Europe and eastern Canada, beginning in the latter part of the 19th century. Treaties with First Nations bands cleared the path of settlement, placing adults on reserves and introducing a system of residential schooling after 1890 to 'civilize' indigenous children. The destructive heritage of the schools and complex questions of governance pose unique challenges for child protection. The *Canada Act* of 1982 severed Canada's constitution from Britain and brought into law the Canadian *Charter of Rights and Freedoms*.

PREVALENCE OF PHYSICAL PUNISHMENT

The physical punishment of children in Canada appears to be a relatively common practice, but its actual prevalence is difficult to estimate. Studies show considerable variation depending upon how the question is asked and who is providing the answers. National surveys range from 21% (Decima, 1988) to 50% (Canadian Press, 2002). Regional surveys show much higher levels, ranging from 70% to 85% (Ateah & Durrant, 2005; Ateah & Parkin, 2002; Clément, Bouchard, Jetté, & Laferrière, 2000; Lenton, 1990). Whatever its prevalence, physical punishment remains acceptable under Canadian law.

LEGAL CONTEXT

Canada is a federal state, with power to enact criminal law resting with the federal government. Jurisdiction over civil matters, including education and child protection, rests with the 10 Provinces and the 3 Territories—but, for First Nations children, the federal government.

Section 43 of the *Criminal Code* (s. 43) gives parents and teachers a defense to child assault if the assault is reasonable and corrective:

> Every school teacher, parent or person standing in the place of a parent is justified in using force by way of correction toward a pupil or child, as the case may be, who is under his care, if the force does not exceed what is reasonable in the circumstances.

Canada shares the origins of its defense with common law and civil law nations. From ancient times, beating was seen as a necessary aid to education, piety, and obedience (Helmholtz, 1993; Scott, 1938; Stone, 1979). The law was in full support. A 365 Roman edict set limits on "domestic correction" by prohibiting "extremely severe castigation" and limiting it to "minors" (McGillivray, 1998). An annotation to the edict as it appears in Justinian's *Corpus Juris Civilis* (529) explains that a "flogging" administered by a magistrate or parent is not punished as an assault because "it is inflicted for the purpose of correction not for the sake of insult." This is reproduced in Bracton's *Laws and Customs of England* (c.1235, v. 2, 298–300) as English common law. It is reflected in Blackstone's 1769 dictum that the father's power is "much more moderate" than in ancient Rome but "still sufficient to keep children in order and obedience. He may lawfully correct his child, being under age, in a reasonable manner, for this is for the benefit of his education" (Book I, Ch. 16). Codified with other defenses to assault by Lord Blackburn for the 1879 Imperial Draft Code Commission, it was enacted in Canada's first *Criminal Code* in 1892. Apart from removing masters and apprentices in 1955, there has been no substantive change to the 365 edict in over 1,600 years. The courts have considerable freedom to interpret the law. In child assault cases, this interpretive freedom combined with the vagueness of the defense has created a legal lottery in which severe assaults might be excused and minor assaults punished.

Over the past 150 years, evolving notions of childhood, the rediscovery of the connection between physical punishment and child injury, and the rise of the children's rights movement have inspired reform efforts. These initiatives span three eras. The first centered on limiting physical punishment in the schools at a time when parental punishment was fully accepted. The second saw prohibition of school corporal punishment, a growing recognition that physical punishment is part of a spectrum of abuse, and demands for repeal. The third began with the launch of a legal challenge to s. 43 under Canada's *Charter of Rights and Freedoms*.

1850 TO 1962: "A KIND, FIRM, JUDICIOUS PARENT"

Physical punishment debates from about 1850 to 1960 centered on the schools. Education journals from this period feature articles arguing that physical punishment is always needed (R., 1884), never needed (Schaible, 1857), or needed as "back-up" or for "the bad boy" (Lewis, 1879; McAllister, 1880; R. J., 1884; *Education Journal*, 1891; Payne, 1896). School boards were to ensure that teachers did not exceed the standard of "a judicious parent" set in Ontario in 1856: "To practice such discipline in his school as would be exercised by a judicious parent in his family; avoiding corporal punishment, except when it shall appear to him to be imperatively required" (Hodgins, 1859; Legislative Assembly, 1856). Regulation 298 of The *Upper Canada School Acts* of 1850, 1853 states: "A pupil shall accept such discipline as would be exercised by a kind, firm and judicious parent."[1] This standard was the work of reformer Egerton Ryerson, founder of Canada's system of free mandatory public schooling, and it remains in many provincial/territorial education acts today. According to Ryerson (1865), the notion that a judicious parent uses physical punishment—"there are occasions when it cannot be wisely avoided"—found support in "scripture and common sense." Ryerson considered public debate to be dangerous: "If children when corrected are allowed to suspect that the public sympathy is with them, and not with the master [then] reprehensible behavior and moral deterioration will be the consequence."

During this period, debate began to shift from a focus on the severity of school punishment to the question of whether it should be used at all. Ellen Key's *The Century of the Child* (1909) inspired early 20th-century education debates. She wrote: "The educator to whose mind flogging never presents itself, even as an occasional resource, will naturally direct his whole thought to finding psychological methods of education. Administering corporal punishment demoralizes and stupefies the educator" (Key, 1909, p. 139). "An Old Teacher" disagreed, viewing the rights of "bad" and "good" children differently:

> [T]he boy was rattaned soundly that very day. . . . I did for that boy a true missionary deed. . . . You have no more right to dilly-dally with such a one than has the surgeon the right to let your body die rather than give you pain. Then, too, the good children have rights which you are bound to respect. (1920, p. 25)

Calmerton's (1901) reference to "children's rights" supports her argument that tact, not punishment, "forms the habit of respect for all teachers, which, in a measure, follows through his school-life, even should he pass into the hands of others less mindful of 'Children's Rights'" (p. 214).

While punishment in Canadian schools was subject to vigorous debate from the 1850s to the 1960s, what happened in the home was a matter of paternal authority and, after 1890, agency discretion (McGillivray, 1990, 1992). Social workers viewed their role as maintaining the family unit, children were left with abusive parents, and parents were rarely prosecuted. Parental authority in intact families was unchallenged.

1962 TO 1998: BATTERED CHILDREN AND CHILDREN'S RIGHTS

Despite Ambroise Tardieu's detailed forensic accounts of parentally-induced injuries to children in 1860 (Wolff, 1988), it was not until publication of *The Battered-Child Syndrome* (Kempe, Silverman, Steele, Droegemueller, & Silver, 1962) a century later that public attention turned to the problem of physical punishment (McGillivray, 1992, 1998; Wolff, 1988). Child protection agencies expanded and apprehension rates skyrocketed. School boards began prohibiting physical punishment. Provinces and territories began amending their education acts. British Columbia was first, in 1973: "The execution of discipline must be similar to that of a 'kind, firm, and judicious parent', but shall not include corporal punishment" (British Columbia, 1973). Nova Scotia followed in 1989, then New Brunswick (1990), Yukon Territory (1990), Prince Edward Island (1993), North-West Territories and Nunavut (1995), Newfoundland (1997), Quebec (1997), Saskatchewan (2005), and Ontario (2009), leaving only Manitoba and Alberta without prohibitions in their education acts today. Despite these provincial/territorial prohibitions, s. 43 of the federal *Criminal Code* still protected teachers from assault charges.

The first calls for the repeal of s. 43 came from within federal government—with one exception: When an agency in Prince Albert, Saskatchewan refused custody of a baby in 1973, the desperate mother threw it off a bridge. Mary Helen Richards, founder of a local Parents Anonymous group, complained to the Social Services Minister (M. H. Richards, personal communication, August 14, 2009). He suggested that she focus on children's rights advocacy and parent support, which inspired her to found the Saskatoon Society for the Protection of Children in 1974. The Society established a Crisis Nursery and lobbied "from the beginning" for repeal of s. 43. "It was always about children's rights" (M. H. Richards, personal communication, August 14, 2009).

Movement at the federal level began with the 1976 House of Commons Standing Committee on Health, Welfare and Social Affairs report, *Child Abuse and Neglect*, which called for "further consideration of section 43." This was followed in 1981 by the Standing Committee's call for "immediate repeal" of s. 43. The Standing Senate Committee on Health, Welfare and Science called for repeal in 1977 and 1980. A Justice Canada Memorandum in 1978 recommended repeal. After hearings across Canada on physical punishment and violence in sports, the Law Reform Commission of Canada (1984) recommended removing the defense from teachers but keeping it for parents to avoid "the engines of law enforcement" being wheeled into the home "for every trivial slap or spanking." Justice Linden, Commission Chair, later explained: "The Commission spent a lot of time consulting around the country and encountered strong views that parents should spank their children" although this "is often a screen for child abuse" (McGillivray, 1988). By 1995, 13 government reports had called for review or repeal (Durrant & Rose-Krasnor, 1995).

The 1989 United Nations *Convention on the Rights of the Child* (CRC), promoted at the 1990 New York World Summit for Children co-chaired by Canadian Prime Minister Brian Mulroney, impelled reform. Canada ratified the CRC in 1991. In January 1993, Federal Justice Minister Kim Campbell prepared Bill C-126, proposing repeal of s. 43. When Mulroney stepped down as Prime Minister in June 1993, Campbell took his place. S. 43 was excised from the bill by her successor, Justice Minister Gilles Blais, as "too controversial" (McGillivray, 1998). Seven more repeal bills were introduced in Parliament between 1994 and 2001 by private members, to no effect. Health Canada's short-lived Children's Bureau sponsored consultations with Federal Justice lawyers, NGOs, and academics in 1993, and a media training workshop in 1994. But the law did not change.

This period saw the formation of child advocacy networks, hundreds of small-scale outreach programs and media events, new research, the founding of the Repeal 43 Committee, and a national workshop on child physical assault (McGillivray, 2004). Justice Ministers after Campbell refused to consider repeal. Questions were raised in the House of Commons about the judgment in the "parking-lot spanking case" (R. v Peterson, 1995), in which the court ruled that the public "bare-bottom spanking" of a 4-year-old girl was reasonable, and that "anger is part and parcel of correcting a child". When questioned about the Peterson case in Parliament, Justice Minister Allan Rock stated that his government had "no intention of changing the Code to outlaw spanking. I think any time a parent behaves toward a child they should do so reasonably and that's exactly what's reflected in the Code" (McGillivray, 1998). That same year, the UN Committee on the Rights of the Child (1995) told Canada that "physical punishment of children in families" should be prohibited, as should its use "in schools and in institutions where children may be placed."

1998 TO 2004: THE CONSTITUTIONAL CHALLENGE TO S. 43

In 1997, the federal Court Challenges Program, which funded legal action for equality rights, granted funds to challenge s. 43 to Ailsa Watkinson, a Professor of Social Work at the University of Regina. Dr. Watkinson chose the Canadian Foundation for Children, Youth and the Law (the Foundation) to take the case. Foundation lawyer Cheryl Milne and senior litigator Paul Schabas, acting pro bono, were counsel. In 1998, the Foundation asked the Ontario Court (General Division; now the Superior Court), for a declaration that s. 43 offends the constitutional guarantees of the Canadian *Charter of Rights and Freedoms* (the *Charter*). The Foundation argued that the defense infringes the child's rights to equal benefit and protection of the law under Section 15 of the *Charter*, security of the person under Section 7, and freedom from cruel or unusual punishment under Section 12. The Foundation also argued on the basis of Canada's obligations under Articles 3, 18, 19, and 28 of the CRC.

Leading experts provided affidavits setting out the social science evidence of the risks and harms of physical punishment. Legal evidence was filed showing that in over a century of judicial interpretation, no coherent standard of reasonable correction had emerged. Criminologist Tammy Landau (2005) filed her study of police response to child assault in three Canadian communities, which mirrored the inconsistencies found in the case law. The Ontario Association of Children's Aid Societies (OACAS), Defense for Children International—Canada, Child Welfare League of Canada, National Youth in Care Network, Society for Children and Youth B. C., Canadian Council of Provincial Child Advocates, Repeal 43 Committee, Canadian Nurses Association, and Canadian Association of Social Workers applied for intervener status in support of the application.[2] Status was granted only to OACAS.

The Attorney General in Right of Canada opposed the application, arguing that although physical punishment is not good for children—"It is never okay to spank children; it is a bad idea and it doesn't work" (Health Canada, 1997)—the Canadian government has chosen to educate parents, not criminalize them. The Canadian Teachers Federation was granted intervener status in support of the government and was permitted to give evidence on the need for physical punishment in the schools, even though its stated policy is that teachers should never use it. Status was also granted to a "Coalition for Family Autonomy", struck for the purposes of the case, consisting of Focus on the Family, R.E.A.L. Women of Canada, Canadian Family Action Coalition, and Home School Legal Defence Association Canada.

In July 2000, Justice McCombs ruled that s. 43 is constitutional and dismissed the application (Canadian Foundation, 2000). The Ontario Court of Appeal heard the Foundation's appeal in September 2001. The court ruled on January 15, 2002 that s. 43 permits "parents and teachers to apply strictly limited corrective force to children without criminal sanctions so that they can carry out their important responsibilities to train and nurture children without the harm that such sanctions would bring to them, to their tasks, and to the families concerned" (Canadian Foundation, 2002). According to the court, the law offends no right of the child.[3]

The Supreme Court of Canada heard the appeal of the lower court's decision on June 6, 2003. The Foundation's interveners were joined by the Québec Commission des droits de la personne et des droits de la jeunesse,[4] on its own behalf and representing the Canadian Counsel of Provincial Child Advocates. In its October 2003 Concluding Observations, the UN Committee on the Rights of the Child expressed "deep concern" that Canada had taken "no action to remove section 43 of the Criminal Code" and recommended "legislation to remove the existing authorization of the use of 'reasonable force' in disciplining children and explicitly prohibit all forms of violence against children, however light".

The Supreme Court delivered its decision on January 30, 2004 (Canadian Foundation, 2004). After narrowing the scope of the defense to exclude teachers and force that risks or causes physical harm, or is used in anger or frustration or by someone with "an abusive personality" or with a child under 2 or over 12 years or incapable of learning from physical punishment, or with an object or on the head, or of a degrading, inhumane, or harmful nature, six of nine judges agreed that s. 43 offends no right of the child.[5] S. 43 remains in the *Criminal Code*—but the definition of "reasonable force" has been narrowed.[6] Chief Justice McLachlin, speaking for the majority of justices, said that s. 43 protects children by preventing parents from going to jail. She interpreted the 1995 statement of the UN Committee on the Rights of the Child that physical punishment within families should be prohibited as permitting mild physical punishment.

The Supreme Court's decision was widely denounced (Anand, 2004; Carter 2005; Durrant, 2007; Leckey, 2005; McGillivray, 2004; McGillivray & Durrant, 2006; Mosoff and Grant, 2005; Sykes 2006). It leaves a "gaping hole" in children's rights jurisprudence (Milne, 2004), it frustrates agency attempts to counsel parents (Bernstein, 2006) and its criteria are "worthy of Dr. Seuss" (McGillivray, 2010a, 2010b). The decision and its aftermath convinced Canadian children's rights advocates to abandon any notion that the defense can be rewritten. The aim is full repeal.

AFTER THE CHALLENGE

Does the Supreme Court ruling effectively distinguish reasonable force from excessive force? Researchers mapped the court's criteria onto a national data set of substantiated physical abuse cases and concluded that the criteria are "arbitrary and not grounded in the reality of child physical maltreatment" (Durrant, Trocmé, Fallon, Milne, & Black, 2009, p. 86). Have the court's criteria lowered the threshold for convictions in child assault cases? A slight trend towards lower tolerance for violence is visible but inconsistencies remain. The criteria are fluid, manipulated for conviction or acquittal according to the judge's views on punishment and the justification given by the accused. Blows to the head and face and physical punishment of teenagers, for example, are not allowed, but the court in R. v. D. K. (2004) acquitted a mother who slapped her 15-year-old daughter in the face, reasoning that the criteria permit minimal force that is transitory and trifling. A 2004 Quebec court used similar reasoning (R. c. D. P.), but other courts have convicted for such blows (R. v. Small, 2005; R. v. Brown, 2005; R. v. C. G., 2009).

Where a parent admits to having used physical punishment, the court may find that the evidence does not prove beyond a reasonable doubt that the force was excessive. In R. v. J. D. B. (2004), a father was acquitted of assaulting his 8-year-old son, as the bruised buttocks may have resulted from tobogganing. The court rejected the child's testimony that he had not been tobogganing and was hit eight times, not three as his father testified. In R. v. S. I. (2004), a woman caring for her cousins of 11 and 13 years was acquitted of assault with a shoe, a bat, a knife, a spoon, and her hand. The judge noted discrepancies in the children's testimony on the number of assaults.

The prohibitions against objects and anger are most consistently applied. The use of belts (R. v. S. J.-B., 2004; R. v. B. W. S., 2006), paddles (R. v. M. U., 2005) and a cooking pot (R. v. Beck, 2008) have resulted in conviction. Force motivated by anger or frustration has also resulted in conviction (R. c. G. O., 2005; R. v. C. M. T. U., 2006; R. v. Olink, 2008; R. v. Power, 2008), while injury to the child is clear evidence that the parent "lost it" (R. v. T. J. R., 2006). As long as physical punishment is legal, limits will be set by individual courts in individual cases and criteria will be bent to fit. The Supreme Court's compromise—keep the defense, narrow the scope—is not a success.

LESSONS LEARNED AND ROOM FOR OPTIMISM

The Government of Canada has not embarked on the public education campaign it had strongly relied upon in defending s.43. Health Canada, responsible for health-related public education, stated that it had no record of projects or money spent for this purpose (personal communication, March 6, 2009). A 2006 survey on public awareness of the Supreme Court decision showed that most adult Canadians (63%) think physical punishment is illegal. Most (66%) know nothing about the decision; of those who do, just 1 in 5 know there are limits on parents' use of physical punishment (Toronto Public Health, 2007). The government's promise of public education is unfulfilled.

Even so, there is room for optimism. Contemporary social consensus is a powerful determinant of physical punishment, the Supreme Court said. Physical punishment is increasingly falling into disfavor. A 2003 opinion survey showed that 63% of adult Canadians support repeal (Toronto Public Health, 2003). This support increased to 71% if guidelines preventing prosecution of minor assault were established. The *Joint Statement on Physical Punishment of Children and Youth* (Durrant, Ensom, and Coalition on Physical Punishment of Children and Youth, 2004), which calls for equal protection for children from physical assault, has been endorsed to date by over 400 organizations from every sector of society. In its report, *Children: The Silenced Citizens*, the Standing Senate Committee on Human Rights (2007) called for the repeal of s. 43 by 2009. Evidence that physical punishment is unacceptable—from the international community, researchers, service providers, academics, and the public—is mounting. The basis of the Supreme Court's decision is eroding.

In 2009, the Senate Standing Committee on Constitutional Affairs adopted Bill S-209 which proposed to amend s. 43 by permitting force where a child's conduct threatens harm, is criminal in nature, or is "excessively offensive or disruptive" but "not merely as physical punishment". The Bill "which in various forms has been before this chamber for nearly 10 years" is "entirely modeled on the New Zealand legislation, trying to ensure protection for parents so that behavior whose primary purpose is to protect children from harming themselves is ensured" (Carstairs, 2009). The proposed amendment fails to distinguish assault from restraint, retains the essence of s. 43, and returns the defense to teachers (McGillivray, Durrant, & Ensom, 2009). It creates new avenues for justifying the use of force, to be litigated over the bodies and rights of children. Given the aftermath of the Supreme Court's decision, this compromise is doomed.

School bans were achieved by trustees and parents pushing for reform over a 35-year period. Until the 1990s, most calls for repeal came from within federal government. The CRC and the Supreme Court's decision brought new voices to the campaign. The Canadian experience suggests that it may be unwise to place much reliance on the good will of politicians, that the courts are not always the best forum for affirming children's rights, and that compromise will not succeed where the issue is as value-laden as child physical punishment. As with all social reform, windows of opportunity open and close unexpectedly. The focus must now be on public education and gaining further support for repeal from institutions dedicated to children's rights and well-being. Central to repeal is the international community's continued condemnation of Canada's failure to repeal its law. The importance of public outreach and steadfast advocacy cannot be overstated.

NOTES

1. The disparity at that time between standards and practices, particularly in the Indian residential schools, is striking (Milloy, 1999).
2. A person, group, or agency with special interest and expertise in a legal question may be granted intervener status by the judge. Attorneys General may intervene as of right in constitutional questions. Interveners have standing in court proceedings to make legal arguments but generally do not have standing to present evidence or to appeal the decision. The Teachers Federation was permitted to present evidence in this case.
3. The confusion between acts of nurture and acts of violence is deeply embedded in the common law. In 2000, the Ontario Court of Appeal ruled that nurturing touch is the common law counterpart of s. 43: "Here, as in s. 43, the common law exception that allows a parent to touch a child in order to care for the child both protects the parent and removes a protection from the child" (*R.* v *A. E.,* 2000, para. 29).
4. Quebec Human Rights and Children's Rights Commission.
5. Three judges disagreed with the majority. Justices Binnie and Deschamps found that s. 43 denies children's rights to equality. Justice Binnie justified this breach under Section 1 of the *Charter* for parents but not teachers. Justice Arbour found that the law unjustifiably breaches the child's right to security of the person, citing the 2003 statement of the UN Committee on the Rights of the Child.
6. The Court defined corporal punishment as "reasonable" if: (1) it is administered by a parent; (2) the child is between the ages of 2 and 12 years inclusive; (3) the child is capable of learning from it; (4) it constitutes "minor corrective force of a transitory and trifling nature"; (5) it does not involve the use of objects or blows or slaps to the head; (6) it is not degrading, inhuman, or harmful; and (7) it is corrective—that is, not the result of the caregiver's "frustration, loss of temper or abusive personality."

REFERENCES

Anand, S. (2004). Reasonable chastisement: A critique of the Supreme Court of Canada's decision in the 'spanking' case. *Alberta Law Review 41*(4), 871–878.

An Old Teacher. (1920). School room methods: A plea for the bad boy. *The Western School Journal, January,* 24–26 [rep., *Popular Educator*].

Ateah, C., & Durrant, J. E. (2005). Maternal use of physical punishment in response to child misbehaviour: Implications for child abuse prevention. *Child Abuse & Neglect, 29,* 177–193.

Ateah, C., & Parkin, C. M. (2002). Childhood experiences with and current attitudes toward corporal punishment. *Canadian Journal of Community Mental Health, 21*, 35–46.
Bernstein, M. M. (2006). The decision of the Supreme Court of Canada upholding the constitutionality of Section 43 of the Criminal Code of Canada: What this decision means to the child welfare sector. *Envision: The Manitoba Journal of Child Welfare, 4*, 66–85.
Blackstone, W. (1769). *Commentaries on the Law of England*. Available at: http://www.lonang.com/exlibris/blackstone/
British Columbia. (1973). *Schools Act*.
Calmerton, G. R. (1901). Tact, then and now. *Educational Journal of Western Canada, 3*(7), 213–215.
Canadian Foundation for Children, Youth and the Law v. Canada. (Attorney General). (2000). 49 O.R. (3d) 662, 188 D.L.R. (4th) 718, 146 C.C.C. (3d) 362, 36 C.R. (5th) 334, 76 C.R.R. (2d) 251, [2000] O.J. No. 2535 (QL), Ontario Superior Court of Justice.
Canadian Foundation for Children, Youth and the Law v. Canada. (Attorney General). (2002). 57 O.R. (3d) 511, 207 D.L.R. (4th) 632, 161 C.C.C. (3d) 178, 154 O.A.C. 144, 48 C.R. (5th) 218, 23 R.F.L. (5th) 101, 90 C.R.R. (2d) 223, [2002] O.J. No. 61 (QL); Ontario Court of Appeal.
Canadian Foundation for Children, Youth and the Law v. Canada. (Attorney General). (2004). 1 *Supreme Court Review, 76*.
Canadian Press and Leger Marketing. (2002). *Child abuse report*. Montréal: Authors.
Carstairs, S. (2009). Speeches, Monday June 22. Available at: http://sen.parl.gc.ca/scarstairs/newsroom/speech2009june22_e.asp
Carter, M. (2005). The constitutional validity of the corporal punishment defense in Canada: A critical analysis of Canadian Foundation for Children, Youth and the Law versus Canada (Attorney-General). *International Journal of Victimology,12*, 189–211.
Clément, M. E., Bouchard, C., Jetté, M., & Laferrière, S. (2000). *La violence familiale dan la vie des enfants du Québec*. Quebec: Institut de la Statistique du Québec.
Committee on the Rights of the Child. (1995). Report adopted by the Committee at its 233rd meeting on June 9, 1995, Ninth Session, CRC/C/43.
Committee on the Rights of the Child. (2003). *Concluding observations*. Consideration of Reports Submitted by State Parties under Article 44 of the Convention, Thirty-fourth Session, CRC/C/15/Add. 215.
Criminal Code, R.S.C., 1953–1954, c. 51.
Decima Research. (1988). *Report to the Institute for the Prevention of Child Abuse on a nation-wide survey of attitudes toward child rearing*. Toronto: Author.
Durrant, J. E. (2007). Corporal punishment. In R. B. Howe & K. Covell (Eds.), *A question of commitment: Children's rights in Canada* (pp. 99–125). Waterloo: Wilfrid Laurier University Press.
Durrant, J. E., & Rose-Krasnor, L. (1995). *Corporal punishment: Research review and policy recommendations*. Ottawa: Department of Health.
Durrant, J. E., Ensom, R., & Coalition on Physical Punishment of Children and Youth. (2004). *Joint statement on physical punishment of children and youth*. Ottawa: Authors. Available at: http://www.toronto.ca/health/pdf/boh_june16_2003_physical_punishment_children_fullreport.pd
Durrant, J. E., Trocmé, N., Fallon, B., Milne, C., & Black, T. (2009). Protection of children from physical maltreatment in Canada: An evaluation of the Supreme Court's definition of reasonable force. *Journal of Aggression, Maltreatment & Trauma, 18*, 64–97.

The Educational Journal. (1891). Editorial notes. V. 4, no. 19 (Feb. 16) 289.
Health Canada. (1997). *Nobody's perfect* [pamphlet].
Helmholz, R. H. (1993). And were there children's rights in early modern England? The canon law and 'intra~family violence' in England, 1400–1640. *International Journal of Children's Rights 1,* 23–32.
Hodgins, J. G. (1859). Department of Public Instructions for Upper Canada. *The laws relating to Common Schools, in the rural sections of Upper Canada.* Toronto: Lovell & Gibson.
Kempe, C. H., Silverman, F. N., Steele, B. F., Droegemueller, W., & Silver, H. K. (1962). The battered-child syndrome. *Journal of the American Medical Association 181,* 17–24.
Key, E. (1909). *The century of the child* (Frances Maro, Trans.). New York: G. Putnam's Sons.
Landau, T. C. (2005). Policing the punishment: Charging practices under Canada's corporal punishment laws. *International Review of Victimology, 12,* 121–138.
Law Reform Commission of Canada. (1984). *Assault.* Working Paper 38. Ottawa: Supply and Services Canada.
Leckey, R. (2005). Embodied dignity. *Oxford University Commonwealth Law Journal, 5,* 63–83.
Legislative Assembly of the Province of Canada. (1856). *Journals 15th February to 1st July.* V. 15 Appendix 58 Rules for teachers. Toronto: G. Desbarats & T. Cary.
Lenton, R. L. (1990). Techniques of child discipline and abuse by parents. *Canadian Review of Sociology and Anthropology, 27,* 157–184.
Lewis, R. (1879). Corporal punishment. *The Canada Educational Monthly and School Chronicle, 1,* 420–422.
McAllister, S. (1880). Public School Department. *The Canada Educational Monthly and School Chronicle, 2,* 284–286.
McGillivray, A. (1988). *The criminalization of child abuse.* LL.M. Thesis. University of Toronto.
McGillivray, A. (1990). Abused children in the courts: Adjusting the scales after Bill C-15. *Manitoba Law Review,* 549–579.
McGillivray, A. (1992). Reconstructing child abuse: Western definition and non-Western experience. In M. D. A. Freeman & P. Veerman (Eds.), *The ideologies of children's rights* (pp. 213–236). Dordrecht, the Netherlands: Martinus Nijhoff.
McGillivray, A. (1998). He'll learn it on his body: Disciplining childhood in Canadian law. *International Journal of Children's Rights, 5,* 193–242.
McGillivray, A. (2004). Child physical assault: Law, equality and intervention. *Manitoba Law Journal, 30,* 133–166.
McGillivray, A. (2010a). Children's rights, paternal power and fiduciary duty: From Roman law to the Supreme Court of Canada. *International Journal of Children's Rights, 18,* 1–34.
McGillivray, A. (2010b). Nowhere to stand: Correction by force in the Supreme Court of Canada. In S. Anand (Ed.), *Paradoxes of children's rights: Essays in honor of Nicholas Bala.* Toronto: Irwin Law.
McGillivray, A., & Durrant, J. E. (2006). Child corporal punishment: Violence, law and rights. In R. Alaggia & C. Vine (Eds.), *Cruel but not unusual: Violence in Canadian families* (pp. 177–200). Waterloo: Wilfrid Laurier University Press.
McGillivray, A., Durrant, J., & Ensom, R. (2009). Changing the child punishment law: Is Bill S-209 a backward step?' *Our Voice in Action: Bulletin of the Ontario Public Health Association, May.* Available at: http://www.opha.on.ca/media/ebulletins/May09/advocacyupdt.shtml

Milloy, J. (1999). *A national crime: The Canadian government and the residential school system—1879 to 1986*. Winnipeg: University of Manitoba Press.

Milne, C. (2004). The limits of children's rights under section 7 of the Charter: Life, no liberty and minimal security of the person. *National Journal of Constitutional Law, 17,* 199–212.

Mosoff, J., & Grant, I. (2005). Upholding corporal punishment: For whose benefit? *Manitoba Law Journal, 31*, 177–199.

Payne, J. L. (1896). The use of corporal punishment. *The Canadian Magazine*, *7,* 477–479.

R., J. (1884). Corporal punishment in schools. *The Canada Educational Monthly and School Magazine, 6,* 10–14.

R. v. *A. E.,* [2000] *Ontario Judgments* No. 2984 (Court of Appeal).

R. v. *B. W. S.*, [2006] *Saskatchewan Judgments* No. 532.

R. v. *Beck,* [2008] *Newfoundland Judgments* No. 110.

R. v. *Brown,* [2005] *Nunavut Judgments* No.10.

R. v. *C. G.*, [2009] *Alberta Judgments* No. 246.

R. v. *C. M. T. U.*, [2006] *British Columbia Judgments* No. 3221.

R. v. *D. K.*, [2004] *Ontario Judgments* No. 4676.

R. c. *D. P.,* [2004] *J. Q. No.10753*

R. c. *G. O.*, [2005] *Judgments de Quebec* No. 7328.

R. v. *J. D. B.*, [2004] *Alberta* Judgments No. 814.

R. v. *M. U.*, [2005] *Ontario Judgments* No. 4577.

R. v. *Olink*, [2008] *Alberta Judgments* No. 283.

R. v. *Peterson*, [1995] *Ontario Judgments* No. 1366.

R. v. *Power*, [2008] *Newfoundland Judgments* No. 266.

R. v. *S. I.*, [2004] *Ontario Judgments* No. 5380.

R. v. *S. J.-B.*, [2004] *Judgments de Quebec* No. 15788.

R. v. *Small,* [2005] *Nova Scotia Judgments* No. 64.

R. v. *T. J. R.*, [2006] *Alberta Judgments* No. 906.

Ryerson, E. (1865). *Reports of the local superintendents of common schools, and of the inspector of grammar schools*. Toronto: Department of Public Instructors for Upper Canada, July.

Schaible, C. (1857). Objections to corporal punishment in the schools. *Journal of education, Upper Canada, 10,* 154–155.

Scott, G. R. (1938). *The history of corporal punishment: A survey of flagellation in its historical, anthropological and sociological aspects*. London: T. Werner Laurie.

Standing Senate Committee on Human Rights. (2007). *Children: The silenced citizens. Effective implementation of Canada's international obligations with respect to the rights of children*. Ottawa: The Committee. Available at: www.senate-senat.ca/rights-droits.asp

Stone, L. (1979). *The family, sex and marriage in England 1500 to 1800*. Harmondsworth, Middlesex: Penguin.

Sykes, K. (2006). Bambi meets Godzilla: Children's rights and parents' rights in Canadian Foundation for Children, Youth and the Law v. Canada. *McGill Law Journal, 51,* 131–166.

Thorne, S. E. (Ed.). (1968). *Bracton on the laws and customs of England* (c. 1235). Cambridge, MA: Belknap Press.

Toronto Public Health. (2003). *National survey on Canadians' attitudes on section 43 of the Criminal Code*. Available at: http://www.toronto.ca/health/pdf/ssl_survey.pdf

Toronto Public Health. (2007). *National survey on Canadians' knowledge of the law on the physical punishment of children (section 43 of the Criminal Code of*

Canada). Available at: www.toronto.ca/health/pdf/summary_report_200703.pdf

United Nations. (1989). *Convention on the rights of the child.* Can. T. S. No. 3, signed May 28, 1990; ratified December 13, 1991.

Upper Canada (Ontario). (1853). *The Upper Canada School Acts (Act of 1850, 1853). The consolidated acts relating to grammar schools in Upper Canada.*

Wolff, L. (1988). *Postcards from the end of the world: Child abuse in Freud's Vienna.* New York: Atheneum.

8 Costa Rica

Ending Physical and Humiliating Punishment in a Central American Country

Milena Grillo

Population:	4,579,000
Type of government:	Democracy, Presidential System
Governing structure:	Four independent, self-governing power branches with national competence and outreach: Executive Power, Legislative Power, Judicial Power and Electoral Power
Child protection system in place:	Yes
Legal system:	Constitution, Family Code, Code for Children and Adolescents
Major religion:	Roman Catholic
Official national language:	Spanish
Ratified United Nations Convention on the Rights of the Child:	1990
Children's Ombudsman:	Yes, operating under the umbrella of the Office of the Ombudsperson

HISTORICAL CONTEXT

Costa Rica is a country located in the midst of the Central American Region. Its origins go back to 1821, when it declared its independence from the Spanish Empire to become a provincial member of a new regional political body, constituted then as the Federal Republic of Central America. In 1856, Costa Rica separated from this body to become a sovereign and independent country. This nation's history attests to the sustainability of its democratic order, one of the strongest in Latin America. Costa Rica holds the record for being the only country in its region making the list of the 23 oldest democracies of the world. The country gained international recognition for abolishing its army in 1948, and then turning this decision into a legal provision under its *Constitutional Charter* of 1949. Ever since that time, the country has directed its national savings to social investment. This explains the country's current position in several international development indices (e.g., 6th in the region on the United Nations Human

Development Index; 3rd worldwide on the Environmental Performance Index). Costa Rica has built a strong coherent legal framework for the protection of children's rights, based on a *Child Rights Charter* adopted in 1949, 30 years before the adoption of the 1979 United Nations *Convention on the Rights of the Child* (CRC). In 2008, the country reformed its law to guarantee full legal protection to children and adolescents from all forms of corporal punishment and humiliating treatment in all settings, including the family.

RELEVANT LEGAL CONTEXT[1]

The main bodies of legislation historically governing children's relations and interests in Costa Rica are Civil Law and Penal Law, both dating from 1841, and Family Law from 1974. These are all based on Roman Law, Canonic Law, and Napoleonic Civil Law. It is from these roots that the national legal framework progressively fine-tuned itself to protect the institution of *pater familiae* for the public good, based on a view of children and women as objects under its exclusive control and possession (Arias Ramos, nd; Brenes Córdoba, 1986).

Canonic Law had an influence on the spirit and wording of the national legislation relevant to the protection of children. A legal framework was established based on a concept of the social order as a set of mandates of interrelated hierarchical authority. Children were subordinated to their parents; wives to husbands; husbands to employers; and wives, husbands, and employers were controlled by Ecclesiastic and Civil legislation. The two main functions of the authority were *prohibiting* and *punishing;* its resolutions were uncontestable, because they were deemed to be the depository of common wisdom and tradition and, therefore, infallible (González Ortega, 1997).

A piece of Civil Law that needs to be referenced here is the *General Code of the Republic* (1841), also named the *Carrillo Code*[2]. This provided the first clear expression of hierarchical authority in national legislation, referring to the lawful use of physical and humiliating punishment against children within the family. Article 143 of this *Code* stated that:

> The son or daughter who, being under patria potestat, leaves the family house without the permission of his or her father, or commits serious or notorious excesses, or shows an ill inclination non-correctible through admonitions and moderate domestic punishments, may be taken by the parents before the Court of the People to be reprehended and made known of his or her duties. Should this son or daughter relapse in the same faults, then the father may, with the knowledge and assistance of the same ruling Judge, place him or her in a correctional house for a period from one month to a year. Equal authority is vested

> onto the mother should she be a widow and for all the situations contemplated in this article; and, in the absence of both parents, onto the grandfather or the grandmother who is a widow. (Carrillo Code, Article 443, 1841)[3]

However, the *Code* did establish some limitations on the exercise of parental authority: Article 446 stated that parents were legally responsible if the allegation of children's misbehavior was unfounded, and if children, pupils, or minors were maltreated. In such cases the Judge was expected to reprimand the guilty, and recommend that order and harmony be restored within the family. This implied the possibility of separation of children from their parents, tutors, or guardians if there was abuse, or if it was in the children's interest. The wording in Article 443, however, created a legal excuse for parents, tutors, and guardians to justify their use of "moderate domestic punishment" against the children in their care. It is this specific provision in this 70-year-old national legislation which is the basis for considering the infliction of "moderate domestic punishments of children" to be a lawful application of parental authority.

This concept of moderate punishment as a lawful parental action expanded through the national legal framework, to become a largely undefined and subjective parameter for determining the appropriateness of various parental acts. From the enactment of the *Civil Code* of 1888 and its reform of 1933 (whereby Article 131 was amended to provide that "The *patria potestad* grants the right to "... moderately correct the children ...") to the enactment of the *Family Code* of 1973,[4] the same provision has been consistently referenced and protected by national legislation. (For a detailed analysis of these reforms see Trejos, 1990).

HUMAN RIGHTS CONTEXT

Human rights instruments and developments were influential in advancing Costa Rica's campaign for law reform. The CRC (especially Articles 19, 28.2, and 37) was ratified by the country in 1990, and in its Concluding Observations on Costa Rica's first report the Committee on the Rights of the Child made specific recommendations to the government to abolish physical punishment. The Committee on the Rights of the Child's *General Comment No. 8* (2006) explicitly affirmed children's right to protection from corporal and other cruel or degrading forms of punishment. The *World Report on Violence against Children* (Pinheiro, 2006) made explicit reference to the increased use of physical violence within families at a global level, and stated clearly that there is an obligation by States to provide children with full legal protection against it.

The research conducted by the Global Initiative to End All Corporal Punishment of Children, the position statement of the American Academy of Pediatrics (1995), and the Resolution adopted by the United Methodist Church (2004) raised public awareness of the issue. These documents were widely disseminated and debated, which led to increased public support for law reform. Selected excerpts were included in a dossier prepared by Paniamor for use by legislators supporting the initiative as they engaged others within the Legislative Congress and amongst their constituencies in the debate.

THE LAW REFORM PROCESS

The campaign to prohibit physical and humiliating punishment (PHP) in Costa Rica began in 2003, involving multiple stakeholders. Prominent politicians, academics, and other individuals made unique contributions, and they, as well as some institutions, should be recognized for the central role they played in the process.

The Role of the Core Group

Among Costa Rica's core group were legislators representing all political parties at the National Legislative Assembly; UNICEF Costa Rica; National Children's Hospital; National Institute for Women; National Commission on Values; Ministry of Public Health; and the Central American Council of Ombudspersons for Children. This group had the capacity to enlist key national allies, and to contradict opposing arguments which presented corporal punishment as an effective tool for preventing children from becoming bad, unproductive adults. Opponents portrayed those who did not hit their children as irresponsible, abandoning parents. A dossier containing research-based information and related documents published by prestigious international institutions, prepared and personally delivered to decision makers, served as a useful tool to counter these arguments.

Special attention was given to informing journalists about the basis for the law reform in a clear and engaging manner. We wanted them first to understand, and then to transmit to the public, why legally banning the use of corporal punishment as a child rearing practice in families was: (1) an issue of equal protection under the law in benefit of children; (2) the first step in preventing children from identifying violence as a means to achieve personal goals; and (3) a step in the country's progress towards achieving full legal protection of children rights, as we committed to when ratifying the CRC 20 years ago (1990).

The Role of Leading Public Institutions

The law reform process began as an initiative of the Children and Adolescents' Section of the Ombudsperson's Office which, in 2003, was headed by a child rights expert, advocate, and Professor of Psychology,[5] Prof. Mario Víquez. His extensive experience working in the government, and the widespread recognition of his professional leadership in the field of child and youth rights, gave him an important role in advocating for reform. Initially he worked from the Office of the Ombudsperson, and later from the National Children's Patronage (Patronato Nacional de la Infancia: PANI), to which he was appointed Executive Director in 2006. PANI is a national government institution responsible for children's and adolescents' issues that played an important part in bringing the law reform initiative to the attention of other government organizations. PANI and the Office of the Ombudsperson formed a partnership to facilitate law reform.

The Role of Civil Society

The work of Fundación Paniamor was central to the advocacy and negotiation that ultimately led to the reform. This is a Costa Rican non-governmental organization (NGO) that has been working in the field of child and youth rights since its inception in 1987. This organization had a strong background in political and social mobilization for the reform of public policy and law.

Save the Children Sweden (SCS) helped to build a network of political and social support. It played a key role in public education within the framework of its multi-country global campaign "Educate without hitting" (Educa sin pegar). This campaign has been implemented in Costa Rica by Paniamor since 2003, in partnership with the public health and education systems.

THE 2008 PROHIBITION

The law reform was intended to change public perceptions of physical punishment as not only harmless to children, but as beneficial to their growth and development. At the time of the reform, physical punishment was widely believed to be not only a parental right but a duty, prescribed by the Holy Scriptures. Therefore, the basis of Costa Rica's law reform was an understanding of physical and humiliating punishment as: (1) a violation of basic human rights to which all persons, including children, are entitled; (2) a form of legalized age-based discrimination; and (3) an expression of instrumental violence, rather than terminal violence[6].

Originally, the law reform proposal was presented as an initiative "to abolish physical punishment and degrading treatment of children". The choice of the word "abolish" was inspired by a landmark national decision to abolish the national army in 1947, which had made the Costa Rican people proud of its democratic system. The word "abolish" was chosen for the law reform initiative, to emphasize the idea that prohibiting physical and humiliating punishment of children would be a new landmark in consolidating democracy—within families. However, after years of debate about the best wording for the initiative, the decision was taken to modify the title to reflect a child rights approach. The law amendment finally approved was titled: *Law on the Right of Children and Adolescents to Discipline Free from Corporal Punishment and Other Forms of Humiliating Treatment* (Law No. 8654 of September 1, 2008). It received majority support from all of the political parties represented at the National Congress.

This law added a new Article (Article 24 bis[7]) to the *Code of Children and Adolescents* (1999), under Chapter I—"The Rights of Personality"[8] (Article 1 of the reform law); and amended Article 143 of the *Family Code*, "Parental Authority: Rights and Duties" (Article 2 of the reform law). The final wording of both amendments, in summary, provides for:

> the right of children and adolescents to receive counseling, education, care and discipline from their parents, tutors, caretakers, or personnel from educational and health institutions, shelters, youth detention and any other type of center, but this is not a legal authorization to those parties for the use of corporal or degrading punishments; and
>
> the obligation of the State, represented by PANI and acting in partnership with the National Integral Protection System and NGOs, to implement awareness raising and educational campaigns and programs to empower parents and other adults to comply with the new legislation. The submission by PANI to the National Council on Children and Adolescents (NCCA) of a periodic report on the advances made in compliance of this mandate is also provided for. The National Integral Protection System and the National Council on Children and Adolescents are structures created under the Code of Children and Adolescents to articulate children's right to protection at the highest level.

The Legislative Commission included an introduction to the final legal amendments that acknowledges the concerns originally expressed by several of its members:

> It is important to state that the amendments hereby addressed are the result of a consensus reached by and between the various organizations promoting the project and those congressmen and congresswomen who initially opposed such initiative, because the final text takes into consideration and incorporates their points of view. (Legislative Ad-hoc Sub Commission, 2008)

IMPLEMENTING THE PROHIBITION

The groundwork for the implementation of the ban was laid long before the law was actually passed. In 2003, in parallel with the launch of the law reform initiative by the Office of the Ombudsperson, Paniamor began to implement the "Educate without Hitting Campaign"[9], with the technical and financial support of SCS and in partnership with public systems with related mandates, specifically the Ministry of Education and the Ministry of Health. Maria Luz Gutiérrez, a Costa Rican legal expert who had directed Paniamor's Violence Prevention Program since 1999, deserves special recognition for her commitment and vision as the campaign coordinator.

The campaign created the capacity for sustained, large-scale parent education and national outreach to families, with a focus on early childhood. The approach used was to "train the trainers"—professionals who would then educate parents. After the first 2 years of implementation, Paniamor began to conduct periodic independent follow-ups of the activities carried out by the trained institutions as part of their regular work program.[10] The 2003–2008 campaign reached 100% of the Child Care National System operating under the Ministry of Health[11] and 65% of the Pre-School Public System operated by the Ministry of Education. The campaign content has become a component of the regular curricula of early childhood parent education programs. In 2008, the Health System initiated a pilot program for children.

SCS is currently supporting Paniamor in the implementation of a 3-year (2009–2011) second phase of the "Educa sin Pegar" campaign to inform and educate parents and communities about the new law and its implications for child-rearing. It is collaborating with PANI in the development and implementation of a national plan of action for awareness-raising, with training and direct support for families to help them comply with the physical punishment prohibition. The working strategy, coordinated by PANI, makes it possible for the core group to count on sustained funding to expand the pilot program for children in the health system to new regions in partnership with other key actors, mainly religious groups and members of the Local Child Integral Protection System.

Both PANI and the Ombudsperson for Children and Adolescents continuously carry out awareness raising activities in support of the enforcement of the law. Both institutions have promoted the coordinated participation of individuals and public organizations, such as NGOs, unions, and national commissions, in drafting and implementing a National Plan of Action. An ad hoc commission was created by PANI in late 2009 with the mandate to draft a plan of action proposal for consideration and approval by the NCCA, before the end of the current government's administration (May 7, 2010). The proposal was drafted by the commission and approved by the Council at its last formal operating session in the current governmental period, on March 25, 2010.

Paniamor, together with UNICEF Costa Rica and two private sector actors, the Entrepreneurial Association for Development and Procter & Gamble Costa Rica,[12] proposed to PANI and the NCCA a national survey on child rearing practices within families.[13] This survey would provide baseline data for an evaluation of the National Plan of Action and help inform the further development of awareness-raising and educational programs. The proposal was accepted and the survey was carried out between November 2009 and January 2010[14]. Its findings were presented to the NCCA and special guests, at the same session where the National Plan was launched.

The findings of the survey confirmed to Paniamor that the passing of the law reform was just the departure point on a longer journey towards the achievement of a cultural change. Of those interviewed, more than half (57.2%) believed that although physical and humiliating punishment should not be used, in some cases there was no alternative. Most people (86%) knew about the new law and 64.3% agreed with it, totally or partially. On the other hand, more than two-thirds (70.4%) believe that child rearing is a private matter to be handled by parents, in which the State should not intervene. The great majority think that as a consequence of the implementation of the new law, children will grow up to be more undisciplined (65.7%), show poorer academic performance (54.6%), be more impulsive (62.9%), and less respectful (62.5%), although they may show more initiative (59.5%) and more self-assurance (53.9%).

The apparent contradiction between majority support for the new legislation and the majority belief that it will have a negative outcome on children clearly reflects how much families need to be empowered with new knowledge and skills in order to implement the legislation. The national stage is therefore set for continued and sustained action, and Paniamor is eager to contribute to achieving this very special cultural revolution. We will move forward in partnership with the Costa Rican State, Save the Children, and other old and new allies, always keeping in mind what we have learned throughout these years. We are committed to supporting family change throughout the nation with understanding and without blame; not prosecuting but supporting; not preaching but providing good quality, respectful support and education.

NOTES

1. This section is based on a larger review on the topic prepared by Prof. Yolanda Bertozzi in 2009 at the request of Paniamor. Yolanda Bertozzi is a Costa Rican expert on family law and has been a member of the consultative advisory group of Fundación PANIAMOR since 2006.
2. This legislation is also formally named the *Carrillo Code* in reference to Braulio Carrillo, Chief of State at the time, who enacted it by Executive Decree.
3. Both the underlining and the translation are by the authors and intended only for the purposes of this work.
4. With the coming into effect of the *Family Code* of 1973, Costa Rica became the second country in the Western world to have a family-specific body of legislation.
5. The Office is an independent public institution.

6. Violence is referred to as "instrumental" whenever it is resorted to by the victimizer as a means to achieve a result other than merely hurting the victim. It is referred to as "terminal" when no other result is expected by the inflicting party than hurting the victim.
7. "Bis" is used when adding a new provision into an existing law, to avoid affecting its original numeric sequence.
8. This is the title to the Section of this Code addressing the protection of fundamental human rights for children.
9. For additional information on the campaign at the Costa Rican level please refer to http://www.protegiendoles.org. At the global level, please refer to http://www.savethechildren.se/
10. So far only outreach and sustainability as a regular institutional program have been evaluated. A 2010 national survey will provide baseline data to assess the impact of the intervention, from that date onwards.
11. This governmental program serves children from 2 to 6 years of age, from socially disadvantaged communities nationwide.
12. The Association is a multi-company national private body promoting Corporate Social Responsibility (CSR) within its members and assessing them on their strategic social investments. It is a long time partner of Paniamor. Procter & Gamble Costa Rica is part of a transnational corporation that applies CSR to early childhood in every country where it operates. It is a new partner both to Paniamor and to UNICEF.
13. http://www.protegiendoles.org/prevention10.htm.
14. InFo Encuesta.

REFERENCES

American Academy of Pediatrics. (1995). Physical punishment. In *Caring for your school-age child: Ages 5 to 12*. Bantam.

Arias Ramos, J. (n.d.). *Derecho Romano*. 6 Ed. Madrid: Ed. Revista de Derecho Privado.

Bertozzi, Y. (2009). *The origins of child family punishment in Costa Rican Legislation*. Working paper prepared at the request of Fundación Paniamor for internal use. Costa Rica, 2009.

Brenes Córdoba, A. (1986). *Tratado de las personas*. Updated version by Gerardo Trejos. San José: Ed. Juricentro.

Committee on the Rights of the Child. (2006). *General Comment No. 8: The Right of the Child to Protection from Corporal Punishment and Other Cruel, Inhuman or Degrading Treatment or Punishment*. CRC/C/GC/8. Available from http://www2.ohchr.org/english/bodies/crc/comments.htm

Family Code of Costa Rica. (Law No. 5.476 of 1974). http://asamblea.racsa.co.cr/biblio/index.htm

General Code of the Republic or The Carrillo Code. (1841). http://asamblea.racsa.co.cr/biblio/index.htm

González Ortega, A. (1997). *Vida cotidiana en la Costa Rica del siglo XIX*. San José: Ed. Universidad de Costa Rica.

Law on the Right of Children and Adolescents to Discipline Free from Corporal Punishment and Other Forms of Humiliating Treatment. (No. 8654 of 2008).

Legislative Ad hoc Subcommission Affirmative Report on Law No. 8654. (File 1534, 2008). http://www.asamblea.go.cr/Centro_de_Informacion/Consultas_SIL/default.aspx

Pinheiro, P. S. (2006). *World report on violence against children.* Geneva: United Nations. Available from http://www.violencestudy.org/IMG/pdf/English.pdf
Trejos, G. (1990). *Costarrican family law.* Volume I. San José. Ed. Juricentro.
United Methodist Church. (2004). *Petition number 41038: Corporal punishment by parents and caretakers.* http://www.umc.org/Calms/petition.asp?mid=2886&Petition=1038

9 Finland
Children's Right to Protection

Sari Husa

Population:	5,300,000
Type of Government:	Democracy, Parliamentary system with President
Governing structure:	Unitary state, no significant regional governmental structures, 342 municipalities with practical responsibility of child protection
Child protection system in place:	Yes
Legal system:	Nordic law with strong civil law influences; Acts (Child Protection, Code); precedents (leading cases) by supreme courts also carry significance in child protection.
Major Religions:	Evangelic-Lutheran Christianity (approximately 80% of the population)
Official Languages:	Finnish (over 90%), Swedish, and in a few Northern municipalities Sámi.
Ratified United Nations Convention on the Rights of the Child:	1991
Children's Ombudsman:	Yes, but with relatively weak powers. Parliamentary Ombudsman also active in child protection.

HISTORICAL CONTEXT

Before 1809, Finland and Sweden shared the same history, and for 600 years Finland was peacefully part of Sweden. Since then there has been significant ongoing interaction between Sweden and Finland in many different fields (legal, political, economic, and cultural). Much of what can be said about other Nordic countries applies also to Finland. In 1809, during the Napoleonic Wars, Sweden was forced to cede Finland to the Russian Empire, not as an independent state, but as a Grand Duchy of Russia with a legislative assembly ("Diet") and a high degree of autonomy. During the 19th century, Finnish nationalism grew and in 1917 Finland declared independence. In 1906, as Russia became politically weak, Finland gained a unicameral Parliament; universal suffrage was implemented for the first time in the world's history and Finnish women became the first in the world to have unrestricted rights to vote and stand for election. In 1917, at a time when the Russian Government was paralyzed due to severe social and political turmoil, Finland declared its independence.

Since then, there has been significant ongoing interaction between Sweden and Finland in the legal, political, economic, and cultural arenas. Today's social ethos, political culture, religion, and legal system in Finland show deep cultural traces of its common past with Sweden. Today the Republic of Finland is an economically prosperous and politically stable uniform state with a well-functioning multiparty system. In international comparisons, Finland ranks very high on life expectancy, literacy, education, peace, prosperity, lack of corruption, protection of fundamental rights, and freedom of the press. Generally speaking, child protection is well-developed and children's social and legal position is well-secured by the state.

However, Finnish child welfare can be traced back to the mercy and charity shown by private persons, the non-corporate public sector and poor relief given by the Church. It has taken time and patience to turn alms into rights, a slow but one-way process. The contemporary child's right to bodily integrity and the prohibition of corporal punishment (since 1983) should be understood in the context of this social change.

THE 18TH CENTURY: THE KINGDOM OF FINLAND-SWEDEN

In the 18th century, the most numerous group in Finland-Sweden were land-owning peasants. The rearing and economic support of their children were the responsibility of a patriarchal community in which the influence and authority of the father extended over all persons living in the household. Inheritance rights were of vital importance, and legitimate and illegitimate children were clearly differentiated. The earliest provisions to protect children are found in the 1734 *Code for Finland-Sweden*, in which the *Inheritance Code* regulated the right and obligation of parents to provide for children, and the appointment of a guardian in case the child's parents died. The *Code* also contained regulations on discipline and child rearing. According to the law, children had to be brought up to become well-behaved, and to have different responsibilities, according to their birth, means, and nature. The *Code* identified the actions that should be taken when a crime was committed by a disorderly child. Children were dealt with in almost the same way as adult criminals. To see the child as a "small adult" was typical of the era; the special nature of childhood was not yet acknowledged. For example, when a child insulted his or her parents, flogging of the child and a public apology were ordered.

The first pedagogical lectures were given in Finland in 1783 by H. G. Porthan, who was a renowned supporter of early child welfare, and they included a requirement for children to respect their parents. The lectures advocated the use of corporal punishment for disobedient children only as a last resort if "nobler" measures did not have their desired effect (Porthan, 1889). So, punishment was not to be used automatically, but only in cases of unruliness.

THE 19TH CENTURY: UNDER RUSSIAN RULE

In 1889, a new *Penal Code* replaced the old one. It contained a regulation reflecting the prevailing attitude to corporal punishment: If a child had committed a punishable offence, parents had to substantiate that they had carried out the physical punishment the judge had ordered. It was parents' *duty* to administer punishment and its administration had to be proven, not merely stated. The *Code* also provided for sanctions, as well as exemptions from sanctions, in cases where the punishment resulted in minor injuries to the child. Physical punishment was considered to be a natural penalty for an offence, misbehavior or crime, particularly when children were under the age of 15. However, it is important to note that children were not singled out for physical punishment at that time; this was a typical penalty for adults as well, so in this respect adults and children could be considered equal. Inflicting punishment within the family was considered to be a private matter, free of governmental or societal interference (Mahkonen, 1991). On the other hand, if it was a question of a penal sanction, the authority was obliged to carry out physical punishment if the parents did not do so.

Although it was expected to abstain from intruding into the family in regard to corporal punishment, the state increasingly became involved in child welfare. The Finnish War of 1809 that led to Finland's annexation by Russia, together with years of failed crops, produced thousands of orphans and child beggars. In 1849, Nicholas I, the Emperor of Russia and Grand Duke of Finland, ordered that unprotected children[1] were to be fostered and their caregivers compensated, partly by the state and partly through the child's labor. Reformatories were provided for children in need of protective care[2].

The state increasingly took responsibility for the maintenance and rearing of foster children, particularly those who were considered to be inclined to disorderliness and crime (Decree on the Less Fortunate, 1852; Pulma, 1987). In 1898, the Finnish Diet passed the *Guardianship Act*, which allowed the separation of a child from parents who did not, or could not, fulfill their child-rearing duties, and ordered the appointment of a guardian to care for the child and his or her property interests. Therefore, the state was intervening into the family and parenting more extensively as time passed.

THE EARLY 20TH CENTURY: THE REPUBLIC OF FINLAND

During the 19th-century era of industrialization and urbanization, it was believed that changing social structures were threatening children's well-being and increasing their tendency to crime. In 1897, the state began to intervene in child-rearing to prevent these unfavorable consequences through a first motion to the Diet. The duty to interfere in family relationships in certain circumstances was first stated in the *Guardianship Act* of 1898. Our Nordic neighbors were a major influence on this legislation. In Scandinavia, the aim has been for the system to define the duty and right of the state to interfere in the care and rearing of children.

The *Guardianship Act 1898* was the foundation for the introduction of the first child welfare act (the *Welfare Act,* January 1, 1936) 40 years later, which specified regulations on the transfer of guardianship. The crucial difference between the *Guardianship Act* and the *Welfare Act* was that the former focused on the deficiencies of parents, while the latter focused on children's behavior and their need for protection and care. The aim of the *Welfare Act* was to remedy children's poor living conditions; lack of, or unsuitability of guardians, and children's deviant behavior. Crime and antisocial behavior were thought to be the consequences of hereditary and environmental factors, so it was believed that criminal behavior would result from insufficient and faulty child-rearing, if the state did not attempt to improve the situation. The *Welfare Act* authorized the state to interfere in family matters, and determined that the child had a right to receive care from the state. The *Act* has been criticized on the basis that it was more focused on protecting the sanctity of marriage and holding families together than on actually protecting the child (Mahkonen, 1991). Undoubtedly, these early legislative developments were focused on the collective, and failed to view children as individuals with genuine rights.

Societal thinking about physical punishment was beginning to change. A ban in elementary schools was enacted in 1914. But its use was still approved in homes. U. Cygnaeus, father of the Finnish elementary school, stated that if a child was physically punished, the parent should be in a composed state and should show compassion for the punishment to have the intended pedagogical effect (Cygnaeus, 1910). In 1942,[3] physical punishment was ended as a sanction ordered by public authorities.

By the 1960s, when the freedom of, and legal safeguards for, individuals were emphasized, social services and child welfare were heavily criticized and polemicized. Several Parliamentary Committees (e.g., KOM 1971:A25) developed guidelines for legislative reform to social services.[4] They recommended a departure from traditional social service thinking, where the emphasis had been on inequality and authority, towards a "customer" orientation. Child welfare had traditionally been seen as an integral part of social services for children and their families, but genuine child welfare was often disregarded in favor of substitute care for the child. The emphasis in the new guidelines was on prevention and support to the family. However, problems arose from the inclusion of both traditional child welfare and special problems related to the care of children in one statute, resulting in the discontinuation of the reform. But legal and social evolution continued.

THE LATE 20TH CENTURY: THE ERA OF CHILDREN'S RIGHTS BEGINS

With the overhaul of the *Penal Code* in the 1970s, the right of caregivers to physically punish their children was finally removed from the statutes. The removal was justified in a Government bill (68/1966) with a regulation stating that allowing corporal punishment encouraged "heavy-handed" caregivers to use unacceptable methods. The regulation was, however, deemed unnecessary because parents' so-called legal right to administer physical punishment was considered to be in force, even though it was not specifically mentioned in the *Act*. Therefore, the right of caregivers to administer physical punishment was removed from the *Penal Code*, but according to the Government bill the right still existed; hence the law was ambiguous. Was there a right to use corporal punishment or was there not?

In 1978, a presentation was made at an annual meeting of medical professionals suggesting that Finland should pay attention to children's right to physical integrity in the forthcoming *International Year of the Child*. Subsequently, the most widely-read national newspaper, *Helsingin Sanomat*, published a lively debate about improving the circumstances of children in Finland. Twenty-seven letters to the editor were published concerning the issue of physical punishment. Most were written by parents, grandparents, or caregivers, and the majority of the writers were opposed to physical punishment. The discussion was wound up, at the request of the newspaper, by L. Pulkkinen, a Professor of Psychology and a well-known researcher in the field of social development and child aggression. She encouraged parents to be gentle, and expressed her concern at how easily child-rearing might slip into physical assault.

The United Nations had declared 1979 the *International Year of the Child*, bringing further attention to the need to develop new laws concerning children in Finland. The President of the Republic and the Parliament expressed a wish for legislative reform. The momentum was increased by a high profile campaign conducted in 1981: "Do Not Hit the Child". In the same year, the Mannerheim League (a child advocacy and welfare non-governmental organization), appointed its first Child Ombudsman.

By the 1980s, it was acknowledged that children sometimes have to be protected from their own parents, and that there was a need for a separate Act to ensure their protection.[5] The challenges of modern society had changed from poverty, homelessness, and loss of parents, to parental alcoholism, neglect, and parenting difficulties, leading to a proposal for a new *Child Custody and Right of Access Act* that would view children as small *persons*, as opposed to the 18th-century view of children as small *adults*. The Act would identify children's needs for shelter, acceptance, tenderness, and understanding from their parents, as well as parents' responsibilities to support and promote their children's growth, autonomy, and increasing responsibility until adulthood. It was in this context that the proposal was made to include in the *Act* an explicit ban on corporal punishment: "The child shall not be subdued, corporally punished or otherwise humiliated."

Debates around the bill included a discussion of the nature of parents' disciplinary authority and the question of whether parents who administered corporal punishment would be guilty of assault. The bill aimed to specify that when the *Custody Act* came into force, parents' disciplinary authority over children would have some limitations and that the *Penal Code* could be applied if necessary.

Before the *Custody Act* was passed, the government invited submissions from public authorities, municipal bodies, church organizations, lawyers and social services. These submissions represented a range of opinions, including the following: (1) there were difficulties in defining corporal punishment, so reform should proceed with caution; (2) corporal punishment only needed to be deleted from the statutory text, and a ban was unnecessary; (3) the commentary on the *Act* should clarify that both physical and mental assault and unreasonable discipline should be identified as unacceptable methods of punishment; (4) a ban on mentally offensive treatment should be included in the law; (5) the text of the *Act* could be interpreted as allowing physical punishment in every-day parenting situations; (6) if the *Act* were re-formulated as, "The child shall not be treated in a way that is physically or mentally insulting", mild hair-pulling and slapping on the wrist would remain acceptable; (7) children's right to physical integrity should be aimed for in stages—public attitudes should be changed before physical punishment was banned; (8) attention should to be paid to the need for supervision and monitoring of parenting behavior; (9) information dissemination, public debate and family education should be emphasized.

Ultimately, the Committee for Legislation (number 11) stated that the statute proposal was in harmony with national and international trends; that it would guarantee the physical integrity of children and their appropriate care; and that it would specify that parents are responsible for setting limits for the child and teaching appropriate rules of behavior. Parliament passed the *Custody Act*, including the ban on physical punishment, in April of 1983. From the point of view of formal law, the problem of the ambiguity in the previous law was resolved.

THE TURN OF THE 21ST CENTURY: THE ERA OF CHILDREN'S RIGHTS CONTINUES

Despite the explicit wording of the 1983 ban, uncertainty about whether the ban in fact referred to physical punishment given for disciplinary purposes remained. This uncertainty was amplified by a case of a stepfather who pulled his 5-year-old step-daughter's hair and slapped her as punishment. In 1991, the lower City Court found the stepfather guilty of assault and imposed a fine, affirming that the law did not permit the corporal punishment of children by parents. But the conviction was appealed. In 1992, the Court of Appeal ruled that: (1) the stepfather was not guilty of deliberate assault because it had not been substantiated that pain had been inflicted for other than disciplinary purposes; and (2) the stepfather was justified in assuming that he was entitled to discipline the child because he lived with the child's mother. The Court of Appeal acquitted the stepfather and released him from the fine ordered by the City Court. The mother appealed this decision to the Supreme Court. In 1993, the Supreme Court (1993:151) ruled that the stepfather had, according to Section 21:7, of the *Penal Code* (1889), repeatedly inflicted a petty assault on his stepdaughter. The commentary on the decision clarified that a parent does not have the right to use physical punishment and that the provision on petty assault can be applied (Husa, 1996, pp. 186–187). The decision eliminated any remaining uncertainty about the interpretation of the ban, supporting and clarifying its meaning. The Supreme Court's decision resulted in the publication of 10 letters to the editor of *Helsingin Sanomat*, only one of which supported the use of physical punishment in child-rearing. It was clear that physical punishment was no longer socially acceptable.

It is significant that the abolition of physical punishment in Finland proceeded regardless of the government in power and its political composition. Governments with a labor majority, those with a conservative majority, and coalition governments have shared similar views, suggesting that the rights of children are a reasonably apolitical issue in Finland.

In 2008, *Helsingin Sanomat* published the news that the European Council recommended the prohibition of corporal punishment in all member countries, which France, for example, opposed. Again, letters were written to the newspaper's editor, but they extended the discussion to include emotional maltreatment, and concerns about parenting under the pressures of working life. Surprisingly, four of these letters supported physical punishment for disciplinary purposes. Was this an indication of increasing support for physical punishment?

Recently, a survey of attitudes was carried out by the Central Union of Child Welfare (Sariola, 2006). In comparison to findings of surveys conducted in the 1980s (Peltoniemi, 1981, 1983), this survey found a substantial decline in support for physical punishment. In the early 1980s, more than half of men approved of physical punishment, while in 2006 less than a third (30%) did. Whereas 40% of women approved of it in the 1980s, only 20% approved of it in 2006. (See also Ellonen et al., 2007 et al., pp. 71–73). The findings also indicated that attitudes towards physical punishment were more positive among people without children, older people, and men.

During the last decade of the 20th century, Finland took additional steps to recognize children's rights. In 1991, Finland ratified the *Convention on the Rights of the Child* (CRC) without reservations (SopS 59/1991). In the 1995 Civil Rights and Freedoms reform, the *Constitutional Act* was amended to comply with international agreements so that the rights of children were acknowledged. Everyone—including children—was accorded full civil rights.

At the start of the new millennium, the final document approved by a special session of the UN General Assembly presumed that Finland would establish a national body to promote implementation of the CRC. The first state Ombudsman for Children (OC) started work on September 1, 2006. The duties of the OC are to: (1) promote the interests of children and the implementation of their rights on a general societal level in cooperation with other agencies and assisted by a Child Advisory Board; (2) submit an annual report to the government on children's well-being and the realization of their rights; (3) influence decision makers to take into account children's perspectives by maintaining contact with children and young people, and conveying their views to professionals working with children, decision makers, and the public; (4) coordinate different agencies working with children; and (5) promote the implementation of the CRC (*Act on the Ombudsman for Children*, 2004). An example of the OC's facilitation of cooperation between different bodies is a survey it commissioned from the Police College and the National Research Institute of Legal Policy on assault against children. This survey led to a more extensive report to which a Central Union of Child Welfare representative also contributed (Ellonen et al., 2007). The report formed the basis for a further project about children as victims of assault. Finland's reports (1995, 1998, and 2003) to the UN Committee on the Rights of the Child also have been facilitated by this type of cooperation.

HAS THE CORPORAL PUNISHMENT BAN HAD AN IMPACT ON VIOLENCE AGAINST CHILDREN?

Several studies of children's experience of violence at home have been carried out in Finland. The first, conducted in 1988, was a survey of 7,439 15- and 16-year-olds (Sariola, 1990, 1992). At that time, 72% of had been subjected to minor violence at home; more than 60% had experienced hair pulling and 25% had been slapped.

In the subsequent generation of teens, this proportion had declined substantially. In 2004, 46% of a sample of 6,160 15- and 16-year-olds reported having been physically punished by their parents at some point in their lives; only 7% had been physically punished during the year preceding the survey

(Ellonen et al., 2007). In a 2008 Internet study of Grade 6 and 9 children, 35% reported having their hair pulled and 10% reported having been slapped (Ellonen, 2008). These findings suggest that the incidence of physical punishment towards children has been dramatically reduced over the past 20 years.

While it is likely that this reduction in children's experience of violence is due, at least in part, to the corporal punishment ban, other legal reforms have also played a role. For example, the *Welfare Act* was reformed in 2007 to emphasize the human rights of children. This *Act* now requires that authorities file child welfare reports, unconstrained by confidentiality requirements. Child welfare authorities are required to make an overall evaluation of the child's best interests, including their mental and physical well-being, when decisions about children are being made.

It is likely that public information campaigns have influenced public attitudes as well. These campaigns include "Do Not Hit the Child"[6], "Fragile Childhood"[7], and the Daphne-program[8] (European Parliament and Council), as well as recommendations for the prevention of interpersonal and domestic violence (RECOGNIZE, PROTECT AND ACT[9]). In addition, the education, social, and health care authorities have offered improved opportunities to recognize and address child assault. For example, since the Government's 2006 decision to undertake a national program to decrease violence, there have been increased efforts to collect information on the nature and development of the violence against children, making it possible to set reduction targets and identify the measures needed to achieve them.

The work of non-governmental organizations (NGOs) has also contributed to the shift in public attitudes. In Finland several NGOs were founded in the 1920s and 1930s which are still active today. Together with state authorities they have taken responsibility for the welfare of children and families. These organizations include the Mannerheim League for Child Welfare, a Swedish speaking NGO in the social and health care sector (founded in 1920), Save the Children Finland (founded in 1921), and the Central Union for Child Welfare in Finland (founded in 1937). These organizations have produced many different bulletins and guides, and developed services for families. In connection with various campaigns, they have raised important issues for public debate. In addition, these organizations have, in cooperation with several public agencies, such as the National Research Institute of Legal Policy and the National Institute for Health and Welfare, disseminated research results on, for example, children's and young peoples' experiences of violence. The NGOs have played a significant role in increasing public awareness and developing legislation.

CONCLUSION

Despite the legal provisions, international agreements, and public education, it remains difficult to completely banish the use of corporal punishment. The issues may be conceived as a question of the tension between the rights of children and the rights of parents. What is the power of children's rights and what kind of decisions do parents make as agents of their rights? Ultimately it is a question of a culture-bound value judgment to decide if it is more important to protect the rights of one party or the other. In Finland, key decisions concerning principles are made by legislators, but regulations about child welfare have traditionally been ambiguous and open to interpretation. In such cases, the judicial system has had to bear the weight of decision making. It is clear that the ban on corporal punishment repaired a defect in the law, stimulated public debate, and consequently made the issue known. Publicity can increase awareness and influence attitudes and thus promote changes in behavior that are reinforced by measures such as creating an Ombudsman for Children post. The abolition of corporal punishment is only one step, albeit an important one, in the evolution towards a world fit for children. This evolution is not yet over in Finland, although the developments of the last 40 years have moved us substantially in this direction.

NOTES

1. The child was designated "unprotected" when the parents neglected the care and rearing of the child, or when the child was deviant to the extent that he or she could not be cared for at home. Orphans and abandoned children also were classified as "unprotected" (Nieminen, 1974).
2. There was need for protective care if a child: (1) had committed an offence for which he or she had not been put on trial or punished; (2) begged or were otherwise defined as vagrant; or (3) was found to be intoxicated, and legal action had not been taken (Nieminen, 1974).
3. At that time an Act for young offenders came into force (1940/262).
4. Extensive legal reforms are preceded by comprehensive preparatory work where several non-governmental organisations are involved together with the Ministry in question. Broadly-based Parliamentary Committees that make use of expert opinions often engage in quite thorough law-drafting before the bill is brought to the Parliament.
5. Finland is part of Central European legal culture along with the other Nordic countries. Unlike Central Europe, however, Finland does not have extensive codified law books but smaller separate Acts.
6. http://www.alalyolasta.fi/
7. http://www.lasinenlapsuus.fi/fi-FI/english/
8. http://europa.eu/legislation_summaries/human_rights/fundamental_rights_within_european_union/l33062_en.htm
9. http://www.stm.fi/c/document_library/get_file?folderId=39503&name=DLFE-6425.pdf

REFERENCES

Cygnaeus, U. (1910). *Uno Cygnaeuksen kirjoitukset Suomen kansakoulun perustamisesta ja järjestämisestä*. Helsinki: Kansanvalistusseura.

Ellonen, N. (2008). Lasten ja nuorten väkivaltakokemukset. Tutkimus peruskoulun 6. ja 9. luokan oppilaiden kokemasta väkivallasta. (Children and young people's experiences of violence. Research in primary 6 and 9 class pupils experiencing violence.) *Lasten hyvinvointitiedon II foorumi (Child Welfare Information Forum) 6.10.2008*. Retrieved from http://www.miedu.fi/export/sites/default/lapset_nuoret_perheet/Tapahtumat_ja_aineistot/2008/Ellonen_061008.pdf

Ellonen, N., Kivivuori, J., & Kääriäinen, J. (2007). Lapset ja nuoret väkivallan uhreina. Lapsiin ja nuoriin kohdistuva väkivalta tilastojen ja kyselytutkimusten valossa. (Violence concentrated on children and young people in the light of statistics and questionnaires.) *Poliisiammattikorkeakoulun tiedotteita 64/2007; Oikeuspoliittisen tutkimuslaitoksen tutkimustiedonantoja 80*. (*Police College Press Releases 64/2007; Legal Policy institute 80*.) Helsinki: Oikeuspoliittinen tutkimuslaitos.

Husa, S. (1996). Physical punishment and education in early childhood: The case of Finland. In E. Hujala (Ed.), *Childhood education: International perspectives* (pp. 185–195). Oulu: University of Oulu.

Mahkonen, S. (1991). *Voidaanko lasta lailla suojella?* (*Can the law protect children?*) Helsinki: Lakimiesliiton kustannus.

Nieminen, K. (1974). Pakkohuostaanotot ja oikeusturva. (Compulsory foster care and legal protection.) *Oikeuspoliittinen tutkimuslaitoksen julkaisuja 1*. (Justice Policy Institute Publications, 1.) Helsinki: Oikeuspoliittinen tutkimuslaitos.

Peltoniemi, T. (1981). Lapsen pahoinpitely ja ruumiillinen kuritus Suomessa syksyllä 1981. (Child abuse and corporal punishment in Finland in the autumn of 1981.) *Lapset ja yhteiskunta* (Children and Society), *40*(12), 650–652.

Peltoniemi, T. (1983). Child abuse and physical punishment of children in Finland. *Child Abuse and Neglect, 7*, 33–36.

Porthan, H. G. (1889). Utkast til Undervisningning för Informatorer, rörande deras skydigheter och klocka förhållande (1783). In K. G. Leinberg (Ed.), *Handlingar rörande Finska Skolväsendets historia* (Documents relating to Finnish school system's history; pp. 249–429). Jyväskylä: Jyväskylä Boktryckeri.

Pulma, P. (1987). Kerjuuluvasta perhekuntoutukseen. Lapsuuden yhteiskunnallistuminen ja lastensuojelun kehitys Suomessa. In P. Pulma & O. Turpeinen (Eds.), *Suomen lastensuojelun historia* (*Finnish child protection history*; pp. 11–264). Helsinki: Suomen Lastensuojelun Keskusliitto.

Sariola, H. (1990). Lasten väkivalta- ja seksuaalikokemukset. Kotona koettu väkivalta ja seksuaalikokemukset aikuisten kanssa. Tutkimus suomalaisista peruskoulun 9-luokkalaisista vuonna 1988. (Children of violent and sexual experiences. Finnish 9th-graders in 1988.) *Lastensuojelun Keskusliiton Julkaisuja, 85*. (Central Union for Child Welfare Publications, 85.) Helsinki: Lastensuojelun Keskusliitto.

Sariola, H. (1992). The prevalence and context of family violence against children in Finland. *Child Abuse & Neglect, 16*, 823–832.

Sariola, H. (2006). Väkivaltaa ei mielletä väkivallaksi'jos uhri on lapsi. (Violence is not perceived as violence—if the victim is a child.) *Lastensuojelun Keskusliitto*. (Central Union for Child Welfare.) Retrieved from http://asiakas.poutapilvi.fi/ltk/prodo/files/400/Tutkimus_2006.pdf

OFFICIAL SOURCES

Act concerning Young Criminal Offenders, 1940
Act on Child Custody and Right of Access, 1983
Act on Guardianship, 1898

Act on the Ombudsman for Children, 2004
Child Welfare Act (with numerous changes), 1936
Convention on the Rights of the Child (SopS 59/1991)
Committee for Legislation. Report (number 11) on Governmental Bill on Child Custody and Right of Access 224/1982
Decree on Less Fortunate, 1852
HE 68/1966 (Governmental Bill on Reforming the Penal Code)
HE 224/1982 (Governmental Bill on Child Custody and Right of Access)
KKO 26.11.1993:151 (Decision of Supreme Court)
KOM 1971:A25 (Committee Report on Guardianship)
Penal Code, 1889 (with numerous changes)

10 Germany

Background and Legal Consequences of the Right to be Raised Without Violence

Kai-D. Bussmann

Population:	81,880,000
Type of government:	Democracy, Federal Republic
Governing structure:	Federal Government and 16 federal states
Child protection system in place:	Yes
Legal system:	Criminal law proceeds from the constitutional premise stated in the Basic Law that no act is punishable unless declared so by law before it was committed, Child Protection Acts at national as well as at federal level
Major religions:	Christianity
Official national languages:	German
Ratified United Nations Convention on the Rights of the Child:	1990
Children's Commissioner/ Ombudsman:	Yes, at national as well as at federal level

There were Germans long before there was Germany. Germanic peoples lived for centuries in Western, Central, and Eastern Europe with similar yet not identical languages and culture. Over time these developed into regional principalities and city states. German unification did not come until 1871 under Bismarck. During the late 19th and early 20th centuries Germany saw much industrialization. The international aspirations of the German Empire were a contributing factor to the First World War. The empire was defeated in 1918 and replaced by the Weimar Republic. The financial struggle that followed the First World War in Germany was one of the contributing factors that led to the rise of Hitler as the leader of a New German Empire in the 1930s. His aggressive foreign policy led to the Second World War (1939–1945). Following Germany's defeat in the Second World War the country was divided into British, French, US, and Soviet occupation which led to the formation of two separate states: the German Democratic Republic (East Germany) and the Federal Republic of Germany (West Germany). On October 3, 1990, after 45 years of 'Cold War', Germany was reunified. Berlin was made capital of Germany. As a founding country, Germany had a main role and still plays it in the European Union.

BACKGROUND

When the German legislature introduced an absolute prohibition of corporal punishment, the intention was to follow the Swedish model and make parents more aware of the need to rear their children without violence (Baltz, 2000; Heger & Schomburg, 2000; Peschel-Gutzeit, 2000). The primary goal was to bring about a change in attitudes and to encourage parents to turn immediately to family and parental counseling centers should the need arise. The goal was not to extend the penal or civil consequences beyond existing measures (Bundestags-Drucksache, 1999, pp. 5ff; Däubler-Gmelin, 1999, p. 83), but far more to make a symbolic statement that would increase public understanding of the importance of eliminating violence against children.

For this reason, the current version of the law replaced a prohibition of *"physical and mental abuse"* (§ 1631 II Civil Code [BGB], 1998, translated) introduced shortly before in 1998. This, in turn, had replaced the very vague prohibition of *"degrading childrearing measures"* that had been in force for decades. This 1998 reform was already an attempt to set stronger legal limits, but it still remained too ambiguous. This is because, in everyday German, the term for abuse ("Mishandling") is associated mostly with very severe assaults with highly visible consequences. This was why a new federal government introduced a legal reform 2 years later that now prohibits every kind of violence in childrearing: *"Children have a right to be reared without violence"* (§ 1631 II, 1 Civil Code [BGB]).

The discussion on banning corporal punishment in Germany goes back to the 1970s. This movement was supported by various non-governmental organizations (NGOs) such as the German League for the Child (*Deutsche Liga für das Kind*, Berlin), a nationally operating interdisciplinary network of numerous associations and organizations involved in the field of early childhood. Set up in 1977, the nonprofit League has more than 250 member organizations including scientific societies, pediatric and psychological associations, family and youth welfare associations, and a great number of service organizations.

On January 26, 1990, the German government signed the UN *Convention on the Rights of the Child* (CRC). It was ratified by Parliament on March 3, 1992 and came into force on April 5, 1992. In its 1995 report, the Committee on the Rights of the Child admonished the Federal Republic of Germany as follows: "The Committee encourages the State party to pursue its efforts towards changing attitudes with a view to eradicating all forms of violence against children, including the use of corporal punishment within the family. In this regard, it further encourages that, in the ongoing process of reform of the Civil Code, consideration be given to the incorporation of an absolute ban of corporal punishment" (Committee on the Rights of the Child, 1995). While the impact of the CRC on German legislation was indirect—the prohibition of violence only became law 10 years later—it certainly contributed to the political discussion (for an overview, see Krappmann, 2009), and provides important guiding principles to this day.

The child rights movement is part of a general change in values occurring in all western industrial societies. Analyses of the civilizing process in society (Elias, 1976, 1988) and research on changing values (Neidhardt, 1986; Schneewind & Ruppert, 1998) indicate a growing taboo on violence in general in modern societies and point to the increase in discourses against it. By the 1960s and 1970s, this shift had led most European countries to increasingly accept findings based on developmental psychology indicating that corporal punishment harms a child's development (Rüping & Hüsch, 1979). This change in values, which also had its effect on the educational discussion in Germany, led to the spread of a less authoritarian childrearing style that encouraged parents to rear their children to be autonomous and critical (deMause, 1980; Lederer & Schmidt, 1995). However, while corporal punishment in schools has become a punishable offence in most European countries, corporal punishment of children within the family was generally excluded from these changes. A trend towards strengthening the legal status of children, including within the family, can only be observed in family law since the 1990s.

The general change in societal values has led some scientists to question whether the Swedish ban of corporal punishment has actually been responsible for the reduction of violence that has been documented there (Larzelere & Johnson, 1999; Roberts, 2000). However, a study comparing social trends in five European countries has revealed that prohibition is associated with a larger decline in violent childrearing than is found in countries without prohibitions (see Chapter 24, this volume).

Politically, this breakthrough in Germany only became possible after the long-ruling liberal–conservative coalition gave way to a socialist–green government. It took this change in political power to overcome decades of resistance. In previous legislatures, reform had always foundered on the objections of conservative forces that feared a weakening of parental authority over their children. The strongest resistance to reform came from the conservative Christian groups, particularly ones close to the Catholic Church. From their perspective, if parents were not allowed to hit their children, they would lose an important symbol of their parenthood. There were also fears that more children would now hit their parents. Critics were also apprehensive that parents using corporal punishment would now be accused by their children. A further fear was that such an abolition would make parents uncertain about their legal position: They would no longer know whether they were allowed to grab a child by the arm in order to prevent a fall from a window or running out into a busy street. The most astonishing arguments were raised against reform right up to the final discussions in Parliament. Evidently, it was simply hard for large sectors of the community to give up this important symbol of parental power, even though the majority was clearly against the use of corporal punishment.

Psychologists and social workers were also not always the best of allies in the campaign for an absolute ban. Many of them were particularly disturbed by the idea of a further legal encroachment into parent–child relations and the difficulties that would result for family therapy. This argument was puzzling because parent–child relations are already subject to family law. Nonetheless, there was a particularly strong belief that it would not be possible to promote a shift towards nonviolent childrearing through a legal prohibition of violence.

At the end of the day, the political and legislative consultations on the need to prohibit violence were backed up effectively by the results of empirical research. The studies at Bielefeld by Detlev Frehsee and his team (see, e.g., Bussmann, 1996; Frehsee, 1996) and the Criminological Research Institute of Lower Saxony (*Kriminologischen Forschungsinstituts Niedersachsen*, see e.g., Wetzels, 1997) paid a particularly decisive role in the deliberations of the lawmakers. These findings pointed to the high incidence of severe forms of violence in society, and highlighted the close relation between corporal punishment and youth violence. Further studies were cited confirming how violent childrearing damages a child's further development (see, Bundestags-Drucksache, 1999, pp. 5ff.). In Germany, it was the results of empirical research that finally shifted opinion and overcame resistance (see Bussmann, 2004).

INFORMING THE PUBLIC ABOUT THE PROHIBITION

The legal reform became law in November 2000 and was accompanied by a nationwide campaign, *Mehr Respekt vor Kindern* (More Respect for Children), from September 2000 to the end of 2001. The campaign was designed to publicize the new legislation, make the general public aware of the harmful consequences of violence, and promote a change of attitude towards a new model of nonviolent childrearing characterized by respect and care for the child. One particularly strong concern was to help parents exercise their childrearing responsibilities and show them that there are alternatives to corporal punishment—even in difficult childrearing situations. The campaign, which was flanked by press, radio, and television as well as numerous local family welfare organizations, took a particularly citizen-oriented focus and used high-impact, on-the-spot initiatives designed to address people directly where they lived and inform them about the new childrearing model.

Roughly 500 individual events—not only seminars, lectures, and panel discussions but also street parties, theater presentations, and the like—were organized in more than 35 cities and districts throughout Germany. The aim was to motivate parents and all local organizations and institutions involved in childrearing to engage in a dialogue over childrearing issues and thereby promote the change of attitude intended by the law and encourage a shift towards nonviolent childrearing.

Furthermore, the Federal Ministry of Justice (Bundesministerium der Justiz) and the Federal Ministry for Family Affairs, Senior Citizens, Women and Youth (Bundesministerium für Familie, Senioren, Frauen und Jugend) initiated a comprehensive research program to study the reception and initial consequences of the reform (see, Bussmann, 2004). In October 2001, interviews were held nationwide with representative samples of 3,000 parents of children less than 18 years of age and, in March of the following year, with 2,000 youths aged 12 to 18. The results are comparable with those from questionnaires given to parents in 1994 and 1996 and to youth in 1992. Written surveys were conducted nationwide with representative samples of 1,074 governmental and non-governmental institutions providing counseling or aid in the autumn of 2001 ('expert study'). Additionally, 30 representatives of relevant institutions were interviewed in depth. The results of this research were then compared with the results of earlier studies (see Bussmann, 2004). In summary, the lawmakers applied three strategies to promote the legal reform: (1) nationwide media campaigns; (2) campaigns run by local family welfare organizations (so-called multiplicators); and (3) concomitant research integrated into the publicity campaigns.

RESULTS OF THE FOLLOW-UP SURVEYS IN GERMANY

In 2005, the author was commissioned by the Federal Ministry of Justice (Bundesministerium der Justiz) to carry out a further follow-up survey to assess progress in the implementation of the law (Bussmann, 2007). A representative and nationwide random sampling procedure was used to form the following groups for a survey carried out between January and February 2005: (1) 1,000 parents of children aged 12 to 18; (2) 1,000 adolescents aged 12 to 18; and (3) 350 staff of counseling and welfare services.

The trends in knowledge of the law were markedly positive in all parent groups. On average, it increased to almost 40% between 2001 and 2005. In contrast, no positive trend was found among adolescents. Although knowledge of the reform remained constant at 28% overall, it declined to 25% in the particularly important target group of adolescents exposed to violent childrearing.

As a result, the report recommended more intensive information campaigns in schools and other education institutes in order to achieve a sustained increase in knowledge about the ban, particularly among children and adolescents. Although the incidence of violence in childrearing continues to gradually decline, the number of violence-prone families and, in particular, abused children and adolescents has remained practically unchanged. At the last three measurement times in 2001, 2005, and 2007, the proportion of parents rearing their children with severe violence fluctuated between 13% and 17%.

At the same time, the results of concomitant research in 2005 have shown how the new right to be reared without violence has begun to fulfill its function as a model and orientation aid on various levels—both in families and in the counseling practices of many centers. Nowadays, one can clearly see a general condemnation of the use of violence in childrearing. Hence, from this perspective the law has attained its goal. In 2005, it was a more popular guiding principle in the general population than ever before. This is confirmed by a longitudinal comparison from 1996 up to 2007. In 2005, rearing children without violence was the ideal for more than 90% of parents, and 87% considered that, in the future, any use of violence should be the exception rather than the rule (for 2007 data, see Chapter 24 of this volume).

This change of values has also taken place in the group of parents who are still characterized by a violent childrearing style. It is remarkable to see how this group supports the intention of the law. This development can be seen most clearly in the fact that already in 2005, 76% of these parents wanted to do everything they could to avoid using corporal punishments like slaps on the face in the future compared to 67% in 2001.

The young generation also strongly condemned violence as a means of childrearing in the 2005 study. A total of 91% of adolescents considered that: "Parents should try to talk to their children more, and not be too ready to hit them." The proportion of adolescents who perceive corporal punishment as disrespect for their personality has also increased since the first survey (2005: 54.2%). They increasingly wish to be respected as a subject rather than as a mere object of childrearing.

The ban has not led to any growth in the criminalization of parents, even though its introduction has led to more frequent reactions to abuse in the proximal social environment, and people less frequently simply look the other way. Only 4% of parents who are aware of the legal ban said that they had reported a case of suspected abuse to the police. This is a notable decline compared to the 12% in 1996. The results of this dark figure study unequivocally reject the frequently voiced suspicion that an absolute ban on corporal punishment would lead to a greater criminalization of violent parents.

It is far more the case that the 2002 and 2005 studies confirm that both adolescents and parents who know about the prohibition of violence and strongly suspect that parents are subjecting a child to physical abuse have become far more active. Almost twice as many parents who were informed about the new legal situation reported it to the youth welfare office (2005: 27%) or discussed it with neighbors (2005: 28%). They also more frequently addressed the parents concerned, compared to those who were not informed about the new legal situation.

In addition, the practical experiences of counseling and welfare centers 5 years after the introduction of the prohibition reveal a clear appreciation of the advantages of being able to tell parents the legal limits of their actions. Although 62% of the institutes surveyed reported that they generally continued to persuade parents to refrain from using violence in their childrearing practices by telling them about alternative conflict solutions (almost 90%) and how harmful violence is (62%), almost 40% of these institutes said that they now also point out the new legal situation. The legal ban is being mentioned very often (80%) in the daily work of centers dealing with cases of suspected abuse. Almost 84% of the institutes reported mentioning this norm as an orientation aid for parents when counseling them. When institutes find that counseling is unable to proceed any further, parents lack insight, or offers of assistance are not accepted, then more than 60% of them regularly point out the new legal situation. When compared to the findings of the 2001 study, these figures show a rapid rate of growth.

Moreover, experiences with this practice are positive. For example, more than half of the institutes reported that it makes their own work with clients easier (68%), and that pointing out the existing legal limits seems to greatly facilitate counseling (53%), as families show a greater willingness to accept help. Hence, the legal reform has not only been accepted by counselors and therapists, but became filled with life immediately after its introduction.

GENERAL LEGAL CONSEQUENCES

The present law encompasses not only physical but also mental forms of violence such as withdrawal of affection or publicly humiliating a child. Any type of sanction that violates a child's basic sense of dignity or induces inappropriate shame is now a legally impermissible form of violence. Because some vagueness did remain due to the term "violence," a second phrase in the new law specified this precisely: "*Physical punishments, mental injuries, and other degrading measures are impermissible*" (§ 1631 II, 2 Civil Code [BGB]). The use of any form of violence as punishment is now clearly forbidden. The term "mental injuries" emphasizes that in contrast to the prohibition of "degrading childrearing measures" in force for many years, it is not the caregiver's action that serves as the criterion, but the resulting harm to the child. The law places responsibility onto caregivers to view the effects of their actions from the child's perspective.

Today, any form of corporal punishment is against the law in Germany regardless of how parents may try to justify it. This is just as true for a slap on the face as for a spank on the bottom. In German society, it is no longer possible to say that you are not allowed to hit anybody except your own child.

CONSEQUENCES IN CIVIL LAW

The new ban is restricted to punishment. This means that parents continue to have the right to protect their child from immediate dangers through physical interventions. For example, a parent who grabs a child's arm tightly when in traffic, at an open window, or on the playground is not exercising violence in the sense of the new § 1631 Civil Code (BGB). Naturally, the new law also does not abrogate the rights to self-defense and defense of others (see § 32 Penal Code [StGB]).

What the new law does is grant children the right to be raised without violence. It does not grant children any rights to demand forbearance or obligation from their parents due to the specialty of § 1666 Civil Code (Bundestags-Drucksache, 1999; Riemer, 2006); the intention is far more to promote parents' awareness that children have rights, because the more parents view their children as having no rights, the more they tend to use corporal punishment and mental cruelty. In so many cases, the frequently heard phrase, "My children belong to me" has brought children dangerously close to being considered their parents' property.

Nonetheless, the new law does have legal consequences. Parents can no longer respond to criticism (from neighbors, counseling services, youth offices, etc.) by saying that they alone decide which methods are appropriate for rearing their children. In legal terms, parents no longer have any legal justifications for violent childrearing. All persons who know about such assaults have the right to address the parents concerned. However, they are not obligated to report them to authorities, such as the youth office or the police. The primary intention behind the law is to increase awareness among adults.

However, assessments of compliance with the law are to be taken into account in family law when ascertaining any possible threat to the best interests of a child (see §§ 1666, 1666a Civil Code [BGB]) and can influence child custody decisions (see § 1671 II Nr. 2 Civil Code [BGB]). The prohibition is generally understood to represent a binding and explicit condemnation of traditional childrearing violence. Parents can no longer defend themselves by referring to their general right of care and custody. If there is a threat to the best interests of a child, the family court must take measures necessary to avert it (court instructions, orders, prohibitions, or even suspension of custody). However, the application of this criterion of the best interests of a child ensures a higher intervention threshold for family law, so that isolated minor infringements of § 1631 II BGB will generally not lead to family court measures–at least as long as the severity and frequency of physical assaults is still insufficient to be viewed as abuse of custody. Therefore, family law now takes a clear position against any form of violence while simultaneously avoiding excess intervention (Riemer, 2006). In fact, the law offers additional provisions to help parents cope with conflict situations without violence (see, in detail, Bundestags-Drucksache, 1999, pp. 6–7; Peschel-Gutzeit, 2000).

Paragraph 16 of the Social Welfare Code (in § 16, VIII vol. KJHG) regulating general support for family childrearing has been amended as follows: "*They [family support measures] should also point to ways in which conflict situations within the family can be resolved without violence.*" Time will reveal the extent to which this provision is applied.

CONSEQUENCES IN PENAL LAW

Any use of violence that "represents a gross and inappropriate treatment that impairs the physical well-being of the victim to a not insignificant degree" has long been viewed as a statutorily defined punishable bodily injury according to § 223 Penal Code (StGB). However, the earlier legal justification for parents to use violence for childrearing purposes (so-called right of chastisement) and only avoid using degrading childrearing measures (see § 1631 II Civil Code, before 1998) has now finally been abolished as well. Although the parental right of chastisement in force for many years had already been abolished in 1998 through the prohibition of abuse, this is now underlined unequivocally by the new reform.

Nonetheless, bodily injury has to have achieved a certain degree of intensity. As this degree is generally attained already through, for example, a slap on the face, the prohibition of violence in family childrearing is the same as the prohibition of violence between adults. In other words, parents are now subject to the same restrictions in their relations to their children as to society as a whole. If they subject their children to more than minor violence, they are now committing a punishable bodily injury according to § 223 StGB.

Some penologists, however, still maintain that this fundamental culpability cannot be applied to mild or even moderately severe corporal punishment (see, for details, Bussmann, 2002; Riemer, 2006). Hence, the discussion on consequences in penal law is still ongoing. Whatever the case, the threshold to a punishable bodily injury is certainly lower than it was under the previous law. In 1987, for example, the Federal Supreme Court still failed to view hitting a child with a 1.4-cm thick length of sturdy hosepipe as a clear transgression of the parental right of chastisement. Through the impact of the new law, local penal courts have, in some cases, already applied stricter criteria similar to those in family law—even for a slap on the face—and no longer exempt violent parents so broadly from their penal responsibilities (see Riemer, 2006).

However, in practice, the actual barriers to criminal proceedings lie elsewhere. Although anybody can report an offense, this is not mandatory in Germany either for public officials working in youth and social welfare offices or for persons working in voluntary and church-run counseling services. In addition, there are only two possible ways to commence criminal proceedings. In the first, a *complaint* has to be lodged by the victim, that is, the child or the child's legal representative (usually a parent), and prosecution must lie in the public interest. A child victim has to gain parental consent to make a complaint, which is something that parents are unlikely to grant for a case against themselves.

The second condition is that although anybody can *report* parents for hitting their child, the public prosecutor has to consider prosecution to be imperative because of the *exceptional* public interest (§ 230 I Penal Code [StGB]). Following national guidelines, public prosecutors generally affirm an exceptional public interest in prosecuting bodily injuries in cases of brutal offences, abuse, or major injury (Nr. 233 Guidelines for the Criminal Procedure [RiStBV]). As a result, the intervention threshold is generally very high. Nonetheless, there are special criteria for children. According to Nr. 235 II Guidelines for the Criminal Procedure (RiStBV), exceptional public interest in prosecuting should be affirmed in all cases of child abuse. This use of the term "child abuse," which, in this case, means serious bodily injury to a child, generally means that commencement of action by the public prosecutor is still restricted to severe cases. In less severe cases of childrearing violence, criminal prosecution of parents who strike their children will continue to be improbable in the future. This explains why there have been so very few convictions of parents for giving their children a slap on the face. Although the parents in these cases were then fined for criminal assault, such convictions absolutely remain exceptions (see also Riemer, 2006).

It is particularly important not to overlook the ways in which the centuries-old right of chastisement continues to exert an influence in many people's minds—and this applies to the justice system as well. Despite the great breadth of the legal gray area for criminal assault without any visible injuries—that is, the entire domain of moderate violence—public prosecutors continue to have reservations about prosecuting parents.

Moreover, modern penal law has long had a range of other responses at its disposal. The guidelines for criminal prosecution emphasize the particular importance of supporting the family through socio-educational measures, family therapy, or other interventions. According to Nr. 235 III Guidelines for the Criminal Procedure (RiStBV), public interest in a criminal prosecution can also be dropped in cases of child abuse when such measures are implemented or seem to promise success. Hence, this domain is guided by the principle of providing assistance rather than punishment.

CONCLUSIONS

Any existing worries that prosecutions of parents will proliferate overlook the numerous procedural barriers that effectively prevent such a situation. The legislature can rightly claim that criminalization of parents is not intended and will also not occur in practice, even though every slap technically constitutes a punishable criminal assault. The most likely place to anticipate legal consequences is in the work of the family courts. For both the legal system and citizens, the prohibition of childrearing violence should raise awareness of the harm of childrearing violence. Therefore, in a positive sense, this legal reform is truly a case of symbolic law.

REFERENCES

Baltz, J. (2000). Ächtung der Gewalt in der Erziehung. Gesetzgeberische Initiativen zur Reduzierung von Gewalt im (elterlichen) Erziehungsgeschehen. In *Zeitschrift für die Jugend, 87,* 210–214.

Bundestags-Drucksache. (1999). Entwurf eines Gesetzes zur Ächtung der Gewalt in der Erziehung. In *Bundestags-Drucksache in der 14. Wahlperiode, 14/1247.*

Bussmann, K.-D. (1996). Changes in family sanctioning styles and the impact of abolishing corporal punishment. In D. Frehsee, W. Horn, & K.-D. Bussmann (Eds.), *Family violence against children. A challenge for society* (pp. 39–61). Berlin, New York: de Gruyter.

Bussmann, K.-D. (2002). Das Recht auf gewaltfreie Erziehung aus juristischer und empirischer Sicht. In *Familie, Partnerschaft, Recht, 17,* 289–293.

Bussmann, K.-D. (2004). The subtle impact of a ban of corporal punishment in childrearing: Results of the evaluation of the German prohibition. In *Child Abuse Review,* 13, 292–311.

Bussmann, K.-D. (2007). The impact of prohibiting violence in child rearing. In E. Furuhash (Ed.), *The transformation of the family and violence: The international perspective* (pp. 271–232). Tokyo: Akashi Shoten (in Japanese).

Committee on the Rights of the Child. (1995). *Concluding Observations: Germany Comments.* UN Doc CRC/C15/Add. 43, para. 30.

Däubler-Gmelin, H. (1999). Schwerpunkte der Rechtspolitik in der neuen Legislaturperiode. In *Zeitschrift für Rechtspolitik, 32,* 81–85.

DeMause, L. (1980). *Hört ihr die Kinder weinen. Eine psychogenetische Geschichte der Kindheit.* Frankfurt a. M., Germany: Suhrkamp.

Elias, N. (1976). *Über den Prozess der Zivilisation* (1st ed., Vols. 1 & 2). Frankfurt a. M., Germany: Suhrkamp.

Elias, N. (1988). *Über den Prozess der Zivilisation* (13th. ed., Vols. 1 & 2). Frankfurt a. M., Germany: Suhrkamp.

Frehsee, D. (1996). Violence toward children in the family and the role of law. In D. Frehsee, W. Horn, & K.-D. Bussmann (Eds.), *Family violence against children. A challenge for society* (pp. 3–18). Berlin, New York: de Gruyter.

Heger, M., & Schomburg, G. (2000). Das Gesetz zur Ächtung der Gewalt in der Erziehung und zur Änderung des Kindesunterhaltsrechts. In *Kindschaftsrechtliche Praxis, 6,* 171–175.

Krappmann, L. (2009). 20 Jahre Kinderrechtskonvention—eine Bilanz. In Deutsches Kinderhilfswerk e.V. (Ed.), *Kinderreport Deutschland 2010.* Freiburg, Germany: Family Media.

Larzelere, R. E., & Johnson, B. (1999). Evaluations of the effects of Sweden's spanking ban on physical child abuse rates: A literature review. *Psychological Reports, 85,* 381–392.

Lederer, G., & Schmidt, P. (1995). *Autoritarismus und Gesellschaft. Trendanalysen und vergleichende Jugenduntersuchungen 1945–1993.* Opladen, Germany: Westdeutscher Verlag.

Neidhardt, F. (1986). Gewalt—soziale Bedeutungen und sozialwissenschaftliche Bestimmungen des Begriffs. In Bundeskriminalamt (Ed.), *Was ist Gewalt? Zum Gewaltbegriff im Strafrecht* (Vol. 1, pp. 109–147). Wiesbaden, Germany: Bundeskriminalamt.

Peschel-Gutzeit, L. M. (2000). Es ist geschafft Gewalt in der Erziehung ist verboten! In *Familie, Partnerschaft, Recht,* 05, 231–232.
Riemer, M. (2006). Auswirkungen des Gewaltverbots in der Erziehung nach § 1631 BGB auf das Strafrecht, In *Familie, Partnerschaft, Recht,* 10, 387–392.
Roberts, J. R. (2000). Changing public attitudes towards corporal punishment: The effects of statuary reform in Sweden. *Child Abuse & Neglect,* 8, 1027–1035.
Rüping, H., & Hüsch, U. (1979). Abschied vom "Züchtigungsrecht" des Lehrers. In *Goldammer's Archiv für Strafrecht,* pp. 1–10.
Schneewind, K. A., & Ruppert, S. (1998). *Personality and family development: An integenerational longitudinal comparison* (J. Harrow, trans.). Mahwah, NJ: Lawrence Erlbaum Associates.
Wetzels, P. (1997). Gewalterfahrungen in der Kindheit. Sexueller Missbrauch, körperliche Misshandlung und deren langfristige Konsequenzen. Baden-Baden, Germany: Nomos-Verlag.

11 Lithuania
Changing a Culture of Violence Towards Children

Ieva Kromelyte

Population:	3,349,900
Type of Government:	Democracy, Parliamentary Republic.
Governing structure:	The parliament (Seimas) consists of 141 members elected through a proportional representation system. The elected President is Head of State, appoints Prime Minister and Cabinet.
Child protection system in place:	Yes
Legal system:	Continental legal system processing to mixed. Child rights protection system is regulated by the Constitution, various Codes, laws, Government orders and other legal acts. Supreme Court precedents are also taken into account.
Major Religion:	Roman Catholic (79%)
Official Languages:	Lithuanian
Ratified United Nations Convention on the Rights of the Child:	1995
Children's Ombudsman:	Yes

Lithuania is bordered by Latvia to the north, Belarus to the southeast, Poland and Kaliningrad to the southwest. During the 14th century it was the largest country in Europe. Presented-day Belarus, Ukraine and parts of Poland and Russia were territories of the Grand Duchy of Lithuania. Current Lithuania and Poland were united in 1569, and their union lasted until the 18th century, when the Russian empire annexed it. Lithuania became an independent sovereign state after World War I. In 1940, it was occupied first by the Soviet Union and then by Nazi Germany. Near the end of the war Lithuania was re-occupied by the Soviet Union, and in March 1990 it became the first Soviet Republic to declare its independence. Lithuania had one of the fastest growing economies in the EU prior to the recent financial crisis. It is a member of NATO, the Council of Europe, and the European Union.

Lithuania's achievement of independence and democratic government and its acceptance of the European experience and international treaties have been accompanied by substantial societal shifts. The economic situation, people's consciousness and values, society's approach to children and their rights, and the child welfare system have all changed. Nevertheless, the physical punishment of children is not yet prohibited, despite Lithuania's ratification of the United Nations *Convention on the Rights of the Child* (CRC) in 1995. The CRC obliges state parties to undertake all appropriate legislative, administrative, social, and other measures for the implementation of the rights recognized in the Convention (Article 4) and for the protection of the child from all forms of physical or mental violence (Article 19). This requires the development and implementation of measures at the national and local levels to prevent violence against children, a violence prevention plan, and the creation of a culture without violence.

The *Constitution of the Republic of Lithuania* asserts that the family is the basis of society and the State. Indeed, for children, the family is a smaller society within the larger society, because it provides virtually their entire early experience of social relationships and communication. Furthermore, social, spiritual, moral, and psychological processes take place in families, helping to shape children's personalities and their citizenship in society. It is therefore crucial to promote the health of families, because it is fundamental to the health of the broader society and to the healthy development and well-being of children (United Nations, 1989).

PHYSICAL PUNISHMENT OF CHILDREN IN LITHUANIA

Many adults in Lithuania still believe that physical punishment is an effective way of bringing up children. Yet punishment, especially physical punishment, does not teach children how to behave appropriately, does not motivate them to change their behavior, and has long-term deleterious effects on their physical and mental health (Gershoff, 2002). Children who have experienced physical punishment are more likely than those who have not experienced it to behave aggressively themselves in response to conflict. Children's experience of physical punishment has a significant negative impact on their social competence in areas such as empathy, conflict resolution skills, confidence, and self-control. Nevertheless, many children continue to experience physical punishment at the hands of their parents.

In 2008, Save the Children (2008) carried out a survey of 1,143 children (10 to 15 years of age—59% girls, 41% boys) in Lithuania to gain insight into their family relationships. The findings indicated that almost half (48%) of the children had experienced physical punishment and 5% said that they were constantly being physically punished. About 1 in 4 children (24%) said that they were physically punished for talking back or lying to adults, 1 in 5 (20%) for smoking or drinking alcohol, and 1 in 6 (16%) for disobedience or non-compliance. Many of the children (60%) thought that physical punishment was justified for smoking and taking stimulants or drugs, while a quarter (25%) believed that physical punishment should be used for lying or talking back to adults. Less than a third of the children (29%) believed that physical punishment should never be used.

THE LAW IN LITHUANIA

The Law on Fundamentals of Protection of the Rights of the Child (1996) states that children cannot be tortured, injured, or subjected to cruel treatment, and that their honor and dignity must be upheld (Article 10, Part 1). This law also states that parents and other legal representatives of children may appropriately, according to their judgment, discipline children for not carrying out their duties or for other inappropriate behavior (Article 49, Part 1). However, children may not be subjected to physical or mental torture, or to other cruelty or humiliation. Parents or guardians who violate children's rights through cruel treatment or other abuse of their rights, are subject to civil, administrative, and criminal liability (Article 56 Part 1, *Law on Fundamentals of Protection of the Rights of the Child*, 1996).

The *Civil Code of the Republic of Lithuania* (2000) states that parents have a right and a duty to properly educate and bring up their children, care for their health, and provide spiritual and moral guidance (Article 3.155, Part 2; Article 3.165, Part 1). Having regard for children's physical and mental state, parents are expected to create favorable conditions for children's full and harmonious development. Where parents fail in their duties to bring up their children, abuse their parental authority, treat their children cruelly, neglect them, or harm children by their immoral behavior, the court may make a judgment for a temporary or unlimited restriction of parental power (*Civil Code*, Article 3.180, Part 1).

The *Code of Administrative Offences of the Republic of Lithuania* stipulates that failing to exercise parental authority or using it against children's interests should result in a caution—or in cases of parents who have already been cautioned, a fine (Article 181). Furthermore, parents, guardians or other persons are liable for not reporting children's rights violations to a child protection institution, police or prosecution service.

Children are also protected from violence by the provisions of the *Criminal Code*. Articles 135 to 140 establish that causing minor or severe health impairment, whether intentionally or through negligence, and causing physical pain are criminal acts. This includes violence that causes physical pain or short-term illness but does not leave any marks on the body (Pavilonis, et al., 2001).

Despite these laws aimed at the protection of children, physical punishment is not explicitly prohibited. Such an action does not fall under the definition of physical or psychological torture, or constitute a crime, misdemeanor, or disturbance (Law Institute, 2006). In fact, smacking or hitting a child with a belt is considered to fall under the definition "child nurture", for which parents or guardians are responsible. From the perspective of criminal, administrative, and civil law, physical punishment falls within the private sphere of the family. As a result, many institutions do not investigate complaints of such incidents when there is no visible harm, such as physical injuries or psychological disorders.

To effectively end physical punishment, it is important to change parental attitudes, reduce public tolerance of physical punishment, and clearly explain its consequences. To accomplish these goals, it is necessary to sensitize the public to the fact that physical punishment is a violation of children's rights, explicitly prohibit it in law, and provide an active public educational campaign to help parents learn new approaches to resolving conflict with their children.

EFFORTS TO END PHYSICAL PUNISHMENT OF CHILDREN IN LITHUANIA

The problem of violence against children has been discussed at professional conferences and in children's rights literature in Lithuania for about 10 years. One of the first publications to address physical punishment was a small book entitled, *Does Just Mean Stronger?* (Save the Children, 1999), which was based on papers presented at a conference on violence against children (Law Institute, 2006). This book provided the results of a 1998 survey, which was commissioned by the non-governmental organization (NGO) Save the Children Lithuania, and carried out by the Market and Opinion Research Centre, Vilmorus Ltd. It showed that about half of a sample of 1,002 Lithuanian parents (over the age of 18) said that they had hit their children, although more than half thought that physical punishment did not help children to become better human beings (58%), and that it was not necessary in raising children (57%; Save the Children, 1999, p. 9). Half of the parents (49%) welcomed a ban on physical punishment and 22% had no strong opinion about a ban. At that time, drafts of amendments to the *Criminal Code* and the *Code of Administrative Offences* were prepared by Save the Children Lithuania, aimed at reducing violence against children by using criminal and administrative sanctions. These were presented to the Seimas (the Parliament of Lithuania) by Aloyzas Sakalas (Member of Parliament) on January 27, 1999 (Save the Children, 1999), but unfortunately they were not passed because of lack of political will and shortcomings in legal expertise (Law Institute, 2006).

Another opportunity to prohibit physical punishment was lost in 2000, when the National Program for the Prevention of Sexual Exploitation and Sexual Abuse of Children was approved by the Government of the Republic of Lithuania. This law was intended to tackle the specific problem of sexual violence against children. Although this is a problem that is closely tied to physical punishment, this dimension of the issue was not raised in this Program (Law Institute, 2006).

In its initial report on its implementation of the *Convention on the Rights of the Child* (CRC), the Government of Lithuania did not even mention the issue of physical punishment. The issue was, however, raised by NGOs, who noted that there was a problem of violence against children, but that the state was not capable of solving it (Law Institute, 2006). In its *Concluding Observations* on Lithuania's initial report, the Committee on the Rights of the Child expressed its concern at the widespread use of physical punishment, in particular within the family, and the generally tolerant attitude towards its use. The Committee recommended that Lithuania adopt appropriate legislative measures to explicitly prohibit the use of any form of physical punishment within the family. It also encouraged the development of measures to raise awareness of the harmful effects of physical punishment and to promote positive discipline, consistent with the child's dignity and in conformity with the CRC.

Subsequently, the Centre for Information on Child Rights identified violence against children as one of the most serious problems in Lithuania, and produced a publication entitled, *An Adult is Not Supposed to Hit a Child* (2003). A resolution recommending a ban on physical punishment of children was passed in the name of organizations protecting children's rights.[1]

On February 17, 2005, the Government approved a *Strategy on Child Welfare Policies*, in which the protection of children from all forms of violence and exploitation was established as a priority. The state's obligation to take measures to protect children from violence, exploitation, neglect, or other damage was emphasized. The strategy was based on the vision of an environment for children that is safe and suitable for their development, and which protects them from all forms of violence and exploitation. A *Plan of Measures for the Implementation of the Strategy on Child Welfare Policies* (2005 to 2012) was approved. Clause 1.8 of this Plan stated that a draft of law would be prepared that would explicitly ban physical punishment. But it was the opinion of politicians that it was not necessary to pass a separate law to prohibit physical and other humiliating punishment. As a result, Clause 1.8 of the *Plan* expired. Instead, it was decided that provisions explicitly banning all physical violence would be added to the *Law on the Fundamentals of Child Rights Protection* and harmonized with the *Civil Code* and other laws.

THE CURRENT SITUATION

Long years of lobbying, social campaigns, press releases, research, roundtable discussions, and national and international conferences by NGOs, the Children's Rights Ombudsman and others have culminated in a draft law that would clearly and explicitly prohibit physical punishment of children. This Draft affects Articles 2, 10, 49, 56 and 57 of the *Law on Fundamentals of Protection of the Rights of the Child.*

Article 2, Parts 2 and 3 of the Draft determine that violence against children includes any form of violence. This includes sexual, physical, psychological, or emotional violence; humiliation, exploitation, neglect, or negligence; actual or likely damage to the health, survival, development, or dignity of children; and physical punishment. Physical punishment is defined as any kind of punishment which involves the use of physical force to cause pain or suffering, however minor.

The Draft of Changes to Articles 2, 10, 49, 56 and 57 of the *Law on Fundamentals of Protection of the Rights of the Child* was prepared and presented to the Seimas (the Parliament) on the initiative of Ona Valiukeviciute, a member of the Committee on Human Rights of the Seimas, on March 5, 2009. Between March and November, 2009, the draft was discussed by other Committees of the Seimas, NGOs, the Ministry of Social Affairs and Labour, the Children's Rights Ombudsman Institution and children (the Lithuanian Children's Parliament). The Draft was rejected by Parliament on March 30, 2010 as the majority of politicians decided that it is not necessary to ban corporal punishment. The Draft is now being revised.

The Ministry of Social Affairs and Labor has recently prepared a Draft of the *Law on Protection of Violence within Private Space*. At the beginning of January 2010, the Draft was sent to the institutions concerned to comment on it. The objectives of the *Law* are to define different forms of violence and to determine legal mechanisms (prevention, protection, and rendering of assistance) to protect people from violence within private life. The Government submitted the Draft to Parliament. It is now being discussed by Committees of the Seimas.

EDUCATING SOCIETY AND PARENTS ABOUT THE POSITIVE NURTURE OF CHILDREN

In order to prevent physical punishment and ensure effective child protection, legal regulation is not sufficient. It is equally important to implement educational measures concerning the harms of physical punishment and the value of positive parenting. While parents are often assumed to be innately competent, not all parents do, in fact, have appropriate child-rearing skills. Children's understandings and expectations of social relationships are formed within their families, which provide a model for communicating with others in their neighborhoods, schools, communities, and the broader society. Therefore it is essential to provide accessible and enjoyable parent education programs, and to discourage tolerance of violence within the family. Parent education should be treated as family support, aimed at helping parents form humane relationships with their children, express their feelings and negotiate conflict constructively, and support their children's development.

There has been significant movement in this direction. On April 24, 2008 the Government approved a *National Program for the Prevention of*

Violence against Children and Assistance to Children for the years 2008 to 2010. Clause 1.4 of its annex states that the Ministry of Social Affairs and Labor and the Ministry of Education and Science should prepare recommendations about education for positive parenting in the year 2009, to reduce cases of violence against children. The ministry is planning to prepare Recommendations in the 3rd quarter of the year 2010.

In May 2008, Save the Children (2008b) initiated a social project called "Nurture Responsibly," which aimed to reduce violence against children within families by 50% in 3 years. The project also aimed to change public attitudes about children's upbringing, and to encourage communication within families. The second survey to check whether the project has had positive impact will be carried out at the end of the project (at the end of 2010–beginning of 2011).

Children need to develop within family relationships based on reciprocal understanding and respect. It is therefore important for Lithuania to follow the example of those countries which have banned physical punishment. We have travelled a long way towards achieving this goal, and there is good reason to expect that we will fully accomplish it in the near future.

NOTES

1. Together with Children and for Children, Save the Children Lithuania, the Children's Support Centre, the Lithuanian Welfare Society for People with Intellectual Disability, the Child's Development Centre, and others

REFERENCES

Centre of Information on Child's Rights. (2003). *An adult is not supposed to hit a child* (pp. 3–4). Vilnius: Author.

Committee on the Rights of the Child. (2001). *Concluding observations on the initial report of Lithuania on the implementation of the CRC*. Retrieved from http://www.unhchr.ch/tbs/doc.nsf/(Symbol)/9f3993ec619bdf13c12569ee00353fe4?Opendocument

Gershoff, E. T. (2002). Corporal punishment by parents and associated child behaviours and experiences: A meta-analytic and theoretical review. *Psychological Bulletin*, *4*, 539–579.

Law Institute. (2006). *Outline of the draft of the law prohibiting violence against the child* (pp. 7–23). Vilnius: Author.

Law on Fundamentals of Protection of the Rights of the Child. (1996). *State News*, 33–807.

Law on the Approval and Entry into Force of the Civil Code of the Republic of Lithuania. Civil Code. (2000). *State News*, 74–2262.

Law on the Approval and Entry into Force of the Criminal Code of the Republic of Lithuania. Criminal Code. (2000). *State News*, 89–2741.

National Programme for the Prevention of Violence against Children and Assistance of Children for the year 2008–2010. (2008). *State* News, 51–1892.

Pavilonis, V., et al. (2001). *Criminal Law. Special Part* (2nd edition; pp. 189–197). Vilnius.
Save the Children. (1999). *Does just mean stronger?* Vilnius: Author.
Save the Children. (2008a). *Children's interview on relations in their families.* Retrieved from http://www.augink.lt/media/vaiku_apklausa.ppt
Save the Children. (2008b). *Nurture responsibly.* Retrieved from http://www.augink.lt/index.php?page=apie-augink-atsakingai
United Nations. (1989). *Convention on the Rights of the Child.* Available at www.un.org/documents/ga/res/44/a44r025.htm .

12 Mongolia

A Nation in Transition

Oloncbimeg Dorjpurev[1]

Population:	Approximately 2.7 million (as of May 2010)
Type of government:	Parliamentary republic
Governing structure:	Unitary
Child protection system in place:	No. Although there is Law on the Protection of Children's Rights, there is a lack of an effective mechanism to prevent and protect children from violence, abuse, neglect, and exploitation.
Legal system:	Romano-Germanic or Civil Law
Major religion:	Buddhism
Official national language:	Mongolian
Ratified United Nations Convention on the Rights of the Child:	1990
Children's Commissioner/Ombudsman:	No

HISTORICAL CONTEXT

For a thousand years before Christ, in the eastern part of the north-eastern Asiatic steppe belt, nomadic tribes of Mongol horsemen lived on cattle breeding and hunting. The first great confederation was the Xiongnu, organized in 209 B.C. The Xiongnu were such a persistent threat to the Qin Dynasty in China that the Chinese began work on a massive fortification—the Great Wall of China (Szczepanski, n.d.). Mongolia's fractious tribes were united and the Mongol Empire was founded in 1206 A.D. by Genghis Khan. He and his successors conquered most of Eurasia, including the Middle East and Russia. The Empire continued until 1368 when the Yuan Dynasty, ruled by the Mongols, collapsed. At the end of the 17th century, most of Mongolia had been incorporated into the area ruled by the Manchu Qing Dynasty. During the collapse of the Qing Dynasty in 1911, Mongolia declared independence, and in 1921 the people's revolution won. The Mongolian People's Republic was proclaimed in 1924 and it remained a socialist country until 1990. Since the peaceful democratic revolution of December 1989, the country has been undergoing a transition to a democracy upholding human rights, a multi-party political system and a free market economy, as declared by the new *Constitution* of May 1990.

LEGAL CONTEXT

Prior to the 1990s, no specific law or article either prohibited or permitted corporal punishment of children. The new *Constitution* declares that human rights and freedom are accepted as the highest value and that all persons lawfully residing within Mongolia are equal before the law and the courts (Article 13), and provides for personal liberty and safety. It states that 'no one may be subjected to torture, inhuman, cruel, or degrading treatment' (Article 16). Many subsequent laws have been adopted that regulate new social relationships, and old laws have been reformed to conform to the *Constitution*.

In addition to the *Constitution*, the following laws protect children from violence in principle: *Family Law* (1999), *Law on the Protection of Children's Rights* (1996), *Law on Combating Domestic Violence* (2004), *Law on Prevention of Crime* (1997), *Criminal Code* (2002) and *Civil Code* (2002). Of these, the *Law on the Protection of Children's Rights* is the most significant law in securing the rights of children. It incorporates the principle that "ensuring a child's right to survival, development, protection and participation in social life is a duty of both state and family" and that "a child has a right to grow up healthy, to live in a safe environment, and to be free from abuse". The law also prohibits subjecting a child to "violence or abuse, physically or mentally" (Article 7). However, none of these laws address the issue of corporal punishment specifically. Only the *Education Law* (amended in 2006) prohibits physical and emotional punishment of children in educational settings.

HUMAN RIGHTS CONTEXT

"Human rights" is a new concept in Mongolia, a nation undergoing a transition from 70 years of communism to democracy and human rights. Prior to 1990, the economic, social, and cultural rights of children, women, and workers were given priority over civil and political rights. Despite some recent progress, such as gaining access to free media and democratic elections, many basic human rights are still not guaranteed—in particular, the right to be protected from violence. The law on domestic violence was adopted only in 2004 after almost 10 years of struggle by women's groups.

The adoption of the new *Constitution* facilitated Mongolia's ratification of international human rights conventions. Mongolia is now a party to more than 60 international human rights treaties including the *International*

Covenant on Civil and Political Rights, the *Convention on the Rights of the Child* (CRC), and the *International Convention against Torture, and Other Cruel, Inhuman, Degrading Treatment and Punishment.*

Mongolia submitted its first report to the United Nations Committee on the Rights of the Child in 1995. In its first two reports, the government did not address the issue of corporal punishment of children. In its first *Concluding Observations*, the Committee (1996) expressed its concern that "appropriate measures have not yet been taken to prevent and combat effectively ill-treatment of children within the family" and recommended that Mongolia "take all appropriate measures, including legislative ones, to combat ill-treatment within the family and sexual abuse of children".

In that same year (1996), a new Civil law was introduced on the *Protection of Children's Rights*. This law affirms children's rights to life, development, protection, and participation in social affairs—and specifies the rights and responsibilities of the government, local parliaments, local governors, parents, caregivers, citizens, and organizations. This law states that a government member will be in charge of children's issues at the national level and there will be a national organization, the National Authority for Children[2], to assist the member (Article 16). This law also established the National Council for Children with the mandate to develop state policies on child development and child protection and coordinate their implementation by allocating adequate government resources and encouraging public participation. It also established local Children's Councils at the provincial, city, district, and soum (the smallest administrative unit) levels. While this law makes it illegal to defame, humiliate, denigrate, and assault children (Article 7.4), it does not prohibit corporal punishment explicitly.

As a result, in response to Mongolia's second periodic report, the Committee on the Rights of the Child (2005) urged the government "to prevent and combat the practice of corporal punishment of children in the family, in schools and other institutions and to explicitly prohibit by law corporal punishment in the family" (para. 30). In response to Mongolia's consolidated third and fourth periodic reports, the Committee (2010) again urged the government to "introduce and enforce legislation to prevent and end all forms of corporal punishment of children as a method of discipline in all settings, including in the family and in the alternative childcare system" (para. 38).

THE CAMPAIGN TO PROHIBIT PHYSICAL AND EMOTIONAL PUNISHMENT OF CHILDREN IN THE SCHOOLS

The campaign began with Save the Children's advocacy campaign to amend the *Education Law* from a human rights perspective, making the rights and duties related to children's education clear. At that time, a study was conducted by Save the Children Sweden (South East Asia and the Pacific Regional Office), Save the Children UK in Mongolia, and the Gender Centre for Sustainable Development (GCSD). This study was part of Mongolia's contribution to the *United Nations Secretary-General's Study on Violence against Children* and it focused on physical punishment in schools and institutions. The study was particularly significant because it marked the first time that physical punishment was discussed in Mongolia. In fact, it was the first time the phrase "physical punishment" and "emotional punishment" entered the Mongolian language. The concept was completely new for the country, even for the Save the Children staff, so the study helped them to understand what it was and what children were experiencing. Its findings triggered a campaign to prohibit physical and emotional punishment in schools as the main part of the education law campaign.

The Role of Children

An historic event in the initial stage of the campaign was a strike carried out in 2006 by a group of 40 to 50 students attending a secondary school for children with disabilities. These children went on strike to protest against the discrimination, sexual harassment, and abuse they were experiencing at school. They marched to the Ministry of Education, Science and Culture and met with the Minister, Mr. Tsagaan Puntsag, who listened to their concerns and took action by firing the school director. The strike was well-covered by the media, and drew public attention to the issue of violence against children in schools. This event was highly significant, as it was the first time that the government publicly acknowledged the existence of violence in schools.

Children had a voice in the campaign in other ways, as well. For example, children's views on corporal punishment and their lives as students were broadcast on television programs and in documentaries. Essays written by children about their experiences in schools were published in major newspapers—and adults responded by writing about their experiences as children. Save the Children organized a radio project that gave children the opportunity to conduct research and record interviews that were aired via local radio in Ulaanbaatar city. The content of the radio programs promoted child rights and raised public awareness of physical and emotional punishment. A CD of the interviews was compiled and distributed with a book of black-and-white photos taken by children to illustrate their thoughts about violence, as well as love and care. Children also hosted a talk show on local radio in Ulaanbaatar city, discussing issues of violence and physical and emotional punishment with their peers.

The Role of Research Findings

In addition to the study described above, children with experience in institutional care conducted child-led research and spoke to the media and to decision makers about children's lives, including the discrimination and emotional and physical punishment they experience in care institutions, schools, in the home and on the street. The goal of the child researchers, as defined by them, was to understand the lives of children living in difficult circumstances and convey that knowledge to adults to gain their support and decrease the magnitude of the problems faced by the children (Altangerel et al., 2006).

The child researchers defined their research topics and questions by discussing their lives, their likes and dislikes, their concerns, and things they want to change in age groups and in a large group. They prioritized, grouped, and compiled the topics and questions generated by these discussions. The child researchers chose the one-on-one interview method as they saw it as a method that is most conducive to engaging the interviewee in a peer-to-peer dialogue, allowing the interviewee to express himself/herself more freely, and maintaining confidentiality. They interviewed 76 children.

The research uncovered the prevalence of violence against children everywhere, including schools. Discrimination and punishment in schools was brought up frequently. In fact, during the research design period, while classifying topics, young researchers named the topic of school as "Discrimination" (Dorjsambuu et al., 2006). Quite a number of respondents shared their concerns about other children and their dreams to develop the country of Mongolia, provide nice and warm houses free for the poor and build schools where children are not discriminated against (Dorjsambuu et al., 2006). These initiatives allowed the experiences of children to be told in their own words and they had a powerful impact on adults' understanding of the issue.

The young researchers met with decision makers to present their research reports before and after the amendment to the *Education Law* passed. At their meeting with the State Secretary of the Ministry of Justice and Internal Affairs in 2008, the State Secretary promised that the government would consult with children to revise the *Family Law*. Seeing these children speak publicly through the media about how children live, what they like and dislike, what their thoughts and dreams are and what they want, has encouraged other children to speak up for their rights.

The Role of Non-governmental Organizations

A coalition of non-governmental organizations (NGOs) was established and led by Save the Children. All 22 NGOs that made up the coalition, including the National Centre against Violence, the Open Academy (the lawyers' association), and the Mongolian National Center for Child Rights, actively participated. The coalition comprised not only child rights or child focused NGOs, but also NGOs working in the fields of women's rights, education, democracy, civic participation, open society, law, and justice. The Union of School Directors and the Association of School Social Workers were also members. These NGOs mobilized their resources to raise awareness of the existing laws and regulations related to violence against children in schools. They ran an intensive media campaign, mobilized teachers, drafted a new law, lobbied politicians, and involved children.

Early in the campaign, the coalition promoted the principle of child rights guaranteed under the CRC as its primary rationale for law reform and the key message was, *No Corporal Punishment*. Over time, they began to call attention to the concept of "learning environment", which is wording that was used in the existing law and which was defined as the material environment. The coalition argued that the "learning environment" includes interpersonal relationships, a concept which the public understood. The coalition's initiative was very successful in precipitating a demand for change among the general public.

The Role of Lawyers

Human rights lawyers Mr. Temuujin Khishigdemberel[3] and Mr. Erdenebat Ganbat[4] played a key role in promoting legal reform. At the time, they were lecturers at the Mongolian National State University and were the most competent human rights lawyers in the country. They educated the NGO coalition about the legislative system and process, were involved in drafting the law reform proposal, and served as spokespersons for the coalition at public events and in the media. They were able to explain the legal issues to politicians and the public.

Of course, there were opponents who argued that physical punishment is part of our culture; that we should not be influenced by foreign or Western ideas; that our teachers used to smack us, but we are alright; that "giving" children rights will spoil them and make them badly behaved. Some lawyers and decision makers argued that in Mongolia international laws have the same power as local laws, so there was no need for a legal amendment prohibiting physical punishment. Some politicians dismissed the proposal for law reform as nonsense: "We are Mongolians and we are in Mongolia. What is this about?" "This is just nonsense. It does not make any sense. No need to spend time discussing this." "Then what are we going to do with children, let them get on our heads?" However, these opponents did not constitute a major force.

The Role of Media

During the second post-communist decade, private media were expanding rapidly. The NGO coalition engaged them, through the country's most prominent journalists, in the issues of violence and discrimination in schools. Mr. Zoljargal Gombo, one of the journalists most respected by the public and politicians, worked with Save the Children and produced a series of documentaries on child rights in general, and on corporal punishment in particular. The documentaries focused on what children and parents think about corporal punishment, and whether it exists in schools. To get journalists' attention, we held two competitions for the most effective coverage of violence and corporal punishment, and organized weekly information sessions for representatives of the media. We also submitted opinion pieces and articles to the newspapers, to call attention to the issue. Soon, violence against children in schools became a topic of nationwide debate. While journalists tended to be ambivalent about law reform in the beginning, they became increasingly supportive as time went on. The public response was mixed, but overall it was more positive than negative. In many cases Save the Children paid for the media, but NGOs from various fields used their networks to get discounts from most of the media outlets, and we were invited by media to various interviews and discussions which did not cost us.

THE PROHIBITION OF PHYSICAL AND EMOTIONAL PUNISHMENT IN SCHOOLS

Save the Children initiated the advocacy campaign at the same time the government was in the process of amending the *Education Law* and the Ministry of Education was working on the amendment. At the beginning of the law reform process, the government did not accept the proposals submitted by Save the Children. In November 2005, the Parliament scheduled a session to read the proposed amendment of the government. It was a critical time because if Parliament approved the government's proposed amendment, it would have taken several years to make an additional amendment. In order not to lose the opportunity, Save the Children took urgent action to have the session postponed. They published an article (2005) in the main newspaper highlighting cases of violations of children's rights in schools and pointing out the gaps in the existing law and in the proposed amendment. The article called on Parliament to reconsider the proposed amendment and to revise it to comply with the *Constitution* and international human rights standards. Immediately afterward, Save the Children got an appointment with Mr. Erdenesuren Baatar, former Head of the Standing Committee of Parliament on Education. After the meeting, he organized a meeting of parliamentarians, the Ministry of Education, representatives of civil society groups, and the private sector. Non-state actors brought forward issues regarding their work and their constituencies. Save the Children was the key speaker and made a presentation highlighting the rights of children to education, protection and non-discrimination and the existing situation—using documentaries in which children and parents spoke, produced in collaboration with Mr. Zoljargal Gombo, the respected journalist.

This was the most important milestone in the advocacy campaign. At the meeting, a decision was made to form a new working group in Parliament to revise the proposed Government amendment (Dorjpurev, Sukhbaatar, & Legjiim, 2009). After the meeting, the NGO coalition made changes in its structure, forming a legal working group that worked closely with the Parliamentary working group. In fact, the Parliamentary working group invited a representative of the Advocacy Coalition to join the group—the human rights lawyer, Mr. Erdenebat Ganbat. Mr. Temuujin Khishigdemberel also worked closely with Mr. Lambaa Sambuu, who led the Parliamentary working group. The coalition integrated the proposal with the amendment of the working group in September/October 2006. The Parliamentary working group submitted the proposed amendment to Parliament.

At that time, the country was governed by a Coalition of the Mongolian People's Revolutionary Party (MPRP; the former communist party) and the Democratic Party (a liberal-right party). Mr. Lambaa Sambuu (a Member of Parliament from the Democratic Party) and Mr. Erdenesuren Baatar (a Member of Parliament from MPRP) were the key politicians who drove the proposal through all the steps and Parliamentary processes. Both were influential politicians within their own parties in the fields of education and social affairs. It was important for the NGO coalition to work with both political parties, which composed the majority of Parliament, in order to gain support in both parties.

In December 2006, the Parliament of Mongolia prohibited all forms of violence—including physical and emotional punishment—in schools. This was only the third time in Mongolian history that campaigners in any sphere have achieved change at this level. The prohibition was passed as part of a broader amendment of the *Education Law*. Several other important provisions on child rights that had been proposed by the NGO coalition, such as the right of children to express their views, were also included in the amendment.[5]

TOWARDS BANNING CORPORAL PUNISHMENT IN ALL SETTINGS

In 2006, the *Family Law* was placed on the reform agenda, providing an opportunity to enact a prohibition of physical punishment of children in the home and alternative care settings. Since then, there have been a number of new developments, some of which have slowed progress and others that have facilitated it.

Obstacles to Full Law Reform

Ongoing changes to the political landscape have led to repeated postponements of the drafting and reading of a prohibition. For instance, since 2006, officials in the Ministry of Justice and Home Affairs, which has responsibility for the *Family Law* amendment, have changed at least three times.

Parliamentary elections were held in 2008 (the coalition government, with MPRP as the ruling party, was re-elected) and a Presidential election was held in 2009 (the Democratic Party was elected). During 2009, Save the Children and civil society advocated intensively for full law reform to be passed before the end of that year, but changes to government officials in the fall delayed progress again. In November 2009, the Prime Minister, who was supportive of civil society's engagement in *Family Law* reform, resigned for health reasons. Since then there have been changes in critical Parliamentary posts, including Chairs of standing committees on social policy and justice. Together, these changes have slowed the pace of decision making considerably.

Progress towards Full Law Reform

Alongside these challenges, there have been some very positive developments in recent years, due to initiatives taken by NGOs, government, and children. Advocacy for a complete ban has been part of a broader advocacy campaign for a national child protection system carried out by a new coalition of NGOs consisting of former coalition members, as well as new members, such as Amnesty International. The coalition is led by Save the Children.

The campaign started with an intensive monthly media campaign in which we engaged the media on a daily basis—sometimes several media on the same day. This was accompanied by 2, 10-second slots—*Children Need Protection!* and *A Child Protection System Is the Way Forward*—which were broadcast regularly on some major television stations. Save the Children produced a few documentaries to illustrate the children's vulnerability and risks; the gaps in legislation, services, and the system; and the need for a child protection system. One of these focused on a 10-year-old boy who had been abused by his step father and then committed suicide in 2002. The goal of this media campaign was to create a public demand to influence the election platforms of political parties running in the 2008 Parliamentary election. An important milestone was achieved during this election campaign when the coalition was able to convince other groups of the importance of the issue. For example, the Women's NGOs Network, the largest and the most experienced network in the country, made the creation of a child protection system its first priority for the election campaign.

The Child Protection System coalition held several meetings with leaders of political parties prior to and during the election campaign. The culmination was a breakfast meeting attended by leaders[6] of major political parties at which some of these leaders made speeches in support of child protection. This event was widely covered by the media. Moreover, through the Women's NGO Network, 56 candidates signed a Memorandum of Understanding to work for a national child protection system once they are elected to Parliament. Four major political parties, including the current ruling parties, incorporated child protection issues into their election platforms. The campaign also has resulted in the National Authority for Children developing a *Mid-Term National Child Protection Strategy*, focusing on establishing a child protection system and including law reform to ban all corporal punishment of children.

Children played an important role in the campaign for a national child protection system. They organized several press conferences, spoke to the media, and participated in a televised policy debate in which only politicians usually participate. Projects implemented by Save the Children and some 2006 coalition members have been promoting social monitoring by parents and students of the implementation of the new Education Law, and training lawyers on strategic litigation. In collaboration with Save the Children Sweden and with funding from JICA, the project has introduced Positive Discipline (Durrant, 2007) into the university curriculum that trains future teachers.

Meanwhile, Save the Children and a coalition of NGOs are running a campaign specifically focusing on law reform. After a successful joint law reform campaign in 2006 and the intensified child protection system campaign during the 2008 Parliamentary election, local NGOs began organizing into networks more; two new networks on child protection and child labor were set up in 2008/2009. Currently, more than 30 NGOs representing 5 networks, including women's rights NGOs and the child participation network[7], are mobilized to support a full prohibition. They have undertaken initiatives to raise awareness of politicians, such as organizing a postcard campaign and delivering appeal letters signed by representatives of the five networks.

Another important development has been the establishment of a 15-member group in Parliament with the mandate to focus primarily on children's issues—the Support Group for Child Development, Protection and Participation. The Ministry of Foreign Affairs co-published the United Nations Committee on the Rights of the Child's *General Comment Number 8* (2006) on corporal punishment and has disseminated it to relevant stakeholders, such as the newly established Parliamentary support group for children's issues.

Child participation in the child protection field has grown substantially. Children have been very active in promoting child rights through peer training, meetings and other activities. They have been actively engaged in public and media events promoting positive discipline, by disseminating flyers during SpankOut Day and organizing a children's campaign on child rights for the 20th anniversary of the CRC. Children have organized press conferences and met a number of times with high-ranking government officials to demand the full implementation of the CRC and the amended *Education Law*. These activities have developed through children's councils or child participation groups formed through community-based centers operated by Save the Children. The main purpose was to help children raise their voices and concerns to other children, staff, and other officials—and to contribute to the development, implementation, monitoring, and evaluation of projects that promote community-based child protection systems and child participation in decision making.

In 2005, Save the Children facilitated child-led research and in 2008 it supported a group of 27 children representing various backgrounds and organizations to produce the first shadow report to the Committee on the Rights of the Child on Mongolia's implementation of the CRC. In 2008/2009, a group of 30 children submitted this report, which focused primarily on violence against children, including corporal punishment. It was sent to Geneva for review by the Committee, and it was published and launched in Mongolia to allow children's voices to be heard by the public and by the government. These children continue to advocate for recognition of children's rights. They organized a club whose membership continues to expand,[8] as well as an independent NGO,[9] and they continue working on child protection issues alongside adults.

The Current Legal Situation

Currently, the Ministry of Justice and Home Affairs Working Group is drafting legal amendments to the *Family Law*. The Ministry supports the prohibition of corporal punishment of children in the home and is including it as one of the main amendments to the law. We anticipate that the amendments will be read by Parliament in the spring session of 2011. In May 2010, the national Council for Children approved the *Mid-Term National Child Protection Strategy*. This means that the Government of Mongolia has officially made a commitment to ban corporal punishment in all settings.

The *Criminal Code* is also undergoing revision, presenting an opportunity to prohibit all forms of violence against children. However, the issue of whether corporal punishment can be banned through the *Criminal Code* is still under debate. Although a great step has been taken, as the concept and language are still new in the country, it is unclear whether the proposed wording of the ban will effectively prohibit corporal punishment. The lawyers who worked on the *Education Law* are committed to full prohibition and see amending *the Law on Protection of Children's Rights* as the best opportunity to do so.

The Current Campaign

Some key supporters of full law reform are the Open Academy NGO and academics/lawyers from Otgontenger University (a private university), who are involved in drafting and promoting the *Family Law* amendments. These lawyers conducted a review of the extent to which current domestic laws are in line with international legislation. The review identified gaps in the current legislation and recommended a ban of corporal punishment of children in the home to adjust to the changing nature of a family in contemporary Mongolian society.

Children continue to play an important role in the campaign. They are developing quarterly newsletters for children, which are also informative for adults. Save the Children is working to meaningfully engage children and young people in reviewing the law reform proposals and providing their input to lawmakers. Children provided their comments on the draft Mid-Term Child Protection Strategy and they are now reviewing the *Family Law* amendments. They plan to meet with members of the new parliamentary group on children's issues and the National Human Rights Commission to discuss child rights issues, including the need for full law reform.

Save the Children is gradually but constantly disseminating information about positive discipline to decision makers and the public, along with information about the international trend towards full prohibition and best practice cases. We have piloted positive discipline programs (Durrant, 2007) in some communities of Ulaanbaatar city and Dornod province. Approximately 970 parents of 2,500 children have taken part. According to interviews with the facilitators, positive changes were observed in parents' knowledge and in their attitudes towards communicating with their children. Also, an independent evaluation (Save the Children & Accenture, 2009) confirmed that the programs were highly effective.

Compared with previous years, there recently has been increased public interest and awareness. The media also are engaged. We have developed newspaper and television ads, one of which shows prominent individuals directly urging full prohibition, and we have published a number of newspaper articles on prohibition and on positive discipline. To reach a wide audience, Save the Children produced a series of 15 short lessons on positive discipline for television. Unfortunately, we were able to broadcast it only a few times due to financial constraints and the unwillingness of national broadcasters to air it for a minimal (or no) fee.

Documentaries about positive discipline have been made, targeting both decision makers and the general public. A well-known journalist, Mr. Zoljargal Gombo, produced a series of documentaries on child rights in collaboration with Save the Children. The documentaries focused on raising awareness of child protection issues by illustrating the current condition of vulnerable children, how the state system/structure is responding to child abuse and violence, and what children really need. A photographer, Mr. Davaanyam Delgerjargal, initiated and produced a series of photo exhibitions and documentaries to promote protection rights and positive discipline. He is one of the first graduates of Focus on Kids black-and-white photo training run by Save the Children and he graduated as a producer from the Mongolian Radio and Television Institute. He is now working at the 'Gamma', a leading photography agency in Mongolia. He has organized several independent exhibitions, and focuses on taking photos that raise people's awareness of violence against children, positive discipline, and the type of society children want. We have found that media and visual art are powerful tools that can touch decision makers' hearts.

We have published a variety of materials on positive discipline, including a Mongolian translation of *Positive Discipline: What It Is and How to Do It* (Durrant, 2007). We also have been promoting positive discipline in the education sector, carrying out pilot projects in some schools, and introducing positive discipline into the teacher training curricula.

CONCLUSIONS AND LESSONS LEARNED

When we first begin to talk about corporal punishment on television or radio, or in parent workshops, there are always some people who oppose our ideas, suggesting that Mongolian children and Mongolian parenting are different from those in the rest of the world, especially those in the West. Having a clear and logical framework that explains what positive discipline is and provides a concrete approach (Durrant, 2007) has been very useful in convincing the public about child rights and corporal punishment. At this point, there do not appear to be any major opponents of full law reform.

Mongolia has experienced a remarkable degree of change in a short period of time—from no focus on human rights and no term for "corporal punishment" to a ban on corporal punishment in schools and Parliamentary debate about full law reform. We are amazed by how much change has happened in our country. We have seen that through networking, civil society groups can achieve their common goals. This has been the biggest movement of civil society groups working in diverse fields, and it is extremely valuable to Mongolia's emerging democracy and civic participation. It also has contributed to a change in the society's view of childhood and children. Just one generation ago, children had no concept of human rights or free expression. Today, Mongolian children are learning to stand up for their rights in a democratic and nonviolent way. This new generation will, we hope, create a new culture that respects and values children and their rights. We have seen that change is possible, and that it can happen quickly. In our experience, it is not time that creates change, but people. It has been an exciting and satisfying journey, participating in such important human rights developments in Mongolia. We know that this journey has some distance to go, but we hope that soon we will witness the full prohibition of physical punishment of children in our country.

NOTES

1. The author acknowledges the substantial contributions of Jargal Chuluuntulga, Narantuya Baymbajav, Dulamsuren Erdenebileg, and Bolormaa

Gulgou whose work has been instrumental to the Mongolian campaign and to the writing of this chapter.

2. The National Authority for Children is mandated to organize policy and legislation on child rights, monitor the activities of child development and protection organizations, cooperate with non-governmental organizations (NGOs), organize capacity building activities, monitor the implementation of national programs on child development and protection, collect data, information, and conduct research on child rights.
3. He was elected to Parliament in the 2008 election and he is supporting the prohibition of corporal punishment in the penal system, alternative care, and homes. During the election campaign, he signed a Memorandum of Understanding with SC and other organizations to collaborate on the development of a national child protection system.
4. He later advocated for the development of a national child protection system, and for reforms to the *Criminal Code* and *Family Law*. Since the Presidential Election, Mr. Ganbat has been serving as Legal Advisor to the President of Mongolia.
5. Other major amendments included: (1) school management and teachers shall be responsible for ensuring that the rights and dignity of pupils, including the right to privacy, are respected; (2) the practice in schools to impose illegal fees on children and parents shall be prohibited; (3) school curricula shall be gender sensitive; (4) the state budget allocated to education shall be responsive to different geographical locations and sensitive to the specific learning needs of children with disabilities; and (5) the state shall allocate the same budget for non-formal schools, which enroll the most marginalized children, as for formal schools.
6. Mr. Elbegdorj Tsahia, who was the leader of the Democratic Party and who won the 2009 President election, attended the event.
7. This network was first established by adults in 2006 to integrate the efforts of child participation organizations and promote child participation in Mongolia. The National Network of Child Participation Organizations has 18 NGO members.
8. Children designed their website in November 2009 and update it regularly. www.childforchild.mn (in Mongolian). "Child to Child" is an NGO established and led by children. Initially it started as a children's club ("Child Protection") to campaign on developing a national child protection system. As some of the children grew up and reached the age of 18, the club was registered as an NGO in 2009.

REFERENCES

Altangerel. G., et al. (2006). *Lives of children in difficult circumstances: Child-led research report*. Ulaanbaatar, Mongolia: Save the Children.

Committee on the Rights of the Child. (1996). *Concluding observations: Mongolia*. UN Doc. CRC/C/15/Add.48. Available from: http://www1.umn.edu/humanrts/crc/crc-Mongolia96.htm

Committee on the Rights of the Child. (2005). *Concluding observations: Mongolia*. UN Doc. CRC/C/15/Add.264. Available from: http://www.crin.org/docs/Mongolia COs.doc

Committee on the Rights of the Child. (2006). *General Comment No. 8: The right of the child to protection from corporal punishment and other cruel, inhuman or degrading treatment or punishment*. CRC/C/GC/8. Available from http://www2.ohchr.org/english/bodies/crc/comments.htm

Committee on the Rights of the Child. (2010). *Concluding observations: Mongolia*. UN Doc. CRC/C/MNG/CO/3-4. Available from: http://www.crin.org/docs/Mongolia_01_10.pdf

Dorjpurev. O., Sukhbaatar. E., & Legjiim B. (2009). *Incorporating child rights in national policy: Case story on the advocacy campaign to amend the Law on Education from a child rights perspective*. Ulaanbaatar, Mongolia: Save the Children (in Mongolian).

Dorjsambuu. A., et al. (2006). *Child led research on lives of children in difficult circumstances*. Ulaanbaatar, Mongolia: Save the Children.

Durrant, J. E. (2007). *Positive discipline: What it is and how to do it*. Bangkok: Save the Children Sweden. Available from http://www.cheo.on.ca/uploads/AboutUs/Files/js_positive_discipline.pdf

Government of Mongolia. *The Constitution of Mongolia (2000 amendment)*. Joint legal information system. Available from http://legalinfo.mn/pages/1/page1.php

Save the Children. (2005, November). Human rights in the education sector. *Ardiin Erh*. Ulaanbaatar, Mongolia (in Mongolian).

Save the Children & Accenture. (2009). *Developing and disseminating teaching materials for violence free child rearing practice in Mongolia: Project implementation monitoring survey*. Ulaanbaatar, Mongolia: Save the Children.

Szczepanski, K. (n.d.). *Mongolia profile*. http://asianhistory.about.com/od/mongolia/p/ProfileMongolia.htm

13 The Netherlands

The Law Against Using Violence in Bringing Up Children

Mirjam Elisabeth Blaak

Population:	16,715,999
Type of government:	Parliamentary democracy under a Constitutional Monarch
Governing structure:	The country's government is based on the principles of ministerial responsibility and parliamentary government. The national government comprises three main institutions: the Monarch, the Council of Ministers, and the States General. There also are regional (12 provinces) and local governments.
Child protection system in place:	Yes
Legal system:	The Dutch system of law is based on the French Code Civil with influences from Roman Law and traditional Dutch customary law.
Major religions:	Catholic 31%, Protestant 21%, Muslim 5.5%, other 1.5%, not religious 41%
Official national languages:	Dutch, Frisian
Ratified United Nations Convention on the Rights of the Child:	1995
Children's Commissioner/ Ombudsman:	A law to establish a Children's Ombudsman has passed Dutch parliament on 16th of June 2010. At the time of writing it was not clear yet when the law would enter into force.

HISTORICAL CONTEXT

After centuries of foreign rule by the Romans, Franks, Burgunds, Habsburgs, and Spaniards, in 1648 the Dutch Republic became a free and sovereign state. During the 17th century, known as the 'Golden Age', the Republic became increasingly prosperous and a major colonial power. In 1815, the northern and southern Netherlands—today's Netherlands and Belgium—were combined to form the Kingdom of the Netherlands. In

1830, Belgium seceded and formed a separate kingdom. The Netherlands remained neutral in World War I, but was invaded in World War II by Germany and was occupied for 5 years. Today, the Netherlands is a small, modern, industrialized nation and the world's third largest exporter of food products. The country was a founding member of North Atlantic Treaty Organization (NATO) and the European Union (EU), and participated in the introduction of the Euro in 1999. The capital of the Netherlands is Amsterdam.

The use of physical punishment in the upbringing of children is deeply rooted in the Netherlands. Until the early 21st century, the use of violence in child rearing was accepted, and even considered to be a necessary educational tool. Although the means and harshness of violence against children changed through time, the use of some form of violence did not disappear completely. The abolition of physical punishment unfolded very slowly in the Netherlands, requiring many lively debates and discussions among academics, professionals, and the public. Finally, in April 2007, the Dutch Civil Code was amended to prohibit the use of violence in the upbringing of children, and to set the standard that parents have an obligation to take care of and raise their children without resorting to mental or physical violence or any other degrading treatment (Press Release, Ministry of Justice, April 2007).

THE ROOTS OF ABOLITION

For over 200 years, a double standard dominated Dutch and German public discourse on the physical punishment of children and the prevention of child abuse and neglect. An historical analysis conducted by Herman Baartman (1993), Professor Emeritus at the Free University of Amsterdam, showed that during the 19th and 20th centuries, while fewer and fewer forms of violence were tolerated, the legitimacy of corrective violence against children was maintained. However, thresholds of tolerance did shift with each successive generation (Baartman, 1993). Each generation wrote about the horrifying types of punishment used against children in generations before them; each viewed the previous generation's acts of violence in education as atrocious (p. 60). However, the idea remained that in certain situations, some form of violence against children was considered essential, and even beneficial. Attempts to address this issue twisted endlessly around questions such as: Who is allowed to hit; from what age a child can be hit; when, where, and how one is allowed to hit; and what degree force is acceptable?

The nature of the discussion changed, however, in the 1960s. Following the lead of the American pediatrician, C. Henry Kempe, who published an article about "battered child syndrome" in 1962, Dutch pediatricians began to publish articles on the subject and to raise awareness of child maltreatment (Van Montfoort, 1994). In 1970, a group of concerned people founded the Dutch Society for the Prevention of Child Abuse (VKM) with the mission to inform the Dutch public about maltreatment, and to disseminate academic and clinical research to professionals. They organized conferences, gave lectures, and developed training, information and awareness raising campaigns, becoming the leading organization in the Dutch movement against child maltreatment (Van Montfoort, 1994). The organization was quite successful in raising the awareness of the government, politicians, and the public about the issue, particularly with regard to secondary and tertiary prevention.[1]

In 1972, a Confidential Doctors' Agency was established to receive reports from doctors and anyone else about suspected child maltreatment. Within a few years, doctors were working with social workers to provide information and advice on how to respond in cases of suspected or documented child maltreatment, and how to refer cases to child protection and family agencies, as well as to the justice system. Within 20 years, 14 Confidential Doctors' Agencies covered the whole country.[2]

Although the Netherlands did not ratify the *Convention on the Rights of the Child* (CRC) until 1995, the rights of children had already entered the Dutch debates about child maltreatment and child protection by the late 1970s. Jaap Doek played a significant role in this development. At that time, Doek was Professor of Youth Law at the Free University of Amsterdam and chairman of VKM, and later became one of the founders of the International Society for the Prevention of Child Abuse and Neglect (ISPCAN). He promoted the children's rights perspective with a focus on the right of children to full and healthy development. It was in 1977 that Doek first urged us to stop thinking of hitting children as an acceptable way of correction in the upbringing of children.

In 1984, Doek established a Dutch section of the international organization, Defence for Children International (DCI), which was set up to promote and protect children's rights. In 1987, a short sentence in an article by Jaap Doek provoked a major public debate. He suggested the introduction of a provision in Dutch civil law to make the use of violence unlawful in the care and rearing of children (Doek, 1987b, p. 206). For several days, the topic was discussed in newspapers and on television shows: Experts explained why physical punishment is essential in educating children; children explained that they wanted to stop child maltreatment, but did not see a need to prohibit corporal punishment (Baartman, 1993, pp. 15–16). As quickly as this debate started, it faded away. But from that time on, the proposal to amend the law was known as "Plan-Doek".

As Doek (1987a) explained, his suggestion was not as simple as it was presented in the media. His proposal was not to ban physical punishment in the *Penal Code* with the intent of punishing parents who used it. Rather, referring to law reform in the Scandinavian countries, he proposed the addition of a provision to the *Civil Code* that would make it unlawful for parents to use violence towards their children with the objective of setting a standard to protect children against violence. He also proposed the inclusion of other humiliating treatment of children in the ban: "such a provision includes not only physical violence (including hitting) but also other forms of violence (inter alia, scolding, tormenting, belittling)" (Doek, 1987a, pp. 158–161). He advocated for children's right to be protected from violence, irrespective of its purpose and who used it.

Doek did not stand alone. In its advice to the Dutch government in 1988, the Dutch Council for Youth Policy made a statement that violence in child rearing is disrespectful towards the child. The Council considered the correctional spanking of children to be a form of violence and, although not punishable, fundamentally and morally contemptible. The Council came to this conclusion from a human rights perspective, recognizing the fundamental right of children to physical integrity (Raad voor het Jeugdbeleid, 1988). However, the Council did not go as far as supporting law reform.

By the mid-1990s, the idea of law reform was gaining support. Prominent academics Herman Baartman (1993) and Jan Willems (1999) expressed their agreement with Doek's proposal to amend the *Civil Code* to abolish corporal punishment. From a pedagogical and historical perspective, Baartman (1993) questioned the dominant standards and values which are fundamental to the Dutch vision on the rights and duties of educators, the rights and duties of children and the goals of child rearing. He warned that "everyday forms of violence in the upbringing of children could easily lead to child abuse" (p. 17). Baartman (1993) agreed with Doek on the need to set a legal standard, and even made suggestions for the wording of the text for a new provision in the Dutch *Civil Code*.

Jan de Boer (1994), at that time a legal advisor at the legal department of the Ministry of Justice, also expressed support for law reform. He wrote about the gradual abolition of physical punishment of spouses, employees, prisoners, patients, and soldiers, and wondered why children were still the only persons not protected against physical punishment by Dutch law. It was necessary to set a standard, he argued, by adding a provision to Article 1:247 of the Dutch *Civil Code*.

In 2000, the director of DCI Netherlands, Stan Meuwese, brought together a group of professionals from different disciplines to set up joint activities to mobilize the government to take action against child maltreatment, including a ban on corporal punishment. As a result, psychiatrist Andries van Dantzig started the Reflection and Action Group against Child Abuse, known as RAAK. For about 8 years, this group of concerned professionals actively lobbied politicians and raised awareness about child maltreatment. The main message of RAAK was to address the responsibility of the whole of Dutch society to take care of and educate their children and to oppose violence against children. "Violence against children is not acceptable" is statement number one in RAAK's Ten-Point program (RAAK, 2000).

Also in 2000, an important legal case shone more light on the issue. A father was accused of severe physical maltreatment of his four children.

The Dutch Supreme Court (2000) ruled that there was no evidence that the father had exceeded his disciplinary powers. According to the judges, it was likely that at certain moments the father deliberately used severe violence to correct his children, but this was not sufficient proof that the father's chastisement was unreasonable (also see Willems, 2004, p. 283). Such jurisprudence on chastisement rights, international pressure from the UN Committee on the Rights of the Child, and the results of research in countries which had banned physical punishment of children, all placed pressure on the government to change the law.

In 2001, Jaap Doek began a 6-year term as Chair of the UN Committee on the Rights of the Child. By this time, support for law reform was growing among non-governmental organizations (NGOs), academics, and professionals, who also started to lobby for amendment to the law. Jan Willems (2005), Professor of Children's Rights, went a step further, by proposing to change the constitution as well.

GETTING THE MESSAGE ACROSS TO PARLIAMENT

Over 20 years, the VKM and RAAK kept child maltreatment on the political agenda through public education and awareness-raising campaigns. At the beginning of the 21st century there were some urgent issues to be tackled by the government; for example, in 2001–2002, a bill was put forward to amend the child care law to provide a legal basis for the rights of professionals to report suspected maltreatment to the Advice and Reporting Centres on Child Abuse and Neglect (ARCAN; the former Bureaus for Confidential Doctors) and to lay down the powers and duties of the Centres in law. The tasks of the ARCAN are to provide advice and consultation to professionals and the general public on how to act on suspicions of child maltreatment, and to investigate such reports (NIZW International Centre, 2004).

Members of Parliament took the opportunity to raise other urgent issues concerning child maltreatment, such as mandatory reporting, parent support, and violence in child rearing. Agnes Kant (Socialist Party SP[3]) and Khadija Arib (Labour Party PvdA[4]) asked the government to study the advantages and disadvantages of a legal provision to prohibit the use of violence in child rearing. State Secretary of Justice, Ella Kalsbeek, from the (Labour Party, PvdA) replied that such research was not required, because there was no need for such a ban—and she did not consider "correctional spanking" to be harmful for children.

Ironically, by rejecting a ban, State Secretary Kalsbeek actually promoted it. Her statements, especially the one about "correctional spanking", caused numerous public debates. Ben Rensen, a youth health care physician and a strong advocate for raising awareness of child maltreatment, proclaimed, "If the debate is only addressing correctional spanking, politics deserves a spanking" (RAAK Magazine, 2003, pp. 22–23).

Banning corporal punishment was on the public and political agendas again. But each time a ban was discussed, its opponents focused the debate on justifying and defending reasonable chastisement and lawful correction. They claimed that a specific provision to prohibit violence in bringing up children was unnecessary, because child abuse was already considered a criminal offence in penal law. For example, Ido Weijers, Professor of Youth Law at the University of Utrecht, opposed amendment of the *Civil Code*, as he considered light correctional smacking not to be harmful for children. Therefore, he saw no need for judicial intervention in such cases. From his point of view, the provision in Paragraph 2 of Article 1:247 in the *Dutch Civil Code*,[5] together with the provisions in Articles 300–304 of the Dutch *Penal Code*,[6] were already satisfactory to combat child maltreatment (Weijers, 2005, p. 173).

THE ROLE OF RESEARCH

Reluctantly, State Secretary Kalsbeek ordered the Research and Documentation Centre of the Dutch Ministry of Justice (WODC) to study the effects of legislation to prohibit the use of violence in the upbringing of children in other countries. At the request of the WODC the Dutch Institute for Care and Welfare (NIZW) compiled a report of legal standards in various European countries (Kooijman, Ten Berge, & Oostveen, 2003). In 2003, the report was published and presented to the Minister of Justice, Piet Hein Donner.

The report provided an overview of the history, background, and effects of law reform in four countries: Sweden, Austria, Denmark, and Germany. It also described the debate in the United Kingdom to clarify the arguments against law reform. The authors concluded that a legal standard, in combination with information and support measures, could help to lower the use of violence in the upbringing of children. They made three recommendations: (1) the Dutch government should "formulate a clear standpoint on the importance of protecting children against violence"; (2) in order to commit itself to the norm that no violence in child rearing is acceptable, the government should introduce a rights-based provision in the *Civil Code* prohibiting all forms of violence against children; and (3) in order to "increase acceptance and to enhance the effects of the legislation supplementary measures, such as research and analysis of the effects of the legislation, a public information campaign and a support structure for parents and professionals, are necessary" (Kooijman et al., 2003, pp. 81–83).

The Minister decided not to follow these recommendations. His statement was similar to that of State Secretary Kalsbeek: "a specific provision to prohibit violence in bringing up children will not have an added value to the existing law and practice". However, the discussion did not end there. In December 2003, NIZW and one of the regional Youth Care Bureaus organized a conference for professionals on educating children without violence. Gert van

Harten, spokesperson for the 14 regional Advice and Reporting Centres on Child Abuse and Neglect, advocated law reform to abolish violence in the upbringing of children. Even though it was a clear wish of the advocates, they could not predict that the Minister was about to change his mind.

THE ROLE OF THE UNITED NATIONS *CONVENTION ON THE RIGHTS OF THE CHILD*

While it is not known exactly what led the Minister to change his mind within a year, international pressure clearly played a part. In 1999, the Committee on the Rights of the Child had urged the Dutch government to explicitly prohibit corporal punishment in law. The Committee recommended that the Netherlands, "in line with developments in other European countries, take legislative measures to prohibit the use of all forms of mental and physical violence against children, including corporal punishment, within the family".

In 2003, the Dutch government submitted its next report to the Committee, as did the Children's Rights Coalition, a union of NGOs. It did not escape the notice of the Committee that the law had not been changed. At the 35th session held on January 19, 2004, the Committee called upon the Dutch government to explain why it did not follow this recommendation. Again, the Committee strongly urged the Dutch government to "explicitly prohibit corporal punishment in law . . . and carry out public education campaigns about the negative consequences of ill-treatment of children, and promote positive, non-violent forms of discipline" (para. 44).

The reporting process and the Committee's recommendations contributed to the willingness of the government to review its position. Another international body with a positive influence on the Dutch developments was the Council of Europe and its instruments: the *European Convention on Human Rights and Fundamental Freedoms* (ECHR) and the *European Social Charter* (ESC). The government's explanatory report shows that Article 3 of the ECHR, and Article 17 of the ESC, had an impact on the wording of the new provision (Explanatory Notes, Kamerstukken II, 2005–2006, 30316, Nr. 3).

THE AMENDMENT

When in February 2004, the Minister of Justice announced his intention to reform the legislation to prohibit corporal punishment, it was a surprise. On the 13th of February 2004, in his written answer to questions in the House of Representatives, the Minister of Justice announced that after carefully examining the Dutch situation, his understanding of the problem had changed and he had reconsidered his point of view.

A legislative proposal was developed by the Ministry of Justice for a new law to be included in the Dutch *Civil Code* under Parental Responsibility. The draft bill was submitted for advice to the Council of State, the advisory body for the government and parliament on legislation and governance, a mandatory control mechanism to check draft bills for contraventions of other laws or treaties, and examine their potential impact on citizens. The Council of State challenged the balance between the prohibition of abuse in the Dutch *Penal Code* and the proposed provision (Report of the Council of State, Kamerstukken II, 2005–2006, 30316, Nr. 4). In the opinion of the Council, the expected outcomes of the new provision could also be achieved by strengthening the enforcement of the provision in the *Penal Code*, questioning the need for the proposed law reform. Furthermore, the Council suggested changing the draft text of the provision and gave detailed advice. According to the Council, some of the terms and concepts used needed thorough review, because the definitions in the explanatory report were not clear enough. The Council also said the scope of the law provision was not clear. The Minister of Justice did not follow the Council's advice to reconsider the bill, but took the other suggestions into account and revised the explanatory report.

The main objective of the bill was to set a normative standard. It would no longer be possible for parents to use mental or physical violence or any other degrading treatment in taking care of and raising their children (Press release of the Ministry of Justice, February 11, 2005 and September 9, 2005). Also, setting the standard made it clear to parents that they are responsible for their children's safety. In the legislative proposal, violence was understood as any kind of violence used as a means of discipline that could harm the child's development. As a result of the new standard, it was expected that it would become more difficult for parents who maltreat their children to justify their actions on the basis of parental duty to carry out reasonable chastisement. Therefore, the provision would have an automatic effect in criminal law, although it would not alter child abuse as a punishable offence under the Dutch *Penal Code*.

The Government also aimed to contribute to the prevention of child maltreatment. It was expected that setting a clear standard would raise parents' awareness and could lead parents to consider and discuss the acceptability of their actions towards their children. It also was expected that the standard would make it easier for care providers to raise the topic of childrearing violence with parents, and to provide them with support in learning and using alternative approaches. The Government also expected that the standard would be instrumental in the early identification of child maltreatment by professionals, and in increasing disclosures by children who had experienced violence in their homes (Kamerstukken II, 2005–2006, 30316, Nr. 3 Explanatory Note).

THE PARLIAMENTARY DEBATE

On September 28, 2005, the bill was submitted to the House of Representatives. The majority of political parties expressed their support, but they drew up a long list of critical questions and concerns about the bill's definition of concepts, its scope, and its potential effectiveness. The Liberal Party (VVD)[7] expressed concern that this law should not just have a symbolic effect and asked the minister to give a clear explanation to the parliament of the need for the new provision. Socialist Party Member, Agnes Kant, submitted a motion that a legal provision to prohibit the use of violence in the upbringing of children should be accompanied by a legal provision to provide parenting support. Her motion was not supported by the majority of the House of Representatives. Among the members of parliament, the representatives of the Labour Party (PvdA,) the orthodox Christian Party (SGP)[8], and the Christian Social Party (Christenunie) seemed to be the most critical. They questioned the provision's effectiveness and added value. They also were concerned about a possible infringement of family or religious rights, and questioned whether the proposed provision was in accordance with Article 8 of the *European Convention for the Protection of Human Rights and Fundamental Freedoms* (Kamerstukken II, 2005–2006, 30316, Nr. 6).

Nevertheless, about a year later, the House of Representatives approved the bill and it was sent to the Senate, which also approved the bill. In April 2007, the law of March 8, 2007 was published in the *Bulletin of Acts, Orders and Decrees* (Staatsblad, 2007), the official Government Gazette, and came into force.

After amendment, Article 1:247 states (unofficial translation with the added text in italics): "(1) Parental authority comprises the duty and the right of the parent to care for and raise his or her minor child. (2) Care and upbringing includes the care and the responsibility for the mental and physical wellbeing of the child and *for his or her safety* and fostering of the development of his or her personality. *In the care and upbringing of the child the parents will not use mental or physical violence or any other humiliating treatment.*"

DEVELOPMENTS SINCE LAW REFORM

Finally, after about 30 years of debate, the Dutch government reformed the law to set a normative standard to protect children against violence, but an accompanying campaign to support the law provision has not yet started. Although the Minister of Justice announced the campaign in 2007, it seems to have been forgotten. Only two leaflets about the law are available: Raising Children without Violence, one for parents and one for professionals (Nederlands Jeugdinstituut [Dutch Youth Institute], 2008a and 2008b).

However, since 2007 child maltreatment has been at the top of the political agenda. In that year, the Netherlands' first study on the nature and scope of child abuse was published, based on nationwide incidence and prevalence research conducted at two universities. The University of Leiden had examined professional reports and statistics from ARCAN from the year 2005, arriving at an estimate of 107,200 cases of child maltreatment in that year (IJzendoorn et al., 2007). According to the researchers 4% are faced with sexual abuse, 18% with physical abuse, 12% with emotional abuse, 29% with physical neglect, 27% with emotional neglect and 10% with other forms of maltreatment. Researchers from the Free University estimated a total of 160,700 cases of child maltreatment per year, based on a survey of secondary school students aged 12 to 17 years. The most common forms of maltreatment were psychological aggression (22%) and physical violence (16%) by parents (Lamers-Winkelman, Slot, Bijl, and Vijlbrief, 2007).

Another major development in 2007 was the appointment of André Rouvoet (Christian Social Party; Christenunie) as the first Program Minister for Youth and Family Affairs by the Balkenende IV government. This new Minister is in charge of areas of policy implemented by four other ministries: the Ministry of Health, Welfare and Sports; Ministry of Justice; Ministry of Education, Culture and Science; and the Ministry of Social Affairs and Employment. The Ministries cooperate to reach the goals of the overarching policy program of the Ministry for Youth and Family Affairs. Among the aims of this policy program is to ensure a safe upbringing: "security: unconditional love, respect, attention, boundaries, structure and regularity, a safe home (free from violence, mistreatment, and sexual abuse) and a safe outdoor environment" (Youth and Family Programme, 2007). By 2011, the Ministry, in cooperation with local and regional governments, will have established a national network of neighborhood youth and family centers to provide parenting advice and support. In addition, the Minister adopted a special action plan to combat child maltreatment–Children Safe at Home, which will be implemented nationwide from 2008 to 2010. The focus of all components of the action plan is on primary and secondary prevention.

In 2009, as part of the implementation of the action plan, the government initiated a national public education campaign to increase the identification of child maltreatment. This campaign provided a good opportunity to raise public awareness about the physical punishment ban, and to educate parents about positive parenting and children's rights. However, the campaign is instead focused on identification and reporting of child maltreatment to the Advice and Reporting Centres on Child Abuse and Neglect.

CONCLUSION

The Dutch ban on physical violence against children constitutes a major step towards realizing children's rights and meeting our international obligation to end the corporal punishment and humiliation of children. Now the government must engage fully in awareness-raising and education for parents and other adult caregivers, and progress towards the elimination of violence against children in the home should be monitored (De Vries, 2008). The most valuable actions for the government to take at this time are to initiate a national public awareness campaign and to design and implement an ongoing impact assessment.

NOTES

1. In the mid-1990s, for organizational reasons, the Netherlands Institute for Care and Welfare (NIZW) took over the awareness-raising and educational activities of VKM.
2. In the early 1990s, the government ordered the Confidential Doctors' Agencies and the Child Protection Council to reorganize their role of advising, reporting, and referring cases, and to set up a nationwide uniform model of regional Advice and Reporting Centres on Child Abuse and Neglect (ARCAN). Since the late 1990s, every province or metropolitan region in The Netherlands has an ARCAN. Anyone can contact the ARCAN about suspected child maltreatment.
3. SP stands for Socialitische Partij, Socialist Party.
4. PvdA stands for Partij van de Arbeid, Labour Party.
5. 'Care and upbringing' include the care and responsibility for the mental and corporal well being of the child and fostering the development of its personality.
6. Physical abuse of children is considered an offence under Articles 300 to 306 of the Dutch *Penal Code*. Article 300 (4) states that intentionally injuring a person's health is equivalent to physical abuse, which is punishable by a term of imprisonment of not more than two years, but where serious bodily harm ensues as a result of the act, the offender is liable to a term of imprisonment of not more than four years. Where death ensues as a result of the act, the offender is liable to a term of imprisonment of six years. If the act is premeditated or intentional, the term of imprisonment rises by two or four to five years. The terms of imprisonment prescribed in Articles 300 to 303 may be increased by one-third where the offender commits the serious offence against his mother, his legal father, his spouse or his child (Article 304, Dutch *Criminal Code*).
7. VVD stands for 'Volkspartij voor Vrede en Democratie' (People's Party for Freedom and Democracy).
   SGP stands for "Staatkundige Gereformeerde Partij" (The Reformed Political Party).

REFERENCES

Baartman, H. E. M. (1993). *Opvoeden met alle geweld. Hardnekkige gewoontes en hardhandige opvoeders.* Utrecht: Uitgeverij SWP.

Boer, J. de (1994, March). De pedagogische tik. *Nederlands Juristenblad (NJB), 12*, 389–390.

Committee on the Rights of the Child. (1999). UN Document CRC/C/15/add.114.

Committee on the Rights of the Child. (2004). *Concluding Observations: Netherlands and Aruba.* UN Document CRC/C/15/add. 227. Available at: http://www.crin.org/docs/Netherland and Aruba COs.doc

Doek, J. E. (1980). Juridische aspecten. In W. H. G. Wolters (Ed.), *Het mishandelde kind. Herkenning, hulpverlening, preventie* (p. 57–66). Nijkerk: Uitgeverij Intro. (Original work published 1977)

Doek, J. E. (1987a). Het jonge kind en zijn ouders: slaan, mag dat? In A. P. Van de Nes, F. Lamers-Winkelman, & J. L. Snoep (Eds.), *Werk in uitvoering* (p. 151–162). Aerdenhout: Stichting Medisch Kleuterdagverblijf Margriet.

Doek, J. E. (1987b). Preventie en overheidsbeleid. In R. Haanstra, K. Kooijman, & P. Schoof (Eds.), *Geweld tegen kinderen: Opstellen over preventie en hulpverlening bij kindermishandeling* (p. 195–209). Den Haag: Vereniging tegen Kindermishandeling.

Doek, J. E. (2005). De Nederlandse aanpak van kindermishandeling: Veel drassigheid en weinig voortvarendheid. In H. Baartman, R. Bullens, & J. Willems (Eds.), *Kindermishandeling: De politiek een zorg* (p. 197–213). Amsterdam: Uitgeverij SWP Amsterdam

IJzendoorn, M. H. van, et al. (2007). *Kindermishandeling in Nederland anno 2005: De Nationale prevalentiestudie mishandeling van kinderen en jeugdigen (NPM—2005).* Leiden: Universiteit Leiden.

Kempe, C. H., Silverman, F. N., & Steele, B. F., Droegemuller, W,. & Silver, H. K. (1962). The battered-child syndrome. *Journal of the American Medical Association, 251*, p. 3288–3300.

Kooijman, K., Ten Berge, I. , & Oostveen, A. (2003). *Fysieke bestraffing van kinderen—een inventarisatie van wettelijke verboden in vier Europese landen.* Utrecht: NIZW

Lamers-Winkelman, F., Slot, N. W., Bijl, B., & Vijlbrief, A. C. (2007). *Scholieren over mishandeling. Resultaten van een landelijk onderzoek naar de omvang van kindermishandeling onder leerlingen in het voortgezet onderwijs.* Amsterdam: Vrije Universiteit Amsterdam/PI research.

Montfoort, A. van (1994). *Het topje van de ijsberg. Kinderbescherming en de bestrijding van kindermishandeling in sociaal-juridisch perspectief.* Utrecht: SWP.

NIZW International Centre. (2004). *Factsheet: Child abuse in the Netherlands.* Utrecht: Author.

Nederlands Jeugdinstituut. (2008a). *Opvoeden zonder geweld. Informatie voor beroepskrachten.* Utrecht: Author.

Nederlands Jeugdinstituut. (2008b). *Opvoeden zonder geweld. Informatie voor ouders en andere opvoeders.* Utrecht: Author.

Raad voor het Jeugdbeleid. (1988). *Kindermishandeling vermeldenswaard.* Rijswijk: Ministerie van Welzijn, Volksgezondheid en Sport.

RAAK. (2000). *Manifest over de aanpak van kindermishandeling en voor een kindvriendelijke omgeving.* Amsterdam: Reflectie- en Actiegroep Aanpak Kindermishandeling (RAAK).

RAAK. (2003). RAAK Magazine. *Stop kindermishandeling.* Amsterdam: RAAK.

Supreme Court. (2000, October 10). LJN: AA7402.

Vries, N. H. G. de (2008). Het verbod op het gebruik van geestelijk en lichamelijk geweld in de opvoeding van kinderen: een 'geslaagde' wijziging? *Tijdschrift voor familie—en jeugdrecht, 47*,169–174.

Weijers, I. (2005). Kindermishandeling: geen wetswijziging, wel heldere criteria. *Tijdschrift voor Familie—en Jeugdrecht, 27,* 169–174.

Willems, J. C. M (1999). *Wie zal de opvoeders opvoeden? Kindermishandeling en het recht van het kind op persoonswording.* Den Haag: T.C.M. Asser Press.

Willems, J. C. M. (2004). Geweld is nooit privé—op weg naar een verbod op slaan en ander opvoedingsgeweld. *Nederlands Juristenblad, 6*(February 6), 281–284.

Willems, J. (2005). Een verbod op slaan en de emancipatie van het kind. *Tijdschrift voor Familie en Jeugdrecht, 33,* 94–98.

Youth and Family Programme. (2007, September). *Actieplan aanpak kindermishandeling. kinderen veilig thuis.* Available at www.rijksoverheid.nl.

PARLIAMENTARY AND GOVERNMENT PUBLICATIONS

Press release Ministry of Justice, April 2007
Press release Ministry of Justice, February 11, 2005 and September 9, 2005
Letter of Minister of Justice to the House of Representatives, February 13, 2004
Explanatory Notes, Kamerstukken II, 2005–2006, 30316, Nr. 3
Report of the Council of State, Kamerstukken II, 2005–06, 30316, Nr. 4
Report of the Parliamentary Debate, Kamerstukken II, 2005–2006, 30316, Nr. 6
Staatsblad, April 25, 2007, 145.

14 New Zealand

The Achievements and Challenges of Prohibition

Nicola Taylor, Beth Wood, and Anne B. Smith

Population:	4,354,701
Area:	113,729 square km
Type of government:	Parliamentary democracy under constitutional monarchy, proportional representation (MMP) with 60 electorate MPs and 60 party MPs. One parliamentary chamber, the House of Representatives.
Child protection system in place:	Yes, under Children, Young Persons and Their Families Act, 1989; Care of Children Act, 2004.
Legal system:	Doctrine of precedent and statutory law (based on English Common Law).
Major religions:	Christian 55%; no religion 34%
Official national languages:	English, Māori, New Zealand Sign Language
Ratified United Nations Convention on the Rights of the Child:	1993
Children's Commissioner/Ombudsman:	Yes, since 1989.

New Zealand was settled by the Māori people, 700 to 2,000 years ago. The British colonized the country in the 1800s, dramatically changing its political and economic landscape. The Treaty of Waitangi, signed between Māori and Queen Victoria in 1840, ceded the right to govern New Zealand to the British, but intended to also respect and protect Māori values and treasures (including land, fisheries, and collective family values). Subsequent diseases, wars, and land confiscations, together with urbanization and the imposition of mainstream education and English language requirements, eroded the economic and social well-being of Māori family life. However, a recent renaissance in Māoridom, and respect for the Treaty as the nation's founding document, has revived the language and enabled significant financial settlements to be paid to tribes for past grievances. New Zealand's economy is heavily dependent on agriculture and tourism. It ranks highly on human development, quality of life, life expectancy, literacy, public education, peace, prosperity, economic freedom, ease of doing business, lack of corruption, press freedom, and the protection of civil liberties and political rights.

New Zealand became the first English speaking country to prohibit all physical punishment of children when the *Crimes (Substituted Section 59) Amendment Act 2007* took effect on June 21, 2007. This reform removed the defense provided by the previous law (Section 59, *Crimes Act 1961*) and means that a parent who is prosecuted for assaulting a child can no longer invoke the excuse that the force used was reasonable in the circumstances and for the purpose of correction.

This amendment was, and continues to be, the focus of intense and polarized public, political, media, and academic debate in New Zealand. A 2009 public referendum on the issue resulted in a majority of the voters agreeing that a smack should not be a criminal offense. In this chapter we outline the social and political context of the law reform process, and the journey to its achievement in the face of the (ongoing) campaign against it.

LEGAL CONTEXT

Section 59 of the *Crimes Act 1961* originated in English common law, which itself was based on Roman law (Wood, Hassall, Hook, & Ludbrook, 2008). Historically, fathers had the right of control over the person, education, conduct, and moral development of their children until the age of 21. The common law defense of reasonable chastisement was first given statutory expression in England in 1889, enabling parents to perform their duty of correcting 'what is evil in the child'. During this era, physical punishment was permitted as a means of disciplining not only children, but also wives, servants, apprentices, pupils, criminals, and naval and military staff (Taylor, 2005a). As New Zealand's legal system developed in the 19th century, the right of parents to use reasonable force to correct their children's behavior was initially given statutory effect in Section 68 of the *Criminal Code 1893*, which allowed teachers, naval officers, and parents to use physical punishment without fear of prosecution. These powers were re-enacted in Section 85 of the *Crimes Act 1908* and Section 38 of the *Infants Act 1908* (Wood et al., 2008), and again in Section 59 of the *Crimes Act 1961*, although at that time there was a slight change in wording and the defense for naval officers was moved to a different section of the 1961 statute.

Corporal punishment of pupils by teachers was abolished in state and private schools and in early childhood centers by Section 139A of the *Education Act 1989*[1], which took effect on 23 July 1990. At that time, Section 59 of the *Crimes Act 1961* (entitled Domestic Discipline) was amended to read:

(1) Every parent [of a child and, subject to subsection (3) of this section, every person in the place of the parent of a child, is justified in using

force by way of correction of the child], if the force used is reasonable in the circumstances.

(2) The reasonableness of the force is a question of fact.

(3) Nothing in subsection (1) of this section justifies the use of force towards a child in contravention of section 139A of the Education Act 1989.

This statutory provision remained in effect until June 21, 2007. Its reform began with the drafting of a Member's Bill[2] by Sue Bradford, a Member of Parliament (MP; Green Party), proposing its full repeal. This Bill was drawn from the ballot in June 2005 and gave real momentum to the campaign to prohibit physical punishment of children. Changes to the law would have occurred much more slowly without Bradford's initiative as there was little political will at that time to confront the issue (Wood et al., 2008, p. 167).

The first reading of Bradford's Bill passed through Parliament 48 days after being drawn, with a majority of MPs voting in favor of it (63 for and 54 against). This allowed the Bill to proceed to the Select Committee stage.[3] During the following year (from February 2006 to February 2007), 1,718 public submissions on the Bill were received by the Justice and Electoral Select Committee. Support from the majority of the Select Committee eventually allowed the Bill to go forward to the next stage. However, over this time there was considerable public debate over the nature and extent of the law reform. People opposing the Bill were concerned about State intervention into family life and the possible criminalization of parents who gave their child a 'light and loving smack'. Those supporting the Bill saw it as an opportunity to respect and protect children's right to physical integrity and equality before the law, encourage nonviolent childrearing, and contribute to reducing New Zealand's high rate of child maltreatment deaths.[4]

The second reading of the Bill, on February 21, 2007, was passed after several hours of debate. It was supported by 70 MPs and opposed by 51, allowing the Bill to proceed to a Committee of the House. The amended Bill was then debated line by line in Parliament on March 14, 2007 and March 28, 2007, with the final stages of debate being interrupted by a 3-week Parliamentary recess. During this recess, Prime Minister (PM) Helen Clark and Sue Bradford negotiated a compromise with the Leader of the Opposition (John Key, National Party). Bradford had steadfastly refused to agree to any compromise which would specify in law where and how children could be physically punished, but she expressed willingness to accept amendments which would reassure the public that minor assaults would not lead to parental prosecutions. Discussions between the PM and the Law Commission eventually led to the drafting of an amendment aimed at reducing public anxieties about the criminalization of parents in cases of minor assault. The amendment would affirm that the Police would have the discretion not to prosecute in cases where the force used on the child was inconsequential, which was actually a re-statement of the powers they already held. The PM then spoke to the Leader of the Opposition who agreed to support the amendment. On May 2, 2007 the PM, the Leader of the Opposition and the Leader of a small political party, United Future, held a press conference to announce the accord that had been reached. Parliament then voted overwhelmingly in favor of the Bill, with 113 MPs supporting it and only 8 opposing it.

The purpose of the new *Crimes (Substituted Section 59) Amendment Act 2007* was "to make better provision for children to live in a safe and secure environment free from violence by abolishing the use of parental force for the purpose of correction" (Section 4, Purpose). Section 5 of the *Amendment Act* repealed the previous Section 59 and replaced it with a section entitled 'Section 59 Parental Control' which reads:

> (1) Every parent of a child and every person in place of a parent of the child is justified in using force if the force used is reasonable in the circumstances and is for the purpose of:
> (a) preventing or minimising harm to the child or another person; or preventing the child from engaging or continuing to engage in conduct that amounts to a criminal offence or continuing to engage in conduct that amounts to a criminal offence; or
> (b) preventing the child from engaging or continuing to engage in offensive or disruptive behaviour; or
> (c) performing the normal tasks that are incidental to good care and parenting.

The key phrase of this new provision is in subsection (2), which states very clearly that corrective force is now illegal:

> (2) Nothing in subsection (1) or in any rule of common law justifies the use of force for the purpose of correction.

This reform clearly prohibited the use of physical force to *correct* a child. However, "smacking" may be motivated by both preventive and corrective intent; commentators are uncertain which purpose would be dominant and how the law might be interpreted in such circumstances (Evans, 2009; Roughan, 2009). This issue—whether "smacking" could be used for purposes other than correction—has not yet been tested in the courts. Therefore, children do not yet enjoy the same level of protection as adults (Hornibrook, 2008).

INFLUENCES ON NEW ZEALAND'S LAW REFORM

It is significant that New Zealand was the first English-speaking country to prohibit all physical punishment of children. This issue has been a particularly challenging one for the English-speaking world (see Australia,

Canada, and the United Kingdom, this volume). Several factors converged to make law reform possible in New Zealand.

The Role of the United Nations Committee on the Rights of the Child (CRC)

New Zealand ratified the CRC in 1993. Several of its articles had an important influence on our reform process: *Article 3* requiring 'the best interests of the child' to be paramount; *Article 6* requiring states to promote 'the survival and development of the child'; *Article 19* requiring protection of children from 'all forms of physical or mental violence'; and *Article 37* requiring that children not be subject to 'cruel, inhuman and degrading treatment or punishment'. While not providing enforceable rights, ratification of the CRC imposes obligations on State Parties to comply with its provisions (Taylor, 2005a, 2005b) and to regularly report on their implementation to the UN Committee on the Rights of the Child.[5] The Committee's *General Comment No. 8* (2006) unequivocally states that physical punishment is incompatible with the CRC (Taylor, 2005a). The Committee has urged all ratifying countries to prohibit it and to implement accompanying public education campaigns. The Committee's *Concluding Observations*, issued in response to country reports, have consistently criticized countries without prohibitions. This was so in the Committee's response to the New Zealand Government's first report (1997), and was even more strongly expressed in their response to the government's second report: "The Committee is deeply concerned that despite a review of legislation, the State party has still not amended Section 59 of the Crimes Act, 1961, which allows parents to use reasonable force to discipline their children" (UN Committee on the Rights of the Child, 2003, para. 29). The Committee recommended amending our legislation to make punishment in the home illegal, and strengthening public education campaigns aimed at eliminating physical punishment.

As part of its 2003 review of New Zealand's compliance with the CRC, the Committee asked Action for Children and Youth Aotearoa (ACYA)[6] to review the application of Section 59 in Family Court and criminal court cases. This review revealed inconsistent application in court cases involving parental violence (Hancock, 2004).[7] Section 59 had been successfully used to defend parents for such actions as hitting a child with a bamboo stick, a belt, a hosepipe, and a piece of wood—and for putting a child in metal chains to prevent the child from leaving the house. In each of these cases, a jury had deemed the parent's action to be reasonable corrective force. However, in other similar cases, judges considered the force unreasonable and rejected the Section 59 defense.[8] This inconsistent application of Section 59 persuaded many people that a change in the law was necessary.

The UN Committee's response to New Zealand's periodic reports led the Government to develop a 'work program' to enhance its compliance with the CRC (Wood et al., 2008). However, if this process had been relied upon to bring about the repeal of Section 59, progress would have been slow. The Government was hesitant to prohibit physical punishment by parents as this was such a controversial issue. Instead, in 2003, they announced a public education campaign intended to promote alternatives to physical punishment. A large-scale public education campaign explicitly focused on discouraging physical punishment did not eventuate, but instead evolved into a multi-faceted, lower key national program called *Strategies with Kids, Information for Parents* (SKIP[9]), aimed at encouraging parents of young children to become more aware of alternatives to physical punishment and to use them more. Section 59 was to be reviewed by the Government after the public education campaign had been in operation for 3 years (Wood et al., 2008).

The Role of Children's Commissioners

Significant leadership was provided by the Children's Commissioners, whose role in promoting children's welfare had been initially established in the *Children, Young Persons and their Families Act 1989*. Subsequently, the *Children's Commissioner Act 2003* required Commissioners to give better effect to the CRC, and broadened their powers to safeguard and promote children's rights more generally.[10] All five Commissioners for Children—Dr. Ian Hassall, Laurie O'Reilly, the Hon. Roger McClay, Dr. Cindy Kiro, and Dr. John Angus—have been strong advocates for the repeal of Section 59, and have played a major role in promoting positive discipline and preventing child maltreatment.

The Role of Non-Governmental Organizations

Several non-governmental organizations (NGOs) played an important role in promoting a child rights agenda and urging action on the Government's policy initiatives for children and young people, such as the *Agenda for Children* (Ministry of Social Development, 2002) and the *Youth Development Strategy* (Ministry of Youth Affairs, 2002), and campaigned for the repeal of Section 59. EPOCH New Zealand[11] was established in 1997 and, led by Beth Wood, gained the support of a wide range of other NGOs, including Māori and Pacific organizations, service delivery agencies, professional organizations, and family violence prevention services. The NGOs' strong call for repeal was evident in their submissions to the Select Committee and played a pivotal role in changing the views of parliamentarians (Debski, Buckley, & Russell, 2006). Other NGOs active on this issue were Save the Children New Zealand, UNICEF, Barnardos New Zealand and the Royal New Zealand Plunket Society (Wood et al., 2008). ACYA, chaired by Dr Alison Blaiklock, coordinated the work of a range of agency/ sector representatives and individual advocates to prepare comprehensive

NGO reports to the UN Committee on the Rights of the Child in 1997 and 2003. Both reports highlighted Section 59's violation of several CRC articles and strongly supported repeal.

The Role of Politicians

Engaging key political support was considered critical if the law was ever going to change in New Zealand. Politicians had been lobbied for at least a decade before the law was amended. Over time, a number of individual politicians expressed personal support for reform, but no party in power was willing to take the political risk in the face of substantial public opposition. However, when Sue Bradford's Private Member's Bill was drawn from the ballot, Prime Minister Helen Clark (Labor Party) threw her support behind the Bill's progress through the Parliamentary process. Her role was pivotal. The intensity of feeling that the issue evoked was reflected in prolonged Parliamentary debates. Reform would not have occurred without the support of Sue Bradford, Helen Clark and, at the end, Opposition Leader John Key.[12]

The Role of Research

Research was critical in providing an evidence base for the reform process and informing the public about nonviolent discipline. In 2001, Professor Anne Smith and Dr. Nicola Taylor, from the Children's Issues Centre (CIC) at the University of Otago, met with the Children's Commissioner, Roger McClay, and his research and policy officer, Heather McDonald, to request funding support for a review of the international literature on discipline. The Office of the Children's Commissioner (OCC) then commissioned the CIC to carry out a review, overseen by a reference group of government department officials, NGO representatives, and academics. This approach exemplified the useful nexus between research and policy, as the CIC research team was able to review aspects of the literature that were of particular interest to the officials in their formulation of new policies and programs.[13]

A four-person research team undertook the independent review of research and professional commentary on child discipline. Two reports were produced. First, a summary report was issued to facilitate public access to the findings (Smith, Gollop, Taylor, & Marshall, 2004). It was distributed by the OCC, the CIC, and the Ministry of Social Development and was available free for parents, the public, and professionals. Second, a longer report (Smith, Gollop, Taylor, & Marshall, 2005) was published primarily for an academic and policy audience, covering a wide range of relevant social science and legal research. Both reports were given extensive public coverage following a 2004 National Seminar sponsored by the CIC entitled, *"Stop it, it hurts me": Research and Perspectives on Physical*

Punishment. The literature review findings were presented, as well as the perspectives of the Children's Commissioner (Dr. Cindy Kiro), Māori and Pasifika representatives, and church representatives.[14] The CIC's conclusions, as summarized in a submission on the Bill to the Select Committee, were as follows:

> When [section 59 of the Crimes Act 1961] came into force, the law makers were unaware of the evidence that physically punishing children was a risk to their health, which has since accumulated (see attached references). Just as with other risks to children's health (smoking, cot death) there is a responsibility on the part of the government not to encourage practices which are risky for children. Physical punishment has been shown to be associated with the following outcomes for children: increased aggression and antisocial behaviour; poorer academic achievement; poorer quality parent–child relationships (attachment); adverse mental health outcomes (depression, anxiety, low self esteem); and diminished moral internalization (children's internalization of parental values and ability to control their own behaviour). There is evidence that other methods of parental discipline are much more effective in bringing about favorable outcomes for children. The current law actually fails to prevent children being exposed to parental violence, and indeed provides parents with an excuse for using violence as a means of controlling children's behaviour. The present law therefore contributes to perpetuating a cycle of intergenerational family violence, despite the importance attached by the government to the prevention of family violence (Smith, 2006, p. 2).

While this work was by no means the only research foundation for repealing Section 59,[15] the CIC's efforts were substantial and influential. They provided an evidence-based and child-focused approach to the issue, highlighting the detrimental impact that physical punishment, particularly when frequent and severe, could have on children. The literature review findings were also central to the design and delivery of the SKIP parent education program introduced by the Ministry of Social Development in 2004. On the basis of research literature, six principles of effective discipline were incorporated into the SKIP program, and community-based parent educators were trained through SKIP seminars throughout the country.

Particularly influential research findings came from work conducted by Terry Dobbs, who explored children's previously invisible and unvoiced perspectives on discipline (Dobbs, 2002, 2005a, 2005b, 2007; Dobbs, Smith, & Taylor, 2006). She found that the majority of children (92%) reported being smacked by their parents, and harsh punishment, including the use of implements, was not uncommon in their experience. Children's descriptions of how they felt about being punished were a new and evocative contribution to the law reform debate.

After the Prohibition

More than 2 years have passed since the law reform took effect. Its supporters did not anticipate immediate and widespread improvements in parental disciplinary practices, but there have been some encouraging signs.

Attitudes Towards Physical Punishment

A large-scale survey reported that in 1981, 92% of men and 86% of women endorsed physical punishment in certain circumstances (Ritchie & Ritchie, 1981). In 2007, a survey carried out by the Office of the Children's Commissioner found that the proportion of the public endorsing physical punishment had decreased to 58%, and less than a third of parents agreed that physical punishment should be part of child discipline (Children's Commissioner, 2008; Wood, 2008).

Use of Physical Punishment

A Ministry of Health (2008) survey of 17,000 New Zealanders conducted between 2006 and 2007 asked the primary caregivers of 4,921 children up to the age of 14 years about the types of discipline they had used in the previous 4 weeks. Two out of three parents said they had used explanation or discussion, but only 4.5% of parents had used physical punishment. Fewer than one-third of parents who had used physical punishment considered it effective.

In an interview study conducted with 117 parents of preschoolers, Lawrence and Smith (2009) found that 41% of parents reported using physical punishment at some time, but only 9% thought it was effective. Diaries kept by parents over a 2-week period showed that less than 3% of parents had physically punished their children during that time. Data from the in-depth interviews indicated that most parents only rarely used physical punishment; if they did use it, they felt badly about it and believed it taught children the wrong messages (Lawrence & Smith, 2009).

Attitudes Towards Prohibition

The Children's Commissioner's survey found that 89% of the public agreed that children were entitled to the same protection from assault as adults. While less than half (43%) supported the prohibition, only 28% were opposed (26% were unsure). These findings suggest that the public was not particularly supportive of physical punishment, and less than one-third opposed its prohibition. Lawrence and Smith (2008) obtained virtually identical findings with their sample of 117 parents of preschoolers: 46% were in favor of the new legislation, 27% were opposed, and 27% were unsure. An important finding of this study was that understanding of the law is related to support for it: Of those who were in favor of the reform, 58% said they understood it; of those who were opposed to the reform, 30% said they understood it; and of those who were unsure, 19% said they understood it. This finding suggests that it is important for governments to provide effective public education about the purpose and implementation of prohibitions when they are passed.

The Citizens' Referendum

Despite the low level of opposition to the law reform found in research, a non-binding citizen-initiated referendum was organized in an attempt to overturn the prohibition. The referendum was part of a continuing and well-funded campaign by a former politician, Larry Baldock, and conservative groups, such as Family First (a faith-based organization promoting parental rights). The referendum was held by postal ballot in July 2009, on the question *Should a smack as part of good parental correction be a criminal offence in New Zealand?* The newly elected Prime Minister (John Key[16]) and the Leader of the Opposition (Hon. Phil Goff) publicly criticized the confusing wording of the question, but the referendum proceeded.

Fifty-four percent of eligible voters voted in the referendum, and 87.4% of them answered 'no' to the question posed. While this result has been widely interpreted as an overwhelming condemnation of the new law, the loaded and confusing nature of the referendum's wording, the fact that it did not refer directly to the law, the low voter turnout, and the survey results discussed above give reason to question that interpretation. The Prime Minister has stated several times that the law is working as intended; there is no evidence that good parents are being criminalized for trivial offences; and the Government has no intention of changing the law despite the referendum result. In front of a hostile audience at a Family First forum, Mr. Key emphasized that the new law is important as it sends a message that violence against children is unacceptable (Collins, 2009).

Reviews of the Prohibition's Implementation

Prior to the passage of the prohibition, considerable public anxiety had been expressed (and fomented) about the possibility of parents were being investigated or prosecuted for minor violations. Following the law's passage, opponents claimed that families were being disrupted and stressed due to unnecessary investigations. Two official reviews of the implementation of the law were carried out in late 2009 to determine whether these claims had any empirical basis.

The first review was required under the 2007 reform (Ministry of Social Development, 2009a). Its aim was to report broadly on the impact of the change in the law. In reality there were limited data available as it was too early to track law-related trends beyond police charging practices (Pope,

2008) and court judgments. The review found no evidence "to show that parents are being subjected to unnecessary state intervention for lightly smacking their children or any other unintended consequences of the Act" (Ministry of Social Development, 2009a, p. 15).

The second review was released in December 2009 (Ministry of Social Development, 2009b). It examined the policies and procedures of the Police and of Child, Youth and Family (NZ's statutory child protection service) to determine whether minor infringements of the law were being investigated or prosecuted, and whether existing laws were adequate to deal with more serious offences against children. This review was undertaken by the Chief Executive of the Ministry of Social Development, the Commissioner for Police and an independent psychologist, Mr. Nigel Latta. In conclusion, they state: "We have reviewed the two agencies' policies and procedures and found that they provide effective guidelines for ensuring parents are treated as parliament intended (Ministry of Social Development, 2009b, p. 3).

Reviews of specific cases refuted opponents' claims of unnecessary intervention, as the review team found the investigations to have been appropriate. Recommendations were made to provide additional reassurances to the public. As a result, the Police publish a report every 6 months, monitoring the implementation of the law, that can be viewed on the Police website.[17] Child, Youth and Family recently released a pamphlet to inform parents of what to expect when a social worker investigates a referral.[18]

CONCLUSION

New Zealand is the first—and only—English-speaking nation to prohibit physical punishment of children. It was not an easy journey, but perhaps it will pave the way for our Commonwealth partners (Australia, Canada, and the UK) and the US to join the growing list of countries committed to upholding children's right to protection.

While we have achieved this landmark, it would be incorrect to assume that we have reached the end of the journey. Opponents of the prohibition remain determined and continue to stir up public fear. But the government appears committed to respecting its commitment under the CRC. Through the reform process, the government and NGOs have become much better informed on the issue and we do not anticipate that they will take regressive steps. Research needs to continue to document the impact of the prohibition, and public education about positive discipline is critical (Smith et al., 2004, 2005). At this point, a sustained period of calm reflection and discussion about the intent of the law is needed, together with support to help parents learn ways of raising their children without violence.

Ending physical punishment is part of an evolving process of understanding children's personhood. We hope that New Zealand will soon be a place where the prohibition is regarded with pride by its citizens, and applauded for its congruity with our longstanding tradition of leading social change. Our prohibition is "about changing the social norm—it is about making Aotearoa New Zealand a place where everyone knows it is not okay to hit children" (Wood, 2004, p. 31).

NOTES

1. Interestingly, this was the same year that the United Nations *Convention on the Rights of the Child* was adopted by the UN General Assembly and New Zealand appointed its first Commissioner for Children.
2. In New Zealand, new laws are usually proposed by the Government and these Bills then go onto the legislative agenda. Individual Members of parliament can also propose Bills (Private Members' Bills) that go into a ballot, which usually contains about 40 Bills. Periodically, a Bill will be drawn from the ballot and placed on the legislative agenda.
3. When a Bill has passed "first reading" in the House, it is referred to a Select Committee composed of Members of Parliament who consider it in depth and seek input from the public. The Select Committee formulates conclusions and submits them to Parliament. The Bill is subsequently voted on by the House.
4. At that time, New Zealand had the third highest rate of child maltreatment deaths among OECD countries—13 times higher than that of Spain, the country with the lowest rate (UNICEF, 2003).
5. Two years after ratification and every 5 years thereafter.
6. The NGO which took responsibility for writing a report to the UN Committee on New Zealand's compliance with the CRC.
7. See also: Taylor (2005a).
8. For example, in *R v McFarlane* (1995) 13 CRNZ 354 where a 13-year-old suffered repeated beatings by her father and stepfather. An appeal to the High Court was also unsuccessful in this case—*R v McFarlane* [2001] CA 29/01, per Blanchard, Doogue, Randerson JJ.
9. See: www.skip.govt.nz
10. The role of the Children's Commissioner and his or her staff is to promote the rights, health, welfare, and well-being of children and young people between birth and 18 years, and to promote the CRC in New Zealand.
11. EPOCH = End Physical Punishment of Children.
12. John Key became Prime Minister a year later (2008) when the National Party won the General Election.
13. The Ministry of Social Development was, at the time, developing the new SKIP parenting education program and was keen to learn of research on positive discipline, as well as the effects of physical punishment on children.
14. These presentations were published in a special issue of the CIC's journal, *Childrenz Issues*, entitled *Perspectives on Physical Punishment*, Volume 8(2), 2004.
15. Drs. Jane and James Ritchie (1970, 1978, 1981, 1993, 1997; Ritchie, 2002), from Waikato University, were the first to introduce research on physical punishment into public debate in the 1970s. The Christchurch Health and Development longitudinal study has also made important contributions to the research literature within New Zealand (Fergusson & Lynskey, 1997).
16. As Leader of the Opposition under Helen Clark's government, John Key had originally opposed the law reform, but had accepted the all-party compromise and voted in support of it.

17. http://www.police.govt.nz/search/node/section%2059%20reports
18. http://www.cyf.govt.nz/info-for-parents/when-we-visit.html

REFERENCES

Action for Children and Youth Aotearoa. (2003). *Children and youth in Aotearoa 2003: The second non-governmental organisations' report to the UN Committee on the Rights of the Child.* Auckland: Action for Children and Youth Aotearoa.

Children's Commissioner. (2008). *Omnibus survey report. One year on: Public attitudes and New Zealand's child discipline law.* Retrieved from http://www.occ.org.nz/__data/assets/pdf_file/0008/5669/OCC_UMR-Research_141108.pdf

Collins, S. (2009, September 19). Goff, Key stand firm on smacking. *New Zealand Herald*, p. A7.

Committee on the Rights of the Child. (2006). *General comment no. 8: The right of the child to protection from corporal punishment and other cruel, inhuman or degrading treatment or punishment.* UN Doc. CRC/C/GC/8. Available from http://www2.ohchr.org/english/bodies/crc/comments.htm

Debski, S., Buckley, S., & Russell, M. (2006). *Just who do we think children are? An analysis of submissions to the Justice and Electoral Select Committee, 2006.* Report to Save the Children. Wellington: Health Services Research Centre, School of Government, Victoria University.

Dobbs, T. (2002). *The missing voice: What are children's views of physical discipline?* CHIX 480 Research Study, Children's Issues Centre, University of Otago.

Dobbs, T. (2005a). *Children's insights into family discipline.* Masters thesis, Children's Issues Centre, University of Otago.

Dobbs, T. (2005b). *Insights: Children and young people speak out about family discipline.* Wellington: Save the Children New Zealand.

Dobbs, T. (2007). What do children tell us about physical punishment as a risk factor for child abuse? *Social Policy Journal of New Zealand, 30,* 145–162.

Dobbs, T., Smith A. B., & Taylor, N. J. (2006). 'No, we don't get a say, children just suffer the consequences': Children talk about family discipline. *International Journal of Children's Rights, 14,* 137–156.

Evans, J. (2009, August 6). New Section 59 is clearly a mess. *New Zealand Herald.* Retrieved October 22, 2009, from www.nzherald.co.nz/nz/news/article.cfm?c_id=1&objectid=10588870&pnum=2

Fergusson, D. M., & Lynskey, M. T. (1997). Physical punishment/maltreatment during childhood and adjustment in young adulthood. *Child Abuse & Neglect, 21*(7), 617–630.

Hancock, J. (2004). The application of Section 59 of the Crimes Act in the New Zealand Courts. *Childrenz Issues, 8*(2), 45–51.

Hornibrook, C. (2008). *Parental control and the child's right not to be hit* (Unpublished LLM Thesis). Dunedin: University of Otago Faculty of Law.

Lawrence, J., & Smith, A. B. (2008). Aotearoa/New Zealand families: Their perspectives on child discipline and recent legislative changes. *Childrenz Issues, 12*(2), 17–24.

Lawrence, J., & Smith, A. B. (2009). *Discipline in context: Families' disciplinary practices for children aged under five.* Wellington: Families Commission Blue Skies Report No 30/09.

Ministry of Health. (2008). *A portrait of health—Key results of the 2005/2006 New Zealand Health Survey.* Wellington: Ministry of Health.

Ministry of Social Development. (2002). *New Zealand's Agenda for Children: Making life better for children*. Wellington: Ministry of Social Development.

Ministry of Social Development. (2004, May 6). *SKIP for parents*. Press release from the Minister for Social Development and Employment. Retrieved June 30, 2004, from http://www.msd.govt.nz/media-information/press-releases/2004/pr-2004-05-06.html

Ministry of Social Development. (2009a). Report to the Minister for Social Development and Employment pursuant to S 7(2) of the Crimes (Substituted Section 59) Amendment Act. Retrieved February 22, 2010, from http://www.beehive.govt.nz/sites/all/files/20091110%20CE%20Monitoring%20Report%20on%20s59.pdf

Ministry of Social Development. (2009b). *Review of New Zealand Police and Child, Youth and Family Policies and Procedures relating to the Crimes (Substituted Section 59) Amendment Act*. Retrieved February 22, 2010, from https://www.msd.govt.nz/documents/about-msd-and-our-work/newsroom/media-releases/news/2009/s59-report.pdf

Ministry of Youth Affairs. (2002). *Youth Development Strategy Aotearoa*. Wellington: Ministry of Youth Affairs.

Pope, R. (2008, June 23). *Six month review of Police activity following the enactment of the Crimes (Substituted section 59) Amendment Act 2007*. Wellington: New Zealand Police. Available at: http://www.police.govt.nz/resources/2008/section-59-activity-review/

Ritchie, J. (2002). Parents: Discipline, punishment and child abuse. A four-decade study of child rearing attitudes and practices. *The New Zealand Psychological Society Bulletin, 100*, 30–33.

Ritchie, J., & Ritchie, J. (1970). *Child rearing patterns in New Zealand*. Wellington: A.H. & A.W. Reed.

Ritchie, J., & Ritchie, J. (1978). *Growing up in New Zealand*. Sydney: George Allen & Unwin.

Ritchie, J., & Ritchie, J. (1981). *Spare the rod*. Sydney: George Allen & Unwin.

Ritchie, J., & Ritchie, J. (1993). *Violence in New Zealand*. Wellington: Huia Publishers.

Ritchie, J., & Ritchie, J. (1997). *The next generation: Child rearing in New Zealand*. Auckland: Penguin.

Roughan, J. (2009, August 1). Sinister undertones to referendum instigators. *New Zealand Herald*. Retrieved October 22, 2009, from www.nzherald.co.nz/opinion/news/article.cfm?c_id=466&objectid=10587889

Smith, A. B. (2006). *Submission to the Justice and Electoral Select Committee on the Crimes (Abolition of Force as a Justification for Child Discipline) Amendment Bill*. Dunedin: Children's Issues Centre.

Smith, A. B., Gollop, M. M., Taylor, N. J., & Marshall, K. A. (2004). *Summary Report. The discipline and guidance of children: Messages from research*. Dunedin: Children's Issues Centre and the Office of the Children's Commissioner.

Smith, A. B., Gollop, M. M., Taylor, N. J., & Marshall, K. A. (2005). *The discipline and guidance of children: Messages from research*. Dunedin: Children's Issues Centre and the Office of the Children's Commissioner.

Taylor, N. J. (2005a). International developments. In A. B. Smith, M. M. Gollop, N. J. Taylor, & K. A. Marshall (Eds.), *The discipline and guidance of children: Messages from research* (pp. 101–130). Wellington: Children's Issues Centre and the Office of the Children's Commissioner.

Taylor, N. J. (2005b). Physical punishment of children: International legal developments. *New Zealand Family Law Journal, 5*(1), 14–22.

UNICEF. (2003). *A league table of child maltreatment deaths in rich nations. Innocenti Report Card, Issue No. 5*. Florence, Italy: Innocenti Research Centre, UNICEF.

United Nations Committee on the Rights of the Child. (2003). *Concluding observations of the Committee on the Rights of the Child: New Zealand*. 34th Session, UN Doc CRC/C/15/Add. 216, October 3, Geneva.

Wood, B. (2004). Panellist response to Anne Smith and Cindy Kiro's keynote addresses. *Childrenz Issues, 8*(2), 30–31.

Wood, B. (2008). The long road to reform. *Childrenz Issues, 12*(2), 13–16.

Wood, B., Hassall, I., Hook, G., & Ludbrook, R. (2008). Unreasonable force: New Zealand's journey towards banning the physical punishment of children. Wellington: Save the Children NZ.

ACTS

Care of Children Act 2004
Children, Young Persons and Their Families Act 1989
Crimes Act 1908
Crimes Act 1961
Crimes (Substituted Section 59) Amendment Act 2007
Criminal Code 1893
Education Act 1989
Infants Act 1908

CASES

R v McFarlane (1995) CRNZ 354
R v McFarlane [2001] CA 29/01 CRNZ 354

15 Norway

The Long and Winding Road towards Prohibiting Physical Punishment

Kirsten Sandberg

Population:	4,870,000
Type of government:	Democracy, Constitutional Monarchy
Governing structure:	Parliamentary system, central government with some power to regions and municipalities. The Sámi people have their own parliament with some power.
Child protection system in place:	Yes
Legal system:	Penal Code, Children and Parents' Act, Child Protection Act, etc.
Major religion:	Christian Evangelical Lutheran (State Church)
Official national languages:	Norwegian, and the Sámi language in some areas in the north
Ratified United Nations Convention on the Rights of the Child:	1991
Children's Ombudsman:	Since 1981—the first one in the world.

HISTORICAL CONTEXT

A number of small Norwegian communities were gradually organized into larger regions in the 9th century, and around the year 900 the realm was unified under a king. In the Middle Ages, Vikings from Norway settled in England, France, Ireland, and Iceland. Norway and Denmark formed one kingdom from 1380 to 1814 when Norway had a short period of independence and adopted its constitution. The same year, in the wake of the Napoleonic wars, Norway was united with Sweden under the Swedish king. In 1905, the union was peacefully dissolved and Norway has been independent since. Norway is a country with a high degree of socioeconomic equality, a high standard of living and a rather homogeneous population. About one million people live in the area around Oslo. Quite a few Norwegians live in small communities with well-developed road, air, and ferry transportation and communication systems. The oil in the North Sea has allowed the country's economy to flourish for most of the last 30 years, subsidizing public health and welfare programs. Twice, by referendum, Norway has decided to stay outside the European Union (EU), but it is connected through the European Economic Area (EEA).

In 1896, Norway became the first country in the world to pass a *Child Protection Act* (*Vergerådsloven*), which established a public body to care for children living under difficult conditions, and set out specific measures for those children. The original *Act* was replaced by a new one in 1953, and another in 1992. The system is mainly designed to take care of children who are not cared for adequately by their parents, including children who experience violence in their homes.

Despite Norway's history of protecting children, it has taken a long journey to obtain a total prohibition against physical punishment in the family. The statutory provision giving parents the right to use physical punishment to discipline their children was removed in 1972, leaving the legal situation unclear. An explicit prohibition was not legislated until 1987. But the story does not end there; according to a 2005 Supreme Court ruling, light smacks were still allowed. This ruling was strongly criticized, and gave rise to public pressure demanding that any right to punish children physically be abolished. A legal amendment clearly forbidding all forms of violence against children was passed in 2010.

BACKGROUND

According to the 1685 *Norwegian Act*, the father had the right to hit his children and the master could hit his servants, but even then they were not permitted to use implements such as knives, or to damage the child's health. By the 1891 *Act on the Limitation of the Use of Corporal Punishment*, this right was limited to the moderate use of physical punishment against children under the perpetrator's authority. Although this reform improved children's protection, it sustained parents' right to physically punish their children by forming an exception to the *Penal Code's* general prohibition of violence.

Physical punishment of children in schools and children's institutions was prohibited through the 1930s and 1940s, but the parental right to physically punish children was upheld. The government-appointed committee preparing the *Child Protection Act* of 1953 discussed the removal of this parental right, but concluded that physical punishment was already less common than before and that public education would be more useful than a legal prohibition. In addition, the question was considered to fall under the authority of the *Penal Code* Commission.

1972: REMOVING THE STATUTORY RIGHT OF PARENTS TO PHYSICALLY PUNISH THEIR CHILDREN

It was in 1971 that the removal of the explicit statutory right to use physical punishment (Act of February 25, 1972, No. 3) was initiated by a Member of Parliament representing the Labor Party. She asked the Minister of Justice whether he would remove the parental right to hit children, arguing that it was unfair that children were less protected by the law than adults despite their greater need for protection, and that a civilized country had a duty to prevent the strong from hitting the weak (Interpellasjon from MP Tove Pihl, April 28, 1971). The ensuing Bill (Ot. prp. No. 17 [1971–1972]), the statements submitted during the written hearing, and the Parliamentary debate show that there was disagreement and uncertainty about the potential effects of abolition. Both the Judges' Association and the Ministry of Justice maintained that even if parents' statutory right to physically punish their children was to be abolished, parents would still have a customary law-based right to use such punishment to a certain extent. In Parliament, opinions varied greatly, from wanting to abolish any form of physical punishment because humanity must start in the home, to acknowledging the right of parents to give their children a good beating when necessary, with or without reference to authorization by a higher power (Befring, 1991; Forhandlinger i Ot., 1972; Forhandlinger i Lt., 1972). In 1972, the following law was enacted: "The *Act of June 20, 1891, on the Limitation of the Use of Corporal Punishment* is abolished." No explicit prohibition replaced the Act.

There was ambiguity and uncertainty about the consequences of the abolition of the 1891 Act. It is probably correct to say that parents' right to punish children physically was constrained, but not totally abolished. Two Supreme Court decisions of 1978 support that view (Rt. 1978, p. 1428; Rt. 1978, p. 1506). Legal opinions differed, but by the early 1980s there was general agreement that whipping, caning, and other forms of severe physical punishment were forbidden, whereas a spontaneous slap and other forms of minor physical punishment were not (Backer, 1982; Bratholm, 1980).

THE 1980s: THE DEBATE INTENSIFIES

In 1982, the Ministry of Justice stated that hard-handed physical punishment leading to considerable pain or unnecessary humiliation was unacceptable, even for the purpose of disciplining the child. Thus, beating with a cane or other implement was forbidden, but lighter physical correction might be allowed (Ministry of Justice Law Department, 1982, cited in Ot. prp. No. 8 [1986–1987]). In that same year, the government-appointed Child Abuse Commission proposed a full prohibition. This Commission had been appointed in 1979, as a result of growing concern about physical maltreatment of children in Norway and internationally. In its report of 1982 (NOU, 1982:26), the Commission focused primarily on serious violence, but pointed to its connection to parental responsibility. Referring to the Swedish prohibition of 1979, the Commission recommended a prohibition of physical punishment and other forms of degrading treatment of children.

Also in 1982, the Ombudsman for Children, Målfrid Grude Flekkøy, made a report to the police regarding a publication for parents that recommended spanking, which precipitated a broad debate in the media (Ombudsman for Children, 1985). She also was concerned that parents were publicly admitting to beating their children without any public criticism. She began to promote the Child Abuse Commission's law proposal, meeting with the relevant Ministries in 1982 and 1983. Her office also published newspaper articles that could be used in a public education campaign (Ombudsman for Children, 1985).

At the same time, some Conservative Christian congregations were defending parents' right to physically punish their children, with reference to the Bible. A pastor in a small non-Episcopal church (Hans Bratterud, *Oslo Fullevangeliske Kirke*) became renowned in 1983 for publicly, at the church's own local radio station, encouraging parents to spank their children. He said it should not happen spontaneously but as a deliberate act, and it should not be called violence. Several Church leaders and others from Christian groups argued publicly against his view (Befring, 1991).

Opinion was split among the broader population, as well. A 1983 opinion poll found that 52% of the respondents thought that spanking was appropriate in some situations, while 43% said that they were absolutely against it. Only 5% were absolutely in favor of it, but 63% opposed a full prohibition (Scanfact, cited in the weekly magazine *Hjemmet*, No. 25/1983, see Ot. prp. No. 8 [1986–1987]). Statements by "ordinary people" in the media suggest that the illegality of spanking and hitting children was not well-known.

However, there was a virtual consensus among experts, such as psychologists and psychiatrists, that violence in the upbringing of children was unacceptable. They considered the risk of physical harm as a result of such violence to be greater than the potential positive effects of such methods. Experts asserted a close relationship between physical punishment of children and child maltreatment, and reported evidence that children who had been beaten were likely to become violent themselves (Ot. prp. No. 8 [1986–1987]).

Interestingly, non-governmental organizations (NGOs) were not involved in the debate at that time. According to Melton (1991), there was a "virtual non-existence of strong interest groups on children's issues in Norway" as compared with Denmark and Sweden (pp. 223–224). *Mental Barnehjelp*[1] (*Mental Help to Children*) was the only NGO directly engaged in promoting children's interests (Melton, 1991). Even the domestic advocacy program of *Redd Barna*, the Norwegian affiliate of the international Save the Children, did not begin until 1989.

However, in 1984, an important seminar on children and punishment was organized by the Norwegian Research Council's Centre for Child Research, which gathered researchers and practitioners from a range of fields, including psychology, social anthropology, and law. The Ombudsman for Children, a practicing psychologist, also took part in the seminar. There was broad agreement that parents should not use physical punishment in raising children (Mjaavatn, 1984). It was argued that reciprocity between parents and children was better than parental authority, because it implied equal worth, founded in a sense of community. In this family dynamic, responsibility would be shared, restrictions would not only be one-way, and respect and recognition would be central concepts (Evans, cited in Mjaavatn, 1984).

Also in 1984, the Ministry of Justice prepared a reform bill based on a statement by the Ombudsman for Children about the legal and psychological consequences of physical punishment. However, although the conservative Minister of Justice was in favor of the reform, she was unable to convince the rest of the Cabinet. In cooperation with the Ombudsman, MPs challenged the Cabinet in Parliament, but the Cabinet had several excuses for not sending the Bill to Parliament (Flekkøy, 1991; Ot. prp. No. 8 [1986–1987]). This government, under Willoch, was a coalition among the Conservatives, the Christian Democrats and the Farmers' Party.

THE LAW REFORM OF 1987: A TOTAL PROHIBITION?

In May 1986, a Social Democratic government was elected (Gro Harlem Brundtland's second Cabinet), which represented a key turning point in the process (Melton, 1991). The Bill was finally sent to Parliament in late 1986. However, the proposed provision still left the legal position of children unclear. The Ombudsman for Children became actively involved once again. With her prompting, prominent lawyers published statements supporting a prohibition while pointing to the lack of clarity in the proposed provision, in the newspapers a few days before the final vote in Parliament, and she herself lobbied MPs (Flekkøy, 1991). The amendment was passed early in 1987. On the basis of the Child Abuse Commission's 1982 report, the legislation would probably have been passed soon anyway (Flekkøy, 1991), particularly because there were forces within the Ministry of Justice working for the amendment (Melton, 1991).

The law of 1987 stated: "The child must not be exposed to violence or otherwise be treated so that its physical or mental health is endangered" (*Children and Parents Act,* Section 30, para. 3). Although the 1987 law reform was intended to clarify the legal situation, its interpretation was unclear from the start. An important change was the removal of the term "punishment" from the proposal because the purpose of the violence was deemed irrelevant. In the Bill, hitting and kicking were seen as practical examples of violence. Beating the child with physical objects such as a cane or *ris* (twigs bound together) would definitely be prohibited, as would a blow to the ear or on the bare bottom. However, light slaps on the hand or a trouser-clad bottom as a spontaneous reaction would not be prohibited (Ot. prp. No. 8 [1986–1987]).

The majority of the Parliamentary Committee emphasized that the provision would not imply a total prohibition of the use of physical power against children, introducing discretion with words such as "unnecessary", "illegitimate", and "reasonably". During the Parliamentary debate, MPs sought to draw the line between what was prohibited and what was not. But there were varying opinions and MPs did not always see the legal consequences of their statements. Some used the term "careful slaps"; others said that in the relationship between parents and children, there must be greater tolerance of mild physical reactions than in other relationships. The Minister of Justice, however, stated that the only acceptable use of physical power was as a preventive measure; that is, not as punishment (Forhandlinger i Ot., 1987). Confusion remained even after the Bill was passed.

Legally it is debatable whether the 1987 reform represented any major change, because interpretation of the law already meant that severe physical punishment (spanking and thrashing) was prohibited. The main aim of legislating a prohibition was to make people aware that hitting children was actually prohibited and to change public attitudes (Ot. prp. No. 8 [1986–1987]). The Bill preceding the law reform promisingly stated that the Ministries would follow up with effective public education. The Ministry of Justice referred to the active dissemination work of the Swedish authorities following their 1979 prohibition, and cited the Ombudsman for Children, who had underlined the need for a broad information campaign (Ot. prp. No. 8 [1986–1987]). The need for such a campaign was also emphasized by Law Professor Lucy Smith, in an interview shortly after the law reform had been approved (Hansen, 1987).

However, the Ministries responsible for informing the public about the law reform left the actual work of doing this to the organization *Mental Barnehjelp*, which had been active in working against child maltreatment (NOU, 1982:26). Two leaflets were produced, but too few copies were printed (Befring, 1991; Flekkøy, 1991). Befring describes the leaflets as written in short verses, the text being neither comprehensive nor very informative. *Mental Barnehjelp* considered the campaign to be too limited and too brief (Befring, 1991). While *Mental Barnehjelp* had suggested that information should be disseminated through the media, particularly television, the Ministry was not willing to pay for widespread media coverage (Befring, 1991). Instead a full-page newspaper advertisement appeared in all major Norwegian newspapers (Flekkøy, 1991).

THE 1990s: THE PROHIBITION IS UNQUESTIONED

Physical punishment and law reform received little public attention throughout the 1990s. While in 1992–1993, the Ombudsman for Children, Trond-Viggo Torgersen, received some inquiries from former Jehova's Witnesses who had experienced physical punishment as children, the issue otherwise became invisible.[2] The prohibition was not mentioned in any governmental documents for almost 20 years after the 1987 law reform, although there were reports to Parliament about related issues. It seems to have become a political non-issue.

Satisfaction with the status quo was confirmed in a Government report to Parliament in 2003 that addressed men's violence within the family. It stated that "as opposed to Norway, many countries still allow parents to punish their children physically within certain limits, and in those countries the perpetrators may perceive their violence as legitimate" (St.meld., No. 29, [2002–2003], p. 50). The Government clearly considered that all forms of physical punishment had been prohibited.

2005: LIGHT SLAPS REVISITED

The prohibition was cited by the courts in a few penal cases concerning violence against children for disciplinary purposes, where the threshold was clearly exceeded (Rt. 1989, p. 282; Court of Appeal LG-2004-8436). But in 2005, the Supreme Court decided a case concerning a stepfather who had given his two stepsons some strokes on the bottom with a flat hand as a reaction to their behavior at school (Rt. 2005, p. 1567). The physical punishment was described as powerful, humiliating to the children, and carried out several hours after the boys' violations had taken place. The stepfather was charged with assault, but acquitted in the County Court. That decision was appealed to the Supreme Court. There, the stepfather's actions were found to clearly exceed the limits of the prohibition against physical punishment. However, the Court added: "even if the parents' right to corporally punish their children has been abolished, the Penal Code section 228 does not apply to parents giving their children lighter slaps with disciplinary intent. . . . In deciding what is permissible, one has to consider the force that has been exercised; the degree of spontaneity in the act; and whether the act was degrading" (para. 24). Thus, not only did the Supreme Court allow parents to use "lighter slaps", which are probably somewhat more intense than the "light slaps" discussed at the time of the prohibition, it also introduced a discretionary power for the courts in making those decisions. This ruling re-introduced confusion about what is permitted and what is not, and reduced the pedagogical effect of the prohibition. The requirement of spontaneity, which previously seemed to have been a prerequisite for allowing light slaps, was reduced to one element to be considered in a discretionary decision.

In its decision, the Court referred to the prohibition's preparatory documents, which were then about 20 years old. In the interim, Norway had ratified the UN *Convention on the Rights of the Child* (CRC) in 1991 and incorporated it into the *Human Rights Act* in 2003. There also had been a change in society's attitudes to children. Astonishingly, the Supreme Court stated that its understanding of the law adhered to the CRC standards, rather than using the CRC and the change in public attitudes as a basis for not adhering to the statements in the preparatory documents (criticized by Backer, 2006; Smith, 2006).

Shortly after the Supreme Court released its decision, the Ombudsman for Children, Reidar Hjermann, sent a letter to the Minister of Justice, emphasizing the need for clarification of the legal situation (Ombudsman for Children, 2005). He emphasized that the decision legitimized physical punishment, raised the threshold of unacceptable violence against children, and placed children at risk, as parents could interpret the decision as childrearing advice. Stating that the decision demonstrated that children's physical integrity was not protected to the same extent as that of adults, he pointed out that the UN Committee on the Rights of the Child had clearly stated that any form of physical punishment is incompatible with the CRC. He also drew attention to the fact that many people were surprised to hear that some form of physical disciplining of children was still permissible in Norway.

Plan Norway and the Global Initiative to End All Corporal Punishment of Children both sent inquiries to the Government. In a 2007 statement, the Norwegian Bishops were among the first to take a public stand in the debate, clearly renouncing all use of violence against children and recommending that the term *tukt* (discipline) be removed from the Norwegian translation of the bible[3] (cited in Ot. prp. No. 104 [2008–2009]). A 2007 study found that one quarter of 18-year-olds had experienced at least mild violence from one of their parents, and 8% reported serious violence from one of them (Mossige & Stefansen, 2007).

In November 2007, a Private Members Bill was put forward by a group of MPs demanding that Norwegian law clearly prohibit all physical punishment of children, including "lighter slaps". The proposal was debated in Parliament and ultimately supported with the recognition that amendment might be needed not only to the *Children and Parents Act*, but also to the *Penal Code* (Ot. prp. No. 104 [2008–2009]).

In the subsequent White Paper, the Ministry of Children and Equality assumed that the legal situation was already such that no form of physical punishment of children was permissible, not even as a means of discipline. They considered that the Supreme Court decision might, however, have created an uncertainty and they proposed an amendment to clarify the law. According to the proposal, any use of physical or psychological violence against children would be prohibited, explicitly including the use of violence as punishment for disciplinary purposes (Høringsnotat, 2008).

The written opinions submitted by organizations and bodies on the White Paper proposal demonstrated engagement in the issue and a broad consensus that all violence against children should be prohibited. This situation represented a substantial shift from 20 years earlier, when the prohibition was presented for general discussion only as part of the report from the Child Abuse Commission. At that time, while many organizations supported the amendment, they did not offer further comments (Ot. prp. No. 8 [1986–1987]). Newspaper reports from that time reveal strong views on both sides of the debate (Ombudsman for Children, 1985).

Only the Director of Public Prosecutions opposed the 2008 proposal in the written hearing, arguing that the acts covered were already prohibited under existing law. He supported the good intentions underlying the proposal, but found that it did not clarify what would be punishable under the *Penal Code*. He argued that all forms of physical power in raising children could not be prohibited, and warned against introducing criminal liability for acts that most parents would accept, such as holding a child after he has happily toppled his milk glass at breakfast over and over again (Ot. prp. No. 104 [2008–2009]).

Backed by the otherwise strong support for the amendment, the Ministry upheld its proposal. The Bill mentioned the international discussions on the topic, and referred to the European Union's *Strategy for Children's Rights* (European Parliament, 2008, para. 42); the Council of Europe's recommendation for a Europe-wide ban on corporal punishment of children (2004); and the UN Committee on the Rights of the Child's *General Comment No. 8* on corporal punishment (2006). A clear statement that no physical or psychological punishment was allowed would be the best way to communicate the standard to parents (Ot. prp. No. 104 [2008–2009]). However, because many organizations had pointed to difficulties in interpreting the term "psychological violence", it was replaced by a sentence prohibiting "the use of violence and frightening, harassing or otherwise inconsiderate behaviour" (Ot. prp. No. 104 [2008–2009], p. 39). While many submissions, such as that from the Norwegian Association of Psychologists, emphasized the importance of guidance to parents concerning positive discipline, the Ministry commented that such guidance already existed (Ot. prp. No. 104 [2008–2009], p. 37).

2010: AN UNAMBIGUOUS PROHIBITION

A clear and explicit prohibition of all physical and psychological violence against children was enacted in 2010. The *Children and Parents Act,* Section 30, third paragraph, now reads:

> The child must not be exposed to violence or otherwise be treated so that its physical or mental health is endangered. This includes violence used in raising the child. The use of violence and frightening, harassing or otherwise inconsiderate behaviour towards the child is forbidden.

As before, violations of the prohibition will not be punishable under the *Children and Parents Act*, but they will be punishable under the *Penal*

Code. With reference to the earlier example of the spilled milk, the Bill says that milder forms of holding the child may, in specific circumstances, be accepted. Also, if a little child is outside in the snow without warm clothes, it is permissible to carry her inside. These acts are seen as acts of prevention or care, which are outside the scope of the prohibition. It is still possible for parents to intervene in order to prevent the child from doing harm to his/herself or others. The much debated "lighter slaps", however, are not permitted (Ot. prp. No. 104 [2008–2009]). In its recent revision of the *Penal Code*, the Ministry of Justice considered whether to include a clarification of children's protection against physical punishment, but found it unnecessary because there could be no doubt today that children have the same right as adults to protection from physical violence under the *Penal Code* (Ot. prp. No. 22 [2008–2009]).

CONCLUSION

Norway's journey to a total prohibition of physical punishment of children has been a long one. In 1972 and 1987 there was a willingness in some parts of society to remove parents' right to use violence in bringing up their children, and the law reforms were a move in that direction. But those reforms were not sufficiently clear, and could be interpreted in favor of parents. Within the political system there was ambivalence, and as late as the 1980s Norwegian society did not seem ready to totally prohibit parental physical punishment of children.

Over the years, there has been little awareness in Norwegian society about the connection between protecting children from parental maltreatment and protecting them from physical punishment. But the ratification of the CRC and its subsequent incorporation into Norwegian law through the *Human Rights Act,* has coincided with, and probably also has been an important force in, a general change of attitude towards children. There has been a shift in perspectives on the relationship between parents and children, towards more autonomy for children and greater reciprocity in families, and a realization that children, perhaps more than anyone, merit protection of their physical integrity. Special attention has been given to minority parents and efforts have been made by local health care and welfare authorities to support them in using positive discipline (Neumayer, Meyer, & Sveaass, 2008). It is hoped that the reform of 2010 will be the final destination of this long journey.

NOTES

1. Since 1996: *Voksne for barn* (*Adults for Children*).
2. He had some difficult discussions with the leader of the congregation, who denied that the physical punishment had occurred (Deputy Ombudsman, personal communication, July 6, 2009).

3. While the Norwegian Church had not been in favor of physical punishment in the 1980s, other Christian organizations and congregations were less clear about their positions, and some were quite forcefully in favor at that time.

REFERENCES

Backer, I. L. (1982). *Barneloven. Kommentarutgave* (The Children and Parents Act: A commentary). Oslo: Universitetsforlaget.

Backer, I. L. (2006). Kan foreldrene gi barna en "lett klaps"? (May parents give their children a "light slap"? in *Festskrift til Carl August Fleischer.* Oslo: Universitetsforlaget.

Bratholm, A. (1980). *Strafferett og samfunn* (Criminal Law and Society). Oslo: Universitetsforlaget.

Befring, A. K. (1991). *Om foreldres rett til fysisk refselse av sine barn—i et historisk, atferdsmessig og rettslig perspektiv* (About the parents' right to discipline their children physically—in a historical, behavioural and legal perspective). Unpublished thesis, Law Faculty, University of Oslo.

Court of Appeal Decision. LG-2004-8436. http://websir.lovdata.no/cgi-lex/wiftzsok?bas=nl&emne1=barneloven&button=S%F8k&sok=fast

Council of Europe. (2004). *Recommendation 1666: Europe-wide ban on corporal punishment of children.* http://assembly.coe.int/main.asp?Link=/documents/adoptedtext/ta04/erec1666.htm

European Parliament. (2008, 16 January). *Resolution: Towards an EU strategy on the rights of the child.* Reference INI/2007/2093. http://www.europarl.europa.eu/sides/getDoc.do?type=TA&language=EN&reference=P6-TA-2008-0012

Flekkøy, M. G. (1991). *A voice for children: Speaking out as their Ombudsman.* London: Jessica Kingsley Publishers.

Hansen, I. S. (1987). Kommentar: Om det nye lovtillegget i barneloven (Commentary: About the new addition to the Children and Parents Act). Interview with Målfrid Grude Flekkøy and Lucy Smith. *Foreldre & barn (Parents and Children) 5,* 22–25.

Høringsnotat. (2008). Forslag til endringer i lov 8. April 1981 nr. 7 om barn og foreldre (barnelova) [White Paper proposing amendments of the Children and Parents Act]. *Barne- og likestillingsdepartementet.* http://www.regjeringen.no/mobil/nb/dep/bld/dok/hoyringar/hoeringsdok/2008/horing—-forslag-til-endring-i-barnelove/horingsnotat.html?id=536972

Interpellasjon from MP Tove Pihl. (1971, April 28). Tidende S. 1970–1971, pp. 2555f.

Melton, G. B. (1991). Lessons from Norway: The Children's Ombudsman as a voice for children. *Case Western Reserve Journal of International Law, 23,* 197–254.

Mjaavatn, P. E. (Ed.). (1984). Barn og straff: En artikkelsamling fra et seminar i Oslo 31.10-02.11.1984 (Children and punishment: A collection of articles from a seminar in Oslo). *NAVFs Senter for barneforskning Rapport, 6.*

Mossige, S., & Stefansen, K. (Ed.). (2007). Vold og overgrep mot barn og unge: En selvrapporteringsstudie blant avgangselever i videregående skole (Violence and abuse against children and young people: A self-reporting study among last year pupils in high school). Oslo: *NOVA Rapport* 20.

Neumayer, S. M., Meyer, M. A., & Sveaass, N. (2008). *Forebygging av vold i oppdragelsen. Samarbeid mellom hjelpeapparat og minoritetsforeldre: En kunnskapsoversikt.* (Prevention of violence in upbringing. Cooperation between public services and minority parents: A knowledge overview). Oslo: Nasjonalt kunnskapssenter om vold og traumatisk stress (NKVTS).

NOU. (1982). *Barnemishandling og omsorgssvikt* (Report from the Child Abuse Commission). No. 26 (referred to as NOU 1982: 26).
Ombudsman for Children. (1985). *Barneombudets årsmelding* (Annual Report).
Ombudsman for Children. (2005). *Brev 15.12.2005 til Justisministeren* (Letter December 15, 2005 to the Minister of Justice). http://www.barneombudet.no/temasider/vold_og_ov/vold_og_ov/arkiv/mot_klapsi
Ot. prp. No. 17. (1971–1972). *Om lov om oppheving av lov 20. juni 1891 nr. 1 om Indskrænkning i Anvendelse af legemlig Revselse m.m.* (Bill on abolishment of the Act of June 20, 1891, on the Limitation of the Use of Corporal Punishment).
Ot. prp. No. 8. (1986–1987). *Om lov om endring i barneloven § 30 (vold og annen mishandling av barn)* [Bill on amendment of the Children and Parents Act (violence and other abuse of children)].
Ot. prp. No. 22. (2008–2009). *Om lov om endringer i straffeloven 20. mai 2005 nr. 28.* (Bill on amendments to the Penal Code). http://www.regjeringen.no/nb/dep/jd/dok/regpubl/otprp/2008-2009/otprp-nr-22-2008-2009-.html?id=540219
Ot. prp. No. 104. (2008–2009). *Om lov om endringer i barnelova mv. (flytting, delt bosted, samvær, vold mv.).* [Bill on amendment of the Children and Parents Act (moving, shared residence, contact, violence etc.)]. http://www.regjeringen.no/nb/dep/bld/dok/regpubl/otprp/2008-2009/otprp-nr-104-2008-2009-.html?id=567744
Parliamentary Debates. Forhandlinger i Lt. No. 4, February 15, 1972; Forhandlinger i Ot. No. 28, February 10, 1972; Forhandlinger i Ot. No. 7, January 10, 1987.
Report to Parliament. (2002–2003). *Om familien—forpliktende samliv og foreldreskap.* (Government Report to Parliament: On the family—binding cohabitation and parenthood). St.meld. No. 29. http://www.regjeringen.no/nb/dep/bld/dok/regpubl/stmeld/2002-2003/stmeld-nr-29-2002-2003-.html?id=471301
Smith, L. (2006). En stefars avstraffelse av to gutter–straffeloven § 228, barneloven § 30 og FNs barnekonvensjon artikkel 19. Rt. 2005 s. 1567. (A stepfather's punishment of two boys.) *Nytt i privatretten* (2) s. 14–16.
Supreme Court Decisions. Norsk Retstidende. (Rt.) 1978, p. 1428. http://websir.lovdata.no/cgi-lex/wiftzsok?bas=hrsiv+hrstr&emne1=rt-2005-1567&button=S%F8k&sok=fast;
Rt. 1978, p. 1506. http://websir.lovdata.no/cgi-lex/wiftzsok?bas=hrsiv+hrstr&emne1=rt-1978-1506&button=S%F8k&sok=fast;
Rt. 1989, p. 282. http://websir.lovdata.no/cgi-lex/wiftzsok?bas=hrsiv+hrstr&emne1=rt-1989-282&button=S%F8k&sok=fast;
Rt. 2005, p. 1567. http://websir.lovdata.no/cgi-lex/wiftzsok?bas=hrsiv+hrstr&emne1=rt-2005-1567&button=S%F8k&sok=fast
United Nations Committee on the Rights of the Child. (2006). *General Comment No. 8: The Right of the Child to Protection from Corporal Punishment and Other Cruel or Degrading Forms of Punishment.* http://www2.ohchr.org/english/bodies/crc/comments.htm

ACTS

Norwegian Act, 1685
Act on the Limitation of the Use of Corporal Punishment, 1891
Child Protection Act (*Vergerådsloven*), 1896
Penal Code, 1902
Child Protection Act, 1953
Act of February 25, 1972, No. 3 on abolition of the 1891 Act on the Limitation of the Use of Corporal Punishment

Children and Parents Act, April 8, 1981, No. 7
Act of February 6, 1987, No. 11, *on amendment of the Children and Parents Act Section 30 (violence and other abuse of children)*
Child Protection Act, July 17, 1992, No. 100
Human Rights Act, May 21, 1999, No. 30
Act of August 1, 2003, No. 86, *on amendments of the Human rights Act (incorporation of the Convention on the rights of the Child)*
Act of April 9, 2010, No. 13, *on amendments of the Children and Parents Act*
Penal Code, May 20, 2005, No. 28 (for the most part not in force by July 1, 2010)

16 Romania
Banning Corporal Punishment of Children

Gabriela Alexandrescu

Population:	21, 472, 331 (November 31, 2009), neighbors are Hungary, Serbia, Ukraine, Republic of Moldova, Bulgaria
Type of government:	Republic, Parliamentary democracy with bicameral Parliament
Governing structure:	Central Government and 42 county representatives of the Government
Child protection system in place:	Yes
Legal system:	Law on the Protection and Promotion of the Rights of the Child—272/21.06.2004
Major religions:	Romanian Orthodox (86.7%), Roman Catholic (4.7%), Protestant (5.3)%
Official national language:	Romanian
Ratified United Nations Convention on the Rights of the Child:	1990
Children's Commissioner/Ombudsman:	No

HISTORICAL CONTEXT

The Greek historian Herodotus recorded the earliest written evidence of people (Dacians) living in the territory of present-day Romania in 513 B.C. In 106 A.D., after several confrontations between the Dacians and the Roman Empire, the Dacian Kingdom became a Roman province. Due to its rich resources, especially silver and gold, the Romans heavily colonized the province, but in the 3rd century A.D., with the invasions of migratory populations, the Roman Empire was forced to withdraw from Dacia. Between the 3rd century A.D. and the 14th century A.D., Dacia was invaded successively by nomadic peoples, including the Huns, the Gepids, the Avars, the Pechenegs, and the Cumans. Romanians lived in three distinct principalities: Wallachia, Moldavia, and Transylvania, the latter being part of the Kingdom of Hungary between the 10th and 16th centuries.

In 1878, under the Treaty of Berlin, Romania was recognized as an independent (from the Ottoman/Turkish empire) state by the Great Powers. Prince Carol I was proclaimed the first King of Romania in 1881. The period from 1878 to 1914 was one of stability and progress for Romania. In 1918, at the end of World War I, Romania became unified. In 1947, Romania became a people's republic under a Communist rule. During Nicolae Ceausescu's regime, which began in the late 1960s, it became a socialist republic. That regime was overthrown as a result of the Romanian revolution of December 1989, and the National Salvation Front proclaimed the restoration of democracy and civil liberties. Romania adopted a new constitution and began intensive economic and political reforms. On January 1, 2007, Romania joined the European Union.

THE RATIONALE FOR LAW REFORM

Violence against children exists to some degree in all societies, and Romania is no exception. Historically, violence was one of the most common responses of parents to conflicts with their children. The belief that one must be severe with a child in order to obtain compliance was widespread. *Beating is from Heaven* was one of the popular proverbial sayings in Romania. The family was considered a closed entity into which no one had the right to intervene. Changing such entrenched beliefs requires political will on the part of government, a clear legal framework, and financial and human resources for awareness-raising and education at the population level. Why then would a state embark on such a lengthy and challenging process?

First, children have rights. There is a human-rights imperative for action to prohibit and eliminate corporal punishment and all other forms of violence against children. Second, the consequences of corporal punishment include emotional and physical suffering and the perpetuation of violent attitudes and actions. Third, children's developmental status makes them particularly vulnerable, so they merit special protection from adults. These were the reasons underlying Save the Children Romania's campaign to ban all corporal punishment of children, which began in 2001. At that time, there was not much international experience to draw from, as only 11 countries had enacted prohibitions.

Save the Children Romania was aware that formalizing the prohibition would not automatically change people's behavior towards their children—in fact, it would be just the first step. Still, such a law would challenge traditional attitudes, send a clear message that it was no longer lawful or acceptable to hit a child, and offer professionals a tool for intervention when necessary to protect children against violence.

THE LEGAL CONTEXT

Prior to the prohibition, the laws related to child maltreatment were vague and inadequate. The words *violence against children* or *corporal punishment* were not included in any law.[1]

The *Family Law*,[2] which deals with the rights and obligations of family members, stated that parents had the responsibility to educate and train their children in order to become useful citizens, but provided no guidance for *how* children should be raised and educated. The use of physical force was only an offence if it caused severe harm. Otherwise, the legal framework did not provide any guidance about the relationship between adults (parents/caregivers or professionals) and children.

The Law on Child Protection[3] in force at that time only prohibited parental behavior which would endanger the life or physical development of the child. If parents were proven to show "abusive behaviour" or "severe neglect", they could lose their parental rights. The Criminal Law[4] stipulated penalties for assault (i.e., rape, incest, sexual intercourse with a minor), which were increased if the victim was a member of the family or child. Therefore, the legal framework did provide the means and the right to intervene within the family, but only when a child's development was severely affected.

AFTER THE 1989 REVOLUTION: LEGAL REFORMS AND NEW INTERNATIONAL RELATIONSHIPS

The transition to capitalism brought increased unemployment, unstable prices, poverty, and lack of adequate housing, which put great pressure on adults, and indirectly affected the lives of children. Families with more than two children were facing serious financial problems, which contributed to increased domestic violence. The social protection system was totally unprepared to deal with these issues. There were no services for children who were victims of violence, except to place them in institutions.

Prior to the revolution, Romanian society had perceived children mainly as persons with needs who should play certain roles in the future society, rather than people with rights. Now, after 50 years of communism, Romanian society had to change its views on citizenship and to acknowledge and respect the rights of every human being, irrespective of gender, age, ethnic or religious background, or any other characteristic. Such a change needed time and continuous efforts by the state and civil society. Several significant developments facilitated this shift.

First, Romania ratified the UN *Convention on the Rights of the Child* (CRC) in 1990, which was a milestone for child protection. With ratification, the state assumed responsibility for fully integrating the CRC's provisions into its legal and institutional frameworks. Article 19[5] provided the stimulus for promoting legal reform, even though protection of children from violence was not one of the issues tackled in the first years of the CRC's implementation.

Then, in 1991, Romania adopted its new *Constitution*. This document stipulated the right of children and young people to special protection and assistance in the fulfillment of their rights. It specified situations in which children needed special protective measures, such as children with disabilities, and child exploitation and labor. But there was no mention of protecting children from violence.

In 1999, the Romanian Government submitted its *Second Periodic Report* to the UN Committee on the Rights of the Child. Early in 2003, during the session prior to its formal examination of Romania's report, the Committee reviewed two alternative reports submitted by non-governmental organizations (NGOs), including Save the Children Romania. Subsequently, the Committee addressed 60 additional questions to the Romanian Government. In its Concluding Observations, the Committee recommended that the Romanian government take the following measures: (1) expressly prohibit all corporal punishment of children; (2) promote nonviolent discipline; (3) establish effective procedures and mechanisms to receive, monitor, and investigate and prosecute instances of maltreatment; (4) strengthen the reporting system by training professionals to identify, report, and manage cases of maltreatment; (5) ensure support services for children in legal proceedings; (6) facilitate the physical and psychological recovery and social reintegration of child victims of violence; and (7) reinforce efforts to prevent and combat violence in families, including awareness-raising campaigns (UN Committee on the Rights of the Child, 2003).

Another important event in the international arena was Romania's admission to the European Union. The official accession negotiations began in early 2000. The negotiation agenda for meeting the EU's criteria included social protection issues—child protection, in particular. The child protection system and the reforms necessary to ensure the quality of services were constantly under review by the European Commission, which allocated funds to support the needed reforms.

As a result of the reorganization undergone by the National Authority for Child Protection and Adoption, and pursuant to Government Decision No. 1432/2004, a National Authority for the Protection of Child's Rights (NAPCR) was established. Its mandate is to monitor and promote children's rights, coordinate efforts to enforce children's rights in all areas concerning them, and support the reform of the child welfare system to prevent parent–child separations, while providing special protection to children temporarily or permanently separated from their parents. NAPCR is responsible for the enforcement of children's rights through legislation and intervention in administrative and judicial procedures. It is a legal entity operating as a specialized body within the Ministry of Labor, Social Solidarity and Family.

RESEARCH REVEALS THE REALITIES OF CHILDHOOD

At the turn of the century, official data on the prevalence of violence in the lives of children were scarce. But after the revolution, research began to develop. In one study, conducted by the World Health Organization (WHO), in partnership with the Romanian Government and the National Authority for Child Protection (Browne et al., 2002), 84% of children said that they were physically punished by their parents, of whom 18% reported being beaten frequently. One in five of the children stated that they were beaten with implements. Almost half (47%) of parents said they physically punished their children. Of these, 79% said they hit their children only with the hand; 16% used both hands and implements; 5% used only implements; and 0.5% frequently left visible marks on their children's bodies. An extrapolation of this last finding to the entire population showed that approximately 25,000 children were suffering frequently from injurious corporal punishment.

Violence in schools was also found to be an issue (Browne et al., 2002). The school environment was characterized by poor teacher–pupil communication, subjective evaluations, sarcasm, an authoritarian teacher style, and the use of traditional rather than modern teaching techniques. As there was no law prohibiting physical punishment in schools, teachers with traditional views still physically punished children (e.g., slapping or beating with a stick).

A study conducted by UNICEF (2002) revealed the existence of physical punishment in child protection institutions[6]. Almost half of the children interviewed had experienced such punishment from teachers, administrative staff, or older children.

In 2002, Save the Children Romania carried out a national study on children's attitudes towards, and experiences of, physical punishment (Save the Children Romania, 2002a). The sample was composed of 1,200 children between the ages of 8 and 13 years living in 15 counties, both urban and rural. Of the sample, 4% reported needing medical care as a result of physical punishment by their parents. Substantial proportions described negative feelings resulting from such punishment: 38% reported feeling sad; 21% humiliated; and 17% unprotected, without any possibility of defending themselves when they were hit. Most believed that hitting children is wrong (81%); that authorities should punish adults who were hitting children (76%); and that corporal punishment should be prohibited by law (82%).

In 2003, Save the Children Romania carried out a qualitative study of children's views of physical punishment. The sample consisted of 1,200 children between the ages of 8 and 13. Overall, children expressed very negative views of this practice. For example, a 13-year-old child said:

> It is the worst thing a person can commit. Humans should protect their family, their friends, not make them suffer.

Although these children condemned physical punishment, they understood some of the reasons why it occurs. For example:

> An irrational act by adults, and sometimes by children, which comes from the education received from their parents.
>
> For imposing one's point of view, for being listened to, for making someone comply or because someone doesn't say what another person wants to hear.
>
> Violence is used as a weapon against someone who does not fulfill your wishes.
>
> One reason may be the stress; financial shortcomings may generate violence, especially in families. Usually, parents quarrel because they don't have enough money. Children are growing up and with increasing age they have more needs; misunderstandings take place, stress appears and with all this comes the violence.
>
> Maybe, especially boys and men, when they are little, aren't supposed to express their emotions, and when a man comes home upset from his work, he won't cry in front of his family, instead he will yell at his children or wife.
>
> Parents use violence as a way of teaching children that what they did was wrong.
>
> At school, children are not listened to but threatened; teachers think that by creating tension and fear, pupils will react in a positive manner. If they cannot face the tensions they shouldn't have become teachers!

A number of pragmatic suggestions were provided in answer to the question "What should be done?"

> . . . there is a need for parental education. A solution may be a school for parents, a special one . . . compulsory for pregnant women . . . (for) the entire maternity leave, expectant mothers should participate in different training, because it is far easier to have a child, even to adopt one, than to educate and raise him/her healthy.
>
> To stop child aggression and exploitation, the law should be more severe with those who abuse children. Also, psychological therapy for the abusers is essential, to reduce the chances of their repeating the crime. Changing adults' attitudes through education is important.

These research findings gave impetus to the campaign to abolish physical of punishment of children in Romania.

THE CAMPAIGN

When Save the Children Romania undertook the campaign to prohibit all physical punishment of children, we expected to face strong opposition from people with traditional attitudes towards childrearing. Moreover, we recognized that to change the law and practice, we would need to address the gaps in the child protection system, the scarcity of social workers and other trained personnel to work with children, and professionals' and parents' lack of knowledge about positive discipline.

After a careful analysis of the situation was completed, the priorities for the campaign were identified, which were to: (1) ban corporal punishment of children; and (2) promote the idea of nonviolent relationships between adults and children. The campaign was designed to address the main stakeholders, who were members of the Government and Parliament; professionals who work with and for children; teachers, parents, and other caregivers; and children and youth. Parliamentarians and government authorities were the first target group to be addressed, as law reform was identified as a crucial component in creating a solid base for the prevention of violence against children.

The Role of Parliament

In 2002, three law proposals referring to domestic violence were submitted for debate in Parliament, but none of them made specific reference to children. Save the Children Romania became an advocate for the legal proposal that was most consistent with children's rights. This proposal was initiated by Mrs. Mona Musca, a politician deeply involved in work to end domestic violence. Her support for the cause was an important factor that contributed to the extension of the debates, beyond politicians and parliamentarians, to the media and the public.

The domestic violence legislation was discussed on several occasions until 2003, when agreement was reached on a final version. During the process, Save the Children recognized that this law would not fully address corporal punishment of children because the law on domestic violence could not include provisions on actions taken outside the family (e.g., child protection or educational institutions). Further complicating the situation was the fact that the implementation of the domestic violence law was coordinated by a new central agency, the National Authority for the Protection of Family, while child protection was the responsibility of the National Authority for Child Protection. As debates about a new law on child protection were beginning, Save the Children decided to advocate for the inclusion of an explicit ban on corporal punishment of children in the new law.

The Role of Public Education

In May 2002, in the Parliament Palace, a public debate was organized that brought together parliamentarians, representatives of the Government, NGOs and the media. It was a very important occasion for Save the Children to advocate for children's rights, and for the acceptance of specific legal provisions to protect children who were the victims of violence. The debate generated both supportive and opposing opinions. This was the first time the issue had been openly debated by legislators and other stakeholders.

In order to increase politicians' understanding of the issue, Save the Children sent letters to all members of the Parliament explaining why certain additions to the law were necessary. Included with each letter was a brochure, *For Those Who Still Believe that Beating is from Heaven* (Save the Children Romania, 2002b). The brochure provided the rationale for banning corporal punishment and emphasized the state's responsibility to uphold children's rights. For example, it stated that:

> Romania is not the only country with such a social problem. There are 10 countries which have banned by law the corporal punishment of children.
>
> Corporal punishment of children within the family or in institutions contradicts the provisions of the UN Convention of the Rights of the Child which Romania ratified in 1990 (Save the Children Romania, 2002b).

The brochure included the UN Committee on the Rights of the Child's statement emphasizing the need to stop harmful traditions, and its recommendation that all appropriate legal and other actions be taken to end physical and humiliating punishment of children. The brochure also provided quotes from children, information about why adults hit children, the principles of positive discipline, and recommendations for action.

Psychologists and social workers organized workshops for parents and teachers on positive discipline. Resource materials, including flyers and brochures for parents, were distributed in 15 counties by Save the Children's volunteers. For example, the brochure *You can make it without smacking!* was aimed at raising parents' awareness of the consequences of corporal punishment and promoting positive, effective and nonviolent ways of disciplining children. The principles promoted were: (1) understanding children's need for communication and cooperation; (2) listening to children; (3) informing children about what their parents expect from them; (4) setting clear limits for children's behavior; (5) being consistent; and 6) developing parents' problem-solving skills. Case studies created a link between theory and practice, making the principles easier to understand and apply. For professionals working with children, the *Good Practices Guide for Preventing Child Abuse* was designed and disseminated. This was a more detailed guide that included practical advice and case studies for implementing positive, nonviolent discipline.

The Role of Media

Several activities were carried out in June 2002 that were covered by the mass media: press conferences, a street campaign, and a *Non-Violence Day*. The central message was brief, aimed at the local community, and addressed old attitudes as represented by the proverb, *Beating is from Heaven*. The key image used to disseminate the message was an image of a sad angel with a bruised eye accompanied by the words, *Beating is not from Heaven*.

The Role of Children

Children participated actively in the campaign. In June 2002, the National Children's Forum was held. This is an annual event that brings together children's representatives from different regions of the country and representatives of the central authorities, giving children an opportunity to ask representatives of the responsible governmental institutions their most burning questions. At the 2002 Forum, children asked why corporal punishment was happening, and what the government was going to do about it. As a follow-up, children launched a *Public Appeal for Non-Violence* which was sent to the media and all responsible authorities with the aim of asking for public support of a corporal punishment ban. This half-page document summarized the impact of corporal punishment on children, asked parents and educators for their support, and asked the authorities to take action.

During the Non-Violence Day, children from 15 counties debated physical punishment and their conclusions were gathered by volunteers. An issue of the magazine *Opinion-Yes!* was dedicated to the children's debates on preventing and combating violence.

The Role of the International Community

In 2001, Save the Children Romania was the first Romanian NGO to join the Global Initiative to End All Corporal Punishment of Children, an international alliance aiming to support and work with national NGOs to lobby state governments to ban all forms of corporal punishment, and to develop public education programs. The Global Initiative, endorsed by UNICEF, UNESCO, and former UN High Commissioners for Human Rights, also provides technical assistance to support states with the process of law reform. Joining the Global Initiative brought Save the Children a new perspective on the role that a prohibition could play in reducing violence against children, as well as the knowledge and resources needed to enact one. Other international organizations that were important in the campaign were the Committee on the Rights of the Child and the European Commission. All of these institutions recognized violence against children as a problem that needed immediate intervention and supported Save the Children's campaign.

RESULTS OF THE CAMPAIGN

In 2003, Law 217/2003[7] on domestic violence was approved. It was the first law in Romania on this issue, and was significant because it officially recognized the problem of domestic violence and was the first sign that there was political will to address it. This law established an institutional framework for preventing and combating domestic violence, the National Agency for the Protection of Family and its family assistants, who are obligated to offer immediate assistance in cases where children are maltreated—and to make a report to the National Authority for Child Protection or the local specialized services. This law also provided a legal framework for developing specific services, including shelters for victims of domestic violence.

Just one year later, in 2004, Law 272[8] on the protection and promotion of children's rights was passed. This law explicitly prohibits physical and humiliating punishment:

> Article 28—(1) The child has the right to be shown respect for his or her personality and individuality and may not be made subject to physical punishments or to other humiliating or degrading treatments. (2) Disciplinary measures concerning the child can only be taken in accordance with the child's dignity, and under no circumstances are physical punishments allowed, or punishments which relate to the child's physical and mental development or which may affect the child's emotional status.
>
> Article 90—It is forbidden to enforce physical punishments of any kind or to deprive the child of his or her rights, which may result in endangering the life, physical, mental, spiritual, moral and social development, bodily integrity, and the physical and mental health of the child, both within the family, as well as in any institution which ensures the protection, care and education of children.

An important aspect of this law is that it obliges professionals working directly with children to report any suspicions of maltreatment, which supports early intervention organizations in their efforts to protect children. If the maltreatment was committed by a professional who was providing services to the child, the employer is obligated to make a report to the authorities and the perpetrators are subject to criminal law.[9,10] Also, specific services for children victims of violence, and their families, can be created by local child protection departments or private institutions.

AFTER LAW REFORM

Prohibiting physical punishment in law was just the first step in ensuring that all children are protected against violence. Changing behavior requires knowledge, practice, and motivation. Since 2004, Save the Children Romania has focused a great deal of effort on developing training workshops and materials. We use a *training the trainers* model in order to reach as many parents and teachers as possible. We have developed training kits, as well as guides for parents and for children.

Because the awareness-raising campaign *Beating is not from Heaven!* had a powerful impact on public attitudes prior to the prohibition, the campaign was relaunched with a focus on informing the public about the new law. The message was disseminated through posters, flyers, and a video spot. The aim of this campaign was to raise awareness of the prohibition and of adults' consequent responsibilities. Save the Children Romania has also developed services to assist children who are victims of violence, which are models of good practice for the authorities.

CONCLUSION

Ending corporal punishment of children is a long-term effort requiring the involvement of the state and of civil society. An NGO can contribute to this process by lobbying and offering expertise, but to have impact at the national level, it has to have strong national and international partners and, most of all, perseverance. As the person who coordinated this campaign, I understood from the beginning how important it is to explain to adults why all forms of violence against children are unacceptable, to give them effective tools for communicating with children, and to educate them about the benefits of nonviolent discipline. We have still a long road to travel, but each day we make progress through our ongoing educational initiatives.

NOTES

1. Constitutia Romaniei—http://www.cdep.ro/pls/dic/site.page?id=339
2. Codul Familiei—http://www.cdep.ro/pls/legis/legis_pck.htp_act?ida=37068
3. Legea 108/1998—http://www.cdep.ro/pls/legis/legis_pck.htp_act?ida=17435
4. Codul Penal
5. "States Parties shall take all appropriate legislative, administrative, social and educational measures to protect the child from all forms of physical or mental violence, injury or abuse, neglect or negligent treatment, maltreatment or exploitation, including sexual abuse, while in the care of parent(s), legal guardian(s) or any other person who has the care of the child."
6. Placement centers or children's homes for orphans or other children in need of protection.
7. http://www.protectiasociala.ro/legislatie/1127883943_217_din_2003.pdf
8. http://www.cdep.ro/proiecte/2004/200/20/4/leg_pl224_04.pdf
9. Article 91—(1) Any person who, through the nature of his or her profession, works directly with a child and has suspicions concerning the existence of a case of child abuse or neglect, must notify the public social security service or the general department for social security and child protection in whose area the respective case was identified.
10. Article 96—If the child abuse or neglect was committed by persons who, based on a legal working contract or another type of contract, were providing the protection, upbringing, care and education of the child, the employers of these persons must notify immediately the criminal investigation authorities and must separate the respective persons from the children who are in their care.

REFERENCES

Browne, K., et al. (2002). *Child abuse and neglect in Romanian families: A national prevalence study 2000*. Bucharest: Romanian Government National Authority for Child Protection.

Committee on the Rights of the Child. (2003). *Concluding Observations: Romania, 32 session, 18th March, 2003*. Available from http://www.unhcr.org/refworld/publisher,CRC,CONCOBSERVATIONS,ROM,3f2595c34,0.html

Save the Children Romania. (2002a). *Child abuse and neglect*. Bucharest: Author.

Save the Children Romania. (2002b). *For those who still believe that beating is from Heaven*. Bucharest: Author.

Save the Children Romania. (2003). *Children say NO to violence*. Bucharest: Author.

UNICEF. (2002). *Violenţa, abuz şi neglijare*. Available from http://www.unicef.org/romania/ro/children_2826.html

17 Serbia

Moving Towards the Abolition of Physical Punishment of Children

Jelena Srna and Ivana Stevanović

Serbia (without Kosovo and Metohija) today	
Territory:	88,361 km²
Population:	7,463,157
Type of government:	Democracy, Republic
Governing structure:	Federal government, autonomous provinces and 160 municipalities
Child protection system in place:	Yes
Legal system:	Criminal Code, Family Law, The Law on the Bases of the System of Education and Upbringing, The Law on Juvenile Offenders and Criminal Justice for Juveniles, and others
Major religion:	Christian Orthodox
Official language:	Serbian
Ratified United Nations Convention on the Rights of the Child:	1990
Children's Commissioner/Ombudsman:	Yes. The post of Deputy Ombudsman for Child Rights was created in the Autonomous Region of Vojvodina in 2002 (appointed 2003) and in the Republic of Serbia in 2005 (elected by the Serbian Parliament in 2008)

HISTORICAL CONTEXT

In the 7th century A.D., Serbian people of Slavic origin settled on the Balkan Peninsula. They lived in the Eastern Roman Empire until the beginning of medieval times, when the first Serbian feudal states were founded. At the end of the 14th century, Serbia came under Ottoman Empire rule. The process of its liberation began in 1804.

The first modern state of Serbia was established in 1878. Until then Serbia was part of a series of territorially and socioculturally different states: the Kingdom of Serbia (1878–1912); the Kingdom of Serbia, Croatia and

Slovenia (1918–1929); the Kingdom of Yugoslavia (1929–1941); the Socialistic Federal Republic of Yugoslavia (1945–1991); the Federal Republic of Yugoslavia (1992–2003); and the State Union of Serbia and Montenegro (2003–2006). Most of those states were created out of wars: The Balkan Wars (1912–1914), World Wars I and II, and regional armed conflicts following the breakdown of the former Yugoslavia: Slovenia (1991), Croatia and Bosnia (1992–1995) and Kosovo (1998–1999). The context of frequent, intensive, extreme, ongoing, and violent change has brought tremendous internal and external strain to people living in Serbia (Srna, 2005). As a post-war society in a painful process of transition, the Republic of Serbia (2006 to date) is now developing as a democratic society on the path towards membership in the European Union, but the outcome of these changes is rather distant and uncertain.

In Serbia, the struggle to end physical punishment of children has been motivated by internal and external factors. On the internal level, the fall of the Milosevic regime in October 2000 created suitable conditions for the development of a democratic society and the improvement of human relations. The period of armed conflicts, isolations, and sanctions ended and Serbia has opened up to the world. Carried forward by new enthusiasm, the Government of Serbia has begun working on reform. Parliament has adopted numerous laws to comply with international criteria and standards. In an atmosphere where people have had enough of violence, governmental and non-governmental sectors together have worked on various initiatives which have resulted in the development of a National Strategy for Prevention of Violence (2005).

Despite these favorable social conditions for achieving the prohibition of corporal punishment of children in Serbia, there are also some unfavorable conditions due to the revival of tradition and religion, which are well known reactions to the fall of communism. On the external level, the Council of Europe has been an influential factor in encouraging Serbia to end corporal punishment (Strasbourg Codex, 2007). Today, Serbia is on the path to creating a safer society for children through the explicit prohibition of corporal punishment at home and in all other settings where adults exercise authority over children.

SOCIOCULTURAL CONTEXT

Contemporary attitudes towards child-rearing in Serbia are difficult to understand without knowing about their deep patriarchal roots. A psychological study on the image of the child in Serbian culture (Trebješanin, 2000) provides some insight. This study involved 20 years of comprehensive, multidisciplinary research including the analysis of various ethnographic, linguistic, historiographical, sociological, pedagogical, and psychological data. The findings reveal two complementary models of the child and child rearing in the Serbian culture: mythical/magical (sacral) and secular/practical.

> In both models the child is by nature a small, helpless, irrational, feeble, dependent being whose fate is to rely on adult care. The difference between the models is in the concept of nature and the process of growing up. The first sacral model is closer to the notion of development as a discontinuous, dramatic and uncertain process; the other, secular and practical one is more utilitarian and closer to the common-sense, empirical perception of development as a linear, continuous and safe process of gradually growing up. (Trebješanin, 2000, p. 346)

Traditional Serbian culture cherishes the cult of male, elder, and ancestor. Children, particularly boys, are associated with good fortune, great value, joy, and immeasurable treasure. But the child is also seen as a weak, protected being that is expected to be unquestioningly obedient. The social power of children is rather low, rising on the scale of authority and responsibility with increasing age.

This implicit traditional model of childhood influences Serbian child-rearing practice in families, schools, and other social institutions (Trebješanin, 2000, p. 298). Traditional Serbs consider punishment to be a valuable and necessary method to produce "a good person". Praising children is rare because it is equated with spoiling them, as illustrated by the proverbs: *Not beaten–not taught* and *Praised–spoiled.*

The power of the belief that *the stick comes from Heaven* can be seen in two Serbian customs typical of the second half of the 18th century. The first is *punching pupils on Saturdays* (Čajkanović, 1973, pp. 17–30). On Saturday afternoons, teachers would beat pupils for no reason. Because these beatings were not done as punishment, what were their purpose and meaning? Perhaps they were carried out as prevention. A famous Serbian ethnologist has proposed that the custom stems from the belief that whipping with a hazelwood stick brings something good and beneficial. Whipping is powerful because it means purification (expelling demons), strengthening (by the force of the hazelwood stick totem), development, and making the spirit stronger (as in a Spartan upbringing).

The second custom is *My flesh, your bones* (Janković, 1958, p. 336). When a child would start attending school, parents would tell the teacher (his spiritual parent), "My flesh, your bones" meaning, "Beat my child freely, make him a strong man!" There is evidence that remnants of this practice exist even today. In recent media reports on the treatment of young drug addicts, they have been shown being severely beaten in church institutions, with the blessings of church authorities and parents.

A sociological study examining the transformation of the Yugoslav family between World Wars I and II (Erlih, 1971) showed that the prevalence of parental beating of children was highest in Serbia (almost 90%, and almost 40% frequently and brutally). In a Multiple Indicator Cluster Survey in 2005, 2716 mothers/caretakers of children aged 2 to 14 years were asked a series of questions about the methods they used to discipline their children when they misbehaved (Statistical Office of the Republic of Serbia and Strategic Marketing Research Agency, 2006). Punishment was the most popular method; almost three quarters (73%) of children between 2 and 14 years of age were subjected to at least one form of psychological or physical punishment by their mothers/caretakers or other household members. Two-thirds were exposed to psychological punishment, half to minor physical punishment, and 7% to severe physical punishment.

HUMAN RIGHTS CONTEXT

The Republic of Serbia/SaM/FRY[1] has been a State Party to the *Convention on the Rights of the Child* (CRC; United Nations, 1989) since 1990, and to both of its protocols, the *Optional Protocol on the Sales of Children, Child Prostitution, and Child Pornography* (2002) and the *Optional Protocol on Children in Armed Conflict* (2002). The Republic of Serbia has also been a member state of the Council of Europe since 2003. The Council of Europe Committee of Ministers has condemned corporal punishment and proposed prohibition in a series of recommendations (R[85]4; R[90]2; R[93]2). Also, the revised *European Social Charter* requires all member states to reform their law to prohibit all corporal punishment and other humiliating treatment or punishment of children, and to promote other proactive administrative and educational measures to recognize and realize children's rights to protection. The Republic of Serbia ratified the *European Social Charter* and the *Revised European Social Charter,* both in 2009.

Upon ratification of the *European Convention on Human Rights* (2003), the 47 member states of the Council take on binding obligations to respect the human rights of all people within their jurisdiction, keeping in mind that children are people, and generally more fragile than adults. The realization of the rights of the child to equal protection from assault under the law and to protection from all forms of violence requires clarity in law that no degree or form of corporal punishment is acceptable or lawful, without exception. This means that the explicit prohibition of all corporal punishment and other humiliating and degrading treatment, at home and in all other settings where adults exercise authority over children, is necessary.

The UN Committee on the Rights of the Child is particularly concerned that corporal punishment in the Serbian family remains lawful, and continues to be widely used. The Committee has urged the Republic of Serbia to expressly prohibit and enforce by law all corporal punishment in the family. The state was further encouraged to undertake awareness-raising campaigns and education programs about nonviolent discipline, and to conduct research into the prevalence of corporal punishment of children in the family and other settings (Committee on the Rights of the Child, 2008).

The new position of Ombudsman—Deputy for Child Rights, was created in the Autonomous Region of Vojvodina in 2002 (appointed 2003), and in the Republic of Serbia in 2005 (elected by the Serbian Parliament in 2008). The position of Deputy for Child Rights, Ombudsman, is still in the process of achieving full legitimacy and authority in Serbian society. In 2006, the new Serbian *Constitution* proclaimed the rights of the child for the first time, and prescribed that they should be regulated by law. An important opportunity, however, was missed by not proclaiming the basic principles of the CRC as constitutional principles.

LEGISLATIVE CONTEXT

The use of corporal punishment as a criminal sanction was abolished in Serbia in December 1873 (Grubac, 2004, p. 134). By the end of the 19th century, the use of corporal punishment as a disciplinary measure in Serbian schools was not encouraged (Pavlovic-Lazarevic, 2009, p. 31), but it was not yet prohibited in the *Primary* or *Secondary School Acts* of 1882. These Acts were not clear on the issue, as "measures for re-education" were allowed but corporal punishment was not explicitly mentioned.

In the 1870s, an anonymous author wrote the following in a Serbian professional journal, *The New School*. "In this case we have to come out decisively against the use of corporal punishment in schools, because today even criminals are not beaten" (Janković, 1958). A number of scientific and professional publications indicate that, at the end of the 19th century, Serbian academicians carefully followed, translated, and disseminated the most modern psychological and pedagogical knowledge (Okanović, 1892; Stojanović, 1894). Professionals in Serbia continuously advocated against corporal punishment of children in schools, condemning such practice and pointing to its numerous short-term and long-term damaging effects, and recommending alternative means of discipline (Gašić-Pavišić, 1988; Janković, 1954; Janković, 1958; Smiljanić, 1977; Tešić, 1959; Tešić, 1974).

In 1929 the *Law on Public Schools* in the Kingdom of Yugoslavia explicitly prohibited corporal punishment as a "measure for re-education" (Article 67). Today, corporal punishment remains prohibited in the *Law on Secondary Schools* (1992), the *Law on the Bases of the System of Education and Upbringing* (2003, 2009) and the *Law on Elementary Schools* (1992). If corporal punishment of children occurs in schools, teachers are considered criminally responsible. However, numerous studies have revealed that physical punishment of children still occurs in Serbian schools. Surveys of children show that between 12% and 40% report being physically punished by their teachers and other staff members (Djordjević & Djordjević, 1988; Gašić-Pavišić, 1998; Plut & Popadić, 2006). The rate is at least three times higher in rural schools (Djordjević & Djordjević, 1988). Studies of teachers' reports have found that between 29% and 40% of preschool teachers (Gašić-Pavišić, 1988; Srna, 1998), 38% of elementary school teachers and 20% of secondary school teachers (Gašić-Pavišić, 1998) report the existence of corporal punishment in educational settings.

In current criminal legislation, corporal punishment is unlawful as a criminal sanction and as a disciplinary measure in penal institutions for juveniles (*Criminal Code*, 2005; *Law on Juvenile Offenders and Criminal Justice for Juveniles*, 2005). However, an assessment of the status of the juvenile justice system in the Republic of Serbia and Montenegro revealed that many young offenders had experienced physical punishment during custody in penal institutions (Conragan, 2002). In another study in penal institutions, every third juvenile offender was aware of the use of corporal punishment, and every fourth stated that he or she had been physically punished (Ilić, 1998).

Labor legislation also prohibits corporal punishment and the violation of these norms is a criminal offence, which results in disciplinary action. This law applies to persons of 15 years of age and older, as they can be legally employed provided they have parental consent for jobs that are not detrimental to their health and development.

While the laws regulating disciplinary actions in schools, penal institutions, and workplaces are clear, corporal punishment in social care institutions for children is not explicitly prohibited (*Law on Social Protection and Social Security Providing to Citizens*, 1991). Research on violence in these institutions has found that half or more of the children had been exposed to physical violence by their closest relatives, and 38% remained exposed to violence during their stay in the institution (Kuzmanović, 2002; Vidanović, 1998). More than a quarter (26%) of children in six residential insitutions for children in state care reported that they had experienced physical violence at least once from a staff member, and 17% of adults working in these institutions reported that some of their colleagues were violent towards the children (Plut & Popadić, 2007).

The law relating to physical punishment in the home is ambiguous. The Serbian *Family Act* (2005) states in Article 69(2): "Parents may not subject the child to humiliating actions and punishments which insult the child's human dignity, and have the duty to protect the child from such actions taken by other persons." Family violence is defined in the Article 197 as "behavior by which a member of the family endangers the bodily integrity, mental health or sanctity of another member of the family". The rights of the child are set out in Articles 261 to 273. However, there is no explicit prohibition of all forms of corporal punishment in the *Family Act*. The full harmonization of domestic legislation in this area could be achieved by adopting a comprehensive *Children Act*, an initiative already started by the Ombudsman.

THE CURRENT MOVEMENT TO ABOLISH ALL CORPORAL PUNISHMENT OF CHILDREN

The Serbian campaign was initiated in October 2007 within the context of the Council of Europe's broader initiative, *Building Europe for and with Children*. The Council for Child Rights (a consultancy body of the Government of the Republic of Serbia) and the Deputy Child Rights Ombudsman of the Autonomous Region of Vojvodina supported this initiative.

The Role of Non-Governmental Organizations (NGOS)

The NGOs' initiative for the legal prohibition of corporal punishment demanded that measures be adopted to stop corporal punishment in all settings, particularly in the family and residential institutions for child care and protection. Eighteen Serbian non-governmental organizations (NGOs) supported this initiative, including: the Association for Alternative Child Care in Families—FAMILIA; ASTRA; Beosupport; Centre for Non-Violent Communication; Children's Cultural Centre, Belgrade; Child Rights Centre, Belgrade; Children's Roma Centre; Counseling Centre against Domestic Violence; Friends of the Children in Serbia; REX Cultural Centre; Dreamland, Zrenjanin; ShockArt; Shkart; SOS Phone for Women and Children Victims of Violence; Victimology Society of Serbia and Youth Integration Centre; Save the Children UK Belgrade office; and UNICEF Belgrade office. These NGOs worked independently and cooperatively, to develop pamphlets, posters, and video spots. The official slogan of the Serbian campaign is, *Always Graceful—Never Forceful, For Childhood without Punishment—For Life without Violence.*

When the campaign was launched in October 2007, the NGOs released a declaration (MANIFESTO) to the public. They called for the following measures to be taken: (1) an explicit legal ban on all forms of corporal punishment of children to ensure the protection of children's dignity and their physical and mental integrity; (2) public awareness campaigns aimed at changing the general acceptance of corporal punishment as a legitimate act; (3) educational programs for all adults who are responsible for the care and education of children (including parents, teachers, child protection workers, child care workers, and staff in correctional institutions), with the aim of teaching them about nonviolent methods of child-rearing, and ensuring effective application of such methods; (4) independent reporting mechanisms to enable children to notify the relevant institutions in cases of maltreatment; (5) support programs for children; (6) research on the scope, characteristics, causes, and consequences of corporal punishment, and to use these findings in designing support programs; and (7) involvement of the media, with encouragement of regular and ethical reporting about the issue, organization of public debates on corporal punishment, and promotion of nonviolent child-rearing.

The Role of Government

The Ministry of Social Policy and the Council for Child Rights proclaimed their commitment to the prohibition of corporal punishment in 2008. A *National Strategy for the Prevention and Protection of Children Against Violence* was adopted in December 2008 with the following strategic aims: (1) to create a safe environment where every child has the right to be protected from all forms of violence (including physical and psychological violence, abuse and neglect, inhuman and humiliating acts, sexual abuse and sexual maltreatment, trafficking in human beings, and all other forms of violence and abuse); (2) to establish a national child protection system to prevent all forms of abuse, neglect and violence; and (3) to introduce measures to abolish the corporal punishment of children. At the same time the Government established a working group to propose a mechanism for implementing the *National Strategy for the Prevention and Protection of Children against Violence*. An Action Plan for implementing the *National Strategy* was finalized in early 2009 and Serbian government adopted them in March 2010.

Also, at the end of 2008, the Council for Child Rights and the Council of Europe began to campaign for law reform with the slogan: *Your hands cherish and protect not punish—hands up against corporal punishment of children*. At that time the institution of the Ombudsman of the Republic of Serbia organized a multidisciplinary conference entitled, *Corporal Punishment of Children in Families—What are the Sanctions?*

The Role of Children

While there are no children's NGOs in Serbia, children and young people were members of the NGOs' Initiative, and participated in creating and conducting campaign activities. For example, children who were members of the NGOs' Initiative visited the Ombudsman and Deputy Ombudsman for Child Rights of Republic of Serbia to explain their demands for legal prohibition of corporal punishment and to ask for his support. This action was well covered by electronic and print media, resulting in numerous public debates. However, children's participation has not been systematically sought in the campaign, nor have children been involved in an ongoing way.

The Role of Media

The electronic and print media have shown quite an interest in initiatives to reform the law to prohibit corporal punishment. They have tended to present the issue neutrally, providing space for different opinions both for and against a ban. However, they have not given much space to professionals' opinions. A 2001 study of the visibility and portrayal of children in adult media showed that the inclusion of professionals' views concerning children is rare in the Serbian media[2] (16% of all statements about children in the press and 21% on television), which is four times less than is found in the United States (Korać & Vranješević, 2001). The authors of the study describe how children are typically portrayed by the media:

> Children are members of a rare, helpless and rather endangered species. The members of this species are mostly of indefinite age, sex and social status. All they are capable and fond of doing is playing and having fun. Apart from that, there is little they can do or understand and even less say. We adults are there to protect them from all risks and dangers. That is exactly what we are doing, as far as other responsibilities and financial resources permit, because we are kind, considerate and caring. On the rare occasions when child-related themes appear in the media, they are essentially an opportunity for adults to boast of their good deeds or to complain of the conditions obstructing them, or both. If a child picture or statement accompanies the theme, it usually draws attention to what adults are doing. This is not to say that this is done intentionally, but rather that it reflects *an implicit philosophy of childhood, equally based on traditional conceptions and striking ignorance concerning children.* (Korać & Vranješević, 2001, p. 141; italics added)

The Role of Professionals

While professional voices are united that corporal punishment is unacceptable in school settings, there is more debate about its acceptability in the home. Arguments continue about the appropriate age at which children should be physically punished, the appropriate circumstances, how frequently and how severely they should be punished, and which parts of the body should be targeted. These discussions usually ignore the issue of the long-term consequences of physical punishment and suggest that the short-term end justifies the means (Gašić-Pavišić, 1988).

The majority of Serbian professionals seem to be apathetic about the issue of corporal punishment. A rare example of a professional contribution to the visibility of the corporal punishment in schools issue was a recent exhibition, *From Punishment to Child Rights*, which opened in April 2009 in the Belgrade Educational Museum (Pavlović-Lazarević, 2009). It gave a vivid, multimedia, historical review of the issue of physical punishment as a disciplinary measure in school, raising public awareness and initiating dialogue about the problem of school violence. The exhibition has aroused great interest, which has kept it open for a long time.

CONCLUSION

A comprehensive legal ban on the corporal punishment of children will be but a first step in a long process of making the world a better place for children in Serbia. Further progress, we believe, will be much more challenging due to several characteristics of Serbian society: (1) a general lack of knowledge about child development and effective parenting; (2) powerful traditional values supporting corporal punishment; (3) deep divisions in opinions and ambivalent attitudes towards change; and (4) children's lack of a public voice. We are at the beginning of a complex and delicate process, demanding wisdom and a synergy of powers and resources. This is a process requiring persistence, patience, strong partnerships, and ongoing support from the international community.

NOTES

1. State Union of Serbia and Montenegro; Federal Republic of Yugoslavia.
2. The study assessed 16 highly rated media over 2 months.

REFERENCES

Čajkanović, V. (1973). *Mit i religija u Srba*. Beograd: Srpska književna zadruga.

Committee on the Rights of the Child. (2008). *Concluding Observations on the Republic of Serbia*. UN Doc. CRC/C/SRB/CO/1.

Conragan, C. (2002). *Children in conflict with the law: Victims of the transition–An assessment of the juvenile justice system in the Republic of Serbia and Montenegro*. UNICEF.

Djordjević, B., & Djordjević, J. (1988). *Učenici o svojstvima nastavnika*. Beograd: Prosveta.

Erlih,V. (1971). *Jugoslavenska porodica u tranziciji*. Zagreb: Liber.

Gašić-Pavišić, S. (1988). *Kažnjavanje i dete*. Beograd: Prosveta.

Gašić-Pavišić, S. (1998). Nasilje u školi. u M. Milosavljević, M. (Ur.), *Nasilje nad decom*. Beograd: Fakultet političkih nauka, Univerzitet u Beogradu.

Grubač, M. (2004). *Telesna kazna u Srbiji 1804–1883*. Beograd: Službeni glasnik.

Ilić, Z. (1998). Zlostavljanje dece (mladih) u vaspitnim i vaspitno-popravnim ustanovama. u M. Milosavljević (Ur.), *Nasilje nad decom*. Beograd: Fakultet političkih nauka, Univerzitet u Beogradu.

Janković, M. B. (1954). Iz istorije telesne kazne kod nas u školi. *Savremena škola, IX 3–4*, 196–207.

Janković, M. B. (1958). Još iz istorije telesne kazne kod nas u školi. *Savremena škola, XIII 5–5*, 325–339.

Korać, N.,& Vranješević, J. (2001). *Nevidljivo dete—Slika deteta u medijima.* Beograd: Jugoslovenski centar za prava deteta.
Kuzmanović, B. (Ur). (2002). *Deca bez roditeljskog staranja.* Beograd: Institut za psihologiju, Save the Children UK.
Okanović, S. M. (1892). *Vaspitne kazne i nagrade.* Beograd: Štamparija Petra K Tanaskovića do delijske česme.
Pavlović-Lazarević, G. (2009). *Katalog izložbe: Od kaštiga do ljudskih prava.* Beograd: Pedagoški muzej.
Plut, D., & Popadić, D. (2006). *Škola bez nasilja- ka sigurnom i podsticajnom okruženju za decu.* UNICEF, Institut za psihologiju Filozofskog fakulteta.
Plut, D., & Popadić, D. (2007). *U lavirintu nasilja—istraživanje nasilja u ustanovama za decu bez roditeljskog staranja u Srbiji.* Beograd: Save the Children UK & Institut za psihologiju .
Smiljanić, D. J. (1977). *Naša škola, 1–2,* 147–153.
Srna, J. (1998). Nasilje nad malom decom. u M. Milosavljević (Ur.), *Nasilje nad decom.* Beograd: Fakultet političkih nauka, Univerzitet u Beogradu.
Srna, J. (2005). Towards reconciling with ourselves and others. *Psihologija,* 38, 117–132.
Statistical Office of the Republic of Serbia and Strategic Marketing Research Agency. (2006). *The Republic of Serbia Multiple Indicator Cluster Survey 2005, Final Report,* pp. 58–60. Belgrade: UNICEF.
Stojanović, J. V. (1894). *Metodika školske discipline,* Niš, Prva niška štamparija Ž. Radovanovića.
Strasbourg Codex. (2007). *Eliminating Corporal Punishment—A Human Rights Imperative for Europe children,* 2nd ed., F/67075. Council of Europe Publishing.
Tešić, V. M. (1959). *Da li smemo da primenjujemo telesne kazne.* Beograd: Rad.
Tešić, V. M. (1974). *Moralno vaspitanje u školma Srbije 1830–1878.* Beograd: Zavod za nastavna sredstva.
Trebješanin, Ž. (2000). *Predstava o detetu u srpskoj kulturi.* Beograd: Jugoslovenski centar za prava deteta.
United Nations. (1989). *Convention on the Rights of the Child.* Available at www.un.org/documents/ga/res/44/a44r025.htm
Vidanović, I. (1998). Nasilje nad decom u dečjim domovima. u M. Milosavljević (Ur.), *Nasilje nad decom.* Beograd: Fakultet političkih nauka, Univerzitet u Beogradu.

LIST OF RELEVANT INTERNATIONAL CONTRACTS AND LAWS

The Law on Ratification of the Convention on the Rights of the Child, SFRY Official Gazette—International Contracts, no. 15/90 and FRY Official Gazette, no. 4/96 and 2/97.
The Law on Ratification of the Optional Protocol on the Sales of Children, Child Prostitution, and Child Pornography, FRY Official Gazette—International Contracts, no. 22/02.
The Law on Ratification of the Optional Protocol on Children in Armed Conflict, FRY Official Gazette—International Contracts, 22/02.
The Law on Ratification of the European Convention on Human Rights, FRY Official Gazette—International Contracts, no. 9/03; FRY Official Gazette—International Contracts, no. 5/05.
The Constitution of the Republic of Serbia. Official Gazette of the Republic of Serbia, no. 83/06.

Law on the Abolition of Corporal Punishment. Proceedings of the laws and regulations, no. XXVI1873.

The Law on Public Schools in the Kingdom of Yugoslavia. no. 97.948, December 15, 1929.

The Law on Juvenile Offenders and Criminal Justice for Juveniles. Official Gazette of the Republic of Serbia, no. 85/05.

Criminal Code. Official Gazette of the Republic of Serbia, no. 85/05.

The Law on Elementary Schools 1992. Official Gazette of the Republic of Serbia, no. 50/92, amended 1993, 1994, 1996, 2002, 2003.

The Law on Secondary Schools. Official Gazette of the Republic of Serbia, no. 50/92, 50/93, 67/93, 48/94, 24/96, 23/2002, 25/2002.

The Law on the Bases of the System of Education and Upbringing. Official Gazette of the Republic of Serbia, no. 62/03, 64/03, amended 2004, no. 58/04.

The Law on the Bases of the System of Education and Upbringing. Official Gazette of the Republic of Serbia, no. 84/09.

The Family Act. Official Gazette of the Republic of Serbia, no. 101/05.

The Law on Social Protection and Social Security Providing to Citizens. Official Gazette of the Republic of Serbia, no. 36/91, amended 1993, 1994, 1996, 2001, 2004, 2005.

18 Spain

Banning Physical and Humiliating Punishment in the Home

Pepa Horno Goicoechea

Population:	44,708,000
Type of government:	Democracy, Constitutional Monarchy
Governing structure:	17 provincial governments and 2 territorial governments
Child protection system in place:	Yes
Legal system:	Criminal Code at national level, Child Protection Acts at the provincial/territorial level
Major religion:	Christianity
Official national language:	Spanish, Catalan, Eusquera, Galician
Ratified United Nations Convention on the Rights of the Child:	1990
Children's Commissioner/Ombudsman:	Yes

> If they hit me, I learn to hit.
>
> (12-year-old Spanish girl).

> The other day, my friend's mother smacked him because we crossed the street when the red light was on, but we were afraid of missing our bus and I cannot understand it because when she is alone, she usually does it herself.
>
> (10-year-old Spanish boy).

HISTORICAL CONTEXT

Historically, Spain was one of the great powers of Europe. Different kingdoms, cultures and religions (Judaism, Catholicism, and Islam) had lived together there for centuries. Columbus' voyage to America in 1492 established Spain as the "bridge" between Latin America and Europe. Through the 18th and 19th centuries, Spain underwent many political changes and gradually lost power at the international level. The Catholic Church has been a very powerful force and it continues to be the main religion of Spain. Each of the two main political parties represents almost half of the Spanish population. To understand contemporary Spain it is necessary to know its 20th-century history. The Spanish Civil War, the 40 years of dictatorship that followed, and the social, political, and legal efforts to establish democracy in the last two decades of the 20th century, have shaped modern Spain and its efforts to end violence against children.

The process of law reform to ban physical and humiliating punishment[1] in the home was a long one in Spain. It began with the government's ratification of the United Nations *Convention on the Rights of the Child* (CRC) in 1990, and ended with an explicit prohibition in 2007.

THE 1990s: REFORM BEGINS

Several key reforms were achieved in the 1990s. Physical and humiliating punishment was abolished from schools in 1997. The Spanish *Penal Code,* enacted in 1995, already stated that "any type of violence against children is forbidden". But the *Civil Code* still stated that parents could "correct children reasonably and moderately" (Articles 154, 238). Some judges considered this law to allow physical and humiliating punishment in the home, but others considered physical and humiliating punishment to be a form of violence and viewed the *Penal Code* as being very clear in prohibiting it. Therefore, judges' personal views were influencing the implementation of the law.

In 1997, the Spanish Ministry of Labor and Social Affairs carried out a study of the attitudes of Spaniards towards physical and humiliating punishment (Ministry of Labor and Social Affairs, 1997) with a sample of 3,500 Spaniards, including 1,026 parents. It revealed that 47% of adults living with their children believed that it was essential to hit children sometimes. Among adults living with children, 2% believed that it was essential to hit children often. Women believed in the necessity of physical punishment more than men; (43% and 37%, parents and non-parents, respectively); parents with primary school education approved of it more than parents with a university degree (49% and 5%, respectively); and older adults (aged 30 to 60) approved of it more than young adults (aged 18 to 29; 40% and 32%, respectively).

At the same time, an incidence study was conducted in Madrid (Ministry of Labor and Social Affairs, 1998), showing that 28% of 1,500 parents reported hitting their children within the previous month an average of 3 times, and 3% of parents reported that they had physically punished their children severely.

In its *Concluding Observations* to the Spanish government, the Committee on the Rights of the Child recommended in 1998 and 2002 that the *Civil Code* be clarified so that it could be understood. At that time, the conservative People's Party was the governing party. The government held that the *Penal Code* was already clear in prohibiting all forms of violence against children, including physical and humiliating punishment in the home. Due to the findings of previous research, the government recognized the need for public education on the issue, and supported the first awareness-raising campaign, *Educate, Don't Punish* (Horno, Benito, Suárez, de Miguel, & Save the Children Spain, 2000; Horno, Calderón, Berzal, García, González, & Save the Children Spain, 1999). This campaign ran from 1999 to 2001, coordinated by Save the Children, UNICEF, and the two major parents' associations–one secular (Confederación Española de Asociaciones de Padres y Madres de Alumnos, Spanish Federation of Parents Associations, called CEAPA) and the other Catholic (Confederación Católica de Asociaciones de Padres y Madres de Alumnos, Spanish Federation of Catholic Parents Associations, called CONCAPA).

Approximately 15,000 parents and professionals received training during those 3 years, and more than 200 media interviews were conducted. Materials on positive parenting were developed for parents, for professionals working with families, and for children (see www.savethechildren.es). These materials focused on child rights, child development, and the importance of attachment. They gave information on positive discipline to help parents eliminate violence while maintaining their authority, and improve their nonviolent conflict resolution skills. The campaign also included advocacy and awareness-raising activities, and a roundtable with politicians which took place in Barcelona and was led jointly by Save the Children and the Ministry of Labor and Social Affairs (Del Molino, Horno, Santos, Save the Children Spain, & Ministry of Labor and Social Affairs, 2000).

THE TURN OF THE CENTURY: REFORM STALLS

As a result of the campaign, a working group led by the government was set up in 2000, to examine the issue of law reform, and propose wording for a clarification of the existing Spanish law on physical and humiliating punishment of children. The working group included the Ministry of Justice, the Ministry of Labor and Social Affairs, and Save the Children Spain. Their work progressed quickly towards a re-wording of Articles 154 and 238 of the *Civil Code*. It appeared that the proposed reform was going to be approved, but problems with the text blocked the process some months later, and the campaign ended in 2001 without the law reform being approved.

But Save the Children Spain continued its training and advocacy activities, with some support from UNICEF and the Children's Ombudsmen in Madrid, Baleares Islands, and Catalonia. Save the Children Spain organized a national child consultation, in coordination with the National Childhood Platform, and the Ministry of Labor and Social Affairs[2]. Of the group of 112 children from 6 to 16 years old who participated, 46% said that it is never necessary to hit a child to educate him/her, 41% said it was sometimes necessary and 4% said it is often necessary. In contrast, only 21% said that it is never necessary to shout, while 68% thought shouting was sometimes necessary, and 2% thought it was often necessary. Among this group of children, approximately half thought that mothers (47%) and fathers (46%) have the right to physically punish and shout at their children, while less than one-quarter thought that grandparents (14%) and siblings (17%) had the right to do so. Only 5% of the children thought that teachers have the right to hit and shout at children. They reported that physical and humiliating punishment produces feelings of pain, sadness, anger, fear, guilty, loneliness, and indifference.

In addition, the National Sociological Research Centre conducted a study of public attitudes towards physical punishment in 2004. Only 26% of 2,500 adults (including those living with children and those not living with them) thought that it was necessary to smack *their own children*. But when they were asked whether it was necessary to smack *children in general*, 59% thought it was necessary in some cases.

Between 2001 and 2004, three regional governments (Valencia, Catalonia, and Castilla la Mancha) reformed their child protection laws to abolish physical and humiliating punishment of all children in any context.

2005–2007: REFORM RESURGES

In 2005, Save the Children Spain published a report showing the most common forms of physical and humiliating punishment in Spain, as identified in training workshops for parents, included: slapping; smacking on the bottom; hitting on the head; shaking; insulting; shouting; threatening; pulling hair or ears; pinching; hitting with a ruler or a belt; making comparisons among children; public humiliation; ridiculing; name-calling; indifference; blaming; discriminating against particular children; locking children away in the dark or forcing a child to face the wall (Horno & Save the Children Spain, 2005). This report provoked a great social debate, because it showed similarities with forms of punishment identified in Spain and those found during training activities in other countries in Latin America, as well as in the South and South East Asian regions.

Following the debate that took place in the mass media after this report was published, further developments took place. In November 2005, the government (a party of the left was in power at that time) announced its intention to pursue law reform and reactivated its awareness-raising activities, collaborating with Save the Children Spain on a new campaign called, *To Teach is Not to Hit*, which continues today. This second campaign was based on experiences from the previous campaign. New awareness-raising materials were designed, as well as training and advocacy activities.

The campaign included a conference in the Spanish National Parliament, an International Congress (Save the Children, & Ministry of Labour and Social Affairs, 2006), and a letter to Parliamentarians signed by Save the Children, UNICEF, and the Madrid Regional Community Ombudsman (Save the Children, & Ministry of Labour and Social Affairs, 2005).

Also in 2006, the government reactivated the working group on law reform, which met over the course of a year to develop a concrete proposal. One of the issues that had to be resolved was the controversy related to the word "punishment". This word has particular historical significance in Spain. It is connected in the minds of many to the dictatorship of Francisco Franco, who emerged as the leader of the Nationalists following the Spanish Civil War. He dissolved the Spanish Parliament in 1939 and established an authoritarian regime that lasted until his death in 1978. During these years, dissidence was punished with heavy prison sentences, torture, forced labor and the death penalty, and the law used the word "punishment" to refer to many of these acts. With the transition to democracy following Franco's death, the word "punishment" was intentionally excluded from the new *Civil Code*. The Spanish government did not wish to re-introduce this word into law, so the working group had to find a way of prohibiting physical and humiliating punishment without explicit reference to "punishment".

The text proposed by the working group included a reference to Article 19 of the CRC: "Parents are legally responsible for children. This responsibility will be exercised always in the best interests of children, according to their personality and respecting their physical and psychological integrity". The working group proposed that this legislation be included in a broader reform of the *International Adoption Law*.

The reform bill was presented to Parliament in the last session of 2007. It was discussed in the presence of the President and all Parliamentarians, and it was well covered by the media. There was considerable debate, but the bill was approved by a majority of Parliamentarians. It was opposed by three of the main parties. The right party argued that the reform was unnecessary, and two regional nationalist parties believed that Spanish society was not ready for the reform, reflecting the different positions present in Spanish society. In the end, however, the prohibition was included in the *National Law of International Adoption* (Article 154) in December 2007. This process generated a major public debate that greatly enhanced awareness of the issue.

While the new text does not include a specific reference to physical and humiliating punishment, it does eliminate the concept of "reasonable punishment" and affirms children's right to physical and psychological integrity. One of the most important aspects of the law is that it is part of the *Civil Code*, which regulates the rights and duties of parents but has no penal authority, making the law primarily educational. Unfortunately, the media covered the law as if it was a penal law, suggesting that "now smacking our children will take us to jail". As a result, further effort is required to change social attitudes.

CONCLUSION

The success of the law reform initiative in Spain is the result of a major collective effort led by Save the Children, the Ministry of Labor and Social Affairs, UNICEF, the Spanish Parents' Associations, and the Children's Ombudsmen, particularly in the Madrid Regional Community. In all, 80 organizations were involved. This network was a key element in the success of the Spanish campaign.

It is important to understand that legal reform is only a part of the process of eradicating the physical and humiliating punishment of children. The focus now must remain on education and the promotion of social attitude change, in order to avoid misunderstanding of the purpose of legal reform, which is to guarantee children full protection and full implementation of their human rights.

The Spanish experience has shown that legal reform, education for parents and professionals about positive parenting and awareness-raising activities must be developed simultaneously. A legal framework that includes a total ban on physical and humiliating punishment legitimizes and supports public education efforts. Legal reform alone does not change the hearts of people (Harper, et al., 2005) but without it, work for social change does not have a normative framework to give it credibility. Legal reform gives credibility to social change, and social change requires a legal framework that recognizes children's human rights.

One of the main things learned during this process is that ending the physical and humiliating punishment of children is a particularly difficult challenge because it affects families more than any other form of violence. When it is questioned, parents—including those who are journalists, judges, and politicians—are likely to feel not only that their authority is being questioned, but that their affective relationships, including those with their own parents, are being judged. Success in this effort requires gaining the hearts of the people. The process proceeds heart by heart, and requires a great deal of time, large networks and boundless optimism.

NOTES

1. According to Save the Children's definition, "physical punishment includes hitting a child with the hand or with an object (such as a cane, belt, whip, shoe, and so on); kicking, shaking or throwing a child, pinching or pulling their hair; forcing a child to stay in an uncomfortable or undignified position, or to take excessive physical exercise; burning or scarring a child (and the threat of any of these actions)" (Harper, Horno, Landsdown, et al. 2005, p. 16).

2. www.cis.es

REFERENCES

Del Molino, C., Horno, P., Santos, A., Save the Children Spain, & Ministry of Labour and Social Affairs. (2000). *Una legislación en defensa de los derechos de los niños y niñas: Propuesta de reforma de los artículos 154 y 238 del Código Civil Español* (*Legislation in defence of children's rights: Proposal to reform Articles 154 and 268 of the Spanish Civil Code*). Madrid: Save the Children.

Harper, K., Horno, P., Landsdown, G., Martin. F., Newel, P. Nilson, M., & International Save the Children Alliance. (2005). *Ending physical and humiliating punishment: Manual for action.* Stockholm: International Save the Children Alliance.

Horno, P., Benito, A., Suárez, S., de Miguel, D., & Save the Children Spain. (2000).

Educa, no pegues: Manual de formación para profesionales de ocio y tiempo libre (*Educate, don't punish. Training manual for professionals who work with children*). Madrid: Save the Children.

Horno, P., Calderón, B., Berzal, R., García, L., González, R., & Save the Children Spain. (1999). *Educa, no pegues: Manual de formación para profesionales que trabajan con padres y madres* (*Educate, don't punish. Training manual for professionals who work with parents*). Madrid: Save the Children.

Horno, P., & Save the Children Spain. (2005). *Amor, poder y violencia: un análisis comparativo de los patrones de castigo físico y humillante* (*Love, power and violence: A comparative analysis of physical and humiliating punishment patterns*). Madrid: Save the Children.

Ministry of Labour and Social Affairs. (1997). *Actitudes de los españoles ante el castigo físico infantil* (*Spanish adults' attitudes toward corporal punishment.*) Madrid: Author.

Ministry of Labour and Social Affairs. (1998). *Violencia en ciudades de Latinoamérica y España* (*Violence in Latin-American and Spanish cities*). Madrid: Author.

Save the Children Spain, & Ministry of Labour and Social Affairs. (2005). *Corregir no es pegar*, tríptico para padres y para profesionales (*To teach is not to hit*). (Leaflet) Madrid: Save the Children.

Save the Children, & Ministry of Labour and Social Affairs. (2006). *Emotional children—education in families.* Madrid: Save the Children.

Save the Children Spain, UNICEF, CEAPA, & CONCAPA. (1999). *Educa, no pegues* (*Educate, don't punish*; Public campaign manifesto, general campaign guide, guide for parents, pamphlet, poster, comic for parents and children.) Madrid: Save the Children.

19 Sweden

A 30-Year Ban on Physical Punishment of Children

Staffan Janson, Bodil Långberg, and Birgitta Svensson

Area:	174,000 sq mi (450,000 km²), the third largest country in Western Europe
Population:	9.3 million inhabitants
Languages:	Swedish; recognized minority languages: Sami (Lapp), Finnish, Meänkieli (Tornedalen Finnish), Yiddish, Romani Chib
Form of government:	Constitutional monarchy, parliamentary democracy
Child protection system in place:	Yes
Parliament:	The Riksdag, with 349 members in one chamber.
Major religions:	Church of Sweden (Lutheran) 72.9% but at least 45% of the population can be classified as agnostic or atheist
Ratified United Nations Convention on the Rights of the Child:	1990
Children's Ombudsman:	Since 1993

HISTORICAL CONTEXT

Modern Sweden was established in the 16th century during the reign of King Gustav Vasa, who fought for an independent and unified Sweden. During this time, Gustav Vasa broke with the Roman Catholic Church and established a Protestant Reformation. In the 17th century, Sweden expanded its territories to form the Swedish Empire, which included Norway, Denmark, Estonia, and parts of northern Germany. Over the subsequent two centuries, most of these conquered territories were lost in wars. Since its last war in 1814, Sweden has been at peace and has remained neutral in wartime. During the 19th century, citizens' political influence was strengthened gradually. Voting reform occurred in 1909, which gave men the right to vote. In 1921, women gained the right to vote and run for office. In the middle of the 20th century, Sweden established a general social welfare system, including tax-financed education, child care, health care, pensions, elderly care, and social services.

In 2009, it was 30 years since Sweden introduced a ban on all forms of violent and emotionally abusive treatment of children by their caregivers. In so doing, Sweden became the first country in the world to prohibit violence as a means of child-rearing. The abolition of corporal punishment means that children in Sweden have the same legal rights as adults to integrity and protection from violence and other humiliating treatment.

The background of this historical event will be described in this chapter, as well as the impact this law reform has had on public knowledge, attitudes, and behavior up to the present time.

THE HISTORY OF CORPORAL PUNISHMENT IN SWEDEN

Our knowledge about child abuse in Sweden in former times is limited. Before the 17th century, criminal justice was handled by laymen, and there exists practically no written record of their decisions. Over time, legal cases went from being subjects of negotiation in the local setting, to being handled by experts. From about 1600, Sweden developed a uniform organization of courts with professional judges on municipal and higher levels. Records of testimonies about child maltreatment[1] from that time exist, although they are sparse.

Swedish historians (Österberg & Lindström, 1988) have, however, clarified that as early as the Middle Ages, corporal punishment of children was not supposed to inflict injuries. Physical punishment was to be used to reprove, not as revenge. A clear demarcation was made between 'maltreatment' and 'milder violence' in childrearing, and severe maltreatment was condemned. A number of proverbs dating from the 17th century instruct parents to administer corporal punishment with love, and as a measure to teach children to become good citizens and to fear God. It was to be well-considered, not used in anger. This way of thinking led to some children being beaten at the end of the week for earlier transgressions, an act that would be regarded with disgust in modern Swedish society. Two other ideas that characterized that period were that: (1) boys in particular (but also girls) should be hardened through exposure to hardships such as cold, heat, and hard work, rather than through beatings; and (2) parents should be strict with the youngest children so that they would learn to obey from an early age (Bergenlöv, 2009).

As a Christian country, Sweden was heavily influenced by the tradition of corporal punishment within that faith. It was not until the end of the 19th century, when Sweden became industrialized and secularized, that the legitimacy of corporal punishment was questioned widely. This change occurred earlier in cities than in rural areas, perhaps because homes were more private and isolated in cities than they had been in the earlier agrarian village societies. Urbanization and the rise of the working class meant that many people lost their connection to the local community and the control mechanisms fostered by close contact with neighbors. From 17th- and

18th-century records, we know that neighbors often intervened if children were punished too harshly. In old peasant societies, families consisted of big open households, where many adults knew what was going on and could stop or prevent maltreatment (Bergenlöv, 2009).

THE EVOLUTION OF THE WELFARE STATE

The public spirit of the 18th century was influenced by philosophical ideas such as Humanism and the Enlightenment, with their strong belief in reason. Politics and the state started to focus on the importance of a healthy and strong population (workforce), which in many respects also meant increased care for children. The Swedish Statistical Bureau was founded in 1749, and from that time Sweden has collected detailed statistics on mortality. In the mid 1700s, the infant mortality rate was about 20% (compared to 0.2–0.3 % in 2008). The Swedish state began to take responsibility for the well-being of the population, and started to publish pamphlets on child care, including one by the father of pediatrics, Nils Rosén von Rosenstein. His 1764 handbook was translated into 10 other languages. At this time the first midwives were trained and young unmarried mothers got help so that they did not kill their newborn babies. During the 18th century an understanding of childhood as a specific phase in life evolved. The idea came to predominate that children should be allowed enough space for play and development, and not too many restrictions should be placed on their behavior.

THE 20TH CENTURY: "THE CENTURY OF THE CHILD"

In 1900 the Swedish author, Ellen Key, published her ground-breaking book, *The Century of the Child*, in which she rejected the corporal punishment of children, describing it as stupid and dangerous (Key, 1996). Soon after, in 1902 the first Swedish law on child care was introduced in which the state was given the right to take a child into custody in case of severe physical maltreatment in the home. In 1942, this intervention was extended to include children who were psychologically maltreated by their families. The motivation for these developments was children's need for protection in the case of parental incompetence.

New radical ideas emerged in the 1930s, and scientific discoveries in child development began to replace the traditional religious ethical framework (Myrdal, Åse, & Hirdman, 2002). The role of parents was no longer to demand obedience, but to understand the child. Instead of fear, parenting focused on honesty and confidence. Arguments from the 18th-century Enlightenment were stressed—that corporal punishment created hatred and bitterness across generations, and that it was time to break this devastating cycle of violence. In the 1930s and 1940s, the new welfare state began to take responsibility for children's education through new pedagogy, and for their well-being through reforms in housing, hygiene, medical treatment, and prevention. It was during these years that publicity campaigns about the negative impact of physical and emotional punishment began. Meetings and lectures were organized by non-governmental organizations (NGOs), educational associations and individuals, which engaged parents and other carers in discussions about how to raise children without violence. Physical punishment was also debated on the radio and in newspaper articles, and public awareness was raised about the lasting damage to children that results from violence. It was argued that children should be treated with respect and understanding if they were to grow into responsible citizens. In the 1930s, Swedish newspapers published articles revealing that many children in institutions had been exposed to systematic physical abuse over long periods of time. Ten years later, the regulations governing children's reformatories were changed to include a ban on all forms of corporal punishment.

CHILD WELFARE: A GOVERNMENTAL RESPONSIBILITY

At the beginning of the last century, Sweden was one of the poorest countries in Europe—about one-fifth of the population emigrated to the United States, mainly due to starvation. As late as the 1930s Sweden and Spain had the poorest dwellings in Europe. After World War II, however, Sweden rapidly became wealthy, with a growing welfare state and the healthiest population and the lowest infant mortality rate in the world—a position which it has more or less maintained up to the present day. There is good reason to believe that the welfare state has been an important foundation for more positive attitudes and behaviors towards children, even though many reforms, as described above, came prior to this wealth.

After World War II, the debate about families' social circumstances intensified. The family was at the centre of political discourse and government reforms. The debate not only focused on physically and emotionally abusive treatment in child rearing, but on the government's responsibility for child welfare, with proponents of reform suggesting that violence was rooted in ignorance and poverty. The reformists believed that society was duty-bound to create reasonable living conditions for all children to ensure family well-being. Child benefits, free school lunches, antenatal clinics, pediatric clinics, and school health care were introduced and parents were given information on many issues such as health, nutrition, and parenting.

ENDING CORPORAL PUNISHMENT IN SCHOOLS

The process of ending corporal punishment in public schools began early in Sweden. The oldest preserved Swedish school statute, from the 17th century, states that corporal punishment should be given carefully and that schools are not butchers' benches and pupils are not donkeys—an astonishing limitation on teachers' right to punish for that historical time. The statute also stated that children who make mistakes due to their lack of wisdom should not be punished. However, this did not mean that punishments were uncommon.

In the 1870s, school inspectors advocated against harsh discipline, and a regulation was introduced around 1880 stating that corporal punishment should be given "with an affectionate sincerity and adapted to the pupil's age and personality". In 1918, all corporal punishment was explicitly banned in gymnasiums.[2] In 1928, it was banned from state-run secondary schools. The result of these first bans was that children from wealthy families were the first to escape corporal punishment, as it was not abolished in elementary schools, which most working class and peasant children attended, until 1958 (Committee on Child Abuse, 2001).

The final stage of abolition of physical punishment at school was preceded by heated debates for about 10 years in the Swedish Parliament and petitions to the Swedish King. Even though many Members of Parliament were opposed to physical punishment in principle, they did not believe it could be abolished entirely as a form of discipline. Many members voiced concern over how schools could maintain order if it was banned, and argued that the majority of parents believed teachers should be entitled to hit pupils (Wiberg, 2006). (In contrast, parents today would react promptly if a teacher even gripped a pupil firmly.)

In 1957, a major reform was enacted: all forms of corporal punishment were equated with cruelty under the law. After this it was no longer possible to maintain physical punishment in schools. Many teachers were however skeptics; male teachers of the higher grades opposed abolition, although female teachers in compulsory schools were in favor of it (Wiberg, 2006). While various aspects of schooling are a frequent topic of debate in today's parliament, media and the general public, no political party or school authority would ever consider the reintroduction of physical punishment in schools. It is unanimously agreed that physical punishment by teachers is both ineffective and a violation of pupils' basic rights. One could reflect on why corporal punishment was abolished in schools more than 20 years before it was prohibited in families. The reason is probably that schools are clearly a government responsibility, whereas the family has been seen as private and out of the realm of government intervention.

ENDING CORPORAL PUNISHMENT IN FAMILIES

Older Swedish law was notorious for protecting adults—especially men/fathers—against charges of assault. In a 1664 law, masters were given the right to punish their employees, as well as their wives and children. According to a 1734 law, if parents abused a child to death this was considered manslaughter by mistake, and it did not result in criminal penalties beyond a small fine.

The first limit on the right to inflict punishment came in 1858 when corporal punishment of adults was prohibited. In 1864, the *Penal Code* clearly stated that any maltreatment, however minor, was punishable—and it removed husbands' right to hit their wives. During this same period, it was made clear that masters were not allowed to injure their servants through punishment. But the right to physically punish children remained for some time to come. For example, the law encouraging parents to physically punish children over the age of 6 who had committed crimes was not removed until 1905, and the law allowing corporal punishment of servants under the age of 16 remained until 1920.

Physical punishment of children by their parents was the last to be abolished. As late as 1920 the law stated that: "for the sake of upbringing, parents have the right to chastise the child in a manner that with respect to the age of the child and other circumstances was judged to be necessary" (Ewerlöf & Sverne, 1999). In 1949, a legal amendment changed this entitlement to suitable "means of upbringing" in an attempt to discourage heavy-handed physical punishment. It was not until 1957 that the parental exemption from criminal assault charges was removed from the *Penal Code* (Bergenlöv, 2009). However, the *Parental Code* still allowed parents to inflict some level of physical punishment. In 1966, this law was removed and a cross reference was inserted into the *Penal Code*, to ensure that assault penalties would apply whether the victim was an adult or a child.

Despite these legal changes, however, many parents continued to think that physical punishment was allowed. The debate continued and included politicians, influential pediatricians, social workers, higher state officials, artists, writers, and actors. Inspired by the work of American physicians, reports of severe child abuse began to emerge from Swedish pediatricians in the late 1950s (Frisk, 1964; Selander, 1957). At a joint meeting of pediatricians and social workers in the 1960s, the first proposal for the investigation of child maltreatment was developed, which was an inventory of child abuse cases reported to the social or medical services at the time (Socialstyrelsen, 1969). In the mid-1960s, the mass media published details of two cases of child maltreatment, which initiated a public discussion about parental rights and contributed to the establishment of a non-governmental organization, "Children's Rights in Society" (BRIS), which included well-known Swedish authors and performers, and advocated for children's rights. As a result, the Swedish government commissioned the National Board of Medical and Social Services to investigate the incidence of severe child abuse in Sweden, leading to further discussions in Parliament.

There was also an ongoing debate in the mass media on the issue. Gradually, the focus of the debate shifted from the rights of parents to the rights of children (SOU, 1978). In 1977, the government set up a parliamentary committee to examine children's rights in Sweden. It was this committee that proposed the explicit ban on physical punishment of children in all settings, including the home. Interestingly, although there was much disagreement with the idea within the Conservative Party, the final proposal actually came from two prominent female members of that party—Ingrid Sundberg, a teacher and member of the Swedish UNESCO Council, and Ingrid Diesen, who chaired the European Women's Union. Finally, in March 1979, the Swedish Parliament voted almost unanimously in favor of the proposal, which was to amend the Parents' Code to include an explicit ban on all forms of physical punishment or other emotionally abusive treatment of children. All political parties supported the amendment; the final vote was 259 in favor, 6 against, and 3 abstentions.

THE 1979 BAN

In 1979, the Swedish government added the following paragraph to the *Parental Act, Chapter 6 §1:*

> Children have the right to care, security and a good upbringing. Children are to be treated with respect for their person and individuality and they shall not be subjected to corporal punishment or any other humiliating treatment.

This law prohibits parents from using physical or emotional violence against their children, but it does not prevent parents from restraining their children to prevent harm to themselves or others. While the prohibition in the *Parental Code* does not itself carry penalties, actions that meet the legal criteria of assault are subject to Chapter 3, Section 5 of the Swedish *Penal Code*, which states that a person who inflicts bodily injury, illness, or pain upon another person or renders him or her powerless or in a similar state, shall be sentenced for assault to imprisonment for a maximum of 2 years or, if the crime is petty, to a fine or imprisonment of at most 6 months. The sentence for gross assault is incarceration for a minimum of 1 year up to a maximum of 10 years, regardless of whether the victim is an adult or a child.

Some critics in Parliament predicted that the corporal punishment ban would lead to a large number of Swedes being branded as criminals, which reflected a misunderstanding of the law's intent. Other critics claimed that the law contradicted the Christian faith.[3] Some segments of the population opposing the ban went so far as to petition the European court to overturn it, claiming it infringed the right to respect for private and family life under Article 8 of the European Convention on Human Rights. The European Court dismissed the application, and took the opportunity to criticize countries that permitted corporal punishment in schools (Ewerlöf & Sverne, 1999).

Anyone who, through their work with children and young people in the public or private sector, receives information that a child may be in need of protection is legally obligated to inform social services. Although the law only applies to people who work with children and adolescents, members of the public are urged under Chapter 14, Section 1 of the *Social Services Act* to notify social services if they suspect that a child is being maltreated (Committee on Child Abuse, 2001).

It is part of the social services' mandate to ensure that children grow up in good and secure conditions. Social services are required to assess a child's need for protection when they receive a report of alleged maltreatment. If they have sufficient evidence to believe that the child is being ill-treated, they must intervene to protect the child and prevent any risk of further maltreatment. Thus, a child can receive help, even if a police investigation does not lead to prosecution.

When it is alleged that an assault constituting a crime has been perpetrated against a child, the allegation is investigated by the police, under the supervision of a public prosecutor. The police conduct the interviews, and the public prosecutor decides whether to indict the accused. Sweden, like some other countries, has in recent years moved towards handling such cases in "children's houses", where police officers, prosecutors, social services, forensic scientists, and child psychologists work closely together. The children's house concept puts the needs of the child first, with the aim of raising the quality of investigations to provide better evidence and a stronger basis for decisions. Housing different authorities and agencies under the same roof creates an unbroken chain, which can provide children and their families with the support they need and to which they are entitled. Children and their families may also need protection, support, and assistance from social services and child psychiatry.

The aim of the law was not to punish parents, but to raise awareness. For this reason, the text was placed in the *Parental Code* (a civil code), while penalties for maltreatment are found in the *Penal Code*. Today, all Swedish parents know that they are not allowed to physically punish their children. If they do so, they can be reported to social services who, in most cases, support the family in learning and using different approaches to parenting. In cases that meet the abuse threshold, the report will be passed on to the police, who may prosecute. If a prosecution ends in a conviction, the sentence will depend on the severity of the maltreatment, regardless of the victim's age.

IMPLEMENTATION OF THE BAN

After the Parliamentary vote of 1979, it was important to ensure that the new legislation actually achieved the intended changes on behalf of children. The government launched an extensive publicity campaign with a Ministry of Justice pamphlet, entitled *Can Children Be Raised without Smacking?*, which was distributed to all households with children. The brochure was translated into German, French, English, Arabic, and various other languages, while parents were offered advice and support about parenting without violence. Antenatal clinics, pediatric wards, and well-baby clinics joined the campaign to provide support and information to parents. Information was printed on milk cartons to encourage awareness and discussion in families. Save the Children Sweden and BRIS held debates and printed posters to further raise awareness of the issue.

Before 1982, child abuse in private spaces (homes) could not be prosecuted unless one of the caretakers herself reported or admitted the abuse. From 1982, the law was reformed so that abuse in private spaces (e.g., homes) became liable to public prosecution, meaning that even milder forms of child abuse could be prosecuted even if the abuser did not admit to it. This is particularly important in cases where both a parent (usually a mother) and children are being abused.

In 1990, Sweden became one of the first countries in the world to ratify the United Nations *Convention of the Right of the Child* (CRC). In 1993, a Children's Ombudsman was appointed. In 1999, a national strategy to implement the CRC was set up, and the Swedish Academy of Children's Rights was established at Örebro University to raise awareness of children's rights within academic disciplines, and among municipal and county council officials.

THE IMPACT OF LAW REFORM IN SWEDEN

In 1981, 2 years after the ban on physical punishment—and following an unprecedented publicity campaign—more than 90% of Swedish adults (Ewerlöf & Sverne, 1999) were aware that the law had changed. But did the campaign also produce changes in values and actual behavior?

In the mid-1990s, Sweden, like most other countries, experienced an economic recession. Increasing reports of family violence led pediatricians and social workers to urge further investigation, resulting in the establishment of a Government Committee on Child Abuse, which worked from 1998 to 2002. The Committee both reviewed prior research and conducted research of its own. This research included: (1) interviews with a representative sample of about 2,500 parents carried out using consistent methodology in 1980, 2000, and 2006, where parents were asked about upbringing, conflicts, and punishment of a certain child during the last year using the Conflict Tactics Scale (Straus, 1971); (2) surveys of representative samples of children (11, 14, and 16 years of age) carried out in 1994, 2000, and 2006–2007 about their experiences of corporal punishment and attitudes to it; (3) a study of 20-year-olds about lifetime experiences of corporal punishment, neglect, sexual abuse, and bullying at school; and (4) tracking of adult attitudes towards corporal punishment since 1965 (Edfeldt, 1985; Karlberg & Taranger, 1976; Stattin, Janson, Klackenberg-Larsson, & Magnusson, 1995; Janson, Långberg, & Svensson, 2007).

The Committee concluded in its report, *Child Assault—Prevention and Action* (Janson, 2001), that most preschool children in the 1960s had been smacked by their parents once or several times per year, and that one-third were smacked regularly, but by the 1970s the data indicated that less than half of children had ever experienced physical punishment. This trend continued into the 1980s, when the figure fell to around one-third. In 1994, 35% of middle-school pupils said they had been smacked at some time, but after 2000 this figure fell to 13% to 14%, and remained steady from 2006. Not only has the number of children who are physically punished fallen, but children are physically punished less often and only rarely with implements (1% to 1.5%). Thus, children in the 2000s are smacked considerably less often and with less force than children in the 1980s. (For detailed analyses of these trends, see Durrant & Janson, 2005; Gilbert et al., 2009; Janson, 2005; Janson, Långberg, & Svensson, 2007).

Figure 19.1 illustrates the decline in parents' use of physical punishment, and the accompanying decline in positive attitudes towards it, that occurred between the 1960s and the 2000s. It also shows a narrowing gap between the percentage of parents who are positive to physical punishment and the percentage who actually inflict physical punishment. Interviews with parents in 1980, 2000, and 2006 have revealed a steady decline in the more serious forms of physical punishment, such as punching and the use of implements. Harsh punishment with the potential to cause serious

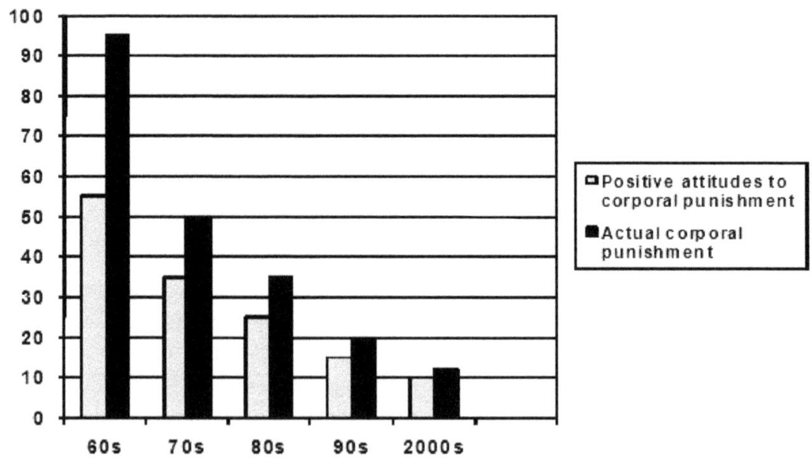

Figure 19.1 Percentage of parents who had physically punished their preschool children, and who held positive attitudes towards physical punishment (Janson, Långberg, & Svensson, 2007).

injury has decreased substantially, and is now reported by less than 1% of Swedish parents (Janson, Moniruzzaman, & Hjern, 2007).

In Sweden, almost an entire generation who experienced physical punishment themselves as children refrained from inflicting it when they became parents. There has been a tremendous change in attitudes and behavior in Sweden during the last 40 to 50 years. In the 1960s, corporal punishment was seen as a justified and useful tool in bringing up children; today most parents look upon such behavior as deviant. This is an unprecedented shift in attitudes and behavior in Sweden in such a short period of time. These rates of physical punishment are probably among the lowest in the world (Gilbert et al., 2009), even though our definition of corporal punishment is quite broad including such behavior as boxing ears, which is not included in other definitions (Janson et al., 2007).

HAS THE LAW HAD ANY ADVERSE EFFECTS?

Critics of law reform sometimes assert that immigrants will have difficulty following the law. Indeed, many immigrants to Sweden find it difficult initially to understand how it is possible to raise children without physical punishment. However, their attitudes and behaviors seem to change quickly when they are well integrated into Swedish society, learn the Swedish language, and enter the work force (Janson, Långberg, & Svensson, 2007).

Critics also have claimed that parents who are not allowed to smack their children will replace hitting with other humiliating treatment. The results of our studies (Janson et al., 2007) show, on the contrary, that parents who refrain from hitting their children to a greater extent than others also use less humiliating punishments.

Some critics have suggested that if parents are prohibited from inflicting minor forms of physical punishment, they will eventually "explode" with more serious attacks (Larzelere & Johnson, 1999). It is the case that reports to the police of suspected assault on children have increased since the early 1980s, rising by 190% between 1990 and 1999 (Janson, 2001). However, this trend does not indicate an actual increase in assaults on children; rather, it reflects a decreased tolerance of such assaults. Violence, which used to be a family secret, is more likely to be reported today because Swedes are less likely to excuse or minimize the physical abuse of children. A Swedish National Council for Crime Prevention study showed that even though reports to the police have increased, these are reports of minor assault; there has been no increase in severe or moderately severe assaults on children (Nilsson, 2000). During the last 50 years, we have also seen a continuous decline in homicides of children under 15—currently the figure is about 7 children killed each year, which is a very low figure compared to the UK and the US. The majority of children are killed in extended suicides, where a severely depressed father kills the whole family. Homicides due to abuse are rare and the current incidence is, at most, one case a year (Janson, Moniruzzaman, & Hjern, 2007).

Some critics of the physical punishment ban predicted that it would result in the prosecution of large numbers of parents. Contrary to this prediction, the number of prosecutions for assault has not increased (Committee on Child Abuse, 2001). This is partly due to the fact that it is extremely difficult to prosecute crimes committed within the four walls of a home, where there are no witnesses other than the perpetrator and the child; the legal system does not allow a lower burden of proof in cases of assault on children than in other criminal cases. Furthermore, many reports lead to children and parents receiving support and protection, rather than to prosecution; social services investigate all allegations of child maltreatment, assess the family's need for support and the child's need for protection, and provide a range of supportive and preventive measures.

Many adults used to believe (and some still do) that youth crime can be combated through the use of force. If this is the case, a prohibition on the use of force should lead to an increase in youth crime. The Swedish National Council for Crime Prevention (BRÅ) monitors youth crime data and distributes information on crime and crime prevention. The Council reports a decrease in youth crime since the mid-1990s, due primarily to youngsters committing fewer thefts and criminal damage offences. Participation in violent crime has remained relatively constant (BRÅ, 2006). The vast majority of young people who commit a crime in Sweden do not end up becoming habitual criminals; the small group who do are responsible for a large proportion of offenses. There is no evidence that criminality is rising among young people in Sweden, and our researchers, politicians, and government are jointly focused on improving interventions to prevent young people engaging in crime. Children's personality and behavioral patterns develop through a constant interplay of genetic and environmental factors (BRÅ, 2001). The ability of parents to provide good care is crucial to the child's development. If parents have difficulty in developing emotional relationships with children or are violent towards children, the risk of children developing serious psychosocial problems increases, and the risk of future engagement in criminal behavior increases (Stattin et al., 1998).

LESSONS LEARNED

The extraordinary change in parental behavior that has been witnessed in Sweden over the last 50 years is probably due to a variety of factors. Swedish society has seen many changes, such as an improved welfare system, greater equality between the sexes and the generations, and improved support for parents with young children. Young children increasingly attend early childhood (day care) centers, which facilitates the detection and prevention of child abuse. Antenatal and children's clinics work hard to raise awareness and provide support to families, in order to prevent violence. And when physical punishment was prohibited, parents discovered alternative ways to resolve conflicts with their children.

These explanations, however, may not represent the whole picture. How is it that Sweden has been so successful in reducing the frequency of corporal punishment of children to such low levels? The Swedish historian Eva Bergenlöv discusses this topic from a different perspective in her newly published book, *Children Who Have Suffered* (Bergenlöv, 2009). Although the development of the Swedish welfare state in the 20th century was probably very important, the roots of the change may be found even earlier. Sweden has a unique history of independent peasants who have not been subordinate to the aristocracy, the church or the state, resulting in more direct contact between ordinary people and the government. Sweden's autonomy in social affairs and economic issues has been very important, quite different from many other countries, where the family and other relationships are the basis for social trust. While welfare in many other states depends on hierarchies, dependencies, and commitments between individuals, in Sweden it is built upon the individual's direct relation to the state.

In Sweden, social ties and love are perceived to be linked with equity and respect for others' autonomy. So the culture already values autonomy and self-reliance separately for men, women, and children, making it possible to institute reforms which in other cultures would have been seen as hostile to families. The prohibition of corporal punishment of children is related to our history, and the typical ways that Swedish people have interacted with the state. Our society has a long history of helping children to become good citizens. Love and compassion for the individual character of the child have always been valued. More recently, adults' empathy with children has been stressed. Religious norms have been replaced, to a large extent, by scientific research findings and an emphasis on human rights. New insights about parenting have arisen from research in medicine, education, child development, and child psychology. The focus of parenting is no longer on obedience, but on teaching the values of democracy and equality (Law, 2006). This social context promotes the rights of children to physical integrity and dignity. Other countries trying to reform their corporal punishment laws can possibly learn from our experiences.

NOTES

1. Children were generally defined as less than 15 years of age or even younger (Bergenlöv, 2009).
2. A gymnasium is a secondary school comparable to English grammar schools and sixth form colleges or US preparatory high schools.
3. It was not until 2006 that the Nordic religious communities made a common statement condemning corporal punishment. In a Christian Bishops' meeting

in Norway in 2008, a decision was made to revise Biblical texts, which in many respects are quite hostile to children (Todd, 2009).

REFERENCES

Bergenlöv, E. (2009). *Drabbade barn'aga och misshandel i Sverige från reformationen till nutid.* Lund: Nordic Academic Press.

BRÅ. (2006). *Ungdomar och brott åren 1995–2005* (No. 2006:7). Stockholm: Swedish National Council for Crime Prevention.

Committee on Child Abuse. (2001). *Barnmisshandel'att förebygga och åtgärda Stockholm; final report of the government committee on child abuse* (No. SOU 2001:72). Stockholm: Socialstyrelsen.

Durrant, J., & Janson, S. (2005). Law reform, corporal punishment and child abuse: The case of Sweden. *International Review of Victimology, 12*, 139–180.

Edfeldt, Å. (1985). *"Allt vad i gören". Slutrapport från SUSA-projektet om aga och våld i hemmet.* Stockholm: Proprius.

Ewerlöf, G., & Sverne, T. (1999). *Barnets bästa'om föräldrars och samhällets ansvar.* Stockholm: Norstedts.

Frisk, A. (1964). Misshandlade småbarn. *Läkartidningen, 61*(41), 3005–3011.

Gilbert, R., Spatz Widom, C., Browne, K., Fergusson, D., Webb, E., & Janson, S. (2009). Burden and consequences of child maltreatment in high-income countries. *The Lancet, 373*(9657), 68–81.

Janson, S. (2001). *Barn och misshandel. En rapport om kroppslig bestraffning och annan misshandel i Sverige vid slutet av 1900-talet* (No. SOU 2001:18). Stockholm: Fritzes.

Janson, S. (2005). Response to Beckett, C. (2005). The Swedish myth: The corporal punishment ban and child death statistics. *British Journal of Social Work, 35*, 1411–1415.

Janson, S., Moniruzzaman, S., & Hjern, A. (2007). Kan barnamord förebyggas. *Läkartidningen, 104*(10), 776–781.

Janson, S., Långberg, B., & Svensson, B. (2007). *Våld mot barn 2006–2007. En nationell kartläggning.* Stockholm: Allmänna Barnhuset och Karlstad Universitet.

Karlberg, P., & Taranger, J. (1976). The somatic development of children in a Swedish urban community. A prospective longitudinal study. *Acta Peadiatrica Scandinavica, 258, (Supplement),* 1–148.

Key, E. (1996). *Barnets århundrade.* Stockholm: Informationsförlaget.

Larzelere, R. E., & Johnson, B. (1999). Evaluation of the effects of Sweden's spanking ban on physical child abuse rates: A literature review. *Psychological Reports, 85*, 381–392.

Law, S. (2006). *The war for children's minds.* New York: Routledge.

Myrdal, A., Åse, C., & Hirdman, Y. (2002). *Något kan man väl göra. Texter i urval 1932–1982.* Stockholm: Carlsson.

Nilsson, L. (2000). *Barnmisshandel. En kartläggning av polisanmäld misshandel av små barn.* No. 2000:15. Stockholm: BRÅ.

Österberg, E., & Lindström, D. (1988). *Crime and social control in medieval and early modern Swedish towns.* Stockholm: Almqvist & Wiksell International.

Selander, P. (1957). Multipla frakturer hos spädbarn vid förnekat trauma. *Läkartidningen, 54*(9), 611–619.

Socialstyrelsen. (1969). *En utredning om barnmisshandel.* No. 1969:9. Stockholm: Socialstyrelsen.

SOU. (1978). *Barnens rätt. Om förbud mot aga.* No. 1978:10. Stockholm: Statens Offentliga Utredningar.

Stattin, H., Janson, H., Klackenberg-Larsson, I., & Magnusson, D. (1995). Corporal punishment in everyday life: An intergenerational perspective. In J. McCord (Ed.), *Coercion and Punishment in Long-Term Perspectives* (315–347). Cambridge: Cambridge University Press.
Straus, M. (1971). Some social antecedents of physical punishment. A linkage theory interpretation. *Journal of Marriage and the Family, 33,* 658–663.
Swedish National Council for Crime Prevention. (2001). *Criminal development—early risk factors and preventive measures.* No. 2001:15. Stockholm: Swedish National Council for Crime Prevention.
Todd, C. (2009). *Churches for non-violence.* Keynote address to the 11th annual EU-NGO forum on human rights: Violence against children. Stockholm.
Wiberg, R. (2006). Den stora agadebatten: En analys av debatten inför förbudet mot aga i skolan 1958 och i hemmet 1979. Halmstad: Högskolan i Halmstad, sektionen för humaniora.

20 The United Kingdom

The Ongoing Struggle to Achieve Legal Reform

Sharon Owen

Population:	61,855,000 (2009). 2005 estimates by country: England 50,431,700; Wales 2,958,600; Scotland 5,094,800; Northern Ireland 1,724,400
Government:	Constitutional monarchy, parliamentary democracy
Child protection system in place:	Yes
Legal system:	English common law, combining in Scotland with elements of civil law; England and Wales have a combined judicial system; Scotland and Northern Ireland have separate systems
Major religions:	Predominantly Christian (71.8% in 2001); no official religion. Church of England "established" (protected by the state but not "official"); Church of Scotland "national" (exclusive jurisdiction in spiritual matters); no established church in Northern Ireland or Wales
Official national languages:	English (plus Welsh in Wales; plus Scots Gaelic in Scotland)
Ratified United Nations Convention on the Rights of the Child:	1991
Children's Commissioner Ombudsman:	Separate Children's Commissioners in England, Wales, Scotland, and Northern Ireland

POLITICAL CONTEXT[1]

The UK's official name is "the United Kingdom of Great Britain and Northern Ireland", and since 1922 has comprised England, Wales, Scotland, and Northern Ireland. When the Labor government was elected in 1997, referenda held in each of the countries led to the establishment of the Scottish Parliament, the Northern Ireland Assembly and the Welsh Assembly, with the devolution of certain areas of administration, including different legislative powers in each.

Scotland became part of Great Britain under the *Treaty of Union* in 1707, when it lost its previously independent legislative powers. It regained many of these powers following devolution in the late 1990s and is now able to legislate on most areas of domestic policy, the exceptions being foreign affairs, defense and national security, economic and monetary policy, employment, and social security (*Scotland Act 1998*, Schedule 5). It has a separate judicial system, administering civil justice through the sheriff courts and the Court of Session (the supreme civil court) and criminal justice in the sheriff courts, the district courts and the High Court of Justiciary (Carter & Swift, 2009).

The Northern Ireland Assembly dates back to 1973 but was suspended in 1974 under the rule of the British government. In 1998, the referendum endorsed the *Good Friday Agreement*, a political settlement which led to the re-establishment of the Northern Ireland Assembly (*Northern Ireland Act 1998* and *Northern Ireland (Elections) Act 1998*). It has had legislative powers since 1999, with brief periods of suspension due to political unrest (Carter & Swift, 2009).

Wales and England have been united politically and legally since the 16th century (Carter & Swift, 2009). When the Welsh Assembly was formed in 1999 (under the *Government of Wales Act 1998*) it could pass only secondary legislation. In 2006 it was replaced by the National Assembly for Wales (under the *Government of Wales Act 2006*) and can now enact "measures" equivalent to primary legislation in certain areas. This does not include criminal law, which has proved a barrier to achieving prohibition of all corporal punishment in Wales despite the Assembly's commitment to the issue (see next section).

LEGAL CONTEXT FOR PROMOTING PROHIBITION OF CORPORAL PUNISHMENT OF CHILDREN

The campaign to end corporal punishment of children in the UK has been a long one. Corporal punishment is now unlawful in almost all settings outside the family home. But significant and longstanding pressure for complete prohibition from international and regional human rights bodies, and from professionals and organizations working with and for children within the UK, has met with persistent government resistance to removing the "right" of parents to physically punish children in the name of "discipline".

Physical Punishment Outside the Home

The process of prohibiting corporal punishment in settings outside the home spanned the whole of the 20th century. Flogging in the British army was prohibited in 1906, under a Liberal government. In 1948, under a Labor government, "birching" was prohibited as a sentence of the courts, although it remained on the statute books of the Isle of Man for another 30 years. In 1957, flogging in the navy was prohibited, this time under the

Conservatives. In 1967, when Labor had returned to power, corporal punishment was prohibited in prisons and borstals.[2]

Prohibition in schools is more recent. It was achieved in state schools[3] throughout the UK in 1987 under a Conservative government, and extended to private schools under Labor in 1999 in England and Wales, 2000 in Scotland, and 2003 in Northern Ireland. In 2008, it was discovered that the law did not cover small, private, part-time education settings, a loophole which was closed when education law was revised that year. Laws against corporal punishment in alternative care settings have proceeded in a similar piecemeal way. They do not yet extend to private foster care or, in Northern Ireland, to day care institutions and childminding.[4]

Physical Punishment in the Home

Throughout the UK, physical punishment of children is lawful by parents—and by others *in loco parentis* where there is no explicit prohibition. Its legality is enshrined in provisions allowing for "reasonable punishment" in England and Wales (*Children Act 2004*, Section 58) and Northern Ireland (Law Reform (*Miscellaneous Provisions*) (*Northern Ireland*) Order 2006, Article 2) and "justifiable assault" in Scotland (*Criminal Justice (Scotland) Act 2003*, Section 51). These laws reflect the common-law defense for the use of corporal punishment, confirmed by Chief Justice Cockburn in 1860 in a case brought against a teacher when a 13-year-old boy died after being beaten with a thick stick and a skipping rope (*R v Hopley* [1860]):

> By the law of England, a parent . . . may for the purpose of correcting what is evil in the child, inflict moderate and reasonable corporal punishment, always, however, with this condition, that it is reasonable and moderate.

This ruling was confirmed in statute in the first law to protect children from cruelty, the *Prevention of Cruelty to and Protection of Children Act 1889*. During the passage of the bill, various parliamentarians sought to give "reassurance" that the wording aimed to ensure the law did not affect the right of parents and teachers to punish a child (Newell, 1989). There was no debate on the issue when the provision was re-enacted in the *Prevention of Cruelty to Children Act 1894* (Section 24), the *Prevention of Cruelty to Children Act 1904* (Section 28) and the *Children and Young Persons Act 1933* (Section 1). This statutory confirmation was finally repealed by the *Children Act 2004*—but leaving the common-law defense available for parents and others charged with common assault.

Despite assertions that it "does not condone" corporal punishment by parents (e.g., Council of Europe, 2008; Morgan, 2009), the UK government has continued to resist calls to remove completely the defense of "reasonable punishment" in order to give children the same legal protection from assault that adults have, repeatedly claiming this would infringe on adults' right to choose how to bring up their own children in the way they see fit (e.g., Joint Committee on Human Rights, 2004b) and asserting that "smacking isn't violence" (e.g., Joint Committee on Human Rights, 2003; Council of Europe, 2008; Morgan, 2008).

HUMAN RIGHTS CONTEXT

Pressure to reform laws in the UK has come from various sources, primarily the European Court of Human Rights, the European Committee of Social Rights, the Council of Europe and United Nations bodies.

European Court of Human Rights

The European Court of Human Rights (ECHR), which hears cases concerning alleged violations of the *Convention for the Protection of Human Rights and Fundamental Freedoms* (the European Convention on Human Rights), ratified by the UK in 1951, has a long history of involvement in the prohibition of corporal punishment of children in the UK (Council of Europe, 2007). Judicial corporal punishment was finally removed from statute in the Isle of Man after the case of a 15-year-old boy who had been sentenced to be birched was taken to the ECHR (*Tyrer v UK*, 1978). The Court ruled that the punishment amounted to degrading punishment in breach of Article 3 of the *Convention* (prohibition of torture and inhuman or degrading treatment or punishment).

The ECHR also played an important role in prohibiting corporal punishment in schools. In the case of *Campbell and Cosans v UK* (1982), allegations by two parents that the corporal punishment used in their sons' Scottish schools violated Article 3 were rejected because neither boy had actually received corporal punishment. But the Court did find the UK had failed to respect the parents' philosophical convictions against the use of corporal punishment under Article 2 Protocol 1 of the *Convention*, which confirms "the right of parents to ensure such education and teaching in conformity with their own religious and philosophical convictions".

Further cases were taken to the Court in the 1980s by schoolchildren and their parents, alleging breaches of their rights under Article 3 and/or Article 8 (respect for family and private life). In most cases, "friendly settlements" were reached and the UK government agreed to make *ex gratia* payments to the families involved. Corporal punishment was finally abolished in state schools in 1987. When prohibition was extended to private schools, the ECHR, in the case of *Philip Williamson and Others v UK* (2000), rejected unanimously and without a hearing an application by a group of private Christian schools alleging the ban breached parents' rights to freedom of religion and family life.

Corporal punishment in the home was the subject of the case of *A v UK*, which concerned a child who had been beaten with a garden cane by his step-father, causing bruising. The step-father was acquitted in an English court of the charge of "assault occasioning actual bodily harm" on the grounds this was "reasonable chastisement". In a landmark judgment in 1998, the ECHR ruled that UK law thus failed to provide adequate protection, including effective deterrence, to the child from degrading punishment severe enough to be covered by Article 3 of the *Convention*. The UK government accepted the judgment and, eventually, the need for legal reform. But rather than enacting equal protection for children by explicitly and fully repealing the defense, legislation in England and Wales, Northern Ireland, and Scotland was amended over the next 6 years so as to limit the applicability of the defense. Technically, this met the requirement of the now decade-old ruling, because *A v UK* concerned very severe beating and European Court judgments focus on the particular circumstances of the case.

The Committee of Ministers of the Council of Europe is responsible for supervising the execution of Court judgments by the respondent state. Following intense political pressure from the UK government and despite strong representations from UK NGOs and children's commissioners and *A's* legal representatives, the Committee finally closed the case of *A v UK* in 2009 (Council of Europe Committee of Ministers, 2009). For 11 years, the ongoing supervision of the judgment by the Committee helped to keep the issue of corporal punishment on the government agenda. Over that period there have been repeated recommendations from international and European human rights bodies which have unequivocally confirmed the UK must remove the defense completely if it is to meet its obligations under international human rights law. In 2010, the UK government is still resisting this pressure.

European Committee of Social Rights

In 2001, the European Committee of Social Rights, which monitors implementation of the *European Social Charter*, published a general observation that conformity with the *Charter* obliges states to prohibit corporal punishment of children in all settings, including the family (European Committee of Social Rights, 2001). In 2005 the UK, which ratified the *Charter* in 1962, was found to be in breach of its obligations under Article 17 because corporal punishment in the home is not prohibited (European Committee of Social Rights, 2005).

Following visits to the UK in February and March/April 2008, the Council of Europe Commissioner for Human Rights, Thomas Hammarberg, published a memorandum reviewing the issue of corporal punishment in which he heavily criticized laws which allow "reasonable punishment" and "justifiable assault", as well as the absence of an explicit ban on corporal punishment of children in custody (Council of Europe, 2008). He wrote that as long as corporal punishment remains lawful, the government's statement that it does not condone smacking "lacks credibility".

United Nations Bodies

The United Nations (UN) Committee on the Rights of the Child has three times followed its examination of reports by the UK government with recommendations to remove the "reasonable chastisement/punishment" defense from UK law (Committee on the Rights of the Child, 1995, 2002, and 2008). Prohibition in the family has also been recommended by the Committee on the Elimination of Discrimination against Women (2008) and the Committee on Economic and Social Rights (2002, 2009).

The UK was among the first states to be examined on its human rights record by the UN Human Rights Council in the Universal Periodic Review process. Concern at the lack of prohibition of corporal punishment in the family was expressed by a number of states and strong recommendations were made to enact full prohibition (Human Rights Council, 2008).

THE CAMPAIGN FOR LAW REFORM

The campaign to end corporal punishment in the home began shortly after prohibition was achieved in all state schools, when the Society of Teachers Opposed to Physical Punishment (STOPP) transferred its remaining funds to the newly formed organization EPOCH—End Physical Punishment of Children. The campaign is now pursued throughout the UK by the Children Are Unbeatable! (CAU) Alliance of more than 600 organizations and projects, including all the major children's charities and professional associations concerned with safeguarding children, and many prominent individuals (www.childrenareunbeatable.org.uk). There are linked but separately coordinated campaigns in Northern Ireland, Scotland, and Wales, and there is an associated young people's campaign.[5] The government's responsibility to implement the *A v UK* judgment provided major opportunities for CAU to campaign for the removal of the legal defenses for physical punishment of children.

CAU's policy is to use any credible parliamentary opportunity to seek to achieve equal protection for children. Activities are focused on building support among parliamentarians in all parties and among professionals and others working with and for children. To support calls for law reform, CAU responds to government consultations; commissions and disseminates research; and engages in relevant public debate, for example following high profile cases of child fatalities. A growing group of young supporters campaigns with the Alliance. Young people speak directly to MPs and policy makers, participate in conferences, speak at meetings, and tell other children about the campaign.

Support for prohibition has steadily grown among faith groups. The Churches' Network for Non-violence (www.churchesfornon-violence.org) was established in 2005 to engage faith communities in the campaign against corporal punishment in the UK and worldwide, and works closely with CAU. By 2009, around 50 UK bishops and other high level religious offices had formally signed their support for law reform.

PROGRESS TOWARDS LAW REFORM IN ENGLAND AND WALES

In January 2000, the government launched a consultation in England and Wales on the "reasonable chastisement" defense (Department of Health, 2000b). But the consultation document itself stated that while the government "accepts the need for change . . . we do *not* consider that the right way forward is to make unlawful all smacking and other forms of physical rebuke and this paper explicitly rules out this possibility" (para. 1.5). The consultation aimed to answer two questions: "First, within the context of a modern family policy in a responsible society, where should we draw the line as to what physical punishment of children is acceptable within the family setting? Second, how do we achieve that position in law?" (para. 1.6).

The official analysis of responses to the consultation in England and Wales noted that "the overwhelming majority of voluntary organizations, local authorities and education and health related organizations . . . opposed the physical punishment of children outright" (Department of Health, 2000a, para. 21), and that 30% of individuals and under 10% of religious organizations held this view. The government concluded no further change to the law was necessary because it "would not command widespread public support or . . . be capable of consistent enforcement" (para. 76). The "reasonable chastisement" defense would be kept under review.

In rejecting law reform, the government argued that the *Human Rights Act 1998*, which incorporates the *European Convention on Human Rights*, is in force and that courts must take account of the judgment in the case of *A v UK*. CAU responded by collating cases in the year since the *Human Rights Act* came into force in which UK courts continued to acquit parents who caused bruising and other injuries on their children (CAU, 2001a).

The government has also relied upon public opinion in rejecting prohibition. When simply asked whether or not smacking should be lawful, the majority oppose law reform. For example, 59% of more than 1,800 respondents agreed that "The law should allow parents to smack their children" (Ipsos MORI, 2007). But when given more detailed information about what law reform means, opinion polls have revealed greater support for reform. A survey of over 1,000 adults in 1999 found that 73% (and 78% of parents with dependent children), supported a change in the law if they were sure that parents would not be prosecuted for "trivial" smacks (Ipsos

MORI, 1999). A poll in 2002 again found a majority supportive of law reform: 97% opposed physical punishment of babies up to 18 months, 78% opposed physical punishment of toddlers under three, 96% opposed the use of implements, and 98% opposed hitting children on the head (Ipsos MORI, 2002). In 2004, a poll of over 2,000 adults found that 71% would support law reform to give children and adult family members the same legal protection from being hit (Ipsos MORI, 2004).

The consultation on the "reasonable chastisement" defense coincided with the death of 8-year-old Victoria Climbié at the hands of her great aunt and her great aunt's partner in 2000. The case was given a high media profile and generated a public outcry. Victoria died despite having had contact with numerous statutory and non-statutory services. Post-mortem examination revealed 128 separate injuries and scars on her body. In 2001, her great aunt and her great aunt's boyfriend were found guilty of murder and sentenced to life imprisonment. The case prompted a public enquiry and a renewed focus on child protection law and policy in the UK.

CAU identified the inquiry into Victoria's death as an opportunity to call for equal protection for children, making a detailed submission to the Inquiry (CAU, 2001b). Noting that one of Victoria's killers had started his torture with disciplinary slaps and that more than one child a week is battered to death in Britain, the National Society for the Prevention of Cruelty to Children (NSPCC) and other CAU organizations pressed Lord Laming, the chair of the inquiry, to propose abolition:

> Outlawing physical punishment would, at a stroke, transform the child protection system. . . . It has to be speculative whether Victoria Climbié herself would have been saved by such a ban, but had Victoria Climbié been sent to Sweden instead of the UK, she would have stood a hugely higher chance of being alive today. Certainly many other UK children at risk of death and serious injury would be saved. (CAU, 2001b)

The inquiry's report provided 108 recommendations (Laming, 2003), but these did not include any change to child protection law or to legislation relating to physical punishment. In contrast, the parliamentary Health Committee strongly recommended that the government "remove the increasingly anomalous reasonable chastisement defence from parents and carers in order fully to protect children from injury and death" (Health Committee, 2003, para. 55). At the same time, the Joint Committee on Human Rights published its report to the government on the *Convention on the Rights of the Child* (CRC; Joint Committee on Human Rights, 2003). It called for complete removal of the defense.

CAU's parliamentary supporters tabled a private member's bill to explicitly repeal the "reasonable chastisement" defense by amending the *Children and Young Persons Act 1933*. It was unsuccessful but symbolized the strengthening of CAU's parliamentary campaign.

The next serious legislative opportunity was provided by the parliamentary passage of a new *Children Bill* in 2004. As presented, it did not cover the issue at all, but a new clause was tabled to repeal the "reasonable chastisement" defense. In light of the government's opposition, CAU pressed for a free vote in parliament, which would allow Members of Parliament (MPs) to vote according to conscience rather than by party line. At this stage, more than 180 MPs and Peers[6] had signed up in support of CAU's aims. There was widespread professional consensus, with more than 350 organizations signed up to CAU, as well as faith groups including Caritas Social Action, the Catholic Children's Society, the Methodist Church, and the United Reform Church.

When the new clause was debated at committee stage in the House of Lords, there were strong speeches in support from Peers, but the amendment was rejected. The government "whipped"[7] Labor Peers to oppose equal protection reform but allowed them a free vote on an alternative proposal to restrict rather than repeal the defense. The parliamentary Joint Committee on Human Rights believed this restriction would not satisfy human rights obligations and, referring to the jurisprudence of the Committee on the Rights of the Child, again called for complete repeal of the defense (Joint Committee on Human Rights, 2004b).

CAU continued to press for equal protection. An open letter from MP campaign supporters to the Leader of the Commons[8] called for a free vote on equal protection and rejected the "compromise" proposal. Noting that Labor MPs had been allowed a free vote when prohibition in schools was achieved, it argued that:

> All professional associations working with children and families agree that giving children equal protection is workable and would provide necessary clarity in the law. They also agree that anything less than equal protection would create legal ambiguity, parental confusion and professional uncertainty.
>
> In this context, the Government's offer of a free vote on [the restriction of the defense] is an insult. This flawed proposal, which would continue to give children less protection, is both unprincipled and, in the view of child protection agencies, unworkable.
>
> We have been allowed to vote according to our conscience on protecting foxes. Protecting children properly is at least as worthy of a free vote. (Hinchliffe et al., 2004)

A statement against the compromise was put before parliament by professional organizations concerned with children and families. They said the proposal did not represent "a safe or workable way forward for children and child protection" and called for equal protection. The statement outlined professionals' concerns that the proposed clause would send the wrong message, would not deter dangerous forms of punishment, would be likely to result in unfair and unnecessary prosecutions, had no clarity or legal certainty, would not satisfy human rights obligations, would not work to change the culture, and would place an unreasonable burden on the medical profession (Association of Directors of Social Services et al., 2004).

The strength of feeling for equal protection and against a compromise law was strong and vocal, but the government resisted. The *Children Act 2004* was passed and Section 58 leaves the defense (now called "reasonable punishment") available to parents and others *in loco parentis*[9] charged with common assault. The defense can no longer be used by those charged with assault occasioning actual bodily harm, unlawfully inflicting grievous bodily harm, causing grievous bodily harm with intent, or cruelty to a child.

These events were at odds with developments in Wales, where there is cross-party support for complete abolition of the defense. Following the recommendations to the UK from the UN Committee on the Rights of the Child in 2002, the National Assembly of Wales issued a Cabinet Statement confirming its intention to communicate its support for law reform to the UK government. Many Welsh Peers and MPs supported the "equal protection" clause in the 2004 campaign, including the lead sponsor for the clause in the House of Lords and two of the four sponsors in the Commons; over 40 Welsh MPs voted in favor of it (Taylor, 2006).

However, law reform cannot be achieved independently in Wales because it would impact on criminal justice, a responsibility that has not been devolved from the UK government. So instead, the Assembly supports the CAU campaign in Wales and continues to press the UK government for removal of the defense. In 2004, the Assembly's views were stated in a paper presented to the Health and Social Services Committee:

> The Assembly Government believes that the current legal defence of "reasonable chastisement" should be ended. We wish to encourage respect for children's rights to human dignity and nonviolent forms of discipline, including through public education programmes. We have made representations to the UK Government about this.
>
> We do not accept that smacking teaches children how to behave as they grow up. Children who are smacked are more likely to believe that the strong get their own way and that violence is an acceptable manner of expressing a view or dealing with anger or frustration.
>
> We believe that we must respect what children themselves have told us: that a smack serves to create distrust, fear and dislike, but is not the best way to instil respect for the adult or acceptance of their values. (Welsh Assembly Government, 2004, pp. 4–5)

In its 2009 progress report on implementing the CRC, the Assembly stated that it "has taken a principled stance against physical punishment of children, and agrees with the view of the UN Committee on the Rights of the Child that corporal punishment should be prohibited by law" (Welsh Assembly Government, 2009, p. 30). The Assembly supports CAU's work promoting positive parenting in Wales, including the launch in 2008 of the *Help at Hand Toolkit* aimed at changing attitudes and behavior regarding physical punishment of children ('Sdim Curo Plant!/Children are Unbeatable! in Wales, 2008; see also Butler & Clutton, 2006). The Assembly also includes the problem of physical punishment of children in its approach to domestic violence (Welsh Assembly Government, 2005).

PROGRESS TOWARDS LAW REFORM IN SCOTLAND

In Scotland, following the decision in the *A v UK* case, a public consultation was held on how the law on physical punishment could be clarified (Scottish Executive, 2000). Analysis of the 220 written responses revealed that 34% were "opposed to any physical punishment and called for a total ban", 17% "supported the right of parents to discipline their children as they see fit and are opposed to any change in the law", and 43% were "prepared to consider the Executive's proposals (to limit rather than remove the defense of 'reasonable chastisement'), albeit often reluctantly" (Scottish Executive, 2002). Most of the 40 children aged 8 to 16 who were consulted in focus groups felt that children under three should not be physically punished but it was acceptable as a last resort for older children (Children in Scotland, 2000). The Scottish Executive proposed to ban corporal punishment of children under the age of 3 and the use of implements on all children (Scottish Executive, 2001).

The *Criminal Justice (Scotland) Bill* was introduced to the Scottish parliament in 2002. It included a provision which would ban all physical punishment of children up to their 3rd birthday and ban the use of implements, shaking, and blows to the head for all children. The Scottish Strategy Group of CAU distributed a briefing to all Members of the Scottish Parliament (MSPs), urging them to endorse the proposals, support the campaign for prohibition of all physical punishment, and encourage the dissemination of information on positive discipline. It outlined the arguments for a total ban and addressed some of the popular misconceptions about prohibition. However, following publication of a report opposing the proposal from a Committee of the Scottish Parliament, the proposal to ban smacking of babies and toddlers was dropped.

In 2003, the *Criminal Justice (Scotland) Act* became law. Section 51 introduced the concept of "justifiable assault" and defines physical punishment of children under 16 by way of blows to the head, shaking and use of implements as unjustifiable. In determining whether an assault is justifiable, courts must take into account "(a) the nature of what was done, the reason for it and the circumstances in which it took place; (b) its duration and frequency; (c) any effect (whether physical or mental) which it has been shown to have had on the child; (d) the child's age; and (e) the child's personal characteristics (including, without prejudice to the generality of this paragraph, sex and state of health) at the time the thing was done". The law was brought into force quietly, with a public information leaflet placed on the Executive website which emphasized that smacking children "is not advisable" because it "can be dangerous", "sets children the wrong example", "has effects which last long after the physical pain dies away", and "is not an effective way to teach children discipline" (Scottish Executive, 2003).

PROGRESS TOWARDS LAW REFORM IN NORTHERN IRELAND

In Northern Ireland, the consultation document on physical punishment law published in response to the decision in the *A v UK* case was clear that obligations under international human rights law would only be fully met by complete removal of the defense (Office of Law Reform, 2001). But the majority of responses rejected removal of the defense, largely because of "religious convictions, a belief that the State should not interfere with family life and the rejection of any linkage between 'reasonable chastisement' and physical abuse" (Office of Law Reform, 2002, p. 58).

In 2002, a resolution to take account of the consultation in England and Wales and the decision not to change the law was debated in the Northern Ireland Assembly. An amendment to the resolution urging the government to take note of developments in Scotland and internationally was defeated. At this time, the devolved powers of the Northern Ireland Assembly were not adequate to enable it to legislate on physical punishment. It was decided that a provision corresponding to Section 58 of the *Children Act 2004* in England and Wales would be introduced in Northern Ireland. Article 2 of the *Law Reform (Miscellaneous Provisions) (Northern Ireland) Order 2006* was adopted by the Parliament in Westminster and provides for the restriction of the defense of "reasonable chastisement" to the summary charge of common assault. The defense can no longer be raised on charges such as wounding, grievous bodily harm, assault occasioning actual bodily harm, or cruelty to a child. The Children's Commissioner in Northern Ireland lost an appeal against the law. The application was rejected in the Court of Appeal on the technical grounds that the Commissioner did not have "victim" status.

GROWING SUPPORT FOR PROHIBITION

In 2005, high profile calls for equal protection were made by MPs at the Labor party conference and in a report from the Commission on Families and the Wellbeing of Children, chaired by Sir Michael Rutter (Commission on Families and the Wellbeing of Children, 2005). In January 2006, the campaign took a major step forward with the publication of a joint statement on physical punishment of children from the four UK commissioners for children and young people, urging "the government and the Scottish Executive to promote consistent legislation throughout the UK to give all children full protection under the law on assault" and promising "our vocal support and also that of the strongest and broadest alliance of professional and other organizations ever formed around an issue for children" (CAU, 2006b).

CAU produced a new report documenting the growing pressure from human rights bodies and parliament's own Joint Committee on Human Rights and summarizing again the arguments for a total ban (CAU, 2006a). The report was welcomed by politicians from both Houses of Parliament. CAU again supported Labor MPs and Peers in calling for a free vote on the issue—more than 170 MPs from all parties signed a House of Commons motion on children's right to equal protection.

GOVERNMENT REVIEW OF THE "REASONABLE PUNISHMENT" LAW

In 2007, the government reviewed the "practical consequences" of Section 58 of the *Children Act 2004* in England and Wales, fulfilling a promise made by the Minister responsible when the legislation was passed (Department for Education and Skills, 2007). CAU briefed supporters and others, encouraging them to make their submissions to the review, and sought to strengthen the involvement of the domestic violence sector, the main women's organizations already having signed up to the campaign.

Responses to the consultation—over 1,400 in all—were overwhelmingly critical of Section 58. A majority in every category of respondent saw no improvement to legal protection of children (only 1% of all respondents thought it had improved protection). When asked to what extent the law deterred parents from using unacceptable levels of physical punishment, the majority in all categories except faith groups felt Section 58 had no deterrent effect. On whether the law had assisted those working with and supporting parents, most (66%) thought it had not assisted at all, only 5% thought it had (Department for Children, Schools and Families, 2007b). The government's report on the consultation noted the strength of negative feeling about Section 58 and its perceived failure to make a positive impact on child protection work: "An overwhelming majority called for children to enjoy the same rights to protection as adults" (Department for Children, Schools and Families, 2007b, p. 3).

But—relying on the results of the public opinion poll strand of the consultation which showed majority public opposition to banning smacking—the government concluded that the law is clear and should not be changed (Department for Children, Schools and Families, 2007a). Government-commissioned research into the views of children aged 4 to 16 revealed that smacking was feared and thought to be ineffective, an abuse of power, and incompatible with parental messages about respect and acceptable behavior (Sherbert Research, 2007). These views were disregarded.

The review of Section 58 coincided with another high profile child death. One-year-old Peter Connelly's death in 2007 led to the largest public outcry about child protection since Victoria Climbié's death. He had lived in the same local authority as Victoria. Like her, he had been known to the authorities. A post-mortem examination revealed a broken back and ribs and other injuries. Peter's mother, her boyfriend, and her boyfriend's brother were convicted of causing or allowing the death of a child. The case led to three inquiries and a nationwide review of social service care. The government decided to introduce legislation relating to the case, but there was no intention to remove the defenses for the use of physical punishment. CAU's analysis of inquiries into child deaths by assault demonstrated that almost all included an element of physical punishment (CAU, 2009b).

DEVELOPMENTS SINCE 2008

In a renewed appeal for action in 2008, CAU sponsored a full-page advertisement in major newspapers and magazines, urging readers to join the campaign for law reform and carrying the names of politicians, policy makers, parents, and professionals working with children and families who support the campaign. The campaign for a free vote continued, and important public figures wrote an open letter to Prime Minister Gordon Brown.

Professional organizations issued a joint statement about the importance of removing the defenses in providing a clear foundation for child protection and the promotion of positive, nonviolent parenting—"full legal reform is the only safe, just and workable way forward". The statement outlined what prohibition would mean in practice, including how reports of physical punishment would be dealt with and how decisions would be made on charging and prosecution. It was signed by the major professional and other organizations working with and for children (Association of Directors of Children's Services et al., 2008).

The introduction of a *Children and Young Persons Bill* to parliament provided another opportunity to pursue prohibition. It was intended to amend the legal framework concerning children in public care and included provisions relating to children's well-being, private fostering, and child deaths. CAU sponsored an amendment which would repeal Section 58 of the *Children Act 2004* and the common law rules supporting the use of force for punishing a child. The Conservatives and the Liberal Democrats supported a free vote on the amendment, which was tabled by MPs from the Labor party, the Conservatives, the Liberal Democrats, and two minority parties. It was anticipated there would have been substantial support for change but the amendment was denied time for debate by the business managers in the House of Commons.

In the same period, the concluding observations of the Committee on the Rights of the Child on the UK's third report (Committee on the Rights of the Child, 2008) and Council of Europe Commissioner for Human Rights Thomas Hammarberg's memorandum on corporal punishment in the UK (Council of Europe, 2008) were issued. In response to their calls for total prohibition, the government reiterated its belief that smacking is not violence (Council of Europe, 2008; Morgan, 2008).

CAU published a detailed briefing arguing that smacking *is* violence, drawing on children's views of how it hurts, highlighting the contradiction with the law on domestic violence, and challenging the idea that smacking has nothing to do with serious child abuse (CAU, 2009b). Addressing the notion that people who kill children are unlikely to be deterred by light smacks being against the law, and in light of Peter Connelly's death, CAU developed the public health argument that serious child abuse might be prevented by tackling widespread low-level violence to children and social tolerance of this. Sending the briefing to a wide range of parliamentarians generated new supporters of the campaign in the House of Commons and the House of Lords. A cross-party group of MPs attempted to table an amendment to another Bill covering issues affecting children in 2009, but it was rejected on the grounds that it was outside the Bill's scope.

As part of its focus on the child protection sector in 2009, CAU invited all local safeguarding children boards (LSCBs) to support the campaign. Informally, there is overwhelming backing for the campaign, and by January 2010, 20 boards had formally signed up to CAU (CAU, 2009a).

In September 2009, following a meeting with CAU to discuss equal protection, the government minister responsible for the issue, Baroness Delyth Morgan, stated in a letter to CAU:

> I do need to repeat that the Government does not intend to ban smacking, nor to allow a free vote should the issue come up again for debate in Parliament since this might facilitate a ban, to which we are opposed as a matter of policy. (Morgan, 2009)

The Minister also requested that her name be removed from the CAU website—she, like her predecessor as responsible Minister in the Department for Children, Schools and Families, had previously signed up as a supporter of the aims of the Alliance.

CONCLUSION

There is extensive support in the UK—among professional and other organizations, within parliament, and increasingly among the public—for law reform to achieve equal protection from assault for children. There is also huge pressure from European and international human rights treaty monitoring bodies. The UK is now one of only four countries in the European

Union not to have enacted or committed to enacting full prohibition.[10] CAU will continue to campaign until corporal punishment of children is unlawful in all settings in all parts of the UK. In particular, it is reviewing how to strengthen the legal pressure on the UK to fulfill its human rights obligations. Even government ministers accept in private that this reform is now inevitable; the only question is how long it will take.

NOTES

1. This section is based on Carter, S., & Swift, H. (2009). *UPDATE: A guide to the UK legal system*. Accessed May 19, 2010, from http://www.nyulawglobal.org/globalex/United_Kingdom1.htm
2. "Borstals" were reformatory training (penal) institutions for young people in conflict with the law, originally designed for 16- to 21-year-olds and governed by the prison service.
3. "State schools" are primarily funded and run by the government and provide education to all children free of charge; "private schools" (also known as "public schools" or "fee-paying schools") are run and funded mainly by non-government sources and typically involve parents paying for their child's education.
4. The Northern Ireland Childminding Association defines childminders as "self employed daycare providers who work in their own home to provide care and education for other people's children within a family setting" (http://www.nicma.org/cms/for-childminders, accessed May 19, 2010). They must register with the local Health and Social Services Trust.
5. See http://www.childrenareunbeatable.org.uk/children/home.html
6. Members of the House of Lords are known as "Peers".
7. A "whip" in British politics is an MP who ensures that members of the party vote as the leader desires. To be "whipped" means to be instructed to do this.
8. The Leader of the House of Commons is the person responsible for organizing government business (such as introducing bills and ministerial statements) in the House of Commons.
9. Unless legislation explicitly prohibits them using physical punishment.
10. The others are Belgium, France, and Malta.

REFERENCES

Association of Directors of Children's Services, British Association for the Study and Prevention of Child Abuse and Neglect, Association of British Social Workers, Unite—Community Practitioners' and Health Visitors' Association, NSPCC, Parenting UK, Royal College of Nursing, Safeguarding Children & Young People Forum, and Royal College of Paediatrics and Child Health. (2008). *Implementing equal protection for children: Practical implications of law reform removing the "reasonable punishment" defence*, London: Children Are Unbeatable! Alliance.

Association of Directors of Social Services, British Association for the Study and Prevention of Child Abuse and Neglect, British Association of Social Workers, Community Practitioners' and Health Visitors' Association, NSPCC, Parenting Education and Support Forum, and Royal College of Paediatrics and Child Health. (2004). *Why Clause 56 is not the way forward*. Accessed December 17, 2009, from www.childrenareunbeatable.org.uk/index.html

Butler, V., & Clutton, S. (2006). *"Help at Hand": An evaluation report of a programme of activities promoting alternatives to smacking children.* Commissioned by Children are Unbeatable! Alliance Funded by New Ideas Fund, Social Justice and Regeneration Division, Welsh Assembly Government.

Carter, S., & Swift, H. (2009). *UPDATE: A guide to the UK legal system.* Accessed May 19, 2010, from http://www.nyulawglobal.org/globalex/United_Kingdom1.htm

CAU. (2001a). "Ministers say law on 'reasonable punishment' won't change in England and Wales". *News.* Accessed December 18, 2009, from www.childrenareunbeatable.org.uk/pages/news/archive.html#Ministers

CAU. (2001b). *Submission to the Victoria Climbié Inquiry by the "Children are unbeatable!" Alliance.* Accessed December 17, 2009, from www.childrenareunbeatable.org.uk/pages/news/climbie.html

CAU. (2006a). *Equal protection from assault is every child's human right.* London: Children Are Unbeatable! Alliance.

CAU. (2006b). "Major step forward as Commissioners back reform", *News.* Accessed December 17, 2009, from www.childrenareunbeatable.org.uk/index.html#Anchor-Major-47857

CAU. (2009a). *Children Are Unbeatable! Newsletter,* Issue 1, December 2009.

CAU. (2009b). *The only safe foundation for child protection is to end legalised violence against children.* London: Children Are Unbeatable! Alliance.

Children in Scotland. (2000). *Physical punishment of children in Scotland: A consultation with children and young people.* Edinburgh: Children in Scotland.

Commission on Families and the Wellbeing of Children. (2005). *Families and the state: Two-way support and responsibilities. An inquiry into the relationship between the state and the family in the upbringing of children.* Bristol, UK: The Policy Press.

Committee on Economic and Social Rights. (2002). *Concluding observations of the Committee on Economic, Social and Cultural Rights: United Kingdom of Great Britain and Northern Ireland, the Crown Dependencies and the Overseas Dependent Territories* (fourth report). E/C.12/1/Add.79, June 5, 2002.

Committee on Economic and Social Rights. (2009). *Concluding observations of the Committee on Economic, Social and Cultural Rights: United Kingdom of Great Britain and Northern Ireland, the Crown Dependencies and the Overseas Dependent Territories* (fourth to fifth report). E/C.12/GBR/CO/5, June 12, 2009.

Committee on the Elimination of Discrimination against Women. (2008). *Concluding observations of the Committee on the Elimination of Discrimination against Women: United Kingdom of Great Britain and Northern Ireland* (fifth and sixth reports). CEDAW/C/GBR/CO/6, July 18, 2008.

Committee on the Rights of the Child. (1995). *Concluding observations: United Kingdom of Great Britain and Northern Ireland* (initial report). CRC/C/15/Add.34, February 15, 1995.

Committee on the Rights of the Child. (2002). *Concluding observations: United Kingdom of Great Britain and Northern Ireland* (second periodic report). CRC/C/15/Add.188, October 9, 2002.

Committee on the Rights of the Child. (2008). *Concluding observations: United Kingdom of Great Britain and Northern Ireland* (third and fourth periodic report). CRC/C/GBR/CO/4, October 20, 2008.

Council of Europe Committee of Ministers. (2009). *Final Resolution CM/ResDH (2009)75 Execution of the judgment of the European Court of Human Rights against United Kingdom.*

Council of Europe. (2007). *Eliminating corporal punishment: A human rights imperative for Europe's children,* 2nd ed. Strasburg: Council of Europe Publishing.

Council of Europe. (2008). *Memorandum by Thomas Hammarberg. Commissioner for Human Rights of the Council of Europe, following his visits to the United Kingdom, February 5–8, 2008 and March 31–April 2, 2008,* CommDH (2008) October 9, 2008 and October 28, 2008. Strasbourg: Council of Europe.

Department for Children, Schools and Families. (2007a). *Review of Section 58 of the Children Act 2004*. London: Author.
Department for Children, Schools and Families. (2007b). *Section 58 of the Children Act 2004 Review (consultation): Analysis of responses to the consultation document*. London: Author.
Department for Education and Skills. (2007). *Section 58 of Children Act 2004 Review (Consultation)*. London: Author.
Department of Health. (2000a). *Analysis of responses to the "Protecting children, supporting parents" consultation document*. London: Author.
Department of Health. (2000b). *Protecting children, supporting parents: A consultation document on the physical punishment of children*. London: Author.
European Committee of Social Rights. (2001). *Conclusions XV–2, Vol. 1*. Strasbourg: Council of Europe Publishing.
European Committee of Social Rights. (2005). *Conclusions XVII–2, Vol. 2*. Strasbourg: Council of Europe Publishing.
Health Committee. (2003). *The Victoria Climbié Inquiry Report: Sixth Report of Session 2002–03*. London: The Stationery Office.
Hinchliffe, D., et al. (2004). "Open letter to Rt Hon Peter Hain MP, Leader of the House of Commons". Accessed May 19, 2010, from http://www.childrenareunbeatable.org.uk/index.html
Human Rights Council. (2008). *Report of the Working Group on the Universal Periodic Review: United Kingdom of Great Britain and Northern Ireland*. A/HRC/8/25, May 23, 2008.
Ipsos MORI. (1999). *Strong parental support for anti-smacking law*. Report for NSPCC. Accessed December 17, 2009, from www.ipsos-mori.com/researchpublications/researcharchive/poll.aspx?oItemId=1930
Ipsos MORI. (2002). *Physical punishment of children: Summary of findings*. Report for NSPCC. Accessed December 17, 2009, from www.childrenareunbeatable.org.uk/pages/news/nspcc0202.html
Ipsos MORI. (2004). *Public backs equality law change for children*. Report for CAU. Accessed December 17, 2009, from www.ipsos-mori.com/researchpublications/researcharchive/poll.aspx?oItemId=604
Ipsos MORI. (2007). *A study into the views of parents on the physical punishment of children*. Report for the Department for Children, Schools and Families. Accessed March 14, 2010, from http://publications.dcsf.gov.uk/eOrderingDownload/Section58-Parental-Survey.pdf
Joint Committee on Human Rights. (2003). *The UN Convention on the Rights of the Child: Tenth report of session 2002–03*. London: The Stationery Office.
Joint Committee on Human Rights. (2004a). *Children Bill: Nineteenth report of session 2003–04*. London: The Stationery Office.
Joint Committee on Human Rights. (2004b). *Scrutiny of Bills: Twelfth report of session 2003–04*. London: The Stationery Office.
Laming, W. H. (2003). *The Victoria Climbié Inquiry: Report of an inquiry by Lord Laming*. London.
Morgan, D. (2008). Comments by Baroness Morgan during parliamentary debate. *Hansard* House of Lords, October 16, 2008, Cols 822–824.
Morgan, D. (2009). Letter to CAU, September 4, 2009.
Newell, P. (1989). *Children are people too: The case against physical punishment*. London: Bedford Square Press.
Office of Law Reform. (2001). *Physical punishment in the home—thinking about the issues, looking at the evidence: A consultation paper for Northern Ireland, summary version*. Belfast: Office of Law Reform.
Office of Law Reform. (2002). *"Physical punishment in the home—thinking about the issues, looking at the evidence": Analysis of responses*. Belfast: Office of Law Reform/Department of Finance and Personnel.

Scottish Executive. (2000). *The physical punishment of children in Scotland: A consultation*. Edinburgh: Scottish Executive.
Scottish Executive. (2001). *Making Scotland safer: Improving the criminal justice system*. Edinburgh: Scottish Executive.
Scottish Executive. (2002). *The physical punishment of children in Scotland: Analysis of responses*. Edinburgh: Scottish Executive.
Scottish Executive. (2003). *Children, physical punishment and the law: A guide for parents in Scotland*. Edinburgh: Scottish Executive.
'Sdim Curo Plant!/Children are Unbeatable! in Wales. (2008). *Help at Hand Handbook: A toolkit to change attitudes and behaviour around the physical punishment of children*. Cardiff: SCP/CAU; accompanying website http://www.helpathandtoolkit.info/
Sherbert Research. (2007). *A study into children's views on physical discipline and punishment*. Report for the Department for Children, Schools and Families and the Central Office of Information. London: Sherbert Research/COI.
Taylor, J. (2006). Corporal punishment. In R. Croke & A. Crowley (Eds.), *Righting the wrongs: The reality of children's rights in Wales* (pp. 51–55). Cardiff: Save the Children.
Welsh Assembly Government. (2004). *Children and young people: Rights to action*. Cardiff: Welsh Assembly Government.
Welsh Assembly Government. (2005). *Tackling domestic abuse: TheAall Wales National Strategy*. Cardiff: Welsh Assembly Government.
Welsh Assembly Government. (2009). *Rights in action: Implementing children and young people's rights in Wales*. Cardiff: Welsh Assembly Government.

ACTS

Scotland Act 1998
Northern Ireland Act 1998
Northern Ireland (Elections) Act 1998
Government of Wales Act 1998
Government of Wales Act 2006
Children Act 2004
Law Reform (Miscellaneous Provisions) (Northern Ireland) Order 2006
Criminal Justice (Scotland) Act 2003
Prevention of Cruelty to and Protection of Children Act 1889
Prevention of Cruelty to Children Act 1894
Prevention of Cruelty to Children Act 1904
Children and Young Persons Act 1933
Human Rights Act 1998

CASES

R v Hopley [1860]
Tyrer v UK (1978)
Campbell and Cosans v UK (1982)
Philip Williamson and Others v UK (2000)
A v UK (1998)

21 Uruguay

The Landmark Law in Latin America

Maria Clara Galvis and Gaby Reyes[1]

Population:	3,240,000
Area:	176,000 square kilometers
Type of government:	Federal presidential republic, 19 federal States
Governing structure:	National government
Child protection system:	Comprehensive system of protection of children and adolescents against violence (SIPIAV), which articulates the policies and programs of different institutions.
Legal system:	European Continental Law or Romano-Germánico
Major religion:	Secular State, 47.1% Catholic
Official national language:	Spanish
Ratified United Nations Convention on the Rights of the Child:	1990
Children's Commissioner/Ombudsman:	No

HISTORICAL CONTEXT

Before the arrival of the Spanish in 1516, the territory of Uruguay was populated by indigenous nomadic people (the charrúas). The Spanish began to settle at the end of the 16th and early 17th centuries, with the founding of Colonia del Sacramento and Montevideo. During colonization, Uruguay was the subject of disputes between Portugal, Spain, and England. It became independent of those nations between 1811 and 1821, when it was appended to Brazil. Uruguay declared its independence from Brazil in 1825, generating a war which lasted until 1928, the year when the country finally obtained its independence. The first constitution was adopted in 1830. The 19th century was marked by the arrival of immigrants from Europe, the existence of civil conflicts, and sporadic incursions from Brazil and Argentina. From the middle of the 20th century, the White and Colorado parties disputed the Presidency—until 1973, when the military led a coup d'état to control the insurgency movement, the Tupamaro Front for National Liberation. During that period, many disappearances, arrests, and torture took place. Democracy returned in 1984 with an electoral victory for the Colorado Party. The White and Colorado parties held power until 2004, when a leftist coalition, *Frente Amplio,* won the presidential elections. This government, still in power today, has proclaimed its commitment to seeking justice for the inhumane and criminal acts committed by the military dictatorship. According to the *The Economist Intelligence Unit's Index of Democracy* (2007), Uruguay is the most democratic country in Latin America, and it has the third highest human development index in Latin America, after Argentina and Chile (UNDP, 2009), ranking 50th amongst 182 countries.

THE 19TH CENTURY: BANNING PHYSICAL PUNISHMENT IN SCHOOLS

Physical punishment has been partially controlled in Uruguay, although not by law, since 1847 (Bonfanti, 2005). At that time, the public school regulations allowed a maximum of three spanks. In 1877 the *General Regulations for Public Schools* prohibited corporal punishment in schools, under penalty of dismissal for teachers. At the beginning of the 20th century, this ban was reinforced by the imposition of fines for teachers, which helped reduce the prevalence of physical punishment in schools (Bonfanti, 2005).

However, physical punishment remained a cultural practice in care institutions and within the family throughout the 20th century. Today, most Uruguayan adults have experienced some form of physical punishment (Program Arcoiris, 2005a). This is less likely to be the case in the next generation because in 2007, Uruguay became the first Latin American country to prohibit all physical and humiliating punishment of children.

THE PATH TO PROHIBITION

Prior to prohibition, the *Civil Code* gave parents (Article 261) and guardians (Article 384[2] & [3]) the responsibility to "moderately correct" children. If that parental correction was not "adequate" to change the child's behavior, parents or guardians could present the case to a judge who could decide whether the child should be admitted to a correction center (Articles 261 and 384). The lack of clarity about the meaning of "moderate" or "adequate" correction, in a cultural context that accepted physical punishment as a valid method of education and under a concept of parental authority that understands that children are the objects of protection (*Civil Code*, Article 252), permitted a discretional interpretation that opened the door to physical and humiliating punishment. That children were the objects of protection failed to recognize their status as full rights holders (for example having the right to physical integrity in relation to physical punishment).

The legal situation was reflected in public attitudes. In 2005 Arcoiris[2] carried out a survey of 1,500 children and 900 adults responsible for their care (Program Arcoiris, 2005b). The findings showed that most (92%) adults had been physically punished at home as children and 70% justified its use, however 99% were able to identify methods of nonviolent childrearing if a prohibition of physical punishment were to be introduced.[3] Only 36% of the children believed that physical punishment was justified.

The situation began to change in September 2004, when the *Code for Children and Adolescents* was approved by the government. The new Code adapted the legislation to include the principles within the UNCRC. It took 14 years for Uruguay to adapt it after the ratification of the CRC in 1990. It was a long process that took several drafts and went through several working committees before the final version was produced. This new law was an important step in the process of prohibition. In that same month, Arcoiris and Save the Children Sweden held the first Uruguayan colloquium on physical punishment. This event was supported by several state organizations,[4] as well as national[5] and international[6] civil society.

On March 1, 2005 Uruguay's sociopolitical context changed dramatically. For the first time in the country's history, a leftist party was elected, the *Frente Amplio*.[7] This party had a comprehensive policy program based on respect for, and promotion of, human rights. They were elected with a two-thirds parliamentary majority,[8] and they had the political will to adapt domestic legislation to comply with international Human Rights standards. This election was well-timed. Shortly afterward, the *UN Study on Violence against Children* (Pinheiro, 2006) was released with the recommendation that all States prohibit physical punishment in all environments by 2009. In 2007, the UN Committee of the Rights of the Child recommended that Uruguay explicitly prohibit physical punishment in all settings, including the home.

Another important aspect of Uruguayan society is that it allowed citizens easy access to their political representatives. Members of Arcoiris established ongoing contact with legislators. They found that: (1) legislators were uncertain about what the law permitted, due to its ambiguous language ("moderate" and "adequate"); (2) some legislators believed that a new law would be redundant, because a law against domestic violence already existed (Law 17.514 of July 2, 2002); and (3) some feared that a new law would deprive parents and educators of educational tools. Arcoiris shared the findings of their survey with legislators to inform them about the nature and importance of a prohibition. They also educated legislators about the recommendations of the *UN Study on Violence Against Children* and about General Comment 8 of the UN Committee on the Rights of the Child; (4) the Concluding Observations of the committee about Uruguay; and (5) information about the campaign "Raising Children Without Violence is Possible," promoted by Arcoiris.

In 2005, the *Second Colloquium on the Physical Punishment of Children* was held in the Legislative Palace. This was a definitive event for parliamentarians, because the findings of a historical investigation and two surveys carried out by Arcoiris, were presented there. These provided them with the necessary information to clarify the nature of physical punishment, differentiating it from the types of violence that were addressed by the law against domestic violence. Participants in the Colloquium included Civil Society, UNICEF—Uruguay, Save the Children Sweden, the Vice President of the Oriental Republic of Uruguay, and the speaker of the House of Representatives. It was within the framework of the Colloquium that Arcoiris also publicly presented draft legislation to prohibit physical punishment, to the parliament.

Arcoiris also initiated a public awareness campaign, *Raising Children without Violence is Possible*. Its aim was to disseminate information about the effectiveness of nonviolence and to inform the public about the preventive purpose of prohibiting physical punishment. More than 10,000 pamphlets were distributed at events in which authorities, Members of Parliament, technical teams from State socioeducational programs, staff from educational institutions, and the general public, participated. Dissemination of information was facilitated by the media. Save the Children Sweden played a key role by providing interchange and a continuous link between Arcoiris' efforts and other initiatives being undertaken in the region and throughout the world.

2007: A LANDMARK YEAR

In 2007, a Bill was introduced in Parliament that would prohibit "the use of physical punishment or any type of humiliating treatment as a form of correction or discipline, even if it is mild". This law, "*Personal Integrity of Children and Adolescents*" would be placed in the *Code for Children and Adolescents*. It would prohibit physical punishment by parents and all others charged with the care, treatment, education or supervision of children and youth. It also would give authority to the Institute of the Child and Adolescent of Uruguay to provide parent and caregiver education to promote nonviolent childrearing.

The Bill was debated four times. In the two Senate debates (July 3 and August 14) and in the first Representatives debate (October 31), there was unanimous support for the Bill. But final debate in the House was different. The Senate and the House of Representatives were convened as the General Assembly. The date (November 20) had been chosen by the Parliamentary Front for the Rights of Children and Adolescents to coincide with the commemoration of the UN General Assembly's adoption of the CRC. It was during this final debate that all of the representatives from the National Party voted against the proposal, arguing that it was inconvenient, redundant, unnecessary, and sought to do the will of international organizations. In the end, the issue was resolved by the removal of the phrase "even if it is mild" from the Bill. On November 20, 2007, Uruguay became the first Latin American country to legally prohibit physical punishment in Law 18.214,[9] which became popularly known as the "the knock on the head law".

FINAL REFLECTION

In the 2 years since Law 18.214 was approved, advances have been made. For example, the State has recognized the importance of physical punishment of children and adolescents and has begun to monitor it. And in a recent report on violence against children, the Ministry of Social Development (2009) identified physical and humiliating punishment as a form of violence against children. According to the report, 59% of adults reported having used moderate or severe physical punishment in the home; 15% admitted having inflicted severe or very severe punishments. Therefore, physical punishment continues to occur in many children's homes. Achieving effective implementation of the law requires the State to formulate and implement a public policy that will provide education for parents and the wider public on nonviolent childrearing.

NOTES

1. The authors gratefully acknowledge the assistance of Gabriel Rebollo, Rossana Acosta, Andrea Portaro, and Angels Simon in writing this chapter.
2. This organization has worked since 1992 to prevent violence against children through legal and cultural changes.
3. The question was: "Which would be the alternatives educational methods if corporal punishment was forbidden?"
4. Senate Chamber, Representatives Chamber, Minister of Social Development, Council of Primary Education, the Institute of the Child and Adolescent of Uruguay, the Institute of Human Rights of the Universidad de la República, City Council of Montevideo-Secretary of Childhood, National Directorate of the Prevention of Social Crimes.
5. National Association of Non-governmental Organizations, Committee of the Rights of the Child, Uruguayan Network against Domestic and Sexual Violence, and the Commission of Boys and Girls for their Rights.
6. UNICEF Uruguay, Inter-American Institute of the Child.
7. Tabaré Vásquez, the Frente Amplio's presidential candidate, won the election on October 31, 2004.
8. This majority was achieved by the Frente Amplio with the election of 99 representatives and 30 senators.
9. It was promulgated on December 9th and published in the Official Daily on December 31, 2007.

REFERENCES

Bonfanti, D. (2005). In search for an appropriate corrective: Notes for a history of physical punishment against children in Uruguay (1809–1934). Programa Arcoiris—UNICEF, Uruguay.

Civil Code of Uruguay. Approved by Law 16.603, October 11, 1994.

Eastern Republic of Uruguay. National Institute of Statistics. (2009). http://www.ine.gub.uy/enha2006/flash/Flash%206_Religion.pdf.

Ministry of Social Development. (2009). Practices of upbringing and solving family conflicts: Prevalence of ill-treatment against children and adolescents. http://

www.mides.gub.uy/mides/resultadobuscar.jsp?query=PREVALENCIA+MALTRATO&x=4&y=12

Pinheiro, P. (2006). World Report on Violence against Children. Geneva: United Nations Secretary-General's Study on Violence against Children. Retrievable from: www.unviolencestudy.org

Program Arcoiris. (2005a). Current perception of adults responsible for the care of children and adolescents on corporal punishment and its use in Uruguay. Retrievable from: http://extranet.acabarcastigo.org/contenido.php?v_men=22&v_pla=2&v_dgr=1&v_cod=167&v_regiones=5P&v_categorias=25

Program Arcoiris. (2005b). Boys and girls opinion about raising methods in Uruguay. Retrievable from: http://www.sai.org.uy/website/

The Economist Intelligence Unit's Index of Democracy. (2007). Retrievable from: http://www.economist.com/media/pdf/Democracy_Index_2007_v3.pdf

UN Committee on the Rights of the Child. (CRC). UN Committee on the Rights of the Child: Concluding Observations, Uruguay, 5 July 2007, CRC/C/URY/CO/2, retrievable from: http://www.unhcr.org/refworld/docid/469b351d2.html

United Nations Program for Development, UNDP. (2009). HDI rankings. Human Development Report 2009. Retrievable from: http://hdr.undp.org/en/statistics/

Wikipedia. (2009). Retrievable from: http://es.wikipedia.org/wiki/Uruguay

22 Venezuela

The Process of Prohibiting Physical and Humiliating Punishment

Maria Clara Galvis and Gaby Reyes[1]

Population:	28,384,132
Area:	916,445 square kilometers
Type of government:	Federal Presidential Republic; 23 states and a Capital District: Caracas.
Governing structure:	National government, 10 counties, 60 municipalities
Child protection system in place:	Yes. Enshrined in the Organic Law for the Protection of Children and Adolescents (LOPNA), administrative and judicial bodies, the Public Ministry, care institutions, and the Office of the Ombudsman for Children and Adolescents.
Legal system:	European Continental Law or Romano-Germánico
Major religion:	92% Catholic
Official national languages:	Spanish and indigenous languages
Ratified United Nations Convention on the Rights of the Child:	1990
Children's Commissioner Ombudsman:	Yes. Ombudsman for Children and Adolescents (LOPNA, Title III)

HISTORICAL CONTEXT

When Christopher Columbus arrived in 1498, Venezuela was populated by indigenous Arawacos, Caribs, and Chibchas. The land was colonized by Spain in the 16th century; the capital, Caracas, was founded in 1567. Throughout the 16th and 17th centuries, Spaniards continued to arrive, as well as Germans; English, French, and Dutch pirates; and Capuchin, Franciscan, and Jesuit missionaries. By the end of the 18th century, ideas generated by the Enlightenment and the French Revolution had become widespread, and Latin America began to seek independence. Three Venezuelans—Simon Bolívar, Francisco Miranda, and Antonio José de Sucre—were the main leaders of this movement. Venezuela gained its independence in 1810. At that time, Venezuela was integrated with Panama, Colombia, and Ecuador into a territory called Gran Colombia. In 1830, Venezuela separated and became a sovereign country.

Throughout the rest of the 19th century and into the mid 20th century, Venezuela experienced prolonged periods of military and civilian dictatorships and authoritarian governments. Oil was discovered in Venezuela during World War I leading to an economic boom, followed by slumps as the price of oil fluctuated. The first free elections took place in 1947. The elected President, Romulo Gallegos, legalized political parties and trade unions and enacted a liberal Constitution, but in 1948, after a coup d 'état, a Provisional Board took over the Government. Then, in 1952, a military government was imposed. In 1958, free elections were re-established; the parties Democratic Action and Committee of Independent Political Organization came to power. Free elections have been held since that time.

In 1999, Hugo Chávez Frías, of the Fifth Republic movement[2], was elected President and remains in power today. On the *Economist Democracy Index* (Kekic, 2007), Venezuela ranks 93rd out of 167 countries worldwide. It also ranks highly on the Human Development Index (United Nations Development Program, 2009), occupying the 58th position among 182 countries, and 7th among Latin American nations. On December 10, 2007, Venezuela became the second country in Latin America to ban all physical or humiliating punishment of children and adolescents in all settings, including the home.

THE LEGAL AND CULTURAL CONTEXT

The first *Organic Law for the Protection of Children and Adolescents* (LOPNA) was implemented in 1998. It was in this law that corporal and collective punishment in schools was explicitly banned (Article 57). But this law did not prohibit physical punishment in homes. According to Article 358 of LOPNA, the rearing of children included the "ability to apply appropriate corrective measures". Moreover, Article 265 of the *Civil Code* stated that parenting included the "ability to impose [on the minor] appropriate corrections". Article 349 of the *Civil Code* stated that caretakers could "moderately" correct a minor—and if this correction was not adequate to change the minor's behavior, parents and caretakers could bring the situation to the attention of a juvenile judge who, in turn, could take "appropriate measures". But "adequate" and "moderate" corrections were not clearly defined, so physical punishment could easily be legitimated—particularly within a culture that supported it, as was the case in Venezuela.

In 2004, the organization Community Centers of Learning (Cecodap) carried out a study of public perceptions of physical and humiliating punishment, involving 694 children and 205 adults nationwide. It revealed that both adults and children considered it to be "common sense" that corporal punishment was a natural, normal, and necessary part of a good upbringing for children and adolescents (Cecodap & Save the Children Sweden, 2004). Among the types of punishment viewed as acceptable were smacking on the bottom (33% of children and 44% of adults), pinching (21% of children and 6% of adults), hitting with a belt (29% of children and 19% of adults), shouting (28% of children and 9% of adults), insulting, humiliating, throwing water on the child's face, and putting the child under the shower (19% of children and 7 % of adults). The same study revealed that many children believed that parents hit them as an expression of love, and because it would help them to become better people (Trapani, 2007). Parents justified corporal punishment on the basis that it teaches children to understand the concept of respect, and prevents subsequent negative behaviors (Trapani, 2007).

The ambiguity of the law and the broad public acceptance of physical punishment created a context that legitimated violence against children as recently as the mid-2000s. But through public education and awareness raising, this situation was about to change.

THE JOURNEY TO PROHIBITION

The World Social Forum took place in Caracas in January 2006. It was at this event that, for the first time in Venezuela, it was formally recognized that raising children without violence is possible. This was a highly significant achievement that made visible the issue of physical punishment and the importance of its legal prohibition. As part of the Forum, Cecodap carried out two workshops in which it presented a juridical framework for ending legalized violence against children in Latin America.

In March 2006, Cecodap facilitated a workshop which brought together a group of adolescents from different sectors and regions of the country and Mrs. Gabriela Ramírez, President of the Permanent Commission on the Family, Women and Youth[3]. In this workshop, children asked for support for the legal prohibition of physical punishment. At the end of this workshop, the President of the Permanent Commission made a commitment to young people to propose a law concerning violence against children and adolescents.

In accordance with her commitment, the President of the Permanent Commission brought the issue to the National Assembly. According to Article 211 of the *Constitution*,[4] citizens must be consulted during the discussion and approval of proposed legislation. To facilitate this consultation, the National Assembly organizes days of Social Parliamentarianism of the Street[5] to allow citizens an opportunity to offer their opinions about proposed laws during the legislative process. On April 28, 2006, one such day was held to invite discussion of the proposed prohibition of physical punishment. During this event, a group of adolescents spoke about the negative psychological effects of physical punishment, explained to the parliamentary representatives how they wanted to be treated and taught, and asked them to approve the proposed prohibition.

The Parliamentarians were receptive to this request, given that they were involved in an exercise in civil participation of a minority that had historically experienced discrimination—namely children. The event made visible the problems associated with physical and humiliating punishment, and conveyed the rationale for a legal prohibition. However, the National Assembly decided to postpone the adoption of a specific law prohibiting violence against children and instead, decided to prioritize the reform of procedural aspects of LOPNA. Cecodap decided then to abandon the plan for a single law to prohibit punishment. Instead, they would propose that the law reform be carried out within the context of the reform of LOPNA. The political context was favorable at that time, because both the Executive and the Parliament placed priority on issues related to populations that have historically experienced discrimination, and the Legislature had a constitutional duty to allow the participation of different sectors of citizens in the approval of laws.

With the support of a number of Parliamentarians, Cecodap and Save the Children Sweden worked with an advisor to the President of the Permanent Commission on three aspects of the legislation. First, they drafted the text of the law, grounding it in the right to good treatment, and clearly prohibiting physical and humiliating punishment in simple language. Second, they worked on the amendment of Article 358 of LOPNA (responsibility of childrearing) to prohibit "any type of physical or psychological violence or humiliating corrections". Third, they included the prohibition of "any type of physical or humiliating punishment" in Article 56 of LOPNA, which affirms the right of children and adolescents to be respected. In this way, they aimed to ensure that the prohibition of physical and humiliating punishment would be consistent throughout the text of LOPNA. On July 10, 2007, the Assembly passed the law without amendment and it was signed and stamped on August 14.

During the legislative process, the National Assembly received criticism from some parents who believed that the prohibition of physical punishment would leave them without tools for teaching their children. This obstacle was overcome by providing information to Members of Parliament about the effect of physical punishment on children, nonviolent parenting approaches, and the preventive rather than punitive aim of the reform. So committed were the members of Parliament to protecting children's rights, that it was not necessary to involve the media in the advocacy process.

Finally, the President of the Republic promulgated the law. With the publication of the reform in the *Official Gazette* on December 10, 2007, Venezuela became the second country in Latin America to legally ban any type of physical or humiliating punishment of children and adolescents, in all settings. The law states:

> All children and young people have a right to be treated well. This right includes a non-violent education and upbringing based on love, affection, mutual understanding and respect and solidarity. All forms of physical and humiliating punishment are prohibited. (*Law for the Protection of Children and Adolescents,* Article 32A)

Therefore, this law does not simply prohibit physical punishment, but affirms the right of children and youth to good treatment. In addition, the law establishes the duty of the state to "guarantee policies, programs, and means of protection directed at the abolition of all forms of physical or humiliating punishment of children and adolescents". The law defines physical punishment as the use of force "with the intention to cause some level of pain or physical discomfort", and humiliating punishment as "offensive, denigrating, devaluing, stigmatizing or ridiculing treatment". Both physical and humiliating punishment are carried out in the exercise of childrearing or education "with the purpose of correcting, controlling or changing the behavior of a boy, girl or adolescent, for what does not constitute a punishable act".

AFTER THE LAW REFORM

After the reform was achieved, both civil society and the State initiated activities to facilitate its implementation. Cecodap developed a campaign called *A Passport to Good Treatment: To Educate and to Live Without Aggression is Possible.* This campaign promotes nonviolent peer relationships, the elimination of physical and humiliating punishment, and the right to good treatment. They also have disseminated the *Ten Commandments for Good Treatment,* and carried out activities, such as the *Week of Good Treatment towards Boys, Girls and Adolescents.*

The Office of the Ombudsman disseminates information about LOPNA in public schools. It is also conducting a program called *Scholar Defenders,* which is based on the right to good treatment. This program promotes an environment of tolerance and respect among students, parents, and teachers and encourages nonviolent conflict resolution. A second program, *Building Community for Human Rights,* provides education for the broader community about human rights, and teaches the community about legal mechanisms for the defense of rights. The Office of the Ombudsman supports the community in identifying problems and providing the tools to solve them, and trains community and social leaders in the field of childhood and family about childhood, the LOPNA, and nonviolent parenting.

One of the key components of the process that led to the abolition of physical and humiliating punishment in Venezuela was youth participation. Their involvement gave legitimacy and strength to the process, and to the reform itself. As one youth said, participation in the process was "a wonderful experience" that allowed his voice to be heard, included young people's opinions in discussions of the law intended to protect them, and allowed youth to contribute to better protection of children and adolescents in his country. As one youth from MANIA stated, it is important that youth themselves can explain how they wish to be treated, rather than having adults decide for them.

NOTES

1. The authors gratefully acknowledge the assistance of Fernando Pereira, Carlos Trapani, and Angels Simon, in writing this chapter.
2. http://www.mipunto.com/venezuelavirtual/000/000.html
3. Official Entity of the National Assembly. It is responsible for issues related to childhood.
4. Constitution of the Bolivarian Republic of Venezuela (1999). The Bolivarian Republic of Venezuela seeks to establish a democratic, participating, and protagonist society (Constitution, Preamble, & Articles 62 & 70).
5. This is a practice of the National Assembly that permits the citizens to give their opinions about proposed laws during the legislative process.

REFERENCES

Cecodap & Save the Children Sweden. (2004). *Perceptions of physical and emotional punishment*. Retrievable from: http://www.scslat.org/web/noticias_detalle.php?id=E&tip=P&cod=493&are=&sare=&rgc=&srgc=&ani=

Bolivarian Republic of Venezuela. (1998, October). Organic Law for the Protection of Children and Adolescents (LOPNA). *Extraordinary Official Gazette No. 5, 266.*

Bolivarian Republic of Venezuela. (2007, December). Organic Law for the Protection of Children and Adolescents (LOPNA). *Extraordinary Official Gazette No. 5, 859.*

Kekic, L. (2007). *The Economist Intelligence Unit's Index of Democracy.* Retrievable from: http://www.economist.com/media/pdf/Democracy_Index_2007_v3.pdf

Trapani, C. (2007). *Experience of advocacy for legal reform about physical and humiliating punishment against boys, girls and adolescents in Venezuela.* Retrievable from: http://extranet.acabarcastigo.org/contenido.php?v_men=22&v_pla=2&v_dgr=1&v_cod=84

UN Development Program. (2009). *Human Development Report 2009—HDI Rankings.* Retrievable from http://hdr.undp.org/en/statistics/

23 Yemen

Prohibiting Physical and Humiliating Punishment in Schools

Aisha Saeed and Lucienne Maas[1]

Population:	21,000,000
Type of government:	Democracy, same president in place since the late 1970s
Governing structure:	Emerging democracy with strong tribal influences. Recent Local Government elections
Child protection system in place:	Not set up by government, but some small scale pilot community- and project-based- systems set up by agencies like Save the Children.
Legal system:	Combined system with elements of Shari'a (Islamic or canonical law), urf (customary or tribal law), leftover Ottoman and Egyptian influenced codes.
Major religion:	Islam (Sunni and Zayidi/Shi'a)
Official national languages:	Arabic
Ratified United Nations Convention on the Rights of the Child:	1990
Children's Commissioner/ Ombudsman:	No. Children's Parliament in operation since 2004, with child representatives from each of the 21 governorates (similar to provinces).

HISTORICAL CONTEXT

Yemen's history goes back as far as the 3rd millennium B.C., when it was known as Arabia Felix, or happy or blessed Arabia, because it was the source of a range of luxury goods, such as myrrh and frankincense. The most powerful ancient civilization was that of the Sabaeans, ruled by the Queen of Sheba, which was followed by the early Islamic period starting in the early 7th century.

From the 16th century until the 1990s, Europeans, including the Ottomans and the British, struggled to take control of Yemen. Parts of Yemen were occupied for various periods of time, but Yemen was never fully colonized. With the fall of the Imamate in the early 1960s, the republican era started, which involved several civil wars. The Republic of Yemen came into existence in 1990, with the voluntary unification of North and South Yemen. A civil war in 1994 resulted in the dominance of North Yemen.

Yemen is a poor country ranking 140th out of 182 countries on the Human Development Index (United Nations Development Program, 2009). It has very low rates of school enrollment (54%) and adult literacy (59%), and high rates of child (73 per 1,000 live births) and maternal (570 per 100,000 live births) mortality (UNICEF, 2009). Its economy is heavily dependent on limited oil reserves (63% of the central state budget; GoY, 2003). There is ongoing political instability with active conflict in the north and tensions in the south, as well as frequent security incidents.

THE ROLE OF GOVERNMENT

Physical punishment includes hitting a child with the hand or with an object; kicking, shaking, or throwing a child; pinching; hair pulling; forcing a child to stay in an uncomfortable or undignified position, or to take excessive physical exercise; burning or scarring a child; and the threat of any of these actions. Humiliating punishment takes forms such as verbal abuse, ridicule, isolation, or ignoring a child.

The widespread use of physical and humiliating punishment has been a problem in Yemen's education system for many years. Efforts to eradicate it began in South Yemen[2] in the mid-1980s. South Yemen had a socialist government at that time, and its education system was modeled on that of Eastern Europe. Schooling was viewed as the tool for overcoming socioeconomic disparities, and especially tribal hierarchies. When South Yemen's socialist government identified the expansion of education as one of its goals, a small group of staff (teachers and officials) from the Ministry of Education began to raise the issue of physical punishment and to argue for its elimination in schools. This pressure for a ban was not based on empirical evidence that physical punishment had a negative impact on learning outcomes; in fact, research on its prevalence in schools and its developmental outcomes was lacking. Rather, the campaign for a ban was based on the moral principle of nonviolence.

South Yemen's educational system included the use of school councils, which consisted of teachers and parents. They were involved in ensuring that socialist values were disseminated and followed (Lackner, 1985). These councils, especially in urban areas, were actively involved in the campaign to prohibit physical punishment in schools. When North and South Yemen united in 1990, the new unified government set out to retain the best parts of both, and this included the school councils. Although the role of school councils changed, they continued to lobby for a ban.

THE ROLE OF THE UN CONVENTION ON THE RIGHTS OF THE CHILD

Yemen ratified the UN *Convention on the Rights of the Child* (CRC) in 1991, leading to the establishment in 2002 of the *Child Rights Law Number 45*. This law provides the legislative framework for upholding children's rights in Yemen. It provides legal protection for children from all forms of abuse, and guarantees the fulfillment of children's rights in accordance with existing Yemeni and Islamic laws. According to Article 146, Section 1 (*Protection of Children in Difficult Circumstances*) of this law:

> The state works through the Ministry of Labor and Social Affairs and the Higher Council for Motherhood and Childhood to protect children from maltreatment and exposure to physical and psychological torture, and brings the perpetrators to justice taking into consideration the legal and legislative rights of parents to discipline their children.

This law, then, protected children from "maltreatment", but it was not clear whether this included physical punishment. None of the existing legislation referred to physical punishment of children by adults, either in families or in schools. Advocacy became focused on integrating the CRC into Yemeni law and, in particular, on achieving a ban on physical punishment in schools.

THE ROLE OF CIVIL SOCIETY

The involvement of civil society was needed to shift the advocacy efforts from the school level to the government level. This process was facilitated by support for development that was coming from the international community, and by increasing pressure on the government to improve children's lives. Up to that point, the situation of children in Yemen had not changed much since unification. There was an especially strong push to increase the rate of school enrolment and reduce the rate of school dropout.

It was within this context that a small group of international agencies—UNICEF, Save the Children, and the World Health Organization (WHO)—became involved. They decided to support the National Coalition of Non-Governmental Organizations (NGOs) on the Rights of the Child (consisting of more than 40 NGOs), and to work with the Minister of Education and the Higher Council of Motherhood and Childhood[3] to address an aspect of education that is believed to be linked to school dropout—physical punishment by teachers.

At that time, the call to address school dropout was louder than the call to address children's right to be protected from violence, but the two themes reinforced each other. Then, in 2005 the United Nations Committee on the

Rights of the Child, in its *Concluding Observations*, expressed concern about the widespread use of corporal punishment in families and schools in Yemen. Soon after, the *United Nations World Report on Violence against Children* (Pinheiro, 2006) was released and included a recommendation that corporal punishment be prohibited around the globe by 2009. With these events, children's right to be protected from violence became an important component of the campaign for the ban.

Critical support for the campaign came from the Children's Parliament, which was set up in Yemen in 2000. It played an important role in ensuring that the prohibition was passed, through direct appeals to the Yemeni parliament. The Children's Parliament is an independent group of children, supported by a local NGO, who are (s)elected every two years and represent their governorates on children's issues. There are several additional seats for children with disabilities and other children from marginalized groups. They come together on a quarterly basis to discuss issues of concern and present the outcomes of their discussions to the 'real' parliament. They also play an important role in the reporting on the progress of the implementation of the CRC in Yemen; for example, last year they wrote their first alternative report on the CRC and presented it to the CRC committee in Geneva.

THE PROHIBITION

In 2001, a Ministerial Decree banned the use of physical and humiliating punishment in schools in Article 68 of the *Regulations Governing School Punishment*. This decree came into force in 2002 and explicitly prohibits violence, and states that physical punishment and degradation are not permitted.

> Article 1: It is forbidden in all the schools in all governorates of the Yemen Republic to use any physical and psychological punishment that affects the child.
>
> Article 2: Mistakes committed by students should be addressed scientifically and educationally.
>
> Article 3: If any staff are found to practice physical and psychological punishment against students, legal measures will be taken against him/her.
>
> Article 4: All directors of Education Offices in the governorates are responsible to follow up the implementation of this resolution and obligate all Headmasters/mistresses and teachers to follow it.

The subsequent bylaws include the prohibition of the downgrading of marks, the exclusion of students from certain activities, or the isolation of students in a place for a certain time. The student should be informed of the reasons for the disciplinary measures and, interestingly, it is also stated that punishment should not lead the student to hate school. The bylaws also clearly define permissible punishments. "Light" punishment includes verbal warnings and written warnings that are addressed to both student and parents. "Severe" punishment includes temporary suspension and the transfer of the student to another school.

IMPLEMENTING THE PROHIBITION

To facilitate implementation of the Decree, the Ministry of Education has undertaken training for teachers aimed at shifting their attitudes and equipping them with various skills to reduce the use of physical punishment in schools. The training has been carried out with more than 200 teachers. Unfortunately, however, no other measures were taken to support the implementation of the Decree, and a more comprehensive approach is needed.

An important outcome of the Decree was the initiation of research to examine the prevalence and correlates of physical punishment in schools. An early study (carried out in 2003) revealed that 85% of children who failed in school had been exposed to corporal punishment, compared to 54% of children with excellent educational performance (Al Yahri, 2004).

A later study, carried out in late 2008, (Save the Children, 2009) explored corporal punishment in schools and homes in considerable depth. It investigated attitudes towards school and towards discipline among parents and children, as well as parental practices, through a 30-cluster household survey in three governorates using the *Knowledge Attitudes and Practices* (KAP) questionnaire. The sample consisted of 1,199 children of 7 to 17 years of age, and one of their parents. A KAP questionnaire also was administered to a sample of 299 teachers in Grade 1 to 9, each of whom was also observed for one 45-minute session.[4] Additional data were collected to assess the school environment. The findings revealed that 89% of school-age children (7 to 17 years) were enrolled in school (92% of boys and 85% of girls). Of those who were not enrolled in school, 26% said that they had never attended school and 74% had dropped out of school. Of the group who had dropped out, 50% had done so by grade 5.

Attitudes of Parents and Children

Parents of children who had dropped out of school most frequently identified the child's own decision to stop his/her own education as the reason they dropped out. This finding was corroborated by the responses of the children: 63% of those who had dropped out of school said that they themselves had made the decision, with no difference by gender. However, it is not clear why these children decided to stop their schooling. Few identified violence as a main reason.

Perhaps this is because many did not view violence negatively; 25% of parents believed that teachers need to hurt or humiliate children—and 40% believed that parents need to do so—in order to correct their behavior. They were most likely to support physical punishment for younger children, and humiliation for older children. Support for these acts is still being transmitted across generations; 21% of children believed that physical and humiliating punishment is necessary in schools and 45% believed that it is necessary in homes.

Behavior of Teachers

The classroom observations revealed that teachers were often lacking basic skills in classroom management: only 40% of teachers registered the students in class; 64% ensured that students could see a textbook; 50% checked that students were on the right page; 63% moved among the students; 83% used children's names; and 57% used materials other than the textbook. While 70% of teachers were observed praising individual students, only 38% explained to students how to improve their behavior. Therefore, teachers' skills in optimizing students' success and in preventing conflict in the classroom were limited. So it was not surprising to find that, despite the potentially inhibiting effect of being observed, a substantial proportion of teachers used violent approaches to keep order: 21% were observed making verbal threats; 16% made behavioral threats (e.g., to hit a student); 31% shouted; 7% used physical punishment; and 7% used humiliation.

Almost half (48%) of teachers said that there is community violence against school-aged children and 27% had observed the effects of violence on their students (e.g., bruises). Interestingly almost all teachers said that they as teachers have a responsibility to address violence against children in their community, which suggests that they may not consider their own behavior as violence against children.

Experiences of Children

The majority of students reported experiencing physical punishment at school during the month prior to the survey: 60% of students reported being hit with an object (e.g., ruler, stick) on the hands, arms or legs, compared with 65% in 2004; 28% of children reported being hit on their hands without an object; 28% had to kneel or stand for a long time in class; 41% were shouted at by the teacher; and 24% reported other humiliating punishments.

Many children are also experiencing physical violence at home, although the incidence appears to be decreasing: in 2009, 23% of children said their parents had spanked, hit, or slapped them with a hand or object (compared to 39% in 2004). It is possible that the Decree has had an impact on behavior in the home, by delegitimating physical punishment in the eyes of parents. Humiliating punishment, however, appears to be stable: in 2009, 9% of children reported that their parents had called them "dumb or lazy or another bad thing" (compared to 8% in 2004); 16% of children reported that parents shouted or yelled at them (no comparable information from 2004). These findings suggest that not only teachers, but parents and children need to become agents of change, as they were in the 1980s.

CHANGES SINCE THE DECREE

It is not possible yet to draw any firm conclusions about the impact of the Decree on the use of physical and humiliating punishment in schools. The Decree was issued in 2002, the baseline survey was administered in 2004, and the first implementation activities did not start until 2007. Although the second survey took place in early 2009, we would not expect to see substantial changes in teachers' behavior in such a short time. Ongoing data collection and additional educational activities for teachers are required at this point. Furthermore, teachers need to learn more child-centered teaching practices, to know what can be reasonably expected of children of different ages and backgrounds, and to develop the skills to manage their classrooms and engage children in learning. At this time, basic child centered learning practices are not commonly found in Yemeni schools.

It also will be important to implement programs to address children's attitudes and behavior. Data from the Save the Children (2009) survey showed that 1 out of 5 children believed that physical and humiliating punishment is necessary in schools and almost half believed that it is necessary in homes. Children are often left out of programs aimed at changing adult behavior and attitudes. But their beliefs must be addressed in order to produce a generational shift in behavior. Children also need to be taught nonviolent means of resolving conflict that they can carry with them into their adult lives.

Unfortunately, some contextual factors might slow the process of change. Increasing political instability and a worsening economic situation are leading to weakening of support, both from the Ministry of Education and the public at large, for the implementation of government policies. Investment in the social services is stagnating; all ministerial budgets were cut by 50% in 2009. The central government has to compete with traditional society, where tribal leaders and other influential people have substantial power. New legal systems, including international human rights systems such as the CRC, are often in conflict with the tribal system (United Nations, 2007). The decentralization of government powers to the governorates is progressing slowly (World

Bank, 2006), as are local attitudes towards schooling and nonviolent discipline.

CONCLUSION

In Yemen, the Decree prohibiting physical and humiliating punishment in schools was an important starting point for improving the protection of children from violence, and for improving the quality of education. However, to fully implement the Decree, the government must reduce the acceptability of violence and to teach positive means of resolving conflict. Bringing about such changes is difficult in a country where channels of communication are limited; a large proportion of the population is illiterate; the majority of people live in small, often-isolated hamlets; and tribal law plays a more important role in most communities than 'official' government law. Yemen's challenges are great. But the Decree constitutes a very significant step towards eliminating violence in the lives of children in our country.

NOTES

1. The authors acknowledge the valuable comments of Dr. L. Herrera, Institute of Social Sciences, The Hague, Netherlands.
2. At that time, Yemen was divided into two separate countries: the People's Democratic Republic of Yemen in the South and the Yemen Arab Republic in the North.
3. Several Arab countries have such departments, which are umbrella departments 'over seeing' child- and mother-related ministries. In practice they do not have much power other than advocacy.
4. This survey was supported with funds from the Dubai Cares Foundation, as well as UNICEF.

REFERENCES

Al Yahri, A. (2004). *Mental health, education and corporal punishment in Yemeni school aged children*. London: King's College Institute of Psychiatry.

Committee on the Rights of the Child (2005). *Concluding observations: Yemen*. Accessed May 7, 2009 from http://www.unhchr.ch/tbs/doc.nsf/(Symbol)/CRC.C.15.Add.267.En?Opendocument

GoY. (2003). *Yemen millennium development goals progress report*. Sana'a: Technical Group and United Nations Development Program.

Lackner, H. (1985). *P. D. R. Yemen: Outpost of socialist development in Arabia*. London: Ithaca Press.

Pinheiro, P. S. (2006). *World report on violence against children*. Geneva: United Nations. Available from http://www.violencestudy.org/IMG/pdf/English.pdf

Save the Children. (2009). *Schooling in Yemen: A baseline survey*. Unpublished report. Sana'a: Author.

UNICEF (2009). *State of the world's children*. New York: United Nations Children's Fund.
United Nations. (2007). *Development assistance framework—Republic of Yemen 2007–2011*. Sana'a: RoY.
United Nations Development Program. (2009). *Human development report 2009*. http://hdrstats.undp.org/en/countries/country_fact_sheets/cty_fs_YEM.html
World Bank. (2006). *Republic of Yemen. Country social analysis*. Report Number 34008YE. Washington: World Bank.

Part III

Lessons Learned and Pathways to the Future

24 Effects of Banning Corporal Punishment in Europe

A Five-Nation Comparison

Kai-D. Bussmann, Claudia Erthal, and Andreas Schroth

Article 19 of the United Nations *Convention on the Rights of the Child* (CRC) gives children throughout the world the right to be raised without violence. A rapidly growing number of European nations have codified this right in their laws. All of these nations based their legal regulations on the model of Sweden, the first nation in the world to prohibit all corporal punishment of children. The Swedish *Parenthood and Guardianship Code* stipulates: "children may not be subjected to physical punishment or any other injurious or humiliating treatment" (Chapter 6, § 3, Phrase 2, translated).

Several international studies have concluded that this law has helped to shift parental attitudes and to reduce violent childrearing in Sweden (Durrant, 1999, 2005; Edfeldt, 1996; Janson, 2005; Stattin, Janson, Klackenberg-Larsson, & Magnusson, 1998). Due to nationwide public awareness campaigns, more than 90% of the population was familiar with the law one year after its introduction (Newell, 1980; Ziegert, 1983). Since then, Sweden has not scaled down its campaigns to publicize the harmfulness of corporal punishment and the fact that it is against the law. Various non-governmental organizations (NGOs) such as Save the Children Sweden (2001) have continued their campaigns on several levels, directing them towards not only parents but also preschool- and school-aged children. Germany's 2007 prohibition was publicized, but less intensively (Bussmann, 2000, 2004). There, the percentage of the population familiar with the law is far lower than in Sweden, indicating that prohibition needs to be accompanied by intensive information campaigns.

There are many indications that Sweden has a low incidence of childrearing violence. In 1994, only 50% of Swedish children reported experiencing corporal punishment compared with 76% in Germany as late as 2001. Only 3% of Swedish children received resounding slaps on the face and only 1% were beaten severely, whereas the proportions in Germany in 2001 were 9% and 3% respectively). According to the latest studies, only 4% of Swedish 11- to 13-year-olds and 7% of young Swedish adults have ever experienced corporal punishment (Durrant, 2000; Janson, 2003).

Interestingly, several studies document a decline in childrearing violence in other countries as well, even though they have not prohibited corporal punishment, leading to some debate about whether the reduction in violence in Sweden is due to prohibition alone or whether it is due to a general change in values and attitudes within society (Beckett, 2005; Larzelere & Johnson, 1999; Roberts, 2000). For example, Beckett (2005) has suggested that an international comparison of registered child homicides casts doubt on the positive effect of the Swedish prohibition (Beckett, 2005). However, Janson (2005) argues that any international comparison among child homicide statistics will be inaccurate due to differences in definitions and constraints on control of confounding variables. Therefore, a systematic comparative study is needed to evaluate the impact of corporal punishment prohibitions. The impact of prohibiting corporal punishment has been studied in only a few individual nations, and no study has applied the same methodology across nations. To overcome this gap, the German Research Foundation funded the first European comparative study[1], which was conducted in five nations.

METHOD

Selection of Nations

Austria, France, Germany, Spain, and Sweden were selected to reflect the heterogeneity of legal contexts in Europe. Differentiation and selection criteria were: (1) the prohibition of corporal punishment; and (2) the implementation of an information and education campaign.

Corporal punishment was prohibited in Sweden, Austria, and Germany at the time of the survey. German law states: "Children have a right to be brought up without violence. Corporal punishment, mental cruelty, and other humiliating measures are inadmissible" (§ 1631, Phrase 2 BGB, translated). Austrian law states: "The use of violence and the infliction of physical and mental suffering are inadmissible" (§ 146 a ABGB, translated). Although Austria's prohibition has been in place since 1989, its introduction was not accompanied by a nationwide information campaign as in Germany (where the prohibition has been in force since 2000). Therefore, a comparison between these two nations allows an investigation of the impact of information campaigns beyond that of prohibition itself.

Neither Spain nor France had a corporal punishment prohibition at the time of the survey[2], but they differed in terms of information campaigns on the harmfulness of corporal punishment, permitting a comparison of the impact of legal prohibition relative to the impact of information campaigns alone. At the time of the present study, Spain's law stated: "Minors are subject to parental authority. The exercise of this authority must always be oriented toward the well-being of the children in line with their individual personalities. . . . They [the parents] may subject their children to reasonable punishment exercised with restraint" (Código Civil, Book VII, Article 154, translated). However, nationwide campaigns have been publicizing the risks of violent childrearing since 1998, accompanied by appeals from Spanish pediatricians and psychologists. The aim was to raise awareness and shift attitudes (Arruabarrena Madariaga & De Paúl Velasco, 1999; Cerezo & Pons-Salvador, 2002). In France, corporal punishment is not prohibited nor have there been nationwide information campaigns on its risks or on the benefits of nonviolent childrearing. The French *Civil Code* grants parents broad discretionary powers: "Fathers and mothers have the parental authority to protect their child's safety, health, and morals. In this sense, they have the right and the duty to take care of, supervise, and rear their child" (Code Civil, Book 1, Section IX, Articles 371–372). Outside the boundaries of "child abuse", which is just as punishable in France as in the other nations, no constraints are imposed on parents' actions. We hypothesized that if prohibition has an independent effect, Spain and France should be characterized by higher approval, frequency and severity of corporal punishment than Sweden, Austria, or Germany. It was expected that these outcomes would be at similar levels to those seen in Germany in the 1990s, before corporal punishment was prohibited (Bussmann, 2000, 2004).

Of the five countries, we predicted that the lowest approval, frequency, and severity of corporal punishment would be found in Sweden, followed by Austria and Germany. Although corporal punishment has been prohibited longer in Austria, its information campaign has been weaker. Therefore, we predicted that Austria and Germany would not differ in approval, frequency, or severity of corporal punishment. We expected France to have the highest approval, frequency, and severity of corporal punishment. It represents those western industrial nations that have experienced a general change in values but have not undertaken any systematic efforts to reduce corporal punishment. Therefore, if prohibition and information campaigns together optimize impact, France should provide the starkest contrast with Sweden on all corporal punishment measures.

Sample

Face-to-face interviews were conducted with 5,000 parents—a random sample of 1,000 parents in each nation—between October and

December 2007 (except in Austria where interviews continued until March 2008). All parents were older than 25, and lived in private homes with at least one child under the age of 18. To reduce bias, only parents with the nationality of the target country were included. Slight distribution inequalities in the sample were corrected by weighting data on gender and age composition according to their distribution in the nation concerned.

Measures

A standardized questionnaire was used across nations. The variables were measured with 5-, 6- or 7-point Likert scales. On the 5-point attitude scale, we collapsed responses into a dichotomous variable (1, 2 = disagree; 4, 5 = agree). The frequency of corporal punishment, childhood experience of corporal punishment, and violence in the parental relationship were measured as frequency ratings (e.g., 1 = never; 2 = one or two times; 3 = seldom; 4 = sometimes; 5 = often; 6 = very often). The score analyzed from each of these scales was the sum of the frequency ratings.

FINDINGS

Incidence of Corporal Punishment

As Figure 24.1 shows, our hypothesis that Sweden would have the lowest level of corporal punishment was supported. In the case of mild corporal punishment, there were marked differences between Sweden and the nations with and without prohibitions. Whereas 14.1% of Swedish parents reported giving a "mild slap on the face," 49.9% of Austrian parents, 42.6% of German parents, 54.6% of Spanish parents and 71.5% of French parents reported doing so.

Differences between the nations with and without prohibitions emerged for "spanking the child's bottom with the hand." Whereas 4.1% of respondents in Sweden, 16.0% in Austria, and 16.8% in Germany reported administering this punishment, approximately half of parents in Spain and France reported doing so.[3] Therefore, Swedish parents seem to have rejected corporal punishment to a greater extent than parents in Austria or Germany, which have prohibitions but weaker information campaigns—and to a dramatically greater extent than parents in Spain or France, which had not prohibited corporal punishment at the time of the survey.

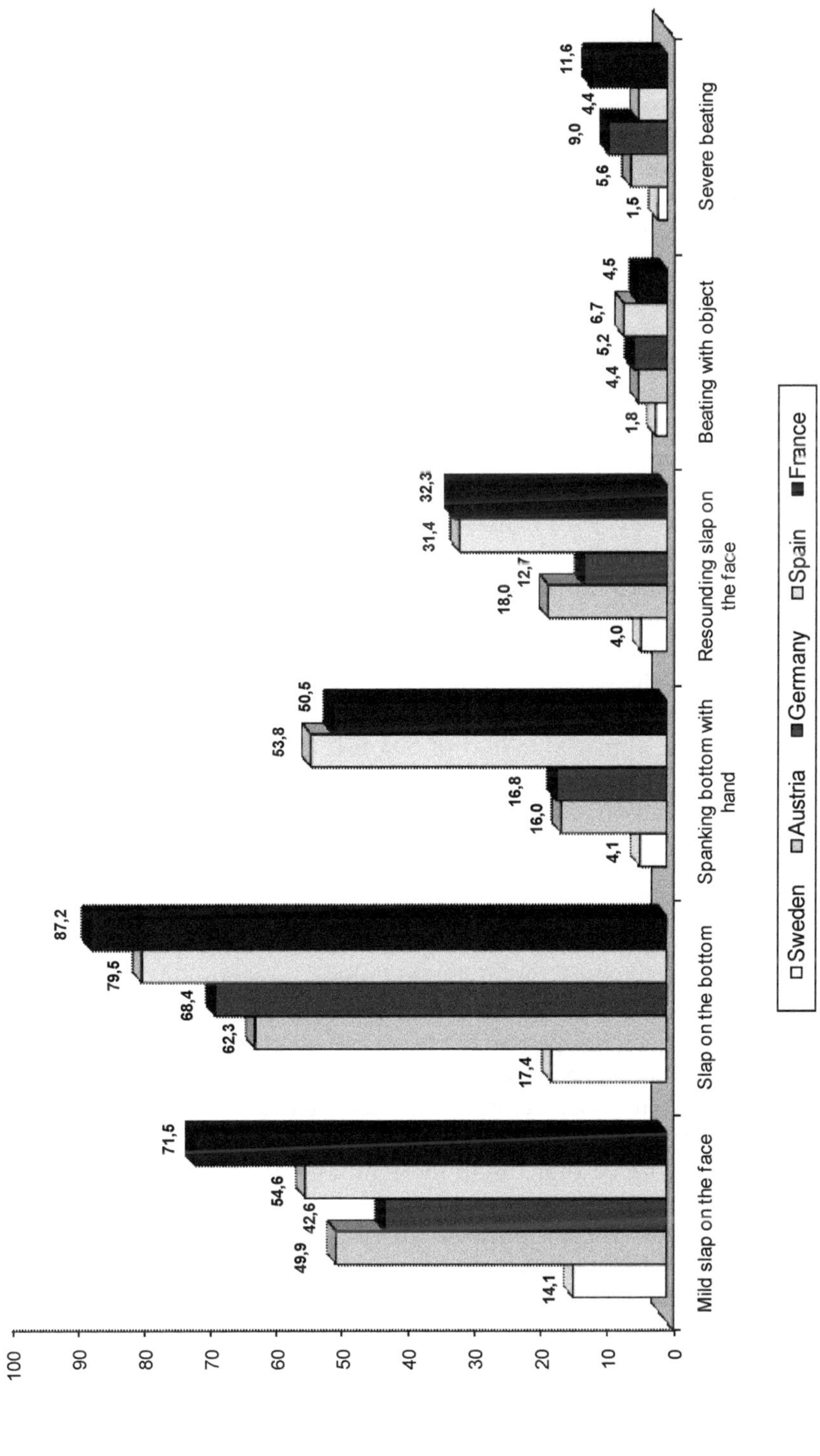

Figure 24.1 Percentages of parents who had used different forms of corporal punishment.

Parenting Subgroups

To distinguish between different parenting subgroups, we subjected all forms of punishment—corporal punishment, not allowing the child to watch television, grounding the child, reducing the child's allowance, shouting at the child, and ignoring and not talking to the child—to a factor analysis (varimax rotation, principal-components, and principal-axis analysis). Each punishment loaded on one of four factors: Prohibitions, Psychological Punishment, Mild Corporal Punishment, and Severe Corporal Punishment (resounding slap on the face, beating with an object, severe beating; see Bussmann, 2000, 2002, 2004, 2005). Then, three parenting subgroups were formed by counting response behaviors rather than being generated on the basis of summative indices: (1) *Nonviolent parents*, who desist from corporal punishment but apply prohibitions and psychological sanctions; (2) *Conventional parents*, who apply all forms of punishment other than severe corporal punishment[4]; and (3) *Violent parents*, who had used severe corporal punishment more than once.

The pattern indicated by the item frequencies (Figure 24.1) was confirmed in these parenting subgroups (Figure 24.2). Three-quarters of Swedish parents reared their children nonviolently; one fifth "conventionally"; and only 3.4% with violence. In contrast, the majority of Austrian (55.8%) and German parents (57.9%) raised their children "conventionally." Although more than one-quarter of the parents in both these nations did not use corporal punishment, approximately 14% of them belonged to the group of violent parents. In contrast, almost one-half of Spanish (47.7%) and French parents (46.7%) were in the "violent" group.

Childhood Experience of Corporal Punishment

Parents were asked about how they had been punished as children. Their reports indicated that they had experienced markedly more violence than they were inflicting on their children—but there were notable between-country differences. More of the *current* generations of children in Austria and Germany have been slapped on the face than was the case in the *previous* generation of children in Sweden. At 39.4%, the proportion of Swedish parents who had been raised without violence exceeds the proportion of Austrian or German parents who are raising their children without violence today—and is twice that found in Spain and almost five times that found in France today.

Table 24.1 presents the proportions of respondents who were raised with and without violence in each country, as well as the proportions that had and had not inflicted violence on their own children, by age cohort. In Sweden, there was an increase in nonviolence and a decrease in violence in the lives of children with each successive cohort. The shifts seen between 1962 and 1973 could be due to the earlier public discussion on the 1957

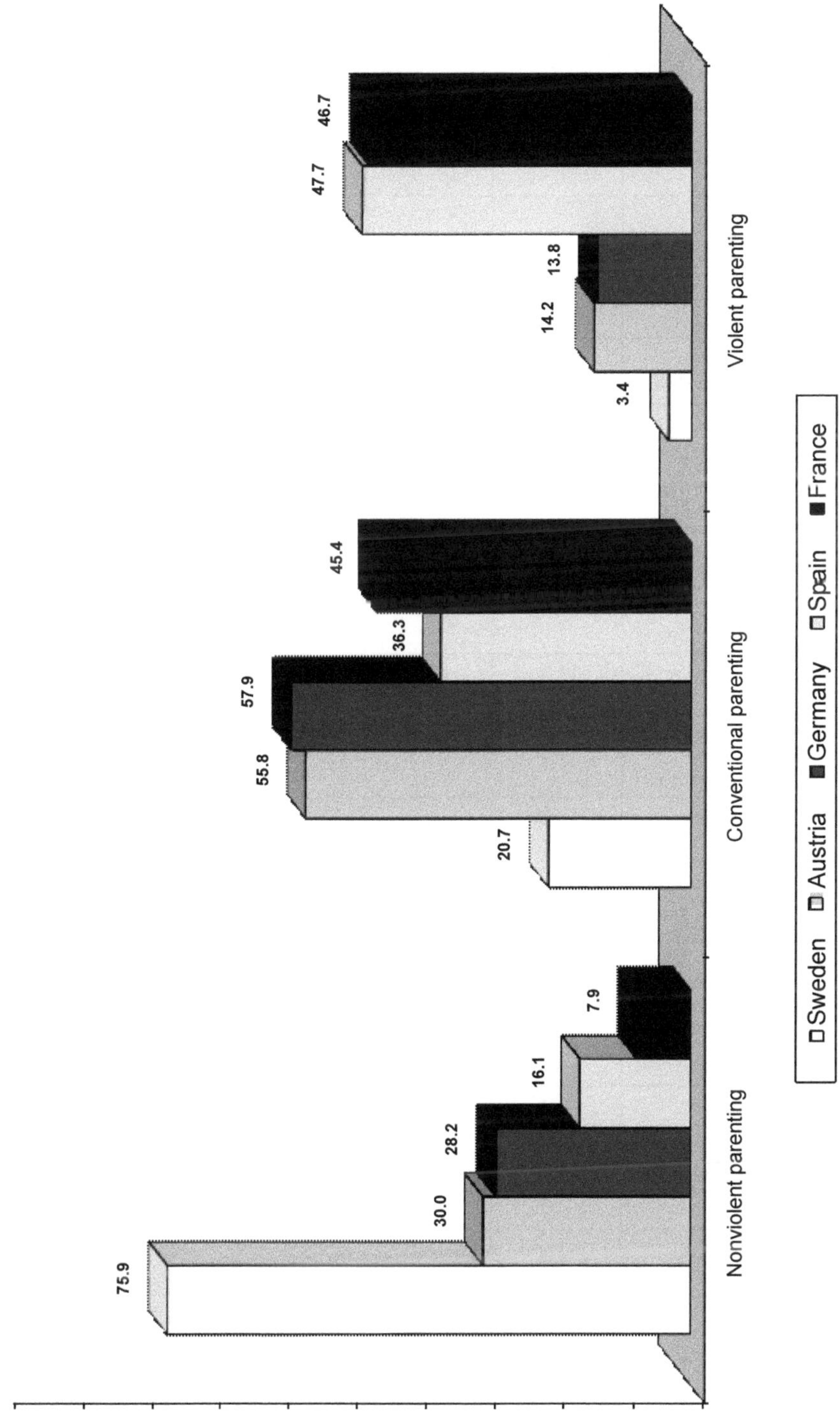

Figure 24.2 Percentage of parents in each parenting subgroup.

Table 24.1 Percentages Reporting Violent and Nonviolent Parenting as Children and as Parents by Age Cohort

		Born before 1962 (older than 46)	Born 1962–1967 (40–45)	Born 1968–1973 (35–39)	Born 1973–1978 (30–34)	Born after 1979 (< 30)
Sweden						
Nonviolent	Own childhood	33.8	38.3	47.3	44.1	45.3
	Today	73.3	75.0	80.1	83.9	89.5
Violent	Own childhood	24.4	19	15.8	16	14.7
	Today	4.4	1.3	2.0	1.2	0.9
Austria:						
Nonviolent	Own childhood	10.5	15.2	9.2	10.0	7.6
	Today	33.8	26.5	26.2	34.2	33.0
Violent	Own childhood	51.3	46.4	42.7	46.4	44.7
	Today	14.5	15.3	15.9	13.8	8.9
Germany:						
Nonviolent	Own childhood	9.2	9.5	13.2	13.3	14.1
	Today	22.4	26.9	31.6	28.4	35.3
Violent	Own childhood	55.5	54.6	45.1	45.2	38.1
	Today	18.8	14.5	8.2	14.1	12.8
Spain:						
Nonviolent	Own childhood	10.2	10.9	5.9	7.5	4.2
	Today	14.3	14.2	14.0	26.9	11.4
Violent	Own childhood	72.4	65.8	72.6	67.6	76.4
	Today	54.4	47.7	46.1	40.3	49.1
France:						
Nonviolent	Own childhood	5.2	3.1	5.2	2.9	2.8
	Today	10.3	6.5	5.8	8.2	9.6
Violent	Own childhood	72.3	75.5	72.0	68.5	67.6
	Today	46.2	49.2	53.1	37.9	41.2

repeal of the criminal defense and the 1966 repeal of the Civil Code paragraph permitting mild corporal punishment. The shifts seen after 1973 are likely due to the 1979 prohibition and its accompanying nationwide information campaign.

It must be pointed out, however, that these are not time-series data. A time series was only simulated by asking the generations in this cross-sectional study to report their experiences retrospectively. Because the passage of time tends to blur memory, even greater differences might have been found using time-series survey data from the time periods in question. Clearly, Sweden has established a decades-long tradition of nonviolent childrearing.

Violence in the Parental Relationship

Empirical studies have shown that a violent parental relationship increases the risk of childrearing violence (Lamnek, Lüdke, & Ottermann, 2006; McGuigan & Pratt, 2001). Therefore, parents in the present study were asked whether they were victims or perpetrators of violence in their relationships. In Sweden, conflicts were far more frequently verbal, and acts of severe violence were markedly less frequent, than in the other countries (Figure 24.3). Acts at the lower threshold of violence (grabbing hard and pushing) were as frequent in Sweden as in Germany and Austria.

Knowledge of Corporal Punishment's Legal Status

Almost 90% of the Swedish respondents knew that corporal punishment had been prohibited in 1979. A large majority interpreted the legal limits accurately, even with regard to mild corporal punishment, which had been socially acceptable until the 1980s (Janson, 2005; Stattin et al., 1998; Straus, 1980). Even a slap on the bottom was known to be prohibited by 94% of Swedish parents. Figure 24.4 presents the proportions of each country sample who believed various acts to be legally permissible.

In Austria and Germany 32% and 31% of respondents, respectively, were aware of the current legal situation. This contrast with Sweden provides evidence of the impact of information campaigns. Other studies have confirmed that only one year after its introduction, the Swedish prohibition was well-known due to the nationwide information campaign that accompanied it (Newell, 1980; Ziegert, 1983). Over the years, Sweden has continued its efforts to make people aware of the harmfulness of corporal punishment and the fact that it is prohibited. Various NGOs have campaigned continuously for many years and on several levels, focusing not only on parents but also on preschool- and school-aged children (Janson, 2005; Save the Children Sweden, 2001).

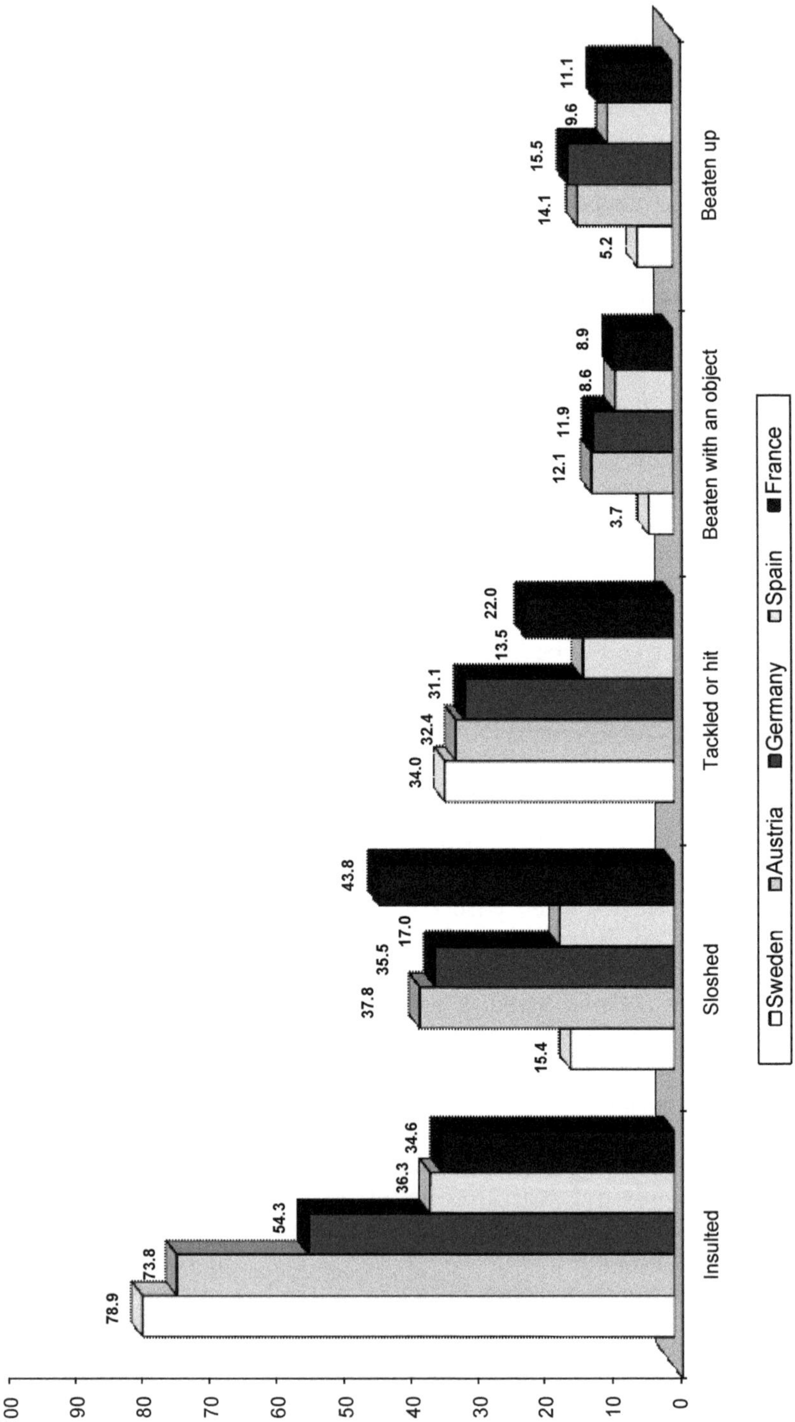

Figure 24.3 Percentages of parents reporting physical assault in the parental relationship.

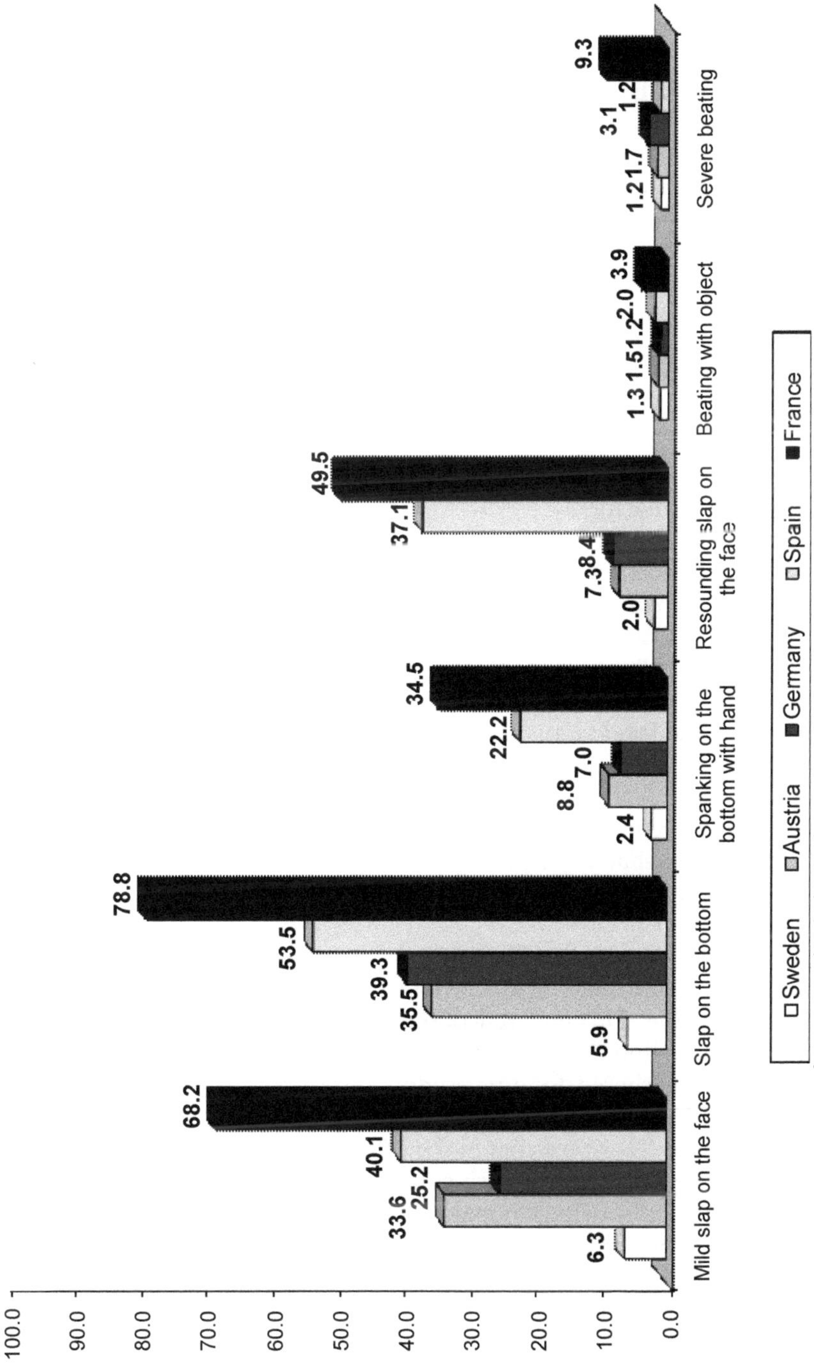

Figure 24.4 Percentages of parents who believe that various acts are legally permissible.

In Austria, there was no nationwide information campaign. In Germany, the government launched a nationwide multimedia strategy to advertise the change in the law under the motto *More Respect for Children*. However, this campaign was limited to the years 2000 and 2002. As a result, there has been no noticeable change in the knowledge about the legal reform since 2001, when approximately 30% of German parents, and almost the same proportion of children and adolescents, knew about the prohibition (Bussmann, 2004). The difference in knowledge between Swedish respondents on the one hand, and Austrian and German parents on the other, demonstrates the necessity of accompanying prohibition with intensive information campaigns—and to maintain them over the long term. Continuous campaigns are needed to anchor the right to nonviolent childrearing and the harmfulness of its alternative in the minds of the population. Also, the Austrian (1989) and German (2007) reforms are more recent than Sweden's, so there has been less time for the norm to shift in those countries. Considering that Sweden repealed its criminal defense in 1957 (Austria in 1977), it has much longer cultural traditions of nonviolent childrearing.

A longitudinal study was carried out in Germany from 1996 to 2007, spanning the period when the 2000 prohibition and its precursor—the *Prohibition of Maltreatment Act* of 1998—were passed. The findings demonstrate how much time is needed to change traditional beliefs about what is right and wrong (Bussmann, 2003, 2005; see Figure 24.5), and how public discussion, legal reform, and value shifts are inextricably intertwined. Beliefs about the legal status of less severe corporal punishment (e.g., mild slap on the face, slap on the bottom) have shifted continuously: The belief that a mild slap on the face is permissible has dropped by more than two-thirds since 2003 and a slap on the bottom by more than one-half. These findings indicate that legal prohibition combined with continuous public discussion can influence beliefs over time, as Swedish findings also indicate (see Janson, 2005).

Although at the time of the survey, Spain had not prohibited corporal punishment, far fewer Spanish than French parents considered it to be legally permissible. This may reflect the public discussions and information campaigns preceding the Spanish legal reform of December 2007 (after the data had been gathered for this study). Severe corporal punishment was believed to be legally permissible by 9% of French parents, compared with between 2% and 3% of parents in the other four countries.

Approximately 38% of Spanish parents and 32% of French parents were aware of awareness-raising campaigns on corporal punishment. This small difference is surprising, considering that Save the Children has been carrying out nationwide information campaigns in Spain since 1998 (Save the Children Spain, 2001), whereas there have not been any such campaigns carried out in France.

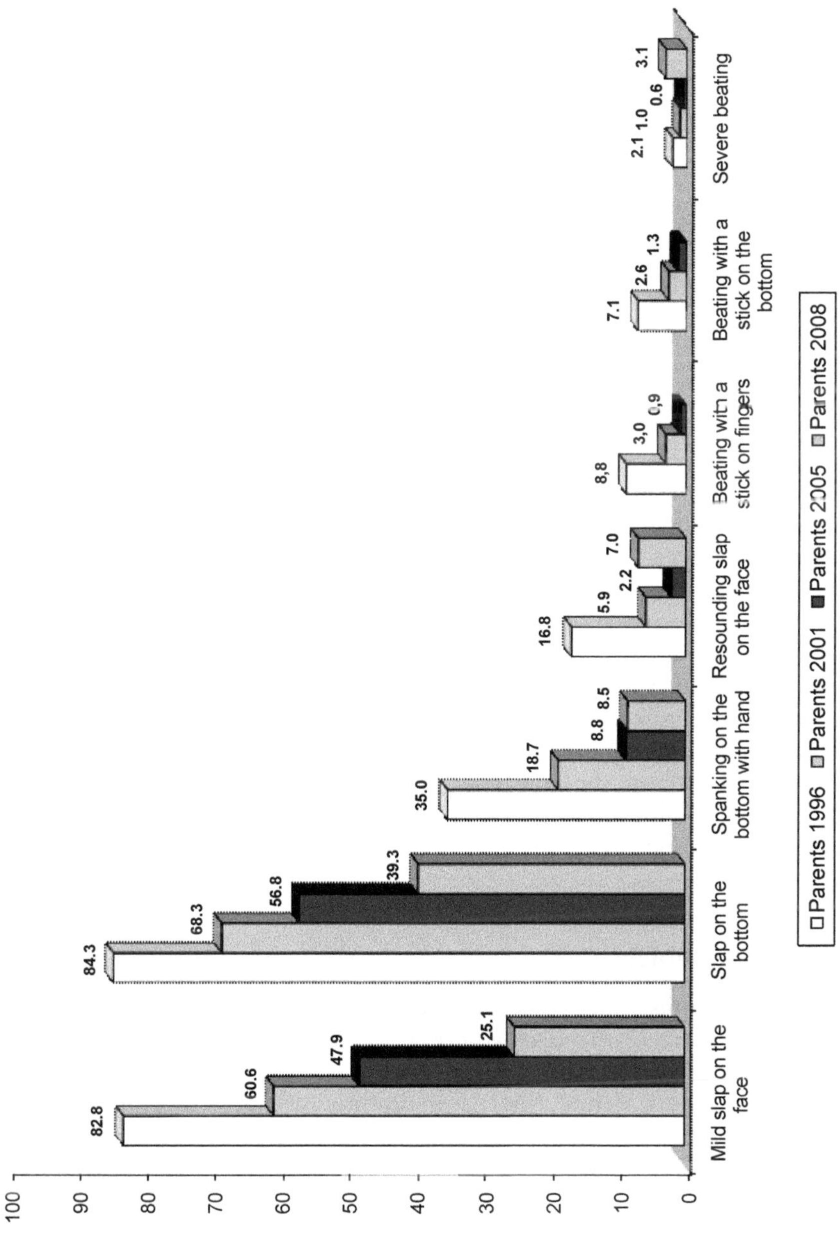

Figure 24.5 Percentages of German parents who believe various acts are legally permissible by year.

Attitudes towards Nonviolent Childrearing

A large majority of parents in all five nations supported the ideal of rearing children without violence—93% in Sweden (Figure 24.6). However, across countries, substantial minorities of respondents believed that they would be unable to rear their children in daily life without some form of mild corporal punishment. This proportion ranged from 15% to 20% in Sweden, Austria, German, and Spain, but was markedly higher in France, at 43%. Therefore, it is not surprising that 53% of French parents are opposed to prohibition (Union des Familles en Europe, 2007).

Attitudes towards Other Disciplinary Responses

Regardless of whether corporal punishment was prohibited in a country, most parents thought it was better to talk with their children than to hit them, which reflects their support for a nonviolent ideal (Figure 24.7). More than two-thirds of the parents were aware that corporal punishment could contribute to a cycle of violence.

A large minority of respondents believed that corporal punishment often happens because of occasional parental helplessness or a lack of alternatives. However, Swedish parents were less likely than parents in other countries to justify its use: Only 4% thought it was an acceptable way of shortening the conflict, and only 6% thought it was an acceptable alternative to not talking to the child. In Austria and Germany, acceptance of these justifications ranged between 13% and 15%. Acceptance of justifications was even higher in Spain and France. For example, 31% of Spanish parents thought corporal punishment was better than not talking to the child, and 27% of French parents thought that "a slap is sometimes the best/quickest way". Therefore, although parents in all nations strove to raise their children without violence, they differed in the ways they justified their violence in their minds.

Definitions of Violence

Findings of previous studies (see Bussmann, 1996, 2004) indicate that parents are not aware of the contradiction between their attitudes towards nonviolent childrearing and their use of corporal punishment, simply because they do not define what they do as violence. It is known from criminological research that the concept of violence is not based on objective observation but on subjective attribution (Neidhardt, 1986). Swedish parents are consistent in their rejection of violence. They are more likely to define mild corporal punishments (e.g., mild slap on the face or bottom) as violence than the parents in other nations who, while rejecting violent childrearing in principle, are less likely to view the violence they do use as violence (Figure 24.8).

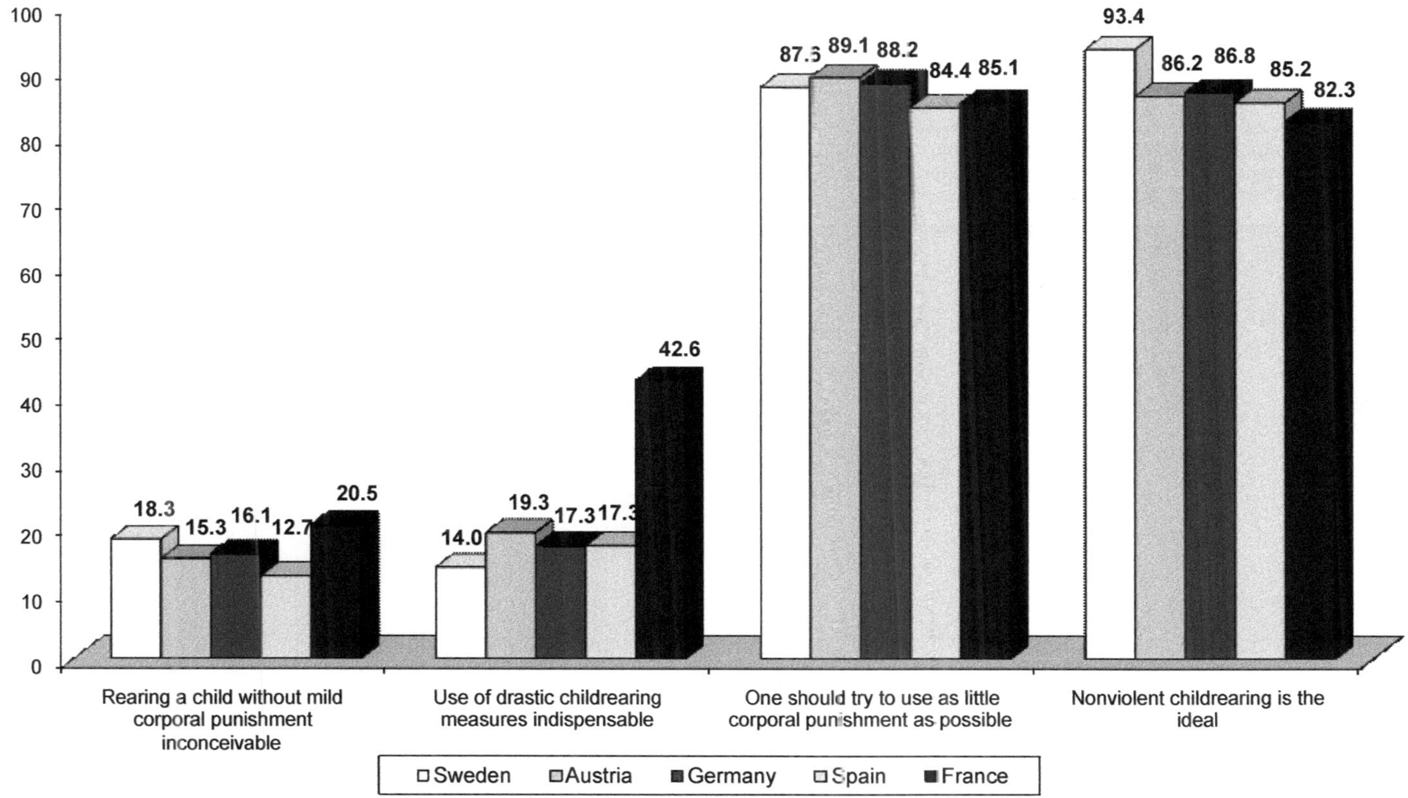

Figure 24.6 Percentages of parents holding various beliefs about childrearing.

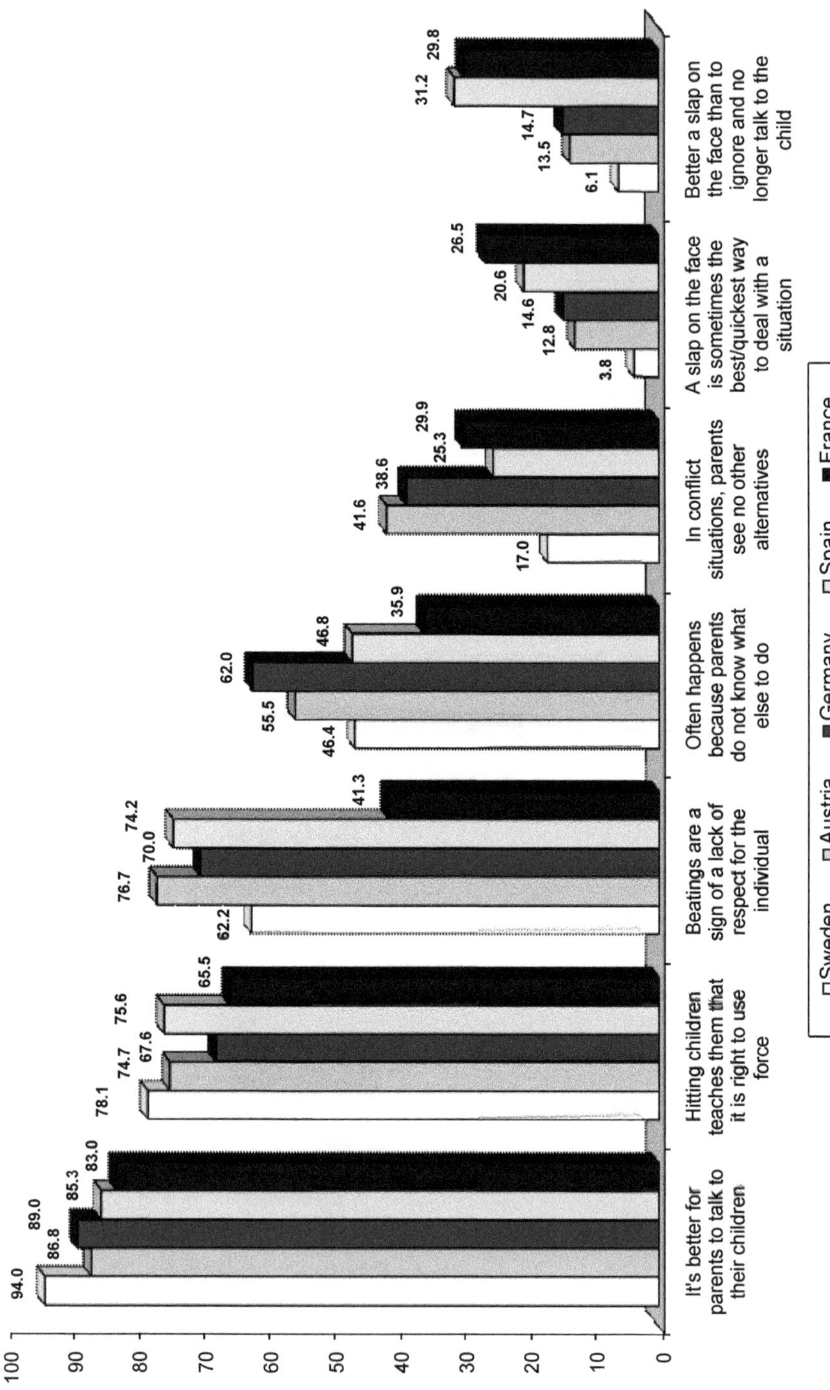

Figure 24.7 Percentages of parents holding various beliefs about corporal punishment.

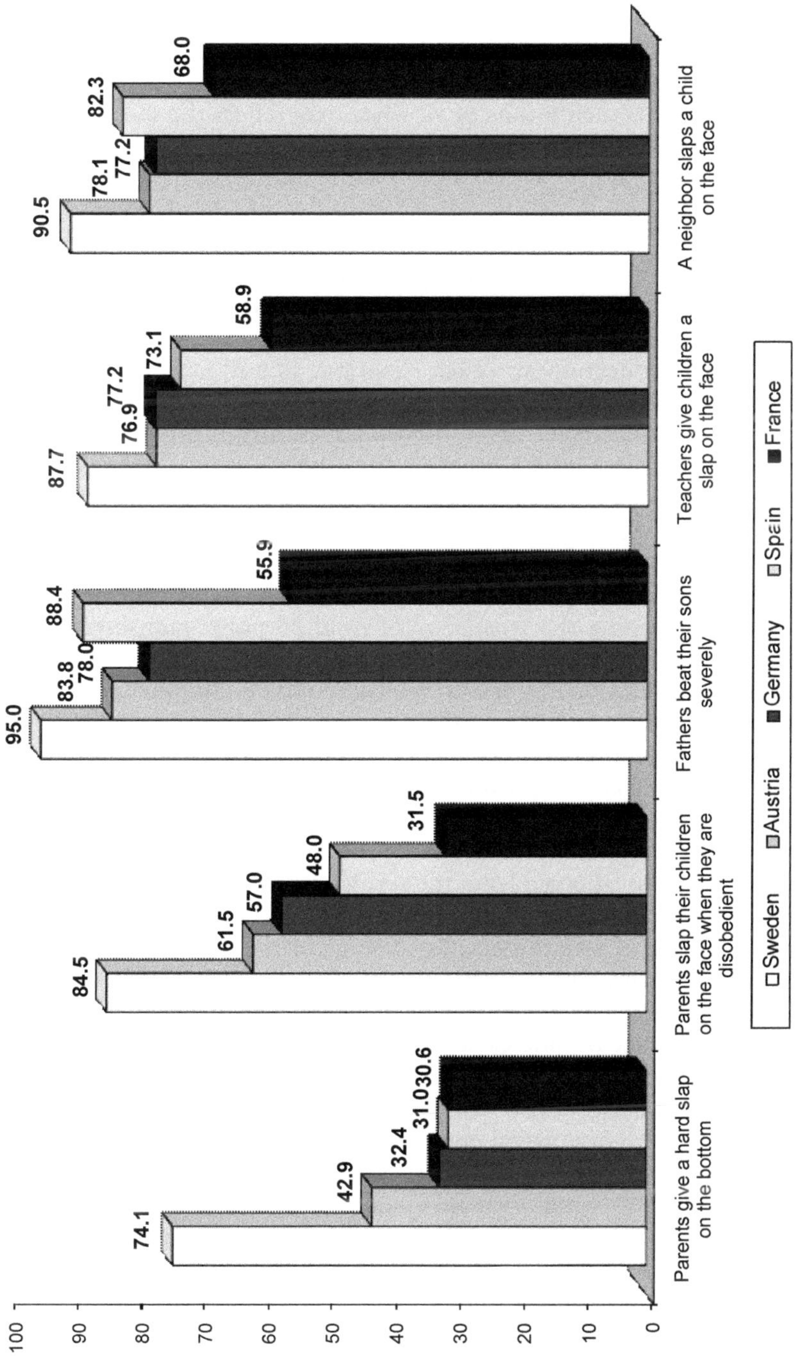

Figure 24.8 Percentages of parents who believe various acts constitute violence.

Definitions of violence did not differ substantially across Spain, Austria, and Germany. French parents, however, considered violence to comprise a much narrower range of acts. Only 56% of French parents defined a severe beating as violence, and only 59% defined a slap by a teacher (which is not forbidden under French law) as violence. The contrast between French and Spanish parents' definitions of violence may reflect the more intensive information campaigns that have been conducted in Spain.

Predictors of Corporal Punishment

For nations with prohibitions (Sweden, Austria, Germany), we performed regression analyses to identify the variables that predict the frequency with which parents administer mild and severe corporal punishment. We entered gender, age, and education into each equation, as well as approval of corporal punishment, knowledge of its legal status, definition of physical violence, childhood experience of mild corporal punishment, and frequency of violence in the parental relationship. Because the results from the three countries were almost identical, they were entered into the model together.

The predictors explained 47% of the variance in the frequency of mild corporal punishment (Table 24.2; note that only significant findings are presented). However, the sociodemographic variables made little or no contribution to explaining the frequency of mild corporal punishment. The strongest predictors were approval of corporal punishment, knowledge of its legal status, definition of physical violence, and childhood experience of mild corporal punishment. While stronger approval of corporal punishment and more frequent childhood experience of it predicted higher frequency of its use, knowledge that it is prohibited predicted lower frequency of its use. This finding suggests that prohibition has an impact on behavior, as earlier studies have already shown for Germany (Bussmann, 2000, 2004).

A similar pattern emerged from the results of the analysis predicting the frequency of severe corporal punishment. The strongest predictors were approval of corporal punishment, knowledge of the legal status of severe corporal punishment, and definition of physical violence. However, in this model, violence in the parental relationship was a stronger predictor than childhood experience of mild or severe corporal punishment.

We then performed path analyses[5] to study the relationships among the predictors of corporal punishment (see, for more detail, Bussmann, 1996, 2004). To begin, we performed exploratory factor analyses applying principal axis factoring (PAF) on the metric scaled items followed by principal component analysis—both with varimax rotation. While some variables showed cross loading on several factors, the factor structure was clearly recognizable.[6] Key variables were generated on the basis of the results of the PAF, theoretical considerations, and the results of earlier studies in Germany to permit longitudinal comparisons. We generated the variables for the path models (Figure 24.9) with summative indices.

Table 24.2 Results of Linear Regression Predicting Frequency of Corporal Punishment in Sweden, Austria, and Germany

	Frequency of corporal punishment				
	mild			severe	
	β	*p*		*β*	*p*
Approval of corporal punishment	.314	.000		.197	.000
Beliefs about what is legally admissible (mild corporal punishment)	-.263	.000		.087	.000
Beliefs about what is legally admissible (severe corporal punishment)	.104	.000		-.214	.000
Childhood experience of corporal punishment (mild)	.221	.000		-.063	.013
Childhood experience of corporal punishment (severe)				.132	.000
Definition of physical violence	-.126	.000			
Definition of maltreatment				-.152	.000
Violence experienced in parental relationship	.114	.000		.221	.000
Education	-.077	.000			
Sex (reference group: women)	-.055	.000			
Age	.045	.001			
Disapproval of corporal punishment	.034	.041			
(Constant)	.908	.000		1.609	.000
Adj. R^2	.467			.293	
Number of cases	2802			2854	

The path analyses were conducted on both single nations and groups of nations, differentiating between mild and severe corporal punishment as target variables. Results were very similar across nations, except that knowledge of corporal punishment's legal status had a much stronger influence in nations with prohibitions. Here, we report only on the most comprehensive model, which is the one that included all nations and predicted severe corporal punishment. This model explained 34% of the variance in severe corporal punishment and is presented in Figure 24.9.

In line with our hypotheses, this path model indicated that parents' knowledge of corporal punishment's legal status had a direct influence on the frequency of severe corporal punishment. It also revealed indirect relations between parents' definitions of violence and their approval of corporal punishment. However, parents' definitions of violence also had a strong indirect effect on frequency of severe corporal punishment through

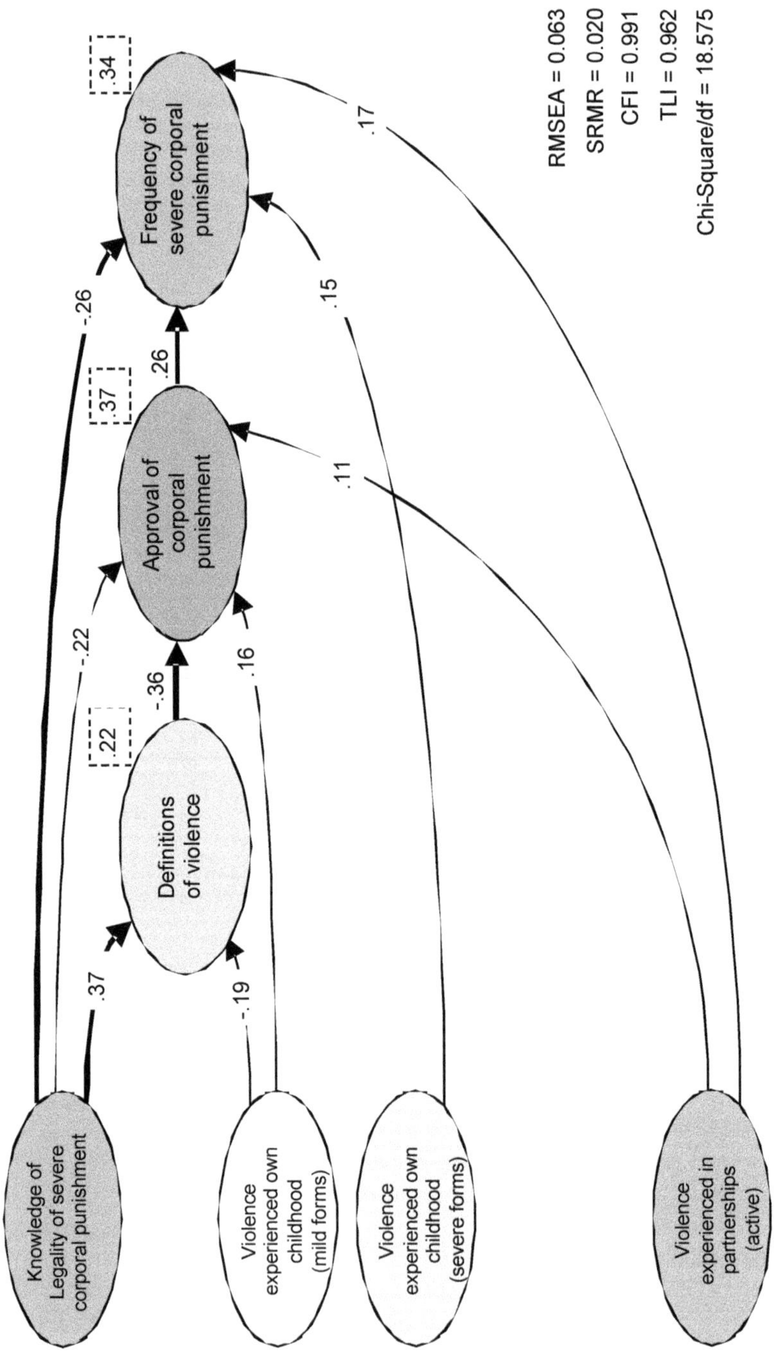

Figure 24.9 Path model predicting severe corporal punishment.

approval of corporal punishment. A lack of knowledge of severe corporal punishment's legal status weakened parents' perceptions of violence, while simultaneously strengthening their approval of its use.

Childhood experience of severe corporal punishment directly increased parents' use of it. Interestingly, childhood experience of mild corporal punishment led to a narrower definition of violence and strengthened approval of corporal punishment. Finally, violence in the parental relationship increased the frequency of severe corporal punishment and strengthened approval of it.

SUMMARY AND CONCLUSION

The results of this first European comparative study indicate that prohibiting corporal punishment is associated with a decline in childrearing violence. Parents in nations with prohibitions use corporal punishment less frequently. The impact of prohibition is not only direct but also indirect, through its influence on broadening definitions of violence and decreasing approval of corporal punishment. Moreover, while childhood experience of corporal punishment and violence in the parental relationship increase the frequency with which parents use corporal punishment, their effect sizes can be markedly weaker than those of the direct and indirect influences of prohibition. Therefore, the significance of prohibition should not be underestimated. The law is a communication medium that can have subtle but lasting and confirmable effects (Bussmann, 1996, 2004).

Our findings also demonstrate that information campaigns alone are less effective than prohibition alone. In Spain, which did not have a prohibition at the time of the survey but did have an information campaign, almost half of parents were raising their children with violence. In comparison, 14% of parents in Austria (which had a ban but no campaign) and Germany (which had a ban and a short-lived campaign) were doing so.

At the same time, the findings from Germany and Austria reveal that prohibition alone is insufficient to fully achieve its potential effects. While 14% of parents there were raising their children with violence, only 3% of Swedish parents were doing so. Clearly, Sweden, which has both prohibited corporal punishment and provided ongoing education about the law and parenting, has had the greatest success in changing attitudes and behavior. The effectiveness of Sweden's approach is seen across generations. At 39%, the proportion of Swedish parents who were raised without violence exceeds the proportion of Austrian or German parents who are raising their children without violence today—and is twice that found in Spain and almost five times that found in France today.

These differences indicate that the changes seen in Sweden go beyond a general change in values. They point to the success of Sweden's very early ban and the prior public discourse on nonviolent childrearing and the harmfulness of corporal punishment. Even the current generation of Swedish parents experienced far less childrearing violence in the 1970s and 1980s than children in the other countries are experiencing in this decade. This early decline in corporal punishment must reflect Sweden's early legal reforms and public discussions. The *Penal Code* defense for caretakers was repealed in 1957 (Durrant, 1996), the paragraph in civil law permitting mild corporal punishment was repealed in 1966—and acceptance of violent childrearing declined between 1965 and 1971 (Durrant, 1996; Edfeldt, 1996). Legally, corporal punishment was considered assault at this point in time. The 1979 ban only clarified a legal situation that had been in place for many years. Therefore, the current generation of Swedish parents grew up during a period when the unacceptability of violent childrearing became increasingly explicit and ongoing information campaigns have maintained public awareness of the law.

In Germany and Austria, where prohibition came later and information campaigns have been less intensive, the trends are similar, but weaker than in Sweden. With regard to Germany, where corporal punishment is prohibited and a short-term information campaign was carried out, the present findings can be compared with those of earlier studies to reveal a continuous decline in the approval of childrearing violence. Continuous campaigns and information measures to promote nonviolent childrearing could strengthen this trend.

France (which has neither prohibited corporal punishment nor conducted information campaigns) provides the starkest contrast to Sweden. In France, where corporal punishment has not been prohibited nor have information campaigns been carried out, parents are three times more likely than parents in the other countries to believe that severe corporal punishment is allowed, and almost half do not define severe beating as violence. One-half of French parents believed that it was impossible to raise a child without at least mild corporal punishment, compared to 15% to 20% of parents in the other countries; 70% of French parents have slapped a child's face and only 8% are raising their children without any form of violence.

An important finding of the present study is that more than 80% of parents in each nation supported the goal of raising their children without violence, suggesting that they would welcome support and information that would help them achieve this goal. The present findings confirm those of previous studies demonstrating that the most effective way of doing this is to implement a clear prohibition accompanied by intensive public education about the law and about positive discipline.

NOTES

1. This line of research was initiated by Detlev Frehsee († 2001) who, together with the current project manager, had carried out parent and youth studies on domestic violence in Germany within a legal context in 1992, 1994, and 1996 (Frehsee, 1992, 1993; Frehsee & Bussmann, 1996; Frehsee, Horn, & Bussmann, 1996).

2. Spain subsequently prohibited corporal punishment in 2007. Spanish parents now must "respect the physical and mental integrity" of their children (Código civil, Book VII, Article 154, amended on December 28, 2007, translated).
3. A similar proportion was found in a recent French survey (Union des Familles en Europe, 2007).
4. Respondents assigned to this group had not administered severe corporal punishment more than once.
5. The path analyses were conducted with AMOS structural equation modeling software in SPSS.
6. Details are available from the first author.

REFERENCES

Arrubarrena Madariaga, M.I., & De Paúl Velasco, J. (1999). *Maltrato a los niños en la familia: Evaluacion y tratamiento*. Madrid : Piramide Ediciones Sa.

Beckett, C. (2005). The Swedish myth: The corporal punishment ban and child death statistics. *British Journal of Social Work, 35*, 125–138.

Bussman, K.-D. (1996). Changes in family sanctioning styles and the impact of abolishing corporal punishment. In D. Frehsee, . Horn, & K.-D. Bussman (eds.), *Family violence against children: A challenge for society* (p. 39–61). Berlin: de Gruyter.

Bussman, K.-D. (2000). Verbot familialer Gewalt gegen Kinder. *Zur Einführung rechtlicher Regelungen sowie zum Strafrecht als Kommunikationsmedium.* Köln: Carl Heymann.

Bussmann, K.-D. (2002). Das Recht auf gewaltfreie Erziehung aus juristischer und empirischer Sicht. *Familie, Partnerschaft und Recht, 7*, 289–293.

Bussmann, K.-D. (2003). Erste Auswirkungen des Gesetzes zur Ächtung der Gewalt in der Erziehung. *IKK-Nachrichten Nr. 1–2*(3), 1–4.

Bussman, K.-D. (2004). The subtle impact of a ban on corporal punishment in childrearing: Results of the evaluation of the German prohibition. *Child Abuse Review, 13*, 292–311.

Bussmann, K.-D. (2005). *Auswirkungen des Verbots von Gewalt in der familialen Erziehung.* Unveröffentlichter Forschungsbericht. Martin-Luther-Universität Halle-Wittenberg.

Cerezo, M.A., Pons-Salvador, G. (2002). *El valor del buen trato a la infancia: Coste Humano, social y económico del maltrato.* Valencia, CSV.

Durrant, J. E. (1996). Public attitudes toward corporal punishment in Canada. In D. Frehsee, W. Horn, & K.-D. Bussmann (Eds.), *Family violence against children. A challenge for society* (pp. 107–118). Berlin, New York: de Gruyter.

Durrant, J. E. (1999). Evaluating the success of Sweden's corporal punishment ban. *Child Abuse & Neglect, 23*, 435–448.

Durrant, J. E. (2000). Trends in youth crime and well-being since the abolition oof corporal punishment in Sweden. *Youth & Society, 31*, 437–455.

Durrant, J. E. (2003). Legal reform and attitudes toward physical punishment in Sweden. *International Journal of Children's Rights, 11*, 147–174.

Durrant, J. E. (2005). *Law reform and corporal punishment in Sweden: Response to Robert Larzelere, The Christian Institute, and Families First.* Winnipeg, Canada: Department of Family Social Sciences, University of Manitoba.

Durrant, J. E., & Janson, S. (2005). Law reform, corporal punishment and child abuse: The case of Sweden. *International Review of Victimology, 12*, 139–158.

Edfeldt, Å. W. (1996). The Swedish 1979 Aga ban plus fifteen. In D. Frehsee, W. Horn, & K.-D. Bussmann (Eds.), *Family violence against children. A challenge for society* (pp. 27–37). Berlin, New York: de Gruyter.

Fiedler, P. (2004). Erinnerung, Vergessen und Dissoziation—neuro- und kognitionspsychologische Perspektiven. In A. Eckhardt-Henn & S. O. Hoffmann (Eds.), *Dissoziative Bewusstseinsstörungen* (S. 46–59). Stuttgart, Deutschland: Schattenhauer.

Janson, S. (2003). *Children and abuse—corporal punishment and other forms of child abuse in Sweden at the end of the second millenium. A scientific report prepared for the National Committee on Child Abuse and Related Issues (English Summary)*. Sweden: Ministry of Health and Social Affairs.

Janson, S. (2005). Response to Beckett, C. (2005). The Swedish myth: The corporal punishment ban and child death statistics. *British Journal of Social Work, 35*, 1411–1415.

Lamnek. S. Lüdke, J., & Otterman, R. (2006). *Tatort Familie: Häusliche Gewalt im gesellschaftlichen Kontext*. Wiesbaden, Germany: VS.

Larzelere, R. I., & Johnson, B. (1999). Evaluation of the effects of Sweden's spanking ban on physical child abuse rates. A literature review. *Psychological Reports, 85*, 381–392.

McGuigan, W.\M., & Pratt, C.C. (2001). The predictive impact of domestic violence on three types of child maltreatment. *Child Abuse & Neglect, 25*, 869–883.

Neidhardt, F. (1986). Gewalt—soziale Bedeutungen und sozialwissenschaftliche Bestimmungen des Begriffs. In Bundeskriminalamt (Hrsg.), *Was ist Gewalt? Zum Gewaltbegriff im Strafrecht, Bd. 1*. (S. 109–147). Wiesbaden, Deutschland: Bundeskriminalamt.

Newell, P. (1980). *Children are people too: The case against physical punishment*. London, UK: NCVO.

Pfeiffer, C., Wetzels, P., & Enzmann, D. (1999). *Innerfamiliäre Gewalt gegen Kinder und Jugendliche und ihre Auswirkungen*. KFN Kriminologisches Forschungsinstitut Niedersachsen Forschungsbericht Nr. 80. Hannover, Deutschland: KFN.

Roberts, J. R. (2000). Changing public attitudes towards corporal punishment: The effects of statuary reform in Sweden. *Child Abuse & Neglect, 24*(8), 1027–1035.

Save the Children Spain (2001). *Educa, no pegues. Campaña para la sesibilización contra el castigi físico a los niños y niñas en la familia. Guía para madres y padres*. Madrid: Author.

Save the Children Sweden (2001). *The first anti-spanking law in the world*. Stockholm: Author.

Stattin, H., Janson, H., Klackenberg-Larsson, I., & Magnusson, D. (1998). Corporal punishment in everyday life: An intergenerational perspective. In J. McCord (Ed.), *Coercion and punishment in long-term perspectives* (pp. 315–347). Cambridge, England: Cambridge University Press.

Straus, M. A. (1980). Victims and aggressors in marital violence. *American Behavioral Scientist, 23*, 681–704.

Union des Familles en Europe. (2007). *Pour ou contre les fessées? Synthèse de l'enquête*. Entnommen August 18, 2008, unter http://www.uniondesfamilles.org/enquete-fessees.htm.

Wetzels, P. (1997). *Gewalterfahrungen in der Kindheit. Sexueller Missbrauch, körperliche Misshandlung und deren langfristige Konsequenzen*. Baden-Baden: Nomos-Verlag.

Ziegert, K. A. (1983). The Swedish prohibition of corporal punishment: A preliminary report. *Journal of Marriage and Family, 45*, 917–926.

25 Witnessing History and Charting the Future

Pathways to Prohibition

Anne B. Smith and Joan E. Durrant

The stories told in this book document a social movement of tremendous historical significance. They bear witness to a paradigm shift in global conceptions of childhood. Every story has revealed a cultural history of violence against children that has been legitimated through law, education, religion, and tradition reaching back centuries. The belief that children learn through physical and emotional pain has been firmly entrenched in societies around the world. It is only now, in our time, that this belief has been seriously challenged. Children in the last 30 years have begun to be viewed as persons, rights bearers and full participants in their families and societies. This movement has been symbolized by the prohibition of physical punishment, a tangible reflection of children's changing status.

As the stories in this book show, the pathway to prohibition is not a uniform one. Each country has charted its own course, within its own cultural and historical frameworks. Yet some common themes have emerged. In this chapter, we reflect on the forces that have propelled law reform across countries and regions. By examining the commonalities, perhaps we can better understand the meaning of this movement and identify the key forces, agencies, structures, and participants that stimulate reform. Our exploration of this book's stories has revealed seven themes that underlie the empowerment of countries to achieve prohibition.

CULTURAL CONSTRUCTIONS OF CHILDREN, CHILDHOOD, AND GENERATIONAL RELATIONSHIPS ARE THE BACKDROP FOR CHANGE OR RESISTANCE

How societies understand children, childhood, and relationships across generations is fundamental to how children are treated and how they participate in their communities. "We are both constructed and construct ourselves" and therefore both have free will and are determined (Stainton Rogers, 1989, p. 23). Social constructions of what is 'normal' and 'appropriate' in the treatment of children are taken for granted and invisible, and therefore difficult to change, but they have a pervasive influence on what happens to children in schools, families, and other places where they live their lives. These attitudes are sensitive and personal. Challenging them is difficult, because people often feel that their own childhood and parenting experiences, and their parents' behavior, are being criticized. The family is widely viewed as a closed and private entity which should not be the object of public scrutiny or government interference, and attempts to change families are interpreted as 'social engineering' or 'the nanny state'. The Committee on the Rights of the Child's *General Comment Number 8*, however, asserts that the child has a right to human dignity, physical integrity, and equal protection under the law, and "the status of the child as an individual person and holder of human rights. The child is not a possession of parents, nor of the State, nor simply an object of concern" (para. 47).

Globally, the use of physical punishment is deeply rooted in most histories of childrearing and education. Even in Sweden, the first country in the world to prohibit physical punishment, children in the 17th century were beaten at the end of the week for earlier transgressions in the belief that this would teach them to become good citizens (Janson, Långberg, & Svensson, Chapter 19). Religion has also been implicated in the perpetuation of physical punishment. In 18th-century Serbia for example (Srna & Stevanovic, Chapter 17), praising children was rare and children were expected to be unquestioningly obedient. The popular proverb, *the stick comes from Heaven*, resulted in the practice of teachers beating children for no reason on Saturdays, in the belief that whipping them would make their spirits stronger.

These long-held beliefs, however, have helped to focus prohibition campaigns on shifting the cultural norm. In Romania, the proverb, *Beating is from Heaven*, was turned on its head by Save the Children in a 2002 publicity campaign entitled, *For Those who Still Believe that Beating Comes from Heaven* (Alexandrescu, Chapter 16). The campaign included an image of a sad angel with a bruised eye, accompanied by the phrase, *Beating is Not from Heaven*. In this way, the traditional phrase that for so long justified physical punishment was used to challenge it.

Mirjam Blaak (Chapter 13), writes that in the Netherlands, it was only in the 21st century that people began to question the use of violence as a beneficial and essential educational tool. She makes the important point that gradual shifts of opinion do take place over centuries, and thresholds of tolerance for violence gradually fall. One of the indicators of this shift appears to be the prohibition of physical punishment in schools. The countries that were among the first to enact school prohibitions—Finland in 1918 (Husa, Chapter 9), Sweden in 1928 (Janson et al., Chapter 15), Norway in the 1930s (Sandberg, Chapter 15)—were also among the first to challenge physical punishment in homes. Yemen, on the other hand, did not prohibit school corporal punishment until 2002—an extraordinary achievement in a country characterized by traditional tribal society, religious observance, geographic isolation for large parts of the population, poverty, and political instability (Saaeed & Maas, Chapter 23). School prohibitions may contribute to a reduction of violence in homes, as physical punishment begins to be redefined as unnecessary and harmful. But even in countries with school prohibitions, there is still a long journey to full abolition.

The cultural justification (even celebration) of physical punishment is still evident in those countries that have been most intransigent. Sir Gerald Fitzmaurice, a privately educated British judge on the European Court of Human Rights, dissented from the judgement of Tyrer v UK in 1978 that punishment in the case was degrading (Newell, Chapter 2). He believed that the corporal punishment of schoolboys was both 'normal' and a matter of 'pride and congratulation' to boys, because it had been part of his own school experience. The fact that the men educated in these schools continue to occupy positions in government and the judiciary may partly explain the slow progress there. Such attitudes were disseminated throughout the British Empire during its colonial period of the 18th and 19th centuries. The legacy of this period is seen in the intergenerational trauma sustained by Indigenous peoples in the residential schools of Canada (McGillivray & Milne, Chapter 7) and Australia (Saunders & Cashmore, Chapter 6). The punitive and oppressive nature of these schools led to the suffering of generations of children.

Every story told in this book provides an illustration of the reification of beliefs in the necessity and justifiability of physical punishment in the language of legislation. Terms such as "reasonable chastisement", "justifiable assault", "force which is reasonable in the circumstances", and "moderate domestic punishment" are infused with the assumption that physical punishment is necessary, desirable, and effective in bringing up obedient and well-behaved children. This language is so entrenched and so powerful that it can be the greatest obstacle to reform. Norway, for example, passed a law in 1987 stating that, "The child must not be exposed to violence or otherwise treated so that its physical or mental health is endangered" (Sandberg, Chapter 15). It was assumed by many, including the government, that this law prohibited physical punishment. But as recently as 2005, "violence" was interpreted by Supreme Court judges as excluding "light smacks". Another period of debate ensued until a new legal amendment was passed in 2010 that clarified the law. This story exemplifies the role that language plays in affirming the belief that physical punishment is not violence. In Canada, the Supreme Court established criteria to distinguish punishment from violence—the body part struck, whether an object was used, and so on (McGillivray & Milne, Chapter 7). They attempted to carve out a zone of "non-violent violence" without realizing that this distinction would not be tolerated for any other age group.

Constructions of childhood changed in the Nordic countries much earlier than in other nations. Janson et al. (Chapter 19) argue that in Sweden this was influenced by a lack of rigid class divisions and a strong independent peasantry. Constructing children as persons deserving of nurturance seems to be linked to the dawning of democracy. In the early 20th century, there were many signs of respect and concern for children and young people's well being in Scandinavia, an area where democratic values are dearly held and where the state has a strong relationship with individuals. Enthusiasm for democracy, equality, and a sense of collective responsibility for children may have assisted early moves to eradicate violent parenting. The later moves towards democracy in other countries like Lithuania, Mongolia, Spain, Serbia, Romania, Uruguay, Venezuela, and Yemen have all been associated with growing concern for the human rights of children and recognition of these rights in law.

In several of the stories, we see the emergence of a visible and exciting sign of the shift from constructions of children as parents' possessions and the objects of adult power, to persons with agency, and children's and young people's participation in the process of law reform. Children played an active role in Mongolia, Venezuela, Uruguay, and Yemen, as well as many other countries. In these cases, children's right to be involved in decisions about their lives was recognized and their participation was facilitated. While the language of law reform is often about "protection", the movement is very much about participation. Indeed, it is only possible to create contexts in which children are supported to find and express their voice when their participation is respected, recognized and encouraged. The efforts of the International Save the Children Alliance to ensure that children's views are heard, to create new research paradigms, and to engage children in their campaigns provide a leading-edge model of social change.

HUMAN RIGHTS ARE THE PRIMARY FOUNDATION OF PROHIBITION

Peter Newell (Chapter 2) documents the human rights imperative to prohibit physical punishment. Human rights treaties have had a profound effect throughout the world, resulting in a transformation of moral imagination and a shared human rights culture (Lauren, 2003). Although traditional agents of authority have consistently resisted prohibition, every story told in this book demonstrates that human rights instruments have consistently facilitated it.

Two instruments in particular have been effective in this area. The first is the *Convention on the Rights of the Child* (CRC; United Nations, 1989) which has led to a reconstruction of childhood, as it views children "as persons with emerging moral and social lives that parents and governments are explicitly charged with respecting" (Woodhouse, 2004, p. 240). The second is the Committee on the Rights of the Child's *General Comment Number 8* (2006) which states unequivocally that corporal punishment is a violation of children's rights. This document has been pivotal in addressing the question of whether corporal punishment is violence. A third important document is the *World Report on Violence against Children* (Pinheiro, 2006), which has made it difficult for governments to deny the suffering of children around the world—and which clearly identifies physical punishment as a form of violence.

Most of the stories told in this book illustrate the important role of these documents in countries' progress towards abolition. In some cases, the Committee on the Rights of the Child's *Concluding Observations* on countries' reports have served as the tipping point by reminding states of their obligations to children. Even where reform has taken many years, the CRC principles, the periodic reporting process, *General Comment Number 8* (2006), and the *World Report on Violence against Children* (Pinheiro, 2006) all have been useful tools for encouraging debate and keeping the issue before the eyes of governments and the public.

Of English-speaking countries, however, only New Zealand has acted on the Committee's admonitions. Its 2003 *Concluding Observations* expressed deep concern at New Zealand's failure to remove the statutory defense. The government developed a 'work program' to enhance future compliance, but this was mainly used to institute a public education campaign, and it is doubtful if the ban in 2007 could have been achieved without a number of other factors coming into play (Taylor, Wood, & Smith, Chapter 14). Australia, Canada, and the United Kingdom have consistently been asked by the Committee to remove their statutory defense, but their only action has been to make modest (if any) efforts at increasing public education about positive discipline (Chapters 5, 7, and 20).

Regional bodies and instruments have also been effective agents of change, and the most successful of these has been the European Union (EU), which has actively supported prohibition efforts with the remarkable result that today only four EU countries (France, Belgium, Malta, and the UK) do not have bans. Even European countries that are not members of the EU have been influenced by the EU's *Strategy for Children*. For example, Norway based the wording of its 2010 amendment on the EU strategy (Sandberg, Chapter 15).

The Council of Europe, which has a wider membership than the EU, also has strongly encouraged its members to prohibit corporal punishment on the basis of the *European Social Charter* (ESC) and rulings of the European Court of Human Rights (ECHR; Newell, Chapter 2). In the Netherlands, these instruments helped the government clarify the wording of its amended legislation in 2007. The ECHR have been supporting a law reform campaign in Serbia since 2007, and in 2008 the Serbian government announced its commitment to law reform and outlined a strategy for implementation.

Africa also has developed its own human rights instruments, including the *African Charter on Human and People's Rights*, and more recently the *African Charter on the Rights and Welfare of the Child* (Vohito, Chapter 5). These instruments have their own reporting mechanisms and have been influential in promoting nonviolent childrearing. Such regional charters may strengthen the influence of international instruments because of their closeness to, and ownership by, local organizations.

KEY AGENTS OF CHANGE ARE ROOTED IN CIVIL SOCIETY

Civil society is that part of a society in which people cooperate with each other and with public authorities to tackle individual and social problems, and ensure that the interests of minorities or groups lacking political and economic power are addressed. Civil society involves "the collective action of civic, service and social organizations and citizens working outside the realm of the state"[1], including non-governmental organizations (NGOs) which are nonprofit organizations, independent of the state. While governments and their officials change regularly, NGOs usually continue, which makes it possible for them to persist in their efforts to bring about change.

Civil society includes alliances of NGOs, united in their efforts to achieve a common goal. There are many examples of cooperation between local and international NGOs on the physical punishment issue. They have worked together on conducting research, changing public opinion, informing and making alliances with government and political leaders, and supporting one another in their efforts. NGOs have been diverse in their composition, including religious, family support, and service organizations, as well as groups of professionals (e.g., social workers, pediatricians, child protection workers).

One very important contribution of NGOs has been their alternative reports to the UN Committee on the Rights of the Child during the Periodic Reporting process. These reports have been instrumental in pointing out where states have failed to meet their obligations under the CRC, and presenting an alternative point of view on states' progress. It is difficult to imagine that any of the legal reforms that have taken place around the world would have occurred without the involvement of local NGOs, and the backup, funding, and leadership of international NGOs that have been involved for decades in bringing this issue to public attention.

In Finland (Husa, Chapter 9), a high profile campaign by the Swedish NGO, the Mannerheim League, was influential in bringing the issue to public attention in 1981 and their appointment of an Ombudsperson for Children helped achieve a ban in 1983. Indeed, much earlier work in the 1920s and 1930s by the Mannerheim League and other organizations concerned with Child Welfare, such as the Central Union for Child Welfare in Finland (founded in 1937), had previously laid the groundwork for concern about children's rights and well being. In contrast, in Norway (Sandberg, Chapter 15) NGOs were not very much involved in promoting children's interests or involved in public debate; perhaps this could explain the sequence of legal reforms that was required to achieve a clear law.

Bussman (Chapter 10) describes how the German League for the Child (*Deutsche Liga für das Kind*) was instrumental in bringing the physical punishment debate to public attention in Germany in the 1970s. This interdisciplinary network included early childhood education, pediatric, family, and youth welfare agencies—more than 250 organizations altogether. It was not until 2000 that Germany instituted a ban, but the work of these NGOs was essential to changing the climate so that reform could occur. In Canada (Chapter 7), McGillivray and Milne describe the formation of child advocacy networks in the 1990s involving "hundreds of small-scale outreach programs and media events, new research, the founding of the Repeal 43 Committee and a national workshop on child assault". An important Canadian document has been the *Joint Statement on Physical Punishment of Children and Youth*[2] (endorsed by 400 professional organizations across the country) which has helped to demonstrate the degree of consensus that exists on the issue among professional organizations.

In the United Kingdom, NGOs have also been tremendously active (Owen, Chapter 20). STOPP was established to advocate for abolition in schools, and when this was finally achieved the organization became EPOCH[3], now an influential international organization. Today, the UK campaign is led by the Children are Unbeatable! Alliance, which includes more than 600 organizations.

In Uruguay, the first South American country to prohibit physical punishment, a local NGO focused on child welfare and justice, Arcoiris, has worked since 1992 to prevent violence against children. With the election of a new government in 2005, Arcoiris saw an opportunity for change. It cooperated with Save the Children Sweden and other NGOs to initiate a full-scale public awareness campaign–meeting with politicians, holding seminars and colloquia, and distributing 10,000 pamphlets. The success of this campaign can be largely attributed to the careful work done by the NGOs with parliamentarians and government officials. Fundación Paniamor was a similar catalyst for change in Costa Rica after many years of effort there (Grillo, Chapter 8).

The International Save the Children Alliance[4] has certainly been at the forefront of this movement. This child-rights-based NGO has well-developed child protection programs all over the world and actively promotes nonviolence in families. They provide consultation to other NGOs, to governments and to communities in their efforts to eradicate violence from children's lives. The Global Initiative to End All Corporal Punishment of Children[5] has served as a clearinghouse of information on law reform internationally, including country-by-country analyses of legal progress, prevalence research gathered from all corners of the world, and human rights resources. This information has been very helpful to making law reform visible and understood by individuals, organizations, and governments.

Some key individuals in the reform movement have been important participants in civil society, but not necessarily involved in NGOs. They tend to be highly respected people, often human rights lawyers or psychologists, who are passionate about children's well-being. It is hard to underestimate the influence of individuals in initiating debates on physical punishment. For example, the Swedish writer Ellen Key's book, *The Century of the Child*, first published in 1900, had a powerful influence in many countries, particularly in Scandinavia (Key, 1996). Other examples of prominent individuals who have led debate and reform, include Archbishop Desmond Tutu in Africa, Mario Viquez in Costa Rica, Lea Pulkkinen in Finland, Temuujin Khishigmdemberel in Mongolia, Ona Valiukeviciiute in Lithuania, Jaap Doek in the Netherlands, and Jane and James Ritchie in New Zealand.

RESEARCH IS A USEFUL TOOL TO HELP BRING ABOUT CHANGE

The evidence demonstrating that physical punishment predicts long-term negative developmental outcomes has been valuable in the campaign for reform, although not without its complications (Durrant, Chapter 4). Although only a small minority of researchers actually advocate physical punishment on the basis of its "beneficial effects" (Larzelere, 1993, 1998), there are other researchers who argue that, while severe physical punishment is a matter for concern, "light smacking" is normative and harmless (Fergusson & Lynskey, 1997). This dichotomy perpetuates the belief that punishment and maltreatment are two distinct and unrelated phenomena, a belief that is not supported empirically. Sometimes, research has been used to justify the status quo. In the United Kingdom, for example, data from public opinion polls showing that the majority opposed a ban were used by the government to conclude that the law was clear and did not need to be changed (Owen, Chapter 20).

Research has, however, been used in many countries in the world as an evidence-based tool to advocate for reform. The developmental correlates of physical punishment, the impact of caregiver attitudes, children's experiences and views, history and case law, and the effect of law reform have all been investigated. Not only academics, but NGOs and international organizations, such as Save the Children, the World Health Organization, and the United Nations (Pinheiro, 2006), have been involved in research. The findings of this research have been widely used to demonstrate the many negative impacts of legal justifications for physical punishment.

Research actually was the genesis of the prohibition movement in many countries. A publication in the early 1960s by Henry Kempe and his colleagues, *The Battered Child*, was profoundly important in making child maltreatment visible (Kempe, Silverman, Steele, Droegemuller, & Silver, 1962). Although widely cited and discussed in the United States, it was in European countries such as Sweden, Finland, and the Netherlands that it galvanized professionals to bring about changes which would prevent such maltreatment. In the Netherlands, the publication of this book stimulated further research into the extent and scope of child abuse (Blaak, Chapter 13), which laid the groundwork for prohibition.

In Germany, research has played a major and continuing role in law reform. Bussman (Chapter 10) shows how the findings of criminological research revealing high levels of violence towards children, and links between corporal punishment and youth crime, were instrumental in the 1990s in changing public opinion. Germany continues to invest in research, supporting ongoing evaluation of the impact of the 2000 prohibition. Swedish research (Janson et al., Chapter 19) has documented a dramatic decline in violence towards children, accompanying the series of reforms ending in the 1979 prohibition. The first systematic comparative study on trends in parental attitudes and behavior in Europe (Bussman, Erthal, & Schroth, Chapter 24) has demonstrated that a combination of prohibition and ongoing public education is associated with the greatest degree of social change. Its findings will be helpful to decision makers contemplating the most effective approach to reducing violence against children in their countries.

Research seminars and conferences, and their accompanying media coverage, have sown the seeds of change in many countries. A 1984 research seminar that gathered researchers in law, psychology, social anthropology, and psychology accelerated progress towards prohibition in Norway (Sandberg, Chapter 15). Similarly, in New Zealand, a 2004 national seminar disseminated the findings of a comprehensive literature review on physical punishment and reviewed case law, which had been requested by the Committee on the Rights of the Child (Taylor, Wood, & Smith, Chapter 14). The seminar's extensive press coverage shocked the public as it revealed the severity of physical punishment that was legally sanctioned in New Zealand, and informed them about its adverse effects.

A 2002 World Health Organization study revealed a high incidence of severe violence towards children in Romania (Alexandrescu, Chapter 16), which helped convince the public of the need for law reform. In Yemen, research showing high levels of physical punishment in schools, and that 85% of children who had failed academically had been physically punished, advanced the decree to abolish school corporal punishment (Saeed & Maas, Chapter 23).

CHANGE CANNOT OCCUR WITHOUT POLITICAL WILL AND APPROPRIATE GOVERNMENT STRUCTURES

Human rights campaigns rely on political will and government action that strikes at the very heart of the relationship between individuals and the state, challenging tradition and entrenched political power and privilege. According to Lauren (2003), major breakthroughs in the struggle for human rights often come in the wake of revolutions, upheavals, and wars.

Human rights visions are rarely strong enough in themselves to provide sufficiently powerful motives to provoke governments into effective action.

This book includes some stories showing the intransigence of governments, and their failure to recognize the human rights of children. Australia, Canada, and the United Kingdom are prime examples. Despite the presence of sympathetic individuals and support from some parliamentarians, efforts to shift the status quo in such countries have been unsuccessful. A particularly disappointing story comes from Canada, where, following Prime Minister Mulroney's chairing the Summit for Children at the United Nations, a 1993 federal bill was introduced to repeal the criminal defense to corrective assault of a child. But this window of opportunity closed again very quickly following a change of government leader (McGillivray & Milne, Chapter 7).

Some government structures are particularly difficult to change. For example in Australia, the federal government has no jurisdiction over criminal law (Saunders & Cashmore, Chapter 6) and in the United Kingdom, despite some devolution, the Welsh Assembly, which supports a ban, has been unable to change the law because of its lack of criminal jurisdiction (Owen, Chapter 20). Canada too has difficulties in changing the status quo, because of its federal/provincial structures (McGillivray & Milne, Chapter 7).

This book, however, demonstrates that many governments, despite varying degrees of resistance and political struggle, have found the political will to act for children. The political leanings of the party in power do not seem to have as powerful an effect as one might imagine. For example, while a socialist government in Venezuela supported prohibition, the UK's Labor government was intransigent on the issue. In Sweden, it was two Conservative Parliamentarians who introduced the prohibition bill, which was supported by all political parties. In Finland, the government itself initiated law reform, launching a public campaign, inviting public debate, and encouraging submissions from all sectors of society. Sari Husa (Chapter 9) points out that prohibition would have proceeded regardless of which government was in power in Finland, because all parties shared a similar view of its necessity. In Norway, however, the election of a Social Democratic government was the impetus for law reform. Prior to that election, a coalition of various parties could not be persuaded to support the bill, despite the Minister of Justice's approval of it (Sandberg, Chapter 15). It was a change of government involving a coalition between the Socialist and Green parties that precipitated law reform in Germany (Bussman, Chapter 10).

It could be argued that it is a strong commitment to democracy that is the necessary, although not sufficient, prerequisite for change. The fall of authoritarian regimes in Lithuania, Mongolia, Romania, Serbia, Spain, Uruguay, and Venezuela has been accompanied by a willingness to promote human rights. Romania, Spain, Uruguay, and Venezuela prohibited physical punishment in the wake of such societal restructuring. Lithuania,

Mongolia, and Serbia are progressing in the same direction. Serbia is emerging from a period of frequent and intense violence and conflict. The fall of the Milošević regime in 2000 was followed by enthusiasm for democracy, rejection of violence, recognition of human rights instruments, and movement towards membership in the European Union (Srna & Stevanovic, Chapter 17). The Ministry of Social Policy declared its commitment to prohibition in 2008. In Mongolia, following 70 years of communist rule, a rapid transition to democracy has brought with it intense interest in human rights (Dorjpurev, Chapter 12). Interestingly, it was a coalition of former communists and a democratic party that proposed a complete ban there, and set up a working group to oversee the process. The Lithuanian government approved a strategy on Child Welfare Policies that resulted in a 2005 plan including a proposed physical punishment ban (Alexandrescu, Chapter 11).

In New Zealand, NGOs and others had promoted law reform for many years, but "no party in power was willing to take the political risk of initiating change" (Taylor et al., Chapter 14). In a substantial way, it was chance that led to the prohibition there. In 2005, a Green Party Private Member's Bill was drawn by ballot—that is, chosen by chance from a collection of Bills. Despite a long and arduous public debate, the Bill was eventually passed with overwhelming cross-party support. However, the then-Labor Prime Minister, Helen Clark, was pivotal in mobilizing this support. New Zealand's story is an exemplar of the importance of a particular configuration of political factors making reform possible.

Ombudsmen or Commissioners for Children have been almost universally important in the journey to prohibition. Encouraged by the UN Committee on the Rights of the Child, these offices are established to provide governments with independent advice on policies supporting the well-being and rights of children. Only in Norway was a State Ombudsman appointed before the CRC came into existence (1983).[6] New Zealand appointed its Commissioner for Children in the year the CRC was adopted (1989), and Sweden appointed its first Ombudsman in 1993. Ombudsmen have been key figures in promoting reform in Costa Rica, Lithuania, New Zealand, Norway, Serbia, Spain, Sweden, and Venezuela. Ieva Kromelyte (Chapter 11), Advisor to the Ombudsman for Children in Lithuania, describes the substantial role of the Office in educating the government and the public about the necessity of reform.

In English-speaking countries outside of New Zealand, however, the impact of Children's Commissioners has been much more limited. The four commissioners for England, Wales, Scotland, and Ireland released a joint statement in 2006 urging the government to abolish physical punishment, but it has gone unheeded (Owen, Chapter 20). Commissioners have been appointed at the state level in Australia, and some of them, particularly the Commissioner from Tasmania, have supported reform, but so far to no avail (Saunders & Cashmore, Chapter 6). Canada does not yet have a

Children's Commissioner or Ombudsman, so there is no voice for children there at the federal level.

EDUCATION AND AWARENESS-RAISING SHOULD PRECEDE, ACCOMPANY, AND FOLLOW LAW REFORM

Global efforts to prohibit physical punishment are premised on principles of fairness and justice: Children should be protected against violence without discrimination. Many countries have used the law to demonstrate their commitment to this principle and to set a nonviolent childrearing standard. Most of the countries with prohibitions have placed them in their civil codes in order to make symbolic statements without threatening criminal penalties. Law reform itself, however, is not enough to bring about changes in the hearts and minds of people.

The Committee on the Rights of the Child (2006, paras. 44–49) acknowledges that prohibition alone will not achieve changes in attitudes and practice, so it is essential for states to carry out "comprehensive awareness-raising of children's right to protection and of the laws that reflect this right" (para. 44). The Committee also recommends that states provide education about positive parenting and relationships to parents, carers, teachers, and others who work with children and families. According to the *World Report on Violence against Children,* "States should ensure that children's rights are disseminated and understood, including by children. Public information campaigns should be used to sensitize the public about the harmful effects that violence has on children" (Pinheiro, 2006, para. VIA4).

Sweden is an outstanding example of a country that made an intensive effort to both explain the prohibition to the public, and provide education and support for parents (Janson et al., Chapter 19). The 1979 law was accompanied by an extensive publicity campaign. Brochures were delivered to all households with children, translated into many languages. Information was printed on milk cartons to encourage families to discuss the issue. Support services were established for parents through antenatal, pediatric, and well-baby clinics. NGOs, particularly Save the Children Sweden and BRIS (*Children's Rights in Society*), supported the government campaign, using posters and debates to raise awareness. In Finland as well, a high-profile campaign led by parliament both accompanied and followed prohibition, supplemented by intensive NGO initiatives (Husi, Chapter 9).

Germany is another country that has made an exemplary investment in public education (*More Respect for Children*). This lengthy campaign, implemented in 2000 and 2001, explained the legislation and promoted positive parenting in difficult situations (Bussman, Chapter 10). This multimedia campaign was carried out in print, on radio and television, and involved community organizations. More than 500 events took place, including street parties, theater events, lectures, debates, and seminars.

In contrast to these countries, Norway made only minimal efforts at public education (Sandberg, Chapter 15), consisting of a few pamphlets and a full-page newspaper advertisement. The government was not prepared to pay for widespread media coverage. The Netherlands government promised to fund education campaigns to accompany law reform, but they did not fulfill this promise (Blaak, Chapter 13). Blaak describes how an MP tried to include a statement about parent support in the new law, but was unsuccessful. In New Zealand, the government has initiated several campaigns against family violence, and provided some community funding for parent education and support (the SKIP programme), but they failed to draw attention to the fact that physical punishment is violence. Indeed the government's main contribution to the debate has been to reassure parents that "light smacking" will not be prosecuted.

Especially in countries where law reform took place without majority public support, public education is critically important. Unfortunately, however, it has been the exception rather than the rule for states to take the lead in explaining the rationale for law reform and helping parents learn positive disciplinary approaches. It is difficult to know why governments have been so reluctant to stand behind their commitment to children in this way. One could argue that the political risk of prohibition could be ameliorated through a campaign that helped the public to appreciate its rationale. In many countries, governments appear to lack courage to stand up for children, even as they pass laws that affirm their rights. Perhaps governments are reluctant to invest financially in matters that do not necessarily pay off politically.

The gap left by government inaction has often been filled by NGOs who have worked to keep the issue in the public eye and ensure that law reform actually improves the lives of children. The stories told in this book provide rich examples of innovative ways that NGOs have kept the issue alive. Paniamor in Costa Rica (Grillo, Chapter 8), for example, implemented a parent education campaign (*Educate without Hitting*) that was included in the regular curriculum of early childhood parent education programs. Arcoiris in Uruguay disseminated information about the preventive purpose of the ban by arranging public events and distributing pamphlets at these events. In Venezuela, Cecodap engaged youth in workshops, and worked with educators, parents, lawyers, and the police to increase their understanding of the issue.

The International Save the Children Alliance has been critical in this regard. It has undertaken a wide range of initiatives to ensure that parent education and support are ongoing in all regions. Costa Rica, Lithuania, Mongolia, Romania, Uruguay, Venezuela, and Yemen provide just some of the examples described in this book.

CHANGES IN THE LAW CAN BRING ABOUT CHANGES IN ATTITUDES AND PRACTICES

The *World Report on Violence against Children* (Pinheiro, 2006) stresses the need for a transformation in the mindset of societies about violence towards children, so it is important to ask how effective reforms have been in changing this mindset. It has certainly been the aim of prohibition to change both attitudes and actual behavior. However, it is not easy to demonstrate the effectiveness of the reforms, partly because some of the changes have been so recent, but also because it is difficult to attribute causality to any one factor. Nevertheless, evidence is accumulating to suggest that law reform, especially if it is accompanied by public education, does have an impact on violence.

Some countries have had the wisdom to fund ongoing research into the outcomes of their changes in laws and policies. Research findings in Sweden (Janson et al., Chapter 19) show that the ban and its accompanying education initiatives have ensured that virtually everyone knows about the law. There is also solid evidence that the levels of violence towards children have fallen considerably since the 1980s. "Almost an entire generation who experienced physical punishment themselves as children refrained from inflicting it once they became parents" (Janson, et al., Chapter 19). Sweden, the first country to prohibit physical punishment over 30 years ago, now has the lowest levels of violence against children in the world.

Recent research in Finland (Husa, Chapter 9) has also shown a steady decline in support for, and use of, physical punishment over the last 20 years. Only 7% of children were shown to have been physically punished in the previous year in a 2007 study. Germany also has initiated comprehensive research to evaluate the impact of prohibition (Bussman, Chapter 10), revealing an increase in parents' knowledge of the law and a reduction of violence in childrearing. Bussman points out that a condemnation of violence in child rearing is now generally accepted in Germany. The majority of children and young people there view corporal punishment as a disrespect for their personality, and are opposed to it. A comparison of the outcomes of various approaches to physical punishment across five European nations has shown that prohibition appears to have a more powerful effect than public education alone, but that its impact is enhanced by public education (Bussman, Erthal, & Schroth, Chapter 24).

It is more difficult to see an impact of the more recent reforms. For example, a 2009 report from Uruguay, where prohibition took place in 2007, showed that more than half of parents there were still physically punishing their children (Reyes & Galvis, Chapter 21). In Costa Rica, where prohibition occurred in 2008, more than half of parents think that there is no alternative to physical punishment in some circumstances, and believe that children will grow up more undisciplined if they are not physically punished (Grillo, Chapter 9). NGOs in both of these countries are using this information to intensify their efforts in public education, which is clearly an essential ingredient in effecting change. In New Zealand, where law reform also took place in 2008, there is some encouraging research showing attitude and behavior change, despite the intensive efforts and publicity campaigns of a well-funded organization that supports physical punishment (Taylor, Wood, & Smith, Chapter 14).

CONCLUDING COMMENTS

Following centuries, if not millennia, of maltreatment and exploitation of children around the world, we are witnesses to one of history's most remarkable social movements—the recognition of children as persons with fundamental human rights, represented symbolically by the end of legal justifications for inflicting pain on their bodies, minds and spirits. This movement will continue to grow, following multiple pathways, as countries come to terms with their past treatment of children and chart their future course. Inevitably, this change will come even to the wealthy English-speaking countries (Australia, Canada, the UK, and the US) who are in an optimal position to create societies fit for children, but have been the most resistant to change.

Children's healthy development depends, first and foremost, on their trust in a safe and secure environment. This must mean, at a minimum, that they do not experience violence at the hands of those entrusted with their care. We close with the words of Professor Paolo Pinheiro (2006, p. 6):

> There should be no more excuses. Member States must act now with urgency to fulfill their human rights obligations and other commitments to ensure protection from all forms of violence. While legal obligations lie with States, all sectors of society, all individuals, share the responsibility of condemning and preventing violence against children and responding to child victims. None of us can look children in the eye if we continue to approve or condone any form of violence against them.

NOTES

1. http://en.wiktionary.org/wiki/civil_society
2. http://www.cheo.on.ca/en/physicalpunishment
3. End all Physical Punishment of Children.
4. http://www.savethechildren.net/alliance/index.html
5. www.endcorporalpunishment.org
6. In Finland there was an NGO-appointed Ombudsman in 1983 but it was not until 2006 that there was a State-appointed one.

REFERENCES

Committee on the Rights of the Child. (2006). *General Comment No. 8. The right of the child to protection from corporal punishment and other cruel or degrading forms of punishment* (Articles 19 and 28; paras. 2 and 37, inter alia). Retrieved from http://www.unhchr.ch/tbs/doc.nsf/(Symbol)/CRC.C.GC.8.En?OpenDocument

Fergusson, D. M., & Lynskey, M. T. (1997). Physical punishment/maltreatment during childhood and adjustment in young adulthood. *Child Abuse and Neglect, 21,* 617–630.

Kempe, C. H., Silverman, F. N., & Steele, B. F., Droegemuller, W., & Silver, H. K. (1962). The battered-child syndrome. *Journal of the American Medical Association 251*, 3288–3300.

Key, E. (1996). *Barnets århundrade.* Stockholm: Informationsförlaget.

Larzelere, R. E. (1993). Response to Oosterhuis: Empirically justified uses of spanking: Toward a discriminating view of corporal punishment. *Journal of Psychology and Theology, 21,* 142–147.

Larzelere, R. E. (1998). Effective vs. counterproductive parental spanking: Toward more light and less heat. *Marriage and Family, 1*, 179–192.

Lauren, P. G. (2003). The evolution of international human rights, 2nd ed. Philadelphia: University of Pennsylvania Press.

Pinheiro, P. (2006). *World report on violence against children.* Geneva: United Nations Secretary-General's Study on Violence against Children.

Stainton Rogers, R. (1989). The social construction of childhood. In W. Stainton Rogers, D. Hevery, J. B. Roche, & E. Ash (Eds.), *Child abuse and neglect: Facing the challenge* (pp. 23–29). London: Batsford.

United Nations (1989). *Convention on the Rights of the Child.* Available at www.un.org/documents/ga/res/44/a44r025/htm.

Woodhouse, B. (2004). Re-visioning rights for children. In P. B. Pufall & R. P. Unsworth (Eds.), *Rethinking childhood* (pp. 229–243). New Brunswick, NJ: Rutgers University Press.

Contributors

Gabriela Alexandrescu (Romania) has been the Executive President of Save the Children Romania since 1994. She leads the development of the organization, which was established after the fall of communism in 1990. She establishes the priorities for Save the Children's work in Romania—programs, lobbying, advocacy, and fundraising. She is a specialist in children's rights and international humanitarian law who led the campaign against corporal punishment in Romania. She is a consultant to the High Level Group for Romanian Children, a member of the Consultative Committee on NGOs of the Romanian Prime Minister, and a member of the Board of the Romanian NGOs' Federation for Development.

Mirjam Elisabeth Blaak (the Netherlands) holds a Master's degree in Social and Medical Anthropology and is a senior children's rights and child protection officer at Defence for Children ECPAT the Netherlands. She is the co-editor of the *Dutch Handbook on International Child and Youth Law*. Since 2001, she has been involved in several national and international research, training, and advocacy projects to improve the implementation of children's rights and to enhance the protection of children against abuse, neglect, and exploitation. In 2006 she joined the editorial board of the Dutch journal, *Child Abuse and Neglect*.

Kai-D. Bussmann (Germany; Prof. Dr. habil. jur.) studied Sociology and Law in Hamburg, Germany; he is now living in Berlin. Since 1997, he has been Professor of Criminal Law and Criminology at the Faculty of Law and Economics at the Martin-Luther University Halle-Wittenberg. One of his research specializations is the impact of prohibiting violence in childrearing. He has authored or co-authored many articles and reports on this subject, and has conducted several research projects on behalf of the Federal Ministry of Justice (Berlin) and the Deutsche Forschungsgemeinschaft (German Research Association, Bonn).

Judy Cashmore (Australia) holds a Ph.D. in Developmental Psychology and a Master's degree in Education. She is an Associate Professor in the Faculty of Law, University of Sydney, and Adjunct Professor at Southern Cross University. Her research focuses on children's involvement in and perceptions of legal proceedings and other processes related to child protection, child sexual assault, and family law. She co-authored a report for the federal government in 1996 on the legal and social aspects of physical punishment in Australia.

Olonchimeg Dorjpurev (Mongolia) has worked in the fields of women's rights, civil society, community development, social services, education, child protection, and inter-communal conflict in Mongolia, the US, and Papua New Guinea. She studied social work at Columbia University and at the Open Society Institute. She was Director of Programs for Save the Children in Mongolia, where she launched advocacy campaigns aimed at banning corporal punishment in schools and developing a national child protection system. Currently, she works for Save the Children in Papua New Guinea, where she is again involved in a campaign to ban corporal punishment.

Joan E. Durrant (Editor), Ph.D., is a Child-Clinical Psychologist and Professor of Family Social Sciences at the University of Manitoba in Canada. Her research focuses on the psychological, cultural, legal, and human rights dimensions of corporal punishment of children. She was the principal researcher and co-author of the Canadian *Joint Statement on Physical Punishment of Children and Youth*; a member of the Research Advisory Committee of the *United Nations Secretary-General's Study on Violence against Children*; and a co-editor of *Eliminating Corporal Punishment: The Way Forward to Constructive Discipline* (UNESCO). She has been active in public education on the prevention of child maltreatment in Canada and internationally.

Claudia Erthal (Chapter 24) is a Sociologist holding a Diplom-Soziologin. Born in Spain, she studied Romance Studies in Münster and Heidelberg, and Sociology in Halle (Saale). Since 2001, she has been research assistant to Professor Dr. Kai-D. Bussmann's Chair of Penal Law and Criminology in the Faculty of Law at the Martin-Luther University Halle-Wittenberg. She is a consultant to the *Heinrich-Böll Foundation*, Saxony-Anhalt, and to the state teacher training and teacher continuing education centre (*Lehrerfort- und Lehrerweiterbildung*) of Saxony-Anhalt.

Maria Clara Galvis (Uruguay and Venezuela) studied Law in Bogotá, Colombia, and holds a postgraduate degree in Constitutional Law from the University of Genoa, Italy. She is currently Professor of International Human Rights Law at Universidad Sergio Arboleda, Universidad Nacional, and

Universidad Santo Tomás, in Bogotá. For more than 9 years she has litigated human rights cases before the Inter-American Commission and the Inter-American Court of Human Rights, including cases related to torture and violence against children. She has provided legal training for local NGOs in the Andean Region about the use of the Inter-American mechanisms for the protection of children.

Pepa Horno Goicoechea (Spain) is a Psychologist and Consultant in Child Development and Child Protection. For more than 11 years, she has worked with Save the Children to coordinate national and international campaigns to prevent and eradicate violence against children, mainly physical and psychological punishment and sexual abuse and exploitation. She has provided training for intervention programs in more than twenty countries in Latin America, Europe, and South and South-East Asia. She is the author of several books on affective and social development and she has coordinated a number of studies on child protection.

Milena Grillo (Costa Rica) is a Law graduate with a specialization in human rights, and holds a Master's degree in Social and Family Violence. In her capacity as the Executive Director of Fundación Paniamor, Milena headed the central role played by this organization in mobilizing local political and social leaders to approve the 2008 law reform guaranteeing full protection of children against corporal punishment and humiliating treatment within the family. She was the recipient of the 1992 Leadership Award granted by the US Child Assault Prevention Program, and the 2005 Latin Trade Bravo Award as Humanitarian of the Year, for her child rights advocacy across the Latin American Region.

Sari Husa (Finland) holds a Master's degree in Education and a Licentiate degree. She has also studied extensively in the field of public law. She has a long-standing professional interest in child protection and childhood education issues, which she has examined from the points of view of university researcher, community social worker, and state civil servant. Since May 2010, she has been working as a social inspector in the Regional State Administrative Agency of Lapland. Throughout her career she has been particularly interested in the complex questions of child discipline and child protection in the context of education.

Staffan Janson (Sweden) is Professor of Social Pediatrics at Karlstad and Örebro Universities. He has experience in preventive health care for children in low income countries and is a consulting expert on child abuse for the Swedish Government and the European Council. He is also a consulting expert on child injuries for the Swedish Rescue Services, a board member of Save the Children Sweden and has since 2007 been involved in the establishment of the Swedish Academy of the Rights of the Child.

Ieva Kromelyte (Lithuania) has been working as a legal adviser to the Children's Rights Ombudsman of the Republic of Lithuania since 2006, focusing on protection of children from violence. She provides legal advice to help solve the existing problems of violence against children, and gives legal and organizational help to those who have experienced violence. A major focus of her work involves cooperation with governmental, non-governmental and other organizations to take measures to ban corporal punishment in Lithuania.

Bodil Långberg (Sweden), BA, Dipl. Publ. Health, is the head of Allmänna Barnhuset, a well renowned national institute for child welfare dating back to the mid-1600s. Between 1998 and 2002, she headed the Swedish Parliamentary Committee on Child Abuse, and from 2002 to 2005 she headed the Parliamentary Committee on Child Injury Prevention. For many years, she served as Secretary General of the national society, Children's Rights in Society (BRIS).

Lucienne Maas (Yemen) is from the Netherlands and has worked for more than 20 years in the Middle East and Afghanistan, mainly for Save the Children. She holds a Master's degree in Education (UK) and Children's Rights (Switzerland). She is working towards a Ph.D. in Development Studies with a focus on schooling, children's decision-making, and drop out (ISS, The Hague, Netherlands). Currently, she is the Program Director of Save the Children in Yemen.

Anne McGillivray (Canada) is Professor of Law at the University of Manitoba. The right of the child to live free of all forms of violence is pivotal in her research and writing. She serves on the board of the *International Journal of Children's Rights*. She was a member of Canada's children's rights delegation to Cuba and the Steering Committee for the *Canadian Incidence Study on Reported Child Abuse and Neglect*. She has addressed Senate committees, government officials, agencies, police, and citizen groups on children's rights and physical punishment.

Cheryl Milne (Canada) is the Executive Director of the David Asper Centre for Constitutional Rights at the Faculty of Law at the University of Toronto. Formerly, she was a legal advocate for children with the legal clinic Justice for Children and Youth in Toronto. There she led the clinic's Charter litigation at the Supreme Court of Canada including the challenge to the corporal punishment defense in the *Criminal Code of Canada* [*Canadian Foundation for Children, Youth and the Law v. Canada* (2004)].

Peter Newell (Chapter 2) is an international advocate for children's rights. He has chaired the NGO Children's Rights Alliance and is Coordinator of the UK Children are Unbeatable! Alliance. He is Joint Coordinator with Thomas Hammarberg, of the Global Initiative to End All Corporal Punishment of Children. He was co-author of UNICEF's *Implementation Handbook on the Convention on the Rights of the Child*, a consultant for UNICEF on children's rights, adviser to the European Network of Ombudspeople for Children, and a member of the NGO Advisory Panel for the United Nations Secretary-General's Study on Violence against Children.

Sharon Owen (United Kingdom), Ph.D., is a freelance consultant on children's rights, particularly the rights to protection from all forms of violence and to education. Since 2002, she has been the Research Coordinator for the Global Initiative to End All Corporal Punishment of Children, as well as undertaking work for UNICEF, Save the Children Sweden, and, in the UK, the child rights Information Network, the Children Are Unbeatable! Alliance, the Centre for Studies on Inclusive Education, and the Open University. She is on the Council of Management of the Children's Rights Alliance for England.

Gaby Reyes (Uruguay and Venezuela) is Social Communicator for Development and a Program Coordinator in the Latin America and the Caribbean Regional Office of Save the Children Sweden. Gaby has a particular interest in social projects concerning violence against children. For more than 6 years she has managed programs related to various forms of violence, such as sexual exploitation, corporal punishment, and violence in virtual environments. She is the author of handbooks about the prevention of sexual exploitation of children and has conducted various studies in Latin America. She also has worked closely with governmental entities and international NGOs, in order to promote public policies to protect children against violence.

Aisha Saeed (Yemen) is a Senior Protection Specialist at Save the Children Yemen. She studied English Language at the University of Bristol and the University of Lancaster, and was a teacher and school inspector for the Yemen Ministry of Education before joining Save the Children, where she has worked since 1997 in Education and Protection. Aisha was part of the UN Study of Violence against Children process, and advocates for children's protection from violence in all settings. Her main interest is working for and with children and advocating for children's rights.

Kirsten Sandberg (Norway) is a Professor of Law at the University of Oslo. She has taught courses on children and the law for several years, focusing on the child–parent relationship and child protection law, and more broadly on the Convention on the Rights of the Child (CRC) and children's rights. She co-edited a book on the implementation of the CRC in Norway. Most of her research falls within child protection law, including her doctoral thesis on the question of returning foster children to their biological parents. She was a member of the National Commission on abuse and neglect in children's institutions between 1945 and 1980. She also cooperates with Save the Children Norway with regard to the CRC and related policy questions.

Bernadette Saunders (Australia) holds a Master's degree in Social Work and a Ph.D. focusing on physical punishment of children and the intergenerational transmission of family violence. She is currently Senior Research Fellow/Lecturer, Faculty of Medicine, Nursing & Health Sciences, Monash University, Victoria. Her research focuses on the physical punishment of children, including children's views; child abuse and child protection; and the media and language. She is currently conducting a hospital study of child abuse and neglect, as well as further research on physical punishment of children, in conjunction with the Faculty of Law at Monash University.

Andreas Schroth (Chapter 24) holds a Diplom-Soziologe and is a qualified Sociologist. He studied Sociology in Halle (Saale). He has worked as a research assistant at the *Institut für Marktforschung Leipzig GmbH* (Institute for Market Research), and at Professor Dr. Helmut Thome's Chair in Methods of Empirical Social Research in the Institute for Sociology at the Martin-Luther University Halle-Wittenberg. Currently, he is a research assistant to Professor Dr. Kai-D. Bussmann's Chair of Penal Law and Criminology in the Faculty of Law at the Martin-Luther University Halle-Wittenberg.

Anne B. Smith (Editor), Ph.D., was the Director of the Children's Issues Centre at the University of Otago in New Zealand for 12 years, and has been a researcher and writer on childhood and child development for many years. Her book, *Understanding Children's Development,* has been read by practitioners in many child-related fields. Anne also led the team which wrote the influential report *The Discipline and Guidance of Children: Messages from Research,* and has been involved in outreach education on physical punishment. She has recently worked on a variety of research projects, including studies of children as citizens, young children's learning in early childhood centers, and family discipline.

Jelena Srna (Serbia), Ph.D., is an Associate Professor in the Department of Psychology at the University of Belgrade in Serbia. She also has worked as a clinical psychologist/family therapist for the past 30 years. She is an expert on war trauma and psychosocial programs for refugee children and their families, and has worked with the Serbian government on several reform projects related to foster care, justice issues and crisis intervention in Serbian schools. Her work in the areas of child abuse and neglect, adolescent suicide attempts, family therapy, war trauma, and reconciliation has been published in six books and numerous book chapters and journal articles.

Ivana Stevanović (Serbia), Ph.D., has worked for 19 years for NGOs on issues of child rights, child trafficking, child abuse, juvenile offending, women's crime, refugees, and victimization. She is a researcher at the Institute of Criminological and Sociological Research in Belgrade, and President of the Child Rights Centre. She has participated in numerous research projects, scientific meetings and congresses, and published many scientific articles. She is a member of the Council of Child Rights for the Government of Serbia, a board member of the Victimology Society of Serbia, and member of a Council for monitoring and promoting criminal proceedings and juvenile justice.

Birgitta Svensson (Sweden) is a Social Worker with a Master's degree in Public Health. She is currently a doctoral student in Public Health at Karlstad University. She is investigating the incidence of child abuse in various populations, and how staff in pre-schools, schools and preventive services respond when they become aware of child abuse and neglect.

Nicola Taylor (New Zealand) is a Senior Research Fellow at the Centre for Research on Children and Families at the University of Otago, where she also holds a part-appointment in the Faculty of Law. Her academic background is in Social Work and Law, and she has a particular interest in socio-legal research concerning children, parents and professionals. She is a board member of the Childwatch International Research Network, and co-edited *Children as Citizens? International Voices* (2009). Nicola has three children, aged 14 to 21.

Sonia Vohito (Africa) is the Africa Coordinator of a joint project of the Global Initiative to End All Corporal Punishment of Children and the African Child Policy Forum in Ethiopia. In this role, she promotes law reforms and supports national campaigns for the prohibition of corporal punishment of children in Africa. Sonia was trained in France and the United Kingdom and holds post-graduate qualifications in International Law and Charity Management. She has extensive advocacy and management experience in the non-governmental sector at the international level. For several years, she worked for women's and human rights organizations in the UK.

Beth Wood (New Zealand) is a retired child advocate who has been very active in engaging public and political support for law reform in New Zealand for nearly 20 years. She is a co-founder of, and spokesperson for, EPOCH New Zealand. After a career in social work, Beth worked for some years in the Office of the Children's Commissioner and later at UNICEF New Zealand, where she was Advocacy Manager. She is co-author of the book *Unreasonable force: New Zealand's journey towards ending physical punishment of children.*

Author Index

Subject Index

For Product Safety Concerns and Information please contact our EU
representative GPSR@taylorandfrancis.com
Taylor & Francis Verlag GmbH, Kaufingerstraße 24, 80331 München, Germany

www.ingramcontent.com/pod-product-compliance
Ingram Content Group UK Ltd.
Pitfield, Milton Keynes, MK11 3LW, UK
UKHW022115190926
475702UK00013B/1452
* 9 7 8 0 4 1 5 8 4 7 9 8 8 *